Early Church Records
of
Chester County
Pennsylvania

Volume 2

*Charlotte Meldrum
& Martha Reamy*

HERITAGE BOOKS
2007

HERITAGE BOOKS
AN IMPRINT OF HERITAGE BOOKS, INC.

Books, CDs, and more—Worldwide

For our listing of thousands of titles see our website
at
www.HeritageBooks.com

Published 2007 by
HERITAGE BOOKS, INC.
Publishing Division
65 East Main Street
Westminster, Maryland 21157-5026

Copyright © 1997 Charlotte Meldrum and Martha Reamy

All rights reserved. No part of this book may be reproduced or transmitted in any form or by any means, electronic or mechanical, including photocopying, recording or by any information storage and retrieval system without written permission from the author, except for the inclusion of brief quotations in a review.

International Standard Book Number: 978-1-58549-159-9

TABLE OF CONTENTS

Introduction v

Uwchland Monthly Meeting 1

East Vincent Reformed Congregation 37

Goshen Monthly Meeting 78

New Garden Monthly Meeting 112

Index 181

INTRODUCTION

Chester, Bucks and Philadelphia counties were the original three counties of Pennsylvania. The first session of court for Chester County was held in 1682. The church records in this book are those which have survived for the region now identified as Chester County. The last county to be carved out of the original Chester County was Delaware County which was formed in 1789 following the movement of the county seat to the town of West Chester.

Society of Friends

The earliest monthly meetings were founded in that part of Chester County which became Delaware County. The monthly meeting for the meetings at Haverford, Merion and Radnor was established in 1684 by Philadelphia Quarterly Meeting. The monthly meeting was originally settled at Haverford and called Haverford Monthly Meeting. In 1698 it began to circulate to Radnor; it 1796 the name of the monthly meeting was changed to Radnor Monthly Meeting. Chester Monthly Meeting was established in 1681 as a monthly meeting for Marcus Hook and Upland. Darby Monthly Meeting was established in 1684 and Concord Monthly Meeting in 1684.

In that part of Chester County which remained Chester County the following monthly meetings were established prior to 1800:

     1. Newark (now Kennet) Monthly Meeting (1686) was first held in New Castle County (now Delaware), later moving to Kennet after a period in Centre. These records, up to 1800, will be published in Early Church Records of Chester County, Vol. 3.

     2. New Garden Monthly Meeting (1718) was formed by the division of Newark Monthly Meeting and included meetings of New Garden, Nottingham and Londongrove. These records were compiled by Gilbert Cope near the beginning of the 1900s. We have generally followed his format including his manner of dating.

     3. Goshen Monthly Meeting (1722) was formed from Chester Monthly Meeting in 1722. At that time it included the particular meetings of Goshen, Newton and Uwchlan, to which Nantmeal and Pikeland were added. These records were also compiled by Gilbert Cope and are published here through 1800.

4. Bradford Monthly Meeting (1737) was established to include the meetings of Bradford and Caln. Volume 1 of *Early Church Records of Chester County* by Martha Reamy consists of abstracts of these records. These were abstracted up to 1800. The book was published in 1995.

5. Sadsbury Monthly Meeting (1737/8) was established by the division of New Garden Monthly Meeting. Records of the 1700s have been published Family Line Publications as vol. 3 of *18th Century Church Records of Lancaster County*.

6. Uwchlan Monthly Meeting (1763) was formed by the division of Goshen Monthly Meeting. These records were also compiled by Gilbert Cope and are published here through 1800.

7. Nottingham Monthly Meeting (1730) was part of the Baltimore Yearly Meeting. It was established by a division of New Garden Monthly Meeting in 1730. A compilation of the records by Alice Beard has been published by Family Line Publications in *Nottingham Quakers, Births, Deaths and Marriages, 1680-1889*. These are records from East and West Nottingham Meeting, Little Britain Meeting, Deer Creek Meeting, Eastland Meeting and the Octorara Meeting.

8. Londongrove Monthly Meeting (1792) was established by a division of New Garden Monthly Meeting. The 18th century records will be compiled and published in vol. 3 of this series.

Presbyterian

The oldest Presbyterian Church in Chester County is the "Great Valley," in Tredyffrin Township where there was a congregation as early as 1710. In its early years the congregation was largely Welsh. A church building was erected in 1720. The first minister was Malachi Jones who was replaced by David Evans in 1720.

The Charlestown Presbyterian Church was erected in 1743 as a result of the Old Side/New Side split of the congregation of Great Valley. Principally involved in the organization of the church were David Humphries, David John, Griffith Jones, Lewis Martin and Anthony Pritchard. In 1791 the two churches united. The Upper Octorara Church in Sadsbury Township was organized in 1720. Prior to 1724 it was supplied by Rev. David Evans and Rev. David Magill. The first regular pastor was Adam Boyd, from County Antrim, Ireland, installed in 1724.

The Old Side/New Side controversy split this congregation with the forming of the Second Congregation of Upper Octorara by the New Side; Rev. Andrew Sterling was pastor from 1747 to 1765. The churches united in 1768.

Fagg's Manor Presbyterian Church was formed in 1730. It was first called New Londonderry, taking its name from the township. Rev. Samuel Blair, native of Ireland, became its first pastor in 1740.

The Rock Presbyterian Church was organized in 1720. The first structure was in Lewisville, Elk Township; the second church was erected by the New Side in 1741 at Fair Hill, Cecil County, Maryland; the third location was in Cecil County near the line with Chester County.

The New London Presbyterian Church was founded in 1728. Its first minister was Rev. Samuel Gelston, native of Ireland.

Doe Run Presbyterian Church was erected in 1740. It had supplies from the new Side Presbytery of New Castle until ca. 1747 when Rev. Andrew Sterling became their pastor.

Baptist

Great Valley - About 1701 several families from Wales settled in the east end of the valley. In 1711 Hugh Davis (born in Cardiganshire) was elected to be their minister; in 1722 a log house was built.

Hephzibah - An anabaptist society met at John Bentley's in Newlin in the early 1720s. Rev. Owen Thomas who settled in Vincent in 1707, preached at John Bentley's. A meting house was built in 1752.

Vincent Baptist Church - This church was organized in 1737 as a branch of the Great Valley Church. It was constituted as a new church in 1771.

London Tract Church - As early as 1729 some members of the Welsh Tract Baptists of New Castle County established a branch in London Britain. In his will dated 1731, Thomas Morris of that township, gave to Owen Thomas and Richard Whitting "2 for the use of the meeting house that is in Indian town in London Britain." In 1780 it was constituted an independent congregation. The records book for 1780 to 1830 was destroyed, used to kindle the fire at the home of John W. Tawresey.

Seventh Day Baptist

The first society of this denomination may have been at Newtown in what was then Chester County, meeting at the house of David Thomas. Another society was formed at Nottingham in Chester County, meeting chiefly at the house of Samuel Bond in Cecil County, Maryland. The other society was established at French Creek in East Nantmeal (now Warwick) Township, Chester County; here a meeting house as built in 1762.

Dunkers (German Baptist)

In the summer of 1724 the few Dunkers in Coventry formed a congregation with the assistance of Bishop Peter Becker of Germantown.

Episcopal (Anglican Church)

St. David's (commonly called Radnor) Episcopal church was established by persons who emigrated from Radnorshire, wales ca. 1685. A church was built in 1715.

St. John's in the Campassville, West Caln Township, was built in 1729. Rev. Richard Backhouse conducted services there once each month from 1729 until 1739, when Rev. John Blackhall became rector of the parish.

St. Peter's, Great Valley was built in 1744 in East Whiteland Township.

St. John's was founded on or before 1744 at Penn Station in Penn Township.

Methodist

The first Methodist minister in Chester County was probably Isaac Rollins; by 1773 he had established several preaching places in the county. In that year Rev. Francis Asbury made his first visit to the county.

In 1774 a society was formed in Goshen, afterwards called the Valley Meeting and later as the Grove, in West Whiteland Township.

Missionaries preached in Uwchland Township in 1772. Benson's Chapel was built near Little Eagle tavern in 1781.

Lutheran

The Zion Lutheran Congregation was formed ca. 1750; the union church was formed with the Reformed about the same time. The early records of this church were lost.

Pikeland (later called St. Peter's) Church was formed around 1771 in West Pikeland Township.

Reformed

A constitution and a register begun in 1743 for Brownback's in East Coventry Township. Pastors included Jacob Lishy (1743-1744), Philip Boehm (1746-1748), Frederick Sasimir Miller (1753-1761), Philip Leydich (1766-1784), Peter Pernisius (1786-1788) and J. Ammann (1792-1797).

Leaving the Zion Union Church, the Reformed congregation erected their own church about a mile away. It was known as Vincent or East Vincent. The register was begun in 1760. The ministers were John Philip Leydich (1753-1765), Nicholas Pomp (1765-1783), Frederick Dällicker (1784-1799) and Frederick Herman Jr. (1799-1821).

Mennonite

A church was built in 1728 in East Coventry Township, about 3 miles from Pottstown. Another was built in the vicinity of Phoenixville, date unknown. In 1772 a meeting house was erected in Phoenixville on Main Street.

Roman Catholic

In the *History of Chester County* by J. Smith Futhey and Gilbert Cope, they state,

> "The first Catholic mission must have been established between the years (when a mission was set up at the residence of Thomas Wilcox at Ivy Mills) and 1757, at which latter date it appears there were in Chester County, under care of Robert Harding, 18 men and 22 women; under care of Theodore Schneider (of Germans?), 13 men and 9 women; of Irish, 9 men and 6 women; under care of Ferdinand Farmer, of Irish, 23 men and 17 women, of Germans, 3 men. Robert harding was a priest residing in Philadelphia, but the location of the others is not stated.

They later add,

> "About the year 1793, at the west end of Gay Street, in West Chester, a little Catholic chapel stood ... . This was a the time called 'Christ's Church,' and in it the holy sacrifice of the Mass was offered up occasionally, when the people would gather from the surrounding

country, and when a priest would come out from Philadelphia (there being no resident pastor until about the year 1840)."

Abbreviations

The following abbreviations are used:

b. - born

d. - died

da - day

dau. - daughter

dec'd - deceased

m. - married

mo - married

The date 1758.12.13 means 13th day of the 12th month of 1758.

Township Map of Chester County

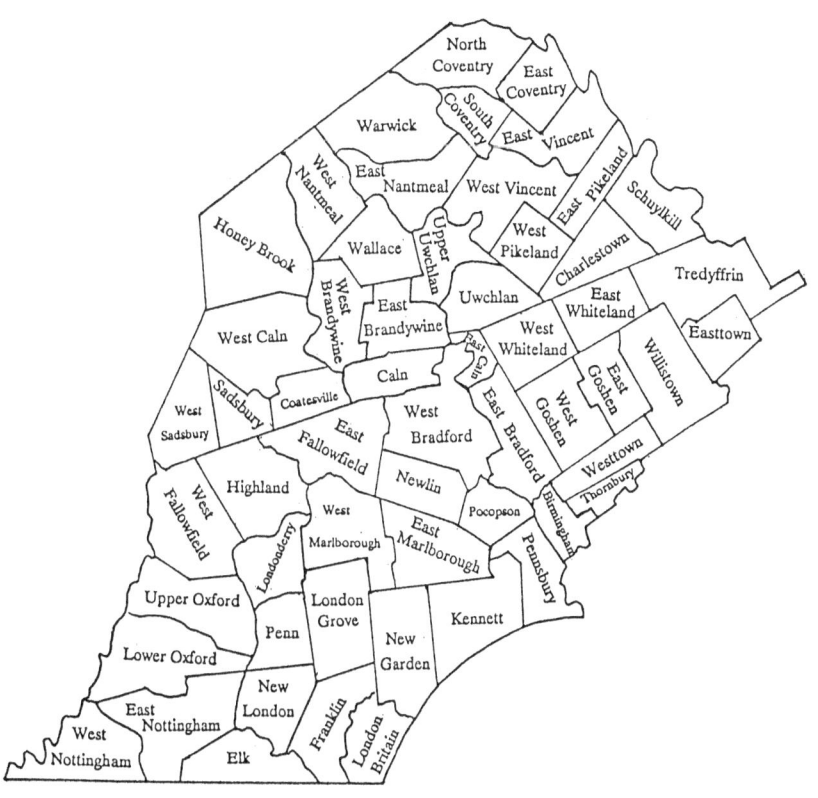

UWCHLAN MONTHLY MEETING
Marriages, Births & Burials 1720-1800

Williams, John and Jane, his wife and their child: Jacob, b. 24th da, 11th mo, 1731/2.
Davies, John and Elizabeth, his wife and their child: Ruth, b. 27th da, 3rd mo, 1723.
Williams, Jacob and Ruth Davies m. 7th da, 10th mo, 1752 and their children: Jane, b. 1st da, 9th mo, 1757, d. 20th da, 10th mo, 1758; Israel, b. 21st da, 9th mo, 1759; Hannah, b. 15th da, 2nd mo, 1762.
Edwards, Rowland and Mary, his wife and their child: John, b. 30th da, 7 mo, 1750.
Michener, John and Mary, his wife and their child: Sarah, b. 13th da, 11th mo, 1750.
Edwards, John and Sarah Michner m. 11th da, 10th mo, 1780 and their children: Mary, b. 24th da, 8th mo, 1781; James, b. 8th da, 8th mo, 1784; John, b. 2nd da, 5th mo, 1788.
Beale, Mary, wife of William Beale, d. 25th da, 8th mo, 1771. William Beale d. 27th da, 11th mo, 1800.
Packer, Phillip and Ann, his wife and their child: James, b. at Prince Town, Middlesex Co., NJ 4th da, 2nd mo, 1726.
Mendenhall, Aaron and Rose, his wife and their child: Rose, b. at East Caln, 4th da, 8th mo, 1733.
Packer, James and Rose Mendenhall m. 1st da, 1st mo, 1751, and their children: Rose, b. 6th da, 12th mo, 1752, d. 23rd da, 10th mo, 1754; Job, b. 27th da, 3rd mo, 1754; Hannah, b. 19th da, 12th mo, 1755; Eli, b. 9th da, 9th mo, 1757; Amos, b. 30th da, 1st mo, 1759, d. 11th da, 8th mo, 1763; Moses, b. 28th da, 4th mo, 1761; Lydia, b. 19th da, 1st mo, 1763; Aaron, b. 5th da, 11th mo, 1764.
Baldwin, John and Hannah, his wife and their child: Joshua, b. at Chester 3rd da, 11th mo, 1721/2, d. 13th da, 5th mo, 1800.
Downing, Thomas and Thomasin, his wife and their child: Sarah, b. 14th da, 8th mo, 1725, d. 16th da, 7th mo, 1745.
Baldwin, Joshua and Sarah Downing m. 7th da, 4th mo, 1744 and their child: Sarah, b. 16th da, 7th mo, 1745.
Baldwin, Joshua and Marcy Brown, dau. of Samuel Brown and Ann, his wife, b. at the Falls in Bucks Co., PA. 12th da, 1st mo, 1722 and d. 22nd da, 1st mo, 1784, m. 11th da, 9th mo, 1747 and their children: Hannah, b. 4th da, 11th mo, 1748/9; John, b. 11th da, 10th mo, 1751, d. 26th da, 12th mo, 1758; Samuel, b. 15th da, 2nd mo, 1754; Rachel, b. 13th da, 7th mo, 1756; Ann, b. 13th da, 12th mo, 1758; Mercy, b. 12th da, 1st mo, 1761; Jane, b. 22nd da, 3rd mo, 1763.
Milhous, Thomas and Sarah, his wife and their child: Thomas Jr, b at

EARLY CHURCH RECORDS OF CHESTER CO.

Newgarden 27th da, 2nd mo, 1731 O.S.

Paschall, William and Hannah, his wife and their child: Elizabeth, b. 5th da, 11th mo, 1729/30. O.S., d. 22nd da, 1st mo, 1758.

Milhous, Thomas Jr. and Elizabeth Paschall m. 7th da, 9th mo, 1751 O.S. and their children: Paschall (son), b. 23rd da, 6th mo, 1752 O.S.; Hannah, b. 19th da, 2nd mo, 1754; Samuel, b. 25th da, 11th mo, 1755; Sarah, b. 28th da, 5th mo, 1757, d. 22nd da, 1st mo, 1758; Seth, b. 22nd da, 10th mo, 1758, d. 25th da, 4th mo, 1759; Isaac, b. 5th da, 6th mo, 1760, d. 27th da, 2nd mo, 1761; Phebe, b. 13th da, 12th mo, 1761; Deborah, b. 31st da, 7th mo, 1764; Enos, b. 6th da, 12th mo, 1766; Susanna, b. 26th da, 6th mo, 1768; Elizabeth, b. 1st da, 12th mo, 1769.

Milhous, Thomas and Sarah, his wife and their children: Robert, b. at Newgarden, Chester Co., PA. 26th da, 11th mo, 1733/4, d. 13th da, 10th mo, 1781.

Merrdith, John and Grace, his wife and their child: Ann, b. 6th da, 6th mo, 1738.

Milhous, Robert and Ann Merrdith and their children: John, b. 16th da, 5th mo, 1757; Dinah, b. 26th da, 3rd mo, 1759; Jesse (son), b. 14th da, 3rd mo, 1761.

Milhous, Thomas and Sarah, his wife and their child: John, b. at Simahoe in Ireland 8th da, 1st mo, 1732/3.

Paschall, William and Hannah, his wife and their child: Margaret, b. at Whiteland, Chester Co., PA. 4th da, 10th mo, 1724.

Milhous, John and Margaret Paschall m. 7th da, 2nd mo, 1749 and their children: Hannah, b. 22nd da, 1st mo, 1749/50, d. 18th da, 11th mo, 1753; Sarah, b. 31st da, 5th mo, 1749/50; William, b. 29th da, 3rd mo, 1753, d. 14th da, 4th mo, 1758; Joanna, b. 24th da, 8th mo, 1754, d. 9th da, 2nd mo, 1758; Mary, b. 31st da, 8th mo, 1760; Lydia, b. 5th da, 2nd mo, 1762, d. 6th da, 3rd mo, 1761; Thomas, b. 16th da, 11th mo, 1765.

Jones, Cadwalader and Ellioner, his wife and their child: Evan, b. 15th da, 10th mo, 1721.

Buffington, Thomas and Ruth, his wife and their child: Susannah, b. 24th da, 5th mo, 1722.

Jones, Evan and Susannah Buffington m. 22nd da, 9th mo, 1744 and their children: Agnes, b. 1st da, 12th mo, 1745/6; Rebecca, b. 14th da, 12th mo, 1748/49; Ruth, b. 18th da, 1st mo, 1750/1; Mary, b. 20th da, 6th mo, 1753; Hannah, b. 3rd da, 18th mo, 1755; Aquila, b. 1st da, 10th mo, 1758; Abner, b. 16th da, 9th mo, 1762.

Jones, Abner, b. 1762, m. 27th of 8th mo, 1789 to Hannah Yearsley, b. 1st da, 3rd mo, 1763 and their children: Susanna, b. 24th da, 5th mo, 1790; Yearsley, b. 23rd da, 8th mo, 1792; Aquila, b. 9th da, 9th mo, 1796.

Davies, John and Eliza, his wife and their child: Amos, b. 1st da, 3rd mo 1728.
Meredith, John and Grace, his wife and their child: Elizabeth, b. 18th da, 9th mo, 1736, d. 7th da, 11th mo, 1768.
Davies, Amos and Elizabeth Meredith m. 5th da, 5th mo, 1757 and their children: Ruth, b. 9th da, 3rd mo, 1758; Joel, b. 6th da, 9th mo, 1759; Grace, b. 25th da, 3rd mo, 1761; Isaac, b. 17th da, 3rd mo, 1765; John, b. 16th da, 2nd mo, 1762; Elisha, b. 2nd da, 1st mo, 1767.
Coates, Moses and Susanna, his wife and their child: Jonathan, b. Newprovidence, Philadelphia Co. PA. 17th da, 11th mo, 1728.
Longstretch, Bartholomew and Ann, his wife and their child: Jane, b. in Warminster, Bucks Co., PA. 23rd da, 11th mo, 1735.
Coates, Jonathan and Jane Longstreth m. 22nd da, 4th mo, 1755 and their children: Ann, b. 12th da, 5th mo, 1757; James, b. 22nd da, 7th mo, 1759; Hannah, b. 5th da, 7th mo, 1761; Jonathan, b. 28th da, 5th mo, 1764; Susanna and Phebe, twins, b. 23rd da, 7th mo, 1766; Kezia, b. 24th da, 2nd mo, 1768; Grace, b. 16th da, 7th mo, 1771; Jane, b. 28th da, 8th mo, 1776; Elizabeth, b. 8th da, 9th mo, 1779.
Coates, Ann, widow of Benjamin, b. 3rd da, 11th mo, 1737/8 and children: Susanna, b. 10th da, 3rd mo, 1776; Benjamin, b. 18th da, 9th mo, 1780.
Longstretch, John and Jane, his wife and their children: Hannah, b. 9th da, 10th mo, 1768; John, b. 10th da, 2nd mo, 1771; Sarah, b. 18th da, 10th mo, 1773; Moses, b. 18th da, 6th mo, 1780; Jane, b. 14th da, 7th mo, 1784.
Lewis, Griffith and Mary, his wife and their child: Samuel, b. 5th da, 8th mo, 1726.
Trotter, William and Hannah, his wife and their child: Margaret, b. 12th da, 2nd mo, 1727.
Lewis, Samuel and Margaret Trotter m. 4th da, 11th mo, 1756 and their children: Hannah, b. 3rd da, 9th mo, 1757, d. 26th 11th mo, 1764; Rebecca, b. 28th da, 10th mo, 1759. Margaret Lewis d. 18th da, 9th mo, 1759.
Lewis, Samuel and Mary, his second wife and their children: Dinah, b. 23rd da, 6th mo, 1766; Griffith, b. 6th da, 12th mo, 1767; Margaret, b. 18th da, 9th mo, 1769, d. 28th, 11 mo, 1770.
Valentine, Thomas and Mary, his wife and their children: Robert, b. at Bally-Brumhill in Ireland 21st da, 7th mo, 1707, d. 21st da, 7th mo, 1786.
Edge, John and Mary, his wife and their child: Rachel, b. at Providence in this county 29th da, 6th mo, 1725, d. 31st da, 1st mo, 1758.

Valentine, Robert and Rachel Edge m. 4th da, 4th mo, 1744 and their children: Thomas, b. 28th da, 3rd mo, 1748, d. 27th da, 3rd mo, 1752; Mary, b. 26th da, 7th mo, 1750, d. 24th da, 3 mo, 1752; Robert, b. 24th da, 6th mo, 1752; Rachel, b. 14th da, 10th mo, 1754; Jane, b. 26th da, 10t, mo, 1756, d. 7th da, 2nd mo, 1757; Sarah, b. 14th da, 10th mo, 1757, d. 7th da, 4th mo, 1758; Phebe, b. 5th da, 6th mo, 1759; George, b. 16th da, 4th mo, 1761, d. 11th da, 7th mo, 1800; Jacob, b. 7th da, 10th mo, 1763; Susanna, b. 26th da, 3rd mo, 1766.

Brown, William and Esther, his wife and their child: James, b. no date.

Elgar, Joseph and Mary, his wife and their child: Elizabeth, b. no date.

Brown, James m. Elizabeth Elgar 14th da, 3rd mo, 1753, and their children: James, b. 4th da, 2nd mo, 1754; Israel, b. 2nd da, 11th mo, 1755; Elisha, b. 16th da, 11th mo, 1757; Esther, b. 3rd da, 6th mo, 1759; Elgar, (son), b. 2nd da, 7th mo, 1761; Miriam, b. 2nd da, 8th mo, 1763; Elizabeth, b. 8th da, 7th mo, 1765; Joseph, b. 15th da, 12th mo, 1767, d. 1768.

Griffith, John and Ann, his wife and their child: Joshua, b. 31st da, 1st mo, 1721.

John, Davis and Elizabeth, his wife and their child: Rachel, b. 10th da, 2nd mo, 1720.

John, Joshua m. Rachel Davis and their children: Lisa, b. 10th da, 3rd mo, 1745, d. 22nd da, 7th mo, 1746; Sarah, b. 13th da, 5th mo, 1747; Elizabeth, b. 15th da, 8th mo, 1749; Sibilla, b. 3rd da, 8th mo, 1753; Abner, b. 22nd da, 8th mo, 1757, d. 18th da, 7th mo, 1758; Rachel, b. 22nd da, 6th mo, 1759; Esaiak, b. 12th da, 7th mo, 1761; Hannah, b. 15th da, 7th mo, 1763; Ann, b. 7th da, 8th mo, 1765.

Lewis, Griffith and Mary, his wife and their children: William, b. 22nd da, 2nd mo, 1724.

Peter Thomas and Elizabeth, his wife: Elizabeth, b. 10th da, 1st mo, 1722/3.

Lewis, William m. Elizabeth Thomas 9th da, 8th mo, 1747, and their children: Mary, b. 11th da, 7th mo, 1748; Rebecca, b. 21st da, 6th mo, 1750; William, b. 24th da, 7th mo, 1752; Elizabeth, b. 29th da, 11th mo, 1755; Sarah, b. 29th da, 7th mo, 1758; Amos, son, b. 29th da, 6th mo, 1761; Hannah, b. 1st da, 3rd mo, 1766.

Starr, James and Hannah, his wife and their children: Sarah, b. 10th da, 12th mo, 1751; Rachel, b. 25th da, 6th mo, 1754; Hannah, b. 9th da, 9th mo, 1756.

Wilson, John and Dinah, his wife and their children: Mary, b. 18th da, 12th mo, 1760; Jehu, b. 1st da, 1st mo, 1763; Seth, b. 7th da, 12th mo, 1764.

Lightfoot, Samuel, son of Samuel Lightfoot, departed this life at Pittsburgh the 30th da, 7th mo, 1759 and was buried there the next day. Certified: James Kenney and Benedict Dorsey.
Lightfoot, Samuel father of the above Samuel Lightfoot, departed this life at his house near Chester the 26th da, 3rd mo, 1777 and was buried in Friends Burying Ground in Chester.
Baldwin, John and Hannah, his wife and their child: John, b. 22nd da, 13th mo, 1719.
Pierce, Caleb and Mary, his wife and their child: Ann, b. 11th da, 11th mo, 1724/5.
Baldwin, John m. Ann Pierce and their children: Mary, b. 17th da, 6th mo, 1744; John, b. 2nd da, 6th mo, 1748, d. 9th da, 9th mo, 1748; Caleb, b. 31st da, 6th mo, 1749; Ann, b. 20th da, 6th mo, 1752.
Martin, Aaron d. 11th da, the 4th mo, [no year given].
Jones, Cadwalader and Elenor, his wife and their children: Cadwalader, b. 8th da, 1st mo, 1724, d. 14th da, 5th mo, 1795, aged 71 years and 2 months.
Gatleif, Charles and his children: Mary, b. 2nd da, 2nd mo, 1731, d. 1st da, 5th mo, 1793 and was bur. the 3rd da, the same.
Jones, Cadwalader m. Mary Gatleif 5th da, 2nd mo, 1750 and their children: Jonathan, b. 12th da, 1st mo, 1750/1; Jesse, b. 25th da, 1st, 1754.
Townsend, Mary (now wife) of Jesse Jones, b. 6th da, 9th mo, 1753.
Meredith, Jno. and Grace, his wife and their child: Enoch, b. 18th da, 6th mo, 1728.
John, Griffith and Ann, his wife and their child: Jane, b. 5th da, 2nd mo, 1725, d. 1st da, 9th mo, 1795.
Meredith, Enoch m. Jane John on 18th da, 12th mo, 1752, and their children: James, b. 1st da, 10th mo, 1753; Elizabeth, b. 30th da, 4th mo, 1755, d. 22nd da, 8th mo, 1759; John, b. 21st da, 3rd mo, 1757, d. 29th da, 8th mo, 1759; Hannah, b. 2nd da, 1st mo, 1759; Ezra, b. 5th da, 11th mo, 1760; Abel, b. 8th da, 8th mo, 1762; Enoch, b. 18th da, 1st mo, 1766; d. 3rd da, 11th mo, 1769; Jane, b. 26th da, 10th mo, 1767; Thomas, b. 20th da, 10th mo, 1770.
Hancock, William and Sarah, his wife and their child: James, b. 2nd da, 9th mo, 1730.
Randal, Joseph and Rebecca, his wife and their child: Elizabeth, b. 11th da, 2nd mo, 1725.
Hancock, James m. Elizabeth Randal 26th da 3rd mo, 1752 and their children: Joseph, b. 11th da, 2nd mo, 1753; William, b. 14th da, 10th mo, 1754, d. 2nd mo, 1755; Sarah, b. 18th da, 6th mo, 1756, d. 10th mo, 1758; Rebekah, b. 22nd da, 10th mo, 1757, d. 3rd mo, 1758;

Elizabeth, b. 2nd da, 2nd mo, 1759; James, b. 21st da, 12th mo, 1760; John, b. 9th da, 11th mo, 1763; Sarah, b. 4th da, 11th mo, 1764; Benjamin, b. 10th da, 5th mo, 1767; Joel, b. 26th da, 4th mo, 1769.

Thomas, Peter and Eliza, his wife and their child: John, b. 7th da, 8th mo, 1717 O.S.

Jones, Cadwalader and wife, Ellinor and their child: Rebekah, b. 1st da, 9th mo, 1718 O.S.

Thomas, John m. Rebekah Jones 28th da, 2nd mo, 1747 and their children: Jehu, b. 29th da, 2nd mo, 1748; Elinor, b. 21st da, 5th mo, 1749; John, b. 3rd da, 12th mo, 1750/1, d. 10th da, 10th mo, 1752; Rebekah, b. 10th da, 8th mo, 1752, d. 28th da, 8th mo, 1754; John, b. 6th da, 4th mo, 1754; Rebekah, b. 10th da, 12th mo, 1755; Sarah, b. 2nd da, 9th mo, 1757; Dinah, b. 5th da, 3rd mo, 1759; Jonah, b. 8th da, 1st mo, 1761; Judah (son), b. 20th da, 8th mo, 1762, d. 3rd mo, 1764.

Downing, Thomas and Thomzin, his wife and their child: Richard, b. 27th da, 2nd mo, 1719.

Edge, John and Mary, his wife and their children: Mary, b. 2nd da, 7th mo, 1721, d. 13th da, 12th mo, 1795.

Downing, Richard m. Mary Edge 23rd da, 3rd mo, 1741, and their children: Hannah, b. 19th da, 1st mo, 1741/2, d. 5th da, 4th 1752; Thomas, b. 13th da, 10th mo, 1743, d. 12th da, 4th mo, 1752; Jane, b. 1st da, 11th mo, 1745, d. 20th da, 4th mo, 1752; John, b. 17th da, 12th mo, 1747/8, d. 20th da, 5th mo, 1748; Richard, b. 4th da, 5th mo, 1750; Mary, b. 31st da, 7th mo, 1752; Thomzin (dau.), b. 26th da, 8th mo, 1754; Jacob, b. 25th da, 10th mo, 1750; William, b. 29 da, 1st mo, 1759; 24th da, 12th mo, 1759; George, b. 8th da, 11th mo, 1760, d. 10th da, 8th mo, 1765; Samuel, b. 4th da, 2nd mo, 1763; m. Jane Ashbridge on 28th da, 10th mo, 1790; Joseph, b. 19th da, 6th mo, 1765.

Downing, Samuel and Jane, b. 11th da, 10th mo, 1764 and their child: George, b. 1st da, 3rd mo, 1802.

Randall, Joseph and Rebecca, his wife and their child: Joseph Randall, b. 16th da, 9th mo, 1734.

Griffith, Benoni and Catherine, his wife and their child: Rachel Griffith, b. 14th da, "the same month" (i.e. 9th mo 1734).

Randall, Joseph M. Rachel Griffith 11th da, 7th mo, 1757 and their children: Hannah, b. 26th da, 8th mo, 1758; Rebecca, b. 25th da, 9th mo, 1760; Sarah, b. 12th da, 2nd mo, 1762; Elizabeth, b. 18th da, 1st mo, 1764; John, b. 4th da, 2nd mo, 1765; Rachel, b. 7th da, 11th mo 1766; Ruth, b. 22nd da, 9th mo, 1768; Joseph, b. 9th da, 8th mo, 1770.

Lightfoot, Samuel and Mary, his wife and their child: William Lightfoot, b. 20th da, 1st mo, 1731.

Ferris, David and Mary, his wife and their child: Mary, b. 17th da, 2nd mo, 1745.
Lightfoot, William and Mary Ferris m. 14th da, 8th mo, 1766 and their children: Susanna, b. 15th da, 8th mo, 1767; Samuel, b. 5th da, 9th mo, 1768; Mary, b. 28th da, 4th mo, 1770; Deborah, b. 26th da, 4th mo, 1773; David, b. 6th da, 2nd mo, 1774; Sarah, b. 22nd da, 7th mo, 1776; William, b. 4th da, 9th mo, 1782.
Cadwalader, David and wife, Mary and their child: Nathan b. 29th da, 1st mo 1725.
Gatlive, Charles and his wife, Mary and their child: Elizabeth, b. 15th da, 2nd mo, 1728, d. 4th da, 1st mo 1772.
Cadwalader, Nathan and Elizabeth Gatlive m. 9th da, 4th mo, 1748 and their children: Charles, b. 2nd da, 3rd mo, 1749; Isaac, b. 27th da, 9th mo, 1751; Judah (son), b. 27th da, 9th mo, 1754; Hannah, b. 24th da, 12th mo, 1755; Nathan, b. 31st da, 1st mo, 1758; Mary, b. 24th da, 3rd mo, 1760; Jesse, b. 23rd da, 3rd mo, 1762; Phebe, b. 11th da, 10th mo, 1764; Elizabeth, b. 14th da, 5th mo, 1768.
John, Samuel and Margaret, his wife and their child: Samuel John, b. 23rd da, 11th mo, 1711/12.
Jenkin, Evan and Sarah, his wife and their child: Ann Jenkin, b. 14th da, 12th mo, 1714/15.
John, Samuel m. Ann Jenkin. Their children: Isaac, b. 19th da, 12th mo, 1738/9; Ruth, b. 24th da, 6th mo, 1741; Samuel, b. 18th da, 9th mo, 1743; Lydia, b. 7th da, 9th mo, 1745; Sarah, b. 23rd da, 8th mo, 1748; Mary, b. 11th da, 8th mo, 1751; Ebenezer, b. 7th da, 9th mo, 1755.
Michem, John, b. 21st da, 4th mo, 1731 O.S. and Jane Stanly, b. 3rd da, 3rd mo, 1744 m. 2nd da, 5th mo, 1762 and their children: Ellen, b. 26th da, 2nd mo, 1763, d. c. 12 years old; Francis (son), b. 11th da, 6th mo, 1764; Ann, b. 25th da, 3rd mo, 1766; Mary, b. 29th da, 2nd mo, 1768; Naomi, b. 6th da, 3rd mo, 1770; John, b. 29th da, 8th mo, 1772; George, b. 2nd da, 3rd mo, 1778.
Meredith, John, b. in Radnorshire, in Wales, 9th da, 2nd mo, 1699 and Grace, dau. of Robert Williams, b. in Goshen in this province 12th da, 3rd mo, 1707, m. 29th da, 9th mo, 1727 and their children: Enoch, b. 18th da, 6th mo, 1728; Simon, b. 12th da, 10th mo, 1729; James, b. 11th da, 10th mo, 1731, d. 11th da, 6th mo, 1741; Fourth son, b. 11th da, 9th mo, 1733, d. 26th da, 9th mo, 1733; Jane, b. 30th da, 11th mo, 1734/5, d. 6th da, 6th mo 1741; Elizabeth, b. 18th da, 9th mo, 1736; Ann, b. 6th da, 5th mo, 1739; Hannah, b. 1st da, 5th mo, 1741; Jane, b. 12th da, 1st mo, 1742/3; Grace, b. 13th da, 11th mo, 1744/5; John, b. 29th da, 4th mo, 1747; Ruth, b. 17th da, 3rd mo, 1750, d. 16th da, 8th mo, 1759. John, father, d. 4th da, 3rd mo 1769; Grace, mother, d. 25th da, 10th mo, 1785.

Kirk, Alfansus and Abigail, his wife and their child: William Kirk, b. 4th da, 1st mo, 1709, d. 3rd da, 3rd mo, 1787.
Buckingham, John and Wife Hannah and their children: Mary, b. before 1734, m. William Kirk d. 9th da, 3rd mo, 1753: Caleb, b. 4th da, 5th mo, 1734; Ruth, b. 16th da, 7th mo, 1736, d. 10th da, 1st mo, 1753; Tamor, b. 25th da, 2nd mo, 1738; Hannah, b. 21st da, 10th mo, 1740, d. 11th da, 4th mo, 1753; Rebecca, b. 31st da, 3rd mo, 1744, d. 8th da, 8th mo, 1752; Rachel, b. 24th da, 6th mo, 1746, d. 24th da, 2nd mo, 1753; Lydia, b. 11th da, 12th mo, 1748/9; Mary and Sarah, twins, b. 1st da, 1st mo, 1751.
Kirk, William and Sibella, dau. of John Davis and Elizabeth, his wife, b. 1st da, 1st mo, 1726, m. 27th da, 3rd mo, 1754 and their children: Isaiah, b. 9th da, 12th mo, 1754; Elizabeth, b. 24th da, 11th mo, 1755; Rebecca, b. 3rd da, 2nd mo, 1758; Ruth, b. 16th da, 4th mo, 1761; Rachel, b. 18th da, 4th mo, 1763; Sibilla, b. 23rd da, 10th mo, 1771.
Trimble, William and Ann, his wife and their child: William, b. 19th da, 9th mo, 1737.
Thomas, Richard and Phebe, his wife and their child: Grace, b. 3rd da, 11th mo, 1742.
Trimble, William and Grace Thomas m. 11th da, 9th mo, 1766 and their children: Richard, b. 15th da, 8th mo, 1767; Susanna, b. 18th da, 9th mo, 1769; Hannah, b. 4th da, 3rd mo, 1772; Lydia, b. 12th da, 8th mo, 1774; Ann, b. 16th da, 2nd mo, 1778.
Trimble, William and Ann, and their children: Phebe, b. 21st da, 7th mo, 1786; John, b. 31st da, 1st mo, 1788; Grace, b. 14th da, 12th mo, 1789; William, b. 13th da, 3rd mo, 1793.
Martin, John and Wife Elizabeth and their child: Thomas Martin, b. in Ireland 21st da, 10th mo, 1714, d. 30th da, 10th mo, 1786.
Jones, Cadwalader and Eleanor, his wife and their child: Sarah Jones, b. 6th da, 2nd mo, 1715, d. 30th da, 6th mo, 1800.
Martin, Thomas and Sarah Jones m. 7th da, 4th mo, 1750, and their children: Eleanor, b. 29th da, 1st mo, 1751; Hannah, b. 12th da, 6th mo, 1753; Susanna, b. 25th da, 11th mo, 1753, d. 21st da, 5th mo, 1758; Aaron, b. 6th da, 2nd mo, 1755; Mary, b. 23rd da, 5th mo, 1756; John, b. 2nd da, 7th mo, 1758.
Cox, Joseph, b. 26th da, 4th mo, 1723 and Catharine, his wife, b. 27th da, 6th mo, 1722, and their children: Hannah, b. 6th da, 9th mo, 1747, d. 1st da, 10th mo, 1747; Mary, b. 8th da, 9th mo, 1748; William, b. 14th da, 8th mo, 1750, d. 23rd da, 8th mo, 1750; Hannah, b. 5th da, 10th mo, 1751; Margaret, b. 6th da, 1st mo, 1753; Benjamin, b. 7th da, 2nd mo, 1756, d. 2nd da, 5th mo, 1757; Benjamin, b. 8th da, 7th mo, 1758; Richard, b. 29th da, 1st mo,

1761; Elizabeth, b. 25th da, 3rd mo, 1763.
Fussell, Bartholomew and Rebekah and their children: Esther, b. 18th da, 3rd mo, 1782; William, b. 30th da, 6th mo, 1783; Sarah, b. 10th da, 9th mo, 1784; Joseph, b. 26th da, 4th mo, 1787; Solomon, b. 28th da, 6th mo, 1789; Jacob, b. 7th da, 2nd mo, 1792; Bartholomew, b. 9th da, 1st mo, 1794; Rebecca, b. 21st da, 4th mo, 1796.
Fussel, Rebecca d. 3rd da, the 4th mo, 1751.
Milhous, Thomas and Wife Sarah: William their son, b. 23rd da, 8th mo, 1738, N.S.
Baldwin, Joshua and wife, Mercy: Hannah their dau., b. 15th da, 1st mo, 1749, N.S.
Mulhous, William and Hannah Baldwin were m. 22nd da, 10th mo, 1767 and their children: Mercy, b. 28th da, 8th mo, 1768; Sarah, b. 4th da, 1st mo, 1771; Samuel, b. 13th da, 4th mo, 1773, d. 7th da, 8th mo, 1778; Rachel, b. 14th da, 1st mo, 1776; Joshua, b. 26th da, 9th mo, 1778, d. 29th da, 8th mo, 1790; Hannah, b. 15th da, 11th mo, 1780; William, b. 4th da, 6th mo, 1783; Phebe, b. 26th da, 5th mo, 1785; Jane, b. 10th da, 6th mo, 1790.
Massey, George and Susannah and their children: Robert, b. 27th da, 12th mo, 1794; Isaac, b. 13th da, 11th mo, 1797; George, b. 12th da, 1st mo, 1801; William, b. 24th da, 12th mo, 1803; Rachel, b. 15th da, 3rd mo, 1806; Isaac, b. 24th da, 8th mo, 1809.
Griffith, John and Mary, his wife and their child: John Griffith their son, b. 13th da, 6th mo, 1737.
Falkner, Jesse and Martha, his wife and their child: Mary Falkner, b. 18th da, 12th mo, 1746/7.
Griffith, John and Mary Falkner m. 11th da, 12th mo, 1768 and their children: Martha, b. 22nd da, 8th mo, 1769; Mary, b. 26th da, 6th mo, 1771; Sibella, b. 10th da, 2nd mo, 1774; Jesse, b. 30th da, 8th mo, 1776, d. 25th 2nd mo, 1777.
Meredith, John and Grace, his wife and their child: Simon Meredith, b. 12th da, 10th mo, 1729.
Pugh, Hugh and Mary, his wife and their child: Dinah Pugh, b. 20th da, 7th mo, 1734.
Meredith, Simon and Dinah Pugh were m. 30th da, 4th mo, 1755 and their children: Mary, b. 6th da, 7th mo, 1756, d. 1st da, 10th mo, 1758; Grace, b. 26th da, 9th mo, 1757, d. 17th da, 5th mo, 1759; Joel, b. 30th da, 3rd mo, 1759; John, b. 6th da, 2nd mo, 1761, d. 30th da, 1st mo, 1775; Mary (2nd), b. 6th da, 11th mo, 1762; Grace (2nd), b. 13th da, 10th mo, 1764; Rebecca, b. 10th da, 8th mo, 1766; James, b. 4th da, 9th mo, 1768; Jese, b. 13th da, 8th mo, 1770; Elizabeth, b. 2nd da, 3rd mo, 1772; Hugh, b. 24th da, 6th mo, 1774; John (2nd), b. 26th da, 12th mo, 1776.
Way, Francis and Elizabeth, his wife and their child: Joshua

Way, b. 27th da, 11th mo, 1737 in Chester Co.
Chandler, Jacob and Martha, his wife and their child: Lydia Chandler, b. 8th da, 12th mo, 1739 at Center in New Castle Co., PA, d. 10th da, 9th mo, 1771.
Way, Joshua and Lydia Chandler m. and their child: Martha, b. 19th da, 3rd mo, 1768.
Cooper, William and Mary, his wife and their child: William Cooper, b. in Kennett 29th da, 6th mo, 1749.
John, Joshua and Rachel, his wife and their child: Sibilla John, b. in Pikeland Township in Chester Co., PA. 3rd da, 8th mo, 1753, d. 6th da, 2nd mo, 1790.
Cooper, William and Sibilla John m. 25th da, 6th mo, 1778 and their children: Mary, b. 25th da, 6th mo, 1779; Rachel, b. 9th da, 4th mo, 1781; Joshua, b. 6th da, 6th mo, 1783; Samuel, b. 5th da, 3rd mo, 1785; Isaac, b. 9th da, 7th mo, 1787; Sibilla, b. 3rd da, 2nd mo, 1790.
Thomas, Reuben of Pikeland Meeting d. 6th da, 4th mo, 1769.
Coates, Susanna of Pikeland Meeting d. 30th da, 11th mo, 1772.
Fussell, Solomon d. 22nd da, 10th mo, 1793.
Starr, Elisabeth d. 14th da, 12th mo, 1799.
Fussell, Sarah d. 21st da, 9th mo, 1800 in the 72nd year of her age.
Starr, Joseph and Rebecca, his wife and their child: Joseph Starr, b. 6th da, 7th mo, 1741.
Longstretch, Bartholomew and Ann, his wife and their child: Elisabeth Longstretch, b. 15th da, 3rd mo, 1741.
Starr, Joseph m. Elisabeth Longstreth 21st da, 6th mo, 1763 and their children: Rebecca, b. 11th da, 7th mo, 1764; Ann, b. 7th da, 9th mo, 1765; Elisabeth, b. 24th da, 4th mo, 1767; Isaac, b. 8th da, 8th mo, 1768; Joseph, b. 5th da, 10th mo, 1769; Sarah, b. 27th da, 11th mo, 1771; John, b. 27th da, 7th mo, 1774; Benjamin, b. 5th da, 2nd mo, 1776; Amy, b. 29th da, 5th mo, 1778; William, b. 8th mo, 1781, d. 31st da, 10th mo, 1786.
Judge, Hugh and wife, Margaret and their child: Hugh, b. Philadelphia, PA. 25th da, 11th mo, 1750.
Hutton, Joseph and wife, Susanna and their child: Susanna, b. in Ireland 20th da, 11th mo, 1753.
Judge, Hugh and Susanna Hutton m. at Uwchlan 12th da, 9th mo, 1776 and their children: Thomas, b. 27th da, 9th mo, 1777; Hannah, b. 21st da, 12 mo, 1778.
Downing, Thomas and Thomzin, his wife and their child: Joseph Downing, b. at Sadsberry in Lancaster Co. 30th da, 4th mo, 1734.
Downing, Joseph and Mary Trimble m. and their children: Thomas, b. 14th da, 10th mo, 1758; Jane, b. 27th da, 7th mo, 1761; Mary, b. 14th da, 10th mo, 1763; Thomzin (dau.), b. 31st da, 3rd mo, 1765;

Joseph, b. 9th da, 4th mo, 1769; James, b. 11th da, 4th mo, 1771; Sarah, b. 1st da, 8th mo, 1773; Richard, b. 26th da, 6th mo, 1775; Ann, b. 1st da, 3rd mo, 1778.
Dunkin, Aaron and Susanna, his wife, and their children: Martha, b. 5th da, 4th mo, 1784; Gulielma, b. 30th da, 7th mo, 1787; Elisabeth, b. 23rd da, 5th mo, 1789.
Dunkin, Aaron d. 7th da, 12th mo, 1791.
Lightfoot, Thomas and Rachel and their child: Susanna, b. 8th da, 1st mo, 1786; Benjamin, b. 12th da, 1st mo, 1787.
Lightfoot, Susanna, wife of Thomas Lightfoot, d. 8th da, 5th mo, 1781.
Lightfoot, Rachel, 2nd wife of Thomas Lightfoot, d. 5th mo, 1790.
Lightfoot, Thomas d. 5th da, 10th mo, 1793.
James Speary d. 5th da, 12th mo, 1774. *James Speary was b. in England and lived some time in the City of London, but I have no other account of his birth or ancestors. [signed] William Lightfoot.*
Jacobs, John and Mary, his wife of New Providence in Philadelphia Co. and their child: Isaac, b. 13th da, 2nd mo, 1741 O.S.
Trimble, William and Ann, his wife of Concord, Chester Co. and their child: Hannah, b. 22nd da, 10th mo, 1743, O.S.
Jacobs, Isaacm. Hannah Trimble 18th da, 9th mo, 1766 and their children: Mary, b. 7th da, 2nd mo, 1768; Ann, b. 14th da, 8th mo, 1769, d. 25th da, 7th mo, 1771; Phebe, b. 9th da, 6th mo, 1771; William, b. 15th da, 8th mo, 1773, d. 4th da, 6th mo, 1795; Hannah, b. 25th da, 12th mo, 1775; Elizabeth, b. 22nd da, 11th mo, 1777; Sarah, b. 4th da, 3rd mo, 1780, d. 23rd da, 2nd mo, 1815; Isaac, b. 14th da, 4th mo, 1782; John, b. 4th da, 7th mo, 1784, d. 12th mo, 1785; Joseph, b. 17th da, 6th mo, 1786; Rachel, b. 3rd da, 9th mo, 1788, d. 21st da, 4th mo, 1796.
Hawley, Joseph b. 6th da, 6th mo, 1760 and Rebecca Meredith, b. 10th da, 8th mo, 1766 m. 23rd da, 5th mo, 1798 and their children: Mary, b. 2nd da, 3rd mo, 1799; Simon, b. 6th da, 4th mo, 1801; Benjamin, b. 13th da, 4th mo, 1803; Joel, b. 7th da, 10th mo, 1804; Jesse, b. 14th da, 2nd mo, 1806; Dinah, b. 30th da, 10th mo, 1808.
Meredith, John and Grace, his wife and their child: John, b. 20th da, 4th mo, 1747.
Jones, Evan and Susanna, his wife and their child: Mary Jones, b. 20th da, 6th mo, 1753, d. 8th da, 5th mo, 1777.
Meredith, John m. Mary Jones 13th da, 6th mo, 1776 and their child: Mary, b. 16th da, 4th mo, 1777, d. 30th da, 9th mo, 1777.
Meredith, John and Elizabeth Kirk, dau. of William and Sybilla Kirk, b. 24th da, 11th mo, 1756, m. 28th da, 10th mo, 1780 and their children: Simon, b. 27th da, 11th mo, 1781; Bulah, b. 5th da, 3rd

mo, 1783; William, b. 18th da, 9th mo, 1784; Isaiah, b. 12th da, 9th mo, 1786; John, b. 18th da, 5th mo, 1788; Enoch, b. 30th da, 3rd mo, 1790, d. 31st da, 12th mo, 1799. Elizabeth Meredith d. in 6th mo, 1794.

Meredith, John and Rebecca Thomas m. 22nd 3rd mo, 1796.

Williams, William and his children: John Williams, b. 8th da, 8th mo, 1749; Sarah, b. 1st da, 1st mo, 1751.

Williams, John and Sarah Kirk m. 21st da, 10th mo, 1772 and their children: Mary, b. 24th da, 7th mo, 1773, d. 19th da, 4th mo, 1776; Katharine, b. 19th da, 7th mo, 1775.

Smedley, William of Middletown and Elizabeth, his wife and their child: Peter, b. 28th da, 1st mo, 1754.

Sharpless, Samuel and Jane, his wife and their child: Phebe, b. 25th da, 5th mo, 1752.

Smedley, Peter and Phebe Sharpless m. 6th da, 6th mo, 1782, and their children: Elizabeth, b. 8th da, 3rd mo, 1783; Joel, b. 22nd da, 8th mo, 1784; Jane, b. 1st da, 1st mo, 1785; Peter, b. 30th da, 11th mo, 1787; William, b. 13th da, 9th mo, 1789; Isaac, b. 29th da, 4th mo, 1791; Samuel, b. 13th da, 8th mo, 1793; Phebe, b. 18th da, 12th mo, 1795; Lydia, b. 22nd da, 11th mo, 1797.

Williams, Edward and Sibbilla, his wife and their child: Daniel, b. 17th da, 5th mo, 1747, O.S.

Humphrey, Owen and Sarah, his wife and their child: Mary, b. 11th da, 4th mo, 1747.

Williams, Daniel and Mary Humphry m. 11th da, 6th mo, 1772 and their children: Sarah, b. 9th da, 4th mo, 1773; Edward, b. 7th da, 11th mo, 1774, d. 5th da, 5th mo, 1775; Sibbilla, b. 10th da, 3rd mo, 1776.

Morris, Edward and, his wife, Hannah and their children: Jonathan, b. 16th da, 2nd mo, 1779; David, b. 17th da, 8th mo, 1781.

Packer, James and Rose, his wife: Job their son, b. 27th da, 3rd mo, 1754.

Lamborn, William and Sarah, his wife and their child: Hannah, b. 21st da, 4th mo, 1754.

Packer, Job and Hannah Lamborn m. at Kennett Meeting House in Chester Co., PA. 28th da, 5th mo, 1778 and their children: Sarah, b. 25th da, 5th mo, 1779; William, b. 14th da, 4th mo, 1780; Hannah, b. 14th da, 4th mo, 1783.

Hallowell, John, son of William and Mary, b. 22th da, 3rd mo, 1788, m. Alice Potts, dau. of Lebelon and Martha, b. 27th da, 10th mo, 1780, and their children: Lebulon, b. 8th da, 7th mo, 1802; William, b. 7th da, 8th mo, 1805; Susanna, b. 27th da, 10th mo, 1806; Martha, b. 23rd da, 12th mo, 1808; Mary, b. 22nd da, 2nd mo, 1810; Daniel, b. 4th da, 3rd mo, 1812; Nathan, b. 2nd da, 7th mo, 1813;

Ann, b. 27th da, 7th mo, 1815.
Rogers, Joseph and Rebecca, his wife of Vincent Township, Chester
  Co., PA and their child: Joseph, b. 25th da, 6th mo, 1719 O.S., d.
  13th da, 6th mo, 1778.
Watson, William and Hannah, his wife of New Providence in
  Philadelphia Co., PA and their child: Hannah, b. 23rd da, 6th mo,
  1717, O.S., d. 6th da, 12th mo, 1778.
Rogers, Joseph and Hannah Watson m. at New Providence 11th mo,
  da, 1741 and their children: Rebekah, b. 23rd da, 12th mo, 1742;
  James, b. 27th da, 2nd mo, 1744; John, b. 4th da, 8th mo, 1746;
  Mary, b. 26th da, 12th mo, 1747; William, b. 3rd da, 6th mo, 1752;
  Jonathan, b. 15th da, 2nd mo, 1755; Hannah, b. 12th da, 1st mo,
  1757.
Thomas, Jonathan, son of Reuben and Rebecca Thomas, b. 6th da, 10th
  mo, 1766.
Thomas, Watson b. 25th da, 12th mo, 1767.
Owen, Elisha, son of Evan and Jane Owen, b. 29th da, 8th mo, 1780.
M'Veagh, Mary b. 28th da, 10th mo, 1758.
M'Veagh, Rachel b. 12th da, 3rd mo, 1768.
M'Veagh, Alice b. 23rd da, 7th mo, 1770.
M'Veagh, Ellen b. 20 da, 2nd mo, 1774.
Butler, William, son of Noble Butler and Rachel, his wife, b. 12th da,
  4th mo, 1732 and Jane Woodward, dau. of James Woodward and
  Ann, his wife, b. 3rd da, 8th mo, 1739 m. at Uwochlen 20th da, 4th
  mo, 1762 and their children: Samuel, b. 24th da, 2nd mo, 1766;
  James, b. 5th da, 7th mo, 1767; Amos, b. 8th da, 5th mo, 1769; Ann,
  b. 6th da, 10th mo, 1770; Rachel, b. 23rd da, 11th mo, 1773; Sarah,
  b. 18th da, 11th mo, 1776; William, b. 8th da, 1st mo, 1780.
Williams, Jonathan b. 31st da, 10th mo, 1761 and Elisabeth Clendenan,
  b. 31st da, 10th mo, 1765 m. 30th da, 4th mo, 1789 and their
  children: William, b. 19th da, 2nd mo, 1790; Isaac, b. 5th da, 6th mo,
  1791; Mary, b. 29th da, 12th mo, 1793; John, b. 23rd da, 3rd mo,
  1796; Mordecai, b. 2nd da, 12th mo, 1798; Deborah, b. 2nd da, 2nd
  mo, 1801.
Starr, James, son of Joseph Starr and Rebecca, his wife, b. 28th da,
  4th mo, 1744 and Sarah Minshall dau. of John Minshall and Sarah,
  his wife, b. 16th da, 4th mo, 1745 m. 13th da, 4th mo, 1769 and
  their children: Ann, b. 18th da, 1st mo, 1770; Aquilla, b. 29th da,
  7th mo, 1771; James and Sarah, twins, b. 16th da, 10th mo, 1772;
  Joseph, b. 21st da, 8th mo, 1774; Rebecca, b. 1st da, 3rd mo, 1776;
  Beulah, b. 11th da, 9th mo, 1778; Mary, b. 13th da, 8th mo, 1780;
  John Minshall, b. 30th da, 11th mo, 1783.
Thomas, Watson and Mary and their children: Julian, b. 20th da, 9th
  mo, 1792; Rebeckah, b. 6th da, 7th mo, 1795; Jonathan, b. 21st da,

11th mo, 1797; George, b. 23rd da, 8th mo, 1801; Charles W., b. 1st da, 9th mo, 1806.

Hilles, William, son of Hugh Hilles and Ann, his wife, of Richland in Bucks Co., PA b. 11th da, 10th mo, 1752 and Rebeckeh Pugh, dau. of Hugh Pugh and Mary, his wife, b. 10th da, the 7th mo, 1745. O.S. m. 24th da, 4th mo, 1776, and their children: Hugh, b. 8th da, 3rd mo, 1778; Mary, b. 31st da, 3rd mo, 1780; Ann, b. 1st da, 11th mo, 1781; Eli, b. 20th da, 7th mo, 1783; David, b. 13th da, 12th mo, 1785; Samuel, b. 20th da, 11th mo, 1788.

Davies, Benjamin b. 27th da, 7th mo, 1736, O.S. and Hannah Davies, b. 17th da, 2nd mo, 1752 m. 31st da, 10th mo, 1771 and their children: John, b. 5th da, 8th mo, 1772; Mary, b. 20th da, 2nd mo, 1775; Elisabeth, b. 15th da, 5th mo, 1777; Hannah, b. 23rd da, 12th mo, 1779; Benjamin, b. 5th da, 8th mo, 1782; Amos, b. 29th da, 10th m. 1785, d. 22nd da, 8th mo, 1799; Tace (dau.), b. 13th da, 4th mo, 1788; Samuel, b. 29th da, 7th mo, 1790; Sabbilla (dau.), b. 12th da, 12th mo, 1792, d. 14th da, 12th mo, 1792; Sarah, b. 2nd da, 7th mo, 1794; Ruth, b. 30th da, 3rd mo, 1797.

Hilles, David, son of Hugh Hilles and Ann, his wife of Richland in Bucks Co., b. 11th da, 9th mo, 1755; Dinah Mulhous dau. of Robert Milhous and Ann, his wife, b. 26th da, 3rd mo, 1759 m. 12th da, 4th mo, 1780 and their children: Ann, b. 9th da, 7th mo, 1781; Robert, b. 23rd da, 12th mo, 1782; Phebe, b. 26th da, 9th mo, 1784; William, b. 26th da, 11th mo, 1786; Rachel, b. 18th da, 1st mo, 1789; Hannah, b. 1st da, 11th mo, 1790; Jesse, b. 26th da, 12th mo, 1792; David and Jonathan, twins, b. 16th da, 11th mo, 1794. Jonathan d. 9th da, 7th mo, 1795; Lydia, b. 6th da, 4th mo, 1796; Nathan, b. 29th da, 8th mo, 1799.

Coates, John Hutchison b. 9th da, 7th mo, 1761 and Hannah Longstreet, b. 9th da, 10th mo, 1768 and their children: Sarah, b. 8th da, 4th mo, 1791; Jane, b. 27th da, 12th mo, 1793; Cyrus, b. 25th da, 2nd mo, 1795; Charles, b. 15th da, 3rd mo, 1797; Aquila, b. 30th da, 10th mo, 1799.

Rogers, Jonathan, son of Joseph Rogers and Hannah, his wife of Vincent in Chester Co., PA. b. 15th da, 2nd mo, 1755 and Ann Jones, dau. of William Jones and Rebeckah, his wife of Whitemarsh in Philadelphia County, PA b. 15th da, 2nd mo, 1758 m. 11th da, 5th mo, 1780 and their children: Charles, b. 22nd da, 1st mo, 1781; William, b. 3rd da, 8th mo, 1782; Hannah, b. 27th da, 1st mo, 1785; Rebeckah, b. 16th da, 10th mo, 1786; Joseph, b. 20th da, 8th mo, 1788; Benjamin, b. 3rd da, 1st mo, 1791; Jonathan, b. 7th da, 2nd mo, 1793; David, b. 5th da, 3rd 1795; Samuel, b. 29th da, 3rd mo, 1800; Ann, b. 20th da, 4th mo, 1802.

Gibbons, Joseph b. 16th da, 10th mo, 1762 and Sarah Milhouse, b. 4th da, 1st mo, 1771 m. 23rd da, 4th mo, 1789, and their children:

William, b. 13th da, 5th mo, 1790; John, b. 11th da, 5th mo, 1792, d. 24th da, 6th mo, 1796; Anna, b. 17th da, 1st mo, 1795, d. 2nd da, 7th mo, 1796; Joseph, b. 14th da, 3rd mo, 1797; Martha, b. 21st da, 9th mo, 1799; Hannah, b. 23rd da, 2nd mo, 1802; Mercy, b. 11th da, 4th mo, 1804.

Hatton, Thomas, son of Joseph Hatton and Susanna, his wife and Sarah Morris, dau. of Jonathan Morris and Mary, his wife and their children: Edward, b. 1st da, 4th mo, 1772; Mary, b. 20th da, 3rd mo, 1774; Joseph, b. 11th da, 10th mo, 1775; Susanna, b. 23rd da, 5th mo, 1778; Thomas, b. 9th da, 9th mo, 1781.

Townsend, Samuel and Priscilla and their children: David, b. 13th da, 12th mo, 1787; Sarah, b. 5th da, 3rd mo, 1789; Rachel, b. 14th da, 8th mo, 1790; Lydia, b. 24th da, 7th mo, 1795; Priscilla, b. 7th da, 3rd mo, 1797; Francis (son), b. 19th da, 11th mo, 1798; Jane, b. 19th da, 7th mo, 1800; Susan, b. 21st da, 2nd mo, 1803; Eliza, b. 14th da, 5th mo, 1805; Thomas J., b. 7th da, 1st mo, 1809.

Thomas, George, son of Richard Thomas and Phebe, his wife, b. 21st da, 2nd mo, 1747, d. 8th mo, 1793 and Sarah Roberts, dau. of John Roberts and Jane, his wife, b. 11th da, 1st mo, 1750 and their children: Jane, b. 18th da, 2nd mo, 1775; Phebe, b. 11th da, 10th mo, 1776; Hannah, b. 7th da, 2nd mo, 1778, d. 28th da, 2nd mo, 1778; Lydia, b. 26th da, 9th mo, 1779; John, b. 29th da, 8th mo, 1781; Elisabeth, b. 24th da, 9th mo, 1783; George, b. 1st da, 8th mo, 1785, d. 31st da, 12th mo, 1785; Sarah, b. 31st da, 12th mo, 1786; Anna, b. 20th da, 1st mo, 1789.

Baldwin, John, son of William Baldwin and Mary, his wife, b. 5th da, 7th mo, 1785 and Lydia Trumble, b. 9th mo, 1793, dau. of William Trumble and Grace, his wife, and their children: William, b. 6th da, 7th mo, 1794; George, b. 3rd da, 12th mo, 1790; Grace, b. 19th da, 8th mo, 1799, d. 21st da, same; Joseph, b. 8th da, 6th mo, 1801; Catharine, b. 9th da, 3rd m. 1804; Thomas, b. 12th da, 12th mo, 1805; Thomas 2nd, b. 9th da, 8th mo, 1807; Lydia Thomas, b. 29th da, 10th mo, 1809; Richard T., b. 3rd da, 9th mo, 1815, d. 11th da, 9th mo, 1815.

Meredith, James, son of Enoch Meredith and Jane, his wife, b. 1st da, 10th mo, 1753 and Rebecca Dolby, dau. of John Dolby and Hannah, his wife, b. 15th da, the 12th mo, 1760 m. 14th da, 10th mo 1784 and their children: Jane, b. 25th da, 6th mo, 1785; Enoch, b. 24th da, 10th mo, 1787, John, b. 1st da, 10th mo, 1790; Abraham, b. 31st da, 1st mo, 1794, d. 21st da, 8th mo, 1794; Isaac, b. 26th da, 11th mo, 1790.

David Renny, jr., b. 4th da, 4th mo, 1773 and Eleanor Maxwell, b. 26th da, 4th mo, 1770 m. 11th da, 10th mo, 1790 and their children: David, b. 14th da, 8th mo, 1799; Maxwell (son), b. 4th da, 2nd mo, 1802.

Rea, Samuel, son of John Rea and Sidney, his wife, b. 15th da, 6th mo, 1749; and Deborah Bane, dau. of Nathan Bane and Mary, his wife, b. 20th da, 9th mo, 1748 m. the 14th da, 4th mo, 1774 and their children: Mary, b. 17th da, 8th mo, 1777; Sidney (dau.), b. 17th da, 4th mo, 1780; John, b. 17th da, 1st mo, 1784; Evan, b. 21st da, 9th mo, 1785, d. 19th da, 4th mo, 1790; Deborah, b. 1st da, 2nd mo, 1787; Samuel, b. 2nd da, 2nd mo, 1790.

Kirk, Isaiah, son of William and Sibille Kirk, b. 9th da, 12th mo, 1754; and Elisabeth Richards m. 12th da, 9th mo, 1787 and their children: Samuel, b. 6th da, 6th mo, 1788; Rachel, b. 19th da, 7th mo, 1790, d. 1st da, 9th mo, 1791; William, b. 27th da, 3rd mo, 1793; Hannah, b. 2nd da, 1st mo, 1797, d. 8th da, 4th mo, 1800; Elisabeth, b. 22nd da, 12th mo, 1798; Mary, b. 13th da, 4th mo, 1804.

Lewis, Griffith, son of Samuel Lewis and Margaret, his wife of West Whiteland Township in Chester County, b. 6th da, 12th mo, 1766 and Lydia Williams, dau. of Ellis Williams and Lydia, his wife, b. 6th da, 8th mo, 1762 m. 9th da, 12th mo, 1789 and their children: Samuel, b. 13th da, 10th mo, 1791; Hannah, b. 1st da, 7th mo, 1793; Mary, b. 27th da, 4th mo, 1799; Nathan, b. 4th da, 10th mo, 1804.

Lewis, John, son of John and Catharine Lewis, b. 10th da, 8th mo, 1737 and Grace Meredith, dau. of John and Grace Meredith, b. 24th da, 1st mo, 1745 m. 28th da, 11th mo, 1775 and their children: Ann, b. 27th da, 8th mo, 1776; Hannah, b. 28th da, 5th mo, 1779; John, b. 29th da, 3rd mo, 1781; Mary, b. 10th da, 4th mo, 1783.

Thomas, Richard, son of Richard Thomas and Phebe, his wife, b. 30th da, 12th mo, 1744; and Thornzin Downing, dau. of Richard Downing and Mary, his wife, b. 26th da, 8th mo, 1754 and their children: Richard, b. 3rd da, 12th mo, 1775; Mary, b. 9th da, 3rd mo, 1778, d. 15th da, 5th mo, 1798; George, b. 21st da, 3rd mo, 1780; Jacob, b. 4th da, 5th mo, 1782; Phebe, b. 8th da, 6th mo, 1784; Thornzin, b. 4th da, 12th mo, 1786; A still-born son, b. 15th da, 11th mo, 1787; Samuel, b. 24th da, 3rd mo, 1783; William, b. no date.

Roberts, John, son of John and Jane Roberts, b. 20th da, 11th mo, 1751 and Elisabeth Jones, dau. of James and Ann Jones, b. 10th da, 9th mo, 1764 m. 23rd da, 11th mo, 1792 and their chidren: John, b. 13th da, 1st mo, 1795; Ann, b. 12th da, 6th mo, 1800.

Thomas, Richard Jr., b. 3rd da, 12th mo, 1775 m. Rebecca Malin and their children: Richard, b. 3rd da, 8th mo, 1800; Lydia, b. 19th da, 6th mo, 1803.

Bonsall, Isaac b. 31st da, 10th mo, 1765; and Mercy Milhous, b. 28th da, 8th mo, 1768 m. 14th da, 9th mo, 1786 and their children: Hannah, b. 30th da, 9th mo, 1787, d. 1st da, 2nd mo, 1791;

William, b. 24th da, 3rd mo, 1790, d. 9th da, 1st mo, 1794; Anna, b. 13th da, 2nd mo, 1792; Edward, b. 28th da, 5th mo, 1794; Joseph, b. 29th da, 10th mo, 1796; Thomas, b. 22nd da, 9th mo, 1798, d. 30th da, 9th mo, 1798; Sidney (dau.), b. 28th da, 9th mo, 1799; Charles, b. 1st da, 10th mo, 1802.

Downing, Richard (the 2nd), b. 4th da, 5th mo, 1750 and Elizabeth, his wife, b. 2nd da, 3rd mo, 1753, and their children: Thomas, b. 21st da, 1st mo, 1773; David, b. 18th da, 12th mo, 1774; Mary, b. 21st da, 9th mo, d. 28th da, same mo, 1770; Richard, b. 26th da, 9th mo, 1778; William, b. 9th da, 1st mo, 1781; Elizabeth, b. 20th da, 10th mo, 1786; Phebe, b. 5th da, 7th mo, 1786.

Downing, Thomas, son of Rd. and Elizabeth, b. 21st da, 1st mo, 1773, and MARY, his wife and their children: Thornzin (dau.), b. 4th da, 4th mo, 1796; George, b. 10th da, 7th mo, 1797; Elizabeth, b. 7th da, 12th mo, 1798; Hester, b. 2nd da, 4th mo, 1800; Mary, b. 13th da, 7th mo, 1804; Thomas, b. 9th da, 2nd mo, 1807.

Downing, Joseph, son of Richard, b. 19th da, 6th mo, 1765 and ANN, his wife and their children: William, b. 29th da, 12th mo, 1791; Samuel, b. 9th da, 12th mo, 1794; Charles, b. 16th da, 10th mo, 1798.

Downing, Richard, son of Richard, b. 26th da, 9th mo, 1778 and Elizabeth, his wife, b. 3rd da, 9th mo, 1777, m. 19th da, 12th mo, 1796 and their children: Hannah, b. 22nd da, 9th mo, 1797, d. 17th da, 10th mo, 1799; Deborah, b. 7th da, 11th mo, 1800; Harriet, b. 6th da, 10th mo, 1802; Miller (son), b. 15th da, 4th mo, 1805.

Elihu Evans and Mary Pugh were m. 15th da, 6th mo, 1763 and their children: Elim b, 16th da, 3rd mo, 1764; Jonathan, b. 26th da, 8th mo, 1765; Rachel, b. 29th da, 9th mo, 1767.

Baldwin, Caleb, son of John, b. 31st da, 6th mo, 1749 and Charity, his wife and their children: Deborah, b. 1st da, 11th mo, 1775; John, b. 13th da, 7th mo, 1778; Samuel, b. 29th da, 6th mo, 1782; Jonathan, b. 29th da, 1st mo, 1792.

Samuel Hains, son of Jacob, b. 14th da, 9th mo, 1772; Phebe, his wife, b. 8th da, 6th mo, 1784 m. 24th da, 10th mo, 1804.

Dillin, William and Sarah John m. 20th da, 5th mo, 1773, d. 16th da, 7th mo, 1795 and their children: Mary, b. 19th da, 1st mo, 1774; Rebecca, b. 24th da, 7th mo, 1775; Hannah, b. 28th da, 7th mo, 1776; Sarah, b. 15th da, 8th mo, 1778; Elisabeth, b. 31st da, 3rd mo, 1780; Isaiah, b. 26th da, 12th mo, 1781; Mercy, b. 28th da, 10th mo, 1783; Owen, b. 27th da, 6th mo, 1785.

Medley, George and Hannah, his wife m. 16th da, 3rd mo, 1785 and their children: Mary, b. 7th da, 2nd mo, 1786; Jane, b. 5th da, 9th mo, 1789; Betty, b. 24th da, 12th mo, 1791 m. --- Woolerton; Hannah, b. 13th da, 2nd mo, 1794; Rachel, b. 4th da, 2nd mo, 1797; m. Robert Moore; Ann, b. 22nd da, 3rd mo, 1799.

Kersey, Jesse and Elizabeth and their children:: Hannah, b. 29th da, 3rd mo, 1791; Lydia, b. 24th da, 11th mo, 1792; Mary, b. 19th da, 5th mo, 1795; Joseph, b. 14th da, 6th mo, 1797; Rachel, b. 29th da, 1st mo, 1800; Sarah, b. 13th da, 11th mo, 1802; Jesse, b. 21st da, 1st mo, 1805; William, b. 9th da, 9th mo, 1807; Elizabeth R., b. 1st da, 11th mo, 1809; Ann, b. 22nd da, 4th mo, 1812; Esther, b. 3rd da, 9th mo, 1815.

Kersey, Hannah sr. d. 26th da, 1st mo, [no year given].

John, Reuben and Lydia Townsend m. 6th da, 12th mo, 1768 and their children: Martha, b. 15th da, 10th mo, 1769; Robert, b. 28th da, 2nd mo, 1771; Joanna, b. 20th da, 1st mo, 1773; Pamela, b. 24th da, 6th mo, 1775; Ann, b. 26th da, 12th mo, 1776; Sarah, b. 5th da, 8th? mo, 1778; Phebe, b. 23rd da, 7th mo, 1780; Lydia, b. 3rd da, 6th mo, 1782, d. 7th da, 10th mo, 1784; Townsend, b. 20th da, 2nd mo, 1784; Israel, b. 16th da, 12th mo, 1787. LYDIA TOWNSEND, d. 31st da, 1st mo, 1798.

Sharpless, Nathan dau. of Jacob, b. 28th da, 9th mo, 1752 m. Rachel Baldwin, b. 13th da, 7th mo, 1756 on 24th da, 4th mo, 1783 and their children: Still-born son, b. 22nd da, 3rd mo, 1784; Mercy, b. 22nd da, 8th mo, 1785, d. 20th da, 8th mo, 1786; Blakey (son), b. 21st da, 6th mo, 1787; Joshua, b. 24th da, 6th mo, 1789; Jacob, b. 3rd da, 8th mo, 1791; Isaac, b. 28th da, 7th mo, 1793; Ann, b. 15th da, 10th mo, 1795; Mercy, b. 30th da, 1st mo, 1798; Rachel, b. 7th da, 7th mo, 1801.

Whelen, John and Martha and their children: Dennis, b. 5th da, 5th mo, 1764; James, b. 21st da, 3rd mo, 1767; Joseph, b. 21st da, 9th mo, 1769, d. 6th mo, 1789; Ann, b. 19th da, 9th mo, 1773, d. 1st mo, 1778; Sarah, b. 16th da, 5th mo, 1776; Phebe, b. 8th da, 12th mo, 1778; Ann, b. 26th da, 3rd mo, 1783.

Buchanan, Thomas, son of George and Mary Buchanan b. 8th da, 8th mo, 1773

Baldwin, Samuel and Mary and their children: Joshua, b. 4th da, 3rd mo, 1780; Mercy, b. 4th da, 10th mo, 1781; George S., b. 4th da, 3rd mo, 1784; Israel, b. 8th da, 2nd mo, 1786; Jane, b. 29th da, 9th mo, 1788; Lydia, b. 19th da, 4th mo, 1789; Isaac, b. 22nd da, 2nd mo, 1791; Samuel S., b. 24th da, 1st mo, 1793.

UWCHLAN MONTHLY MEETING, CERTIFICATES OF REMOVAL
(Issued)
1763 - 1800

9th day 2nd mo, 1763 - Thomas Kirk, lately of Bradford Meeting to Uwchlan Monthly Meeting. Samuel Trimble, lately of Philadelphia Meeting to Uwchlan Monthly Meeting.

9th day 3rd mo, 1763 - Daniel Stanton to Philadelphia Monthly Meeting. *Signed by the following:*

Ann John	John Baldwin	Griffith John
Ruth Roberts	Joseph Kirk	Thomas Downing
Jane Downing	Simon Meredith	James Brown
Jane Owen	John Jacobs Junr.	Joshua Baldwin
Rachel Valentine	James Packer/Parker?	Timothy Kirk
Susanna Brown	Jonathan Coates	David Owen
Susanna Jones	David Williams	Dennis Whelen
Elizabeth Brown	John Milhous	Thomas Martin
Margaret Milhous	William Pearson	William Kirk
Ann John	Thomas Lightfoot Jr.	John Meredith
Mary Beal	William Lightfoot Jr.	Robert Valentine
Jane Coates	Cadwalader Jones	Richard Downing
Elizabeth Milhous	Jacob William	Evan Jones
Jane Wely	John Longstretch	John Thomas
Mary Kirk	Thomas John	Thomas Atherton
Mary Jones	Nathan Cadwalader	Joseph Prichard
Elizabeth Jacobs		

6th da, 4th mo, 1763 - Thomas Lightfoot to Waterford Monthly Meeting in Ireland.

6th da, 4th mo, 1763 - Matthew Taylor to Philadelphia Monthly Meeting.

6th da, 7th mo, 1763 - Elizabeth Brown to Haddonfield Monthly Meeting.

6th da, 7th mo, 1763 - Mary Baldwin, young woman, to Bradford Monthly Meeting.

3rd da, 9th mo, 1763 - Catharine Jones to Newgarden Monthly Meeting.

7th da, 9th mo, 1763 - Thomas Atherton and Abigail, his wife and their children: Richard, Henry and Elizabeth to Warrington Monthly Meeting.

9th da, 11th mo, 1763 - Mary Evans, wife of Elihu Evans to Gwynedd Monthly Meeting.

5th da, 1st mo, 1764 - Benjamin Longstretch, a youth, to Bradford Monthly Meeting.

9th da, 2nd mo, 1764 - Ruth Roberts to Goshen Monthly Meeting.

Mordecai Roberts and Anna Roberts, minor children to reside with Elihu Evans, of the Gwynedd Monthly Meeting.

5th da, 4th mo, 1764 - Mary, wife of Robert Eachus to Sadsbury Monthly Meeting for herself and her three children: Mary, William and Robert.

10th da, 5th mo, 1764 - Hannah, wife of Isaac Thompson, with her husband and their children: Jeremiah, Sarah, Hannah, Isaac and Joseph to Fairfax, VA Monthly Meeting. Hannah Fisher to live with her uncle, Abel John, at Warrington Monthly Meeting.

9th da, 8th mo, 1764 - James Starr and Hannah, his wife and their children: Sarah, Rachal and Hannah to Bradford Monthly Meeting. Mary Martin to Exeter Monthly Meeting.

6th da, 9th mo, 1764 - Abraham Randall, a young man, to Gwynedd Monthly Meeting. Mary, wife of John Darlington to Bradford Monthly Meeting.

4th da, 10th mo, 1764 - Aron Coates and Rachel, his wife and children: Benjamin, Beulah, Grace and Aron to Haverford Monthly Meeting.

10th da, 11th mo, 1764 - Deborah Dawson to Duck Creek Monthly Meeting.

6th da, 12th mo, 1764 - Elizabeth Stalford from Gwynedd Monthly Meeting to Uwchlan Monthly Meeting requests a certificate to Gwynedd Monthly Meeting.

7th da, 3rd mo, 1765 - Sarah, wife of Jonathan Evans to Warrington Monthly Meeting.

4th da, 4th mo, 1765 - Daniel Brown requests a certificate for his son, Thomas placed as an apprentice at Newgarden Monthly Meeting. Joseph Pritchard to Goshen Monthly Meeting.

6th da, 6th mo, 1765 - Robert Hatton, a youth, placed as an apprentice at Philadelphia Monthly Meeting. Joseph Moore to Philadelphia Monthly Meeting.

4th da, 7th mo, 1765 - Aron Coates placed as an apprentice at the Uwchlan Monthly Meeting to Bradford Monthly Meeting. Jane Wely to Exeter Monthly Meeting.

8th da, 8th mo, 1765 - Bathshebba M'Cowen, wife of John, with her husband from Shearman's Valley in Cumberland Co., to Warrington Monthly Meeting in the county of York.

5th da, 9th mo, 1765 - Samuel Stanfield to Cain Creek Monthly Meeting or Newgarden Monthly Meeting in NC along with Mary, his wife and children: Jane, John and Samuel. Robert Benson, a youth placed as an apprentice at Exeter Monthly Meeting.

7th da, 11th mo, 1765 - Joshua Beale, a youth placed as apprentice at Philadelphia Monthly Meeting.

5th da, 12th mo, 1765 - Henry Atherton to Abington Monthly Meeting. Jonathan Brown [meeting name not given].

UWCHLAN MONTHLY MEETING 21

Hannah Ferriss and her husband to Wilmington Monthly Meeting. John Wilson to Newgarden Monthly Meeting with his wife, Joyce?
6th da, 3rd mo, 1766 - Samuel Warner, a youth, from Uwchlan Monthly Meeting to a Monthly Meeting of Friends in Maryland is placed with David Scofield of Kennett Monthly Meeting.
8th da, 5th mo, 1766 - Jacob Bell and Ann, his wife, to Philadelphia Monthly Meeting with children, Deborah and Elizabeth and David Morgan, an apprentice. Levi Randall placed with Richard Goodwin of Goshen Monthly Meeting. Thomas White, jr. who has served most part of his apprenticeship within our meeting to Goshen Monthly Meeting.
5th da, 6th mo, 1766 - John Thomas to Warrington Monthly Meeting with his wife, Rebecca and children: [two oldest] John, Eleanor, also John, Rebecca, Sarah, Dina, Jonah.
10th da, 7th mo, 1766 - William Roberts, a youth to Concord Monthly Meeting.
7th da, 8th mo, 1766 - Joseph James, a youth placed as an apprentice at Gwynedd Monthly Meeting. Lydia Maulsby, wife of John Maulsby to Gwynedd Monthly Meeting.
9th da, 10th mo, 1766 - Samuel Butler from Ireland to Burlington, NJ Monthly Meeting.
6th da, 11th mo, 1766 - Rose Parker to Bradford Monthly Meeting.
4th da, 12th mo, 1766 - Rebecca Shaw to Gwynedd Monthly Meeting.
8th da, 1st mo, 1767 - Hannah Lewis, wife of Henry Lewis, with her husband to Bradford Monthly Meeting.
9th da, 4th mo, 1767 - John Todhunter to Fairfax Monthly Meeting, VA. with wife, Margaret and their seven children: Hannah, Mary, Margaret, Isaac, Jacob, Joseph and Evan. Ezekiel Griffith to Goshen Monthly Meeting.
4th da, 6th mo, 1767 - William Hancock and Sarah, his wife and Jane Hancock, their granddau. to Philadelphia Monthly Meeting. William Brown and Agnes, his wife to Newgarden Monthly Meeting.
9th da, 7th mo, 1767 - Elizabeth Scott, wife of Abram Scott to Kennett Monthly Meeting.
10th of 9th mo, 1767 - Jesse Pennock placed as an apprentice to a Friend belonging to this meeting, is now free and returned to live with his father in New Garden Monthly Meeting.
5th da, 11th mo, 1767 - Susanna Ferree, from Sadsbury Monthly Meeting to Uwchlan.
10th da, 12th mo, 1767 - Joshua Walton to Abington Monthly Meeting.
7th da, 1st mo, 1768 - Samuel Fisher and Ruth, his wife to Warrington

Monthly Meeting. John Edge to Bradford Monthly Meeting.
5th da, 2nd mo, 1768 - Samuel John and Ann, his wife with minor children, Mary and Ebenezer to Warrington Monthly Meeting.
5th da, 5th mo, 1768 - Ruth John to Warrington Monthly Meeting. Samuel John, jr. to Warrington Monthly Meeting. Sarah John to Warrington Monthly Meeting. Walpole Gregory from Philadelphia Monthly Meeting to Burlington Monthly Meeting. Abraham Randal to Concord Monthly Meeting.
9th da, 6th mo, 1768 - Hugh Pugh to Haverford Monthly Meeting. Jane Williams and her son to Warrington Monthly Meeting.
5th da, 1st mo, 1770 - Mary Vernon, recently married to Jonathan Vernon to Chester Monthly Meeting.
8th da, 2nd mo, 1770 - Rachel Garrett to Goshen Monthly Meeting.
10th da, 5th mo, 1770 - James Hancock to Warrington Monthly Meeting with his wife, Elizabeth and their seven children: Joseph, Elizabeth, James, John, Sarah, Benjamin and Joel. Rebecka Jones to New Garden Monthly Meeting. Sarah Brown, a young woman to Haddonfield Monthly Meeting.
7th da, 6th mo, 1770 - Timothy Kirk and Sarah, his wife to Warrington Monthly Meeting with their two youngest children, Ezekiel and Jonathan. Hannah Robison to Exeter Monthly Meeting. Benjamin Chandler with an endorsement from Exeter Monthly Meeting to Wilmington Monthly Meeting.
5th da, 7th mo, 1770 - Mordecai Yarnell, jr. from Philadelphia Monthly Meeting to Chester Monthly Meeting to Uwchlan Monthly Meeting.
9th da, 8th mo, 1770 - Mary Cadwalader, a young woman to Warrington Monthly Meeting. Ann Underwood from Uwchlan Monthly Meeting to New Garden Monthly Meeting.
6th da, 9th mo, 1770 - Ruth Jones, a young woman to Sadsbury Monthly Meeting.
8th da, 11th mo, 1770 - Mary Martin to Goshen Monthly Meeting.
7th da, 2nd mo, 1771. Hannah Townsend to Philadelphia Monthly Meeting with her husband, John Townsend. Ann Park to Bradford Monthly Meeting.
7th of 3rd mo, 1771. Daniel Trimble, who came from the Concord Monthly Meeting to Uwchlan to return to Concord.
4 of 4th mo, 1771. John Milhaus to New Garden Monthly Meeting with Margaret, his wife and children: Sarah, Mary, Ruth, Lyddia and Thomas. Rachel Kirk to Warrington Monthly Meeting.
9th da, 5th mo, 1771. David Williams to Fairfax, VA Monthly Meeting. Jacob Kirk to Warrington Monthly Meeting with Hannah, his wife and their young son, Isaac. Abram Scott to Wrightstown, Bucks

County, PA Monthly Meeting with his wife, Elizabeth and children: Rachel, Amos, Jesse, Rosseter, Esther and Thomas. Catherine Riffell and four of her children: Jonathan, Rachel, Nathan and Isaac to Warrington Monthly Meeting. Kezia Riffell with her parents to Warrington Monthly Meeting. Grace Meredith, the younger to Bradford Monthly Meeting

6th da, 6th mo, 1771. Mordecai Williams and Sarah, his wife to Warrington. Edward Jones to Warrington Monthly Meeting. Mary Davis to Warrington Monthly Meeting

8th da, 8th mo, 1771. Benjamin Parvin from Exeter Monthly Meeting to Wilmington Monthly Meeting. Elizabeth Milhous and her children: Paschal, Hannah, Samuel, Phebe, Deborah, Susanna and Elizabeth to Kennett Monthly Meeting.

10th of 10th mo, 1771. Joseph Randall to Derbe Monthly Meeting.

5th da, 12th mo, 1771. William Trimble and Phebe, his wife to Concord Monthly Meeting. Catherine, wife of Robert Johnston to Concord Monthly Meeting. Anna Wickersham, wife of Jesse Wickersham to Warrington Monthly Meeting. Samuel Clark to New Garden Monthly Meeting.

9th da, 1st mo, 1772. Thomas Duckill to Warrington Monthly Meeting. Sarah Milhous to New Garden Monthly Meeting.

6th da, 2nd mo, 1772. Isaac Morris to Goshen Monthly Meeting.

9th da, 4th mo, 1772. Daniel Brown, who served as a minister at Uwchlan and Susanna, his wife, to Chester Monthly Meeting with children: Joseph, Mary, Margaret, Daniel, John and Joel. Levi Jones to Warrington Monthly Meeting.

7th da, 5th mo, 1772. Robert Valentine, Jr. to Bradford Monthly Meeting. Amos Davies and Agnes, his wife to Kennett Monthly Meeting with their children: Ruth, Joel, Isaac, John and Elisha.

4th da, 4th mo, 1772. Joseph Cox and Catharine, his wife to Goshen Monthly Meeting. Margaret Cox to Goshen Monthly Meeting.

4th da, 6th mo, 1772. Joseph Randall and Rachel, his wife to Goshen Monthly Meeting with their children: Hannah, Rebecca, Sarah, Elizabeth, John, Rachel, Ruth and Joseph. Benjamin Walker, Ruth, his wife and Sarah, their child to Warrington Monthly Meeting.

9th da, 7th mo, 1772. William Morgan and Ann, his wife to Wilmington Monthly Meeting with children: Jesse, Hugh and Rebecca.

6th da, 8th mo, 1772. Mary Hunt, wife of Samuel Hunt, Bradford Monthly Meeting. Hannah Morgan, dau. of William Morgan to Wilmington Monthly Meeting. Elizabeth Morgan, dau. of William

Morgan to Wilmington Monthly Meeting.

10th of 12th mo, 1772. Thomas Atherton, a youth to Philadelphia Monthly Meeting. Hannah, wife of John Davis, with her husband to Warrington Monthly Meeting.

10th of 6th mo, 1773 - William Morgan, a young man to Wilmington Monthly Meeting.

8th da, 7th mo, 1773 - William Hope to The Falls Monthly Meeting in Bucks Co., PA. Thomas Milhous to Kennett Monthly Meeting. Richard Donning, Jr. and wife, Elizabeth to Falls Monthly Meeting in Bucks Co., PA.

4th da, 11th mo, 1773 - Elisha Ellis to Gwynedd Monthly Meeting. Ann Valentine, wife of Robert Valentine, jr., to Bradford Monthly Meeting.

9th da, 12th mo, 1773 - Ann Taylor to New Garden Monthly Meeting.

6th da, 1st mo, 1774 - Sarah Cowgill, a youth, to Goshen Monthly Meeting.

5th da, 5th mo, 1774 - Henry Wells to Hopewell Monthly Meeting, VA. Jacob Mattson and Mary, his wife to Haverford Monthly Meeting with children, Sarah and Hannah.

9th da, 6th mo, 1774 - Mary Weathereld from New Garden Monthly Meeting to Warrington Monthly Meeting. Elizabeth Louden to The Falls Monthly Meeting in Bucks County, PA.

7th da, 7th mo, 1774 - John Suffell and Hannah, his wife to Kennett Monthly Meeting with children: Thomas, Sarah, Jesse and Mary.

8th da, 9th mo, 1774 - Joshua Way and his dau., Martha to Kennett Monthly Meeting.

6th da, 10th mo, 1774 - Ann Underwood to New Garden Monthly Meeting.

10th da, 11th mo, 1774 - Robert Benson to Meeting at Wrightsborough, GA.

8th da, 12th mo, 1774 - Joseph Hudson to Monthly Meeting in Southern District of Philadelphia. Thomas Meteer and Sarah, his wife to The Falls Monthly Meeting in Bucks Co., PA.

5th da, 1st mo, 1775 - Solomon Fussill to Exeter Monthly Meeting.

9th da, 2nd mo, 1775 - Jacob Collins to Pipe Creek Monthly Meeting, MD.

9th da, 3rd mo, 1775 - Jane Lewis, wife of Evan Lewis, to Haverford Monthly Meeting with her husband.

8th da, 6th mo, 1775 - Hannah Cox to Goshen Monthly Meeting. Elizabeth Ives to Exeter Monthly Meeting.

6th da, 7th mo, 1775 - Daniel Warren, a youth, to Wilmington Monthly

Meeting. Mary Buchanan to Bradford Monthly Meeting.
10th da, 8th mo, 1775 - Thomzin Spackman, Wife of George Spackman to Wilmington Monthly Meeting.
7th da, 9th mo, 1775 - Joseph Hatton to Monthly Meeting in Cork, Ireland. Jane Benson, wife of William Benson with her husband to Wrightsborough Monthly Meeting in Ga and their son, William Benson.
7th da, 12th mo, 1775 - Alice Benson with her uncle, William Benson to Wrightsborough Monthly in Ga.
8th da, 2nd mo, 1776 - Susanna Dunkin, wife of Aron Dunkin to Goshen Monthly Meeting.
4th da, 3rd mo, 1776 - Judah Cadwalader, a young man, to the Falls Monthly Meeting in Bucks Co., Pa.
4th da, 4th mo, 1776 - Grace Lewis, wife of John Lewis to Gwynedd Monthly Meeting with her husband.
6th da, 6th mo, 1776 - Ann Tomkin to Abington Monthly Meeting.
10th da, 10th mo, 1776 - Elizabeth Starr, the younger to Abington Monthly Meeting to reside with her uncle. John Forsythe to Concord Monthly Meeting. Mary Trimble, wife of Daniel Trimble, to Concord Monthly Meeting. Ann Trimble to Concord Monthly Meeting. John Forsythe to Concord Monthly Meeting.
5th da, 12th mo, 1776 - Samuel Reese to Exeter Monthly Meeting. Gideon Williamson to Concord Monthly Meeting.
6th da, 2nd mo, 1777 - Townsend Whelen to Philadelphia Monthly Meeting.
8th da, 5th mo, 1777 - Mary Griffith to Warrington Monthly Meeting. John Griffith and Mary, his wife to Hopewell Monthly Meeting, Va, with their Children: Martha, Mary and Sybbilla.
5th da, 6th mo, 1777 - Benjamin Cox, a young man, to Goshen Monthly Meeting.
10th da, 7th mo, 1777 - Joseph Freebee/Freebee? to Exeter Monthly Meeting.
7th da, 8th mo, 1777 - Ellin Thomas, Wife of Abel Thomas to Exeter Monthly Meeting. Bartholomew Fussell to Abington Monthly Meeting.
10th da, 7th mo, 1777 - Hannah Dalby to Goshen Monthly Meeting. Daniel Williams to Wrightsborough Monthly Meeting, Ga with Mary, his wife and children, Sarah and Sibbilla.
9th da, 10th mo, 1777 - Susanna Butler with her husband to Wrightsborough Monthly Meeting, Ga. Abiather Davis to Wrightsborough Monthly Meeting, Ga. John Williams to New Garden Monthly Meeting with his wife, Sarah and their dau.,

Katharine.

6th da, 11th mo, 1777 - William Manfield to Newgarden Monthly Meeting.

8th da, 1st mo, 1778 - Richard Evans and Phebe, his wife and children: Thomas, Sarah, Margaret, Mary and Catherine to Hopewell Monthly Meeting, Va.

5th da, 2nd mo, 1778 - John Butler, a young man, to Wrightsborough Monthly Meeting, Ga. Margaret, wife of John Jones to Wrightsborough Monthly Meeting, Ga.

7th da, 5th mo, 1778 - Hannah Phillips, wife of David Phillips, to Exeter Monthly Meeting.

9th da, 7th mo, 1778 - Thomas Marshall to Concord Monthly Meeting.

6th da, 8th mo, 1778 - Priscilla Yarnall, a youth, dau. of David Yarnall to Goshen Monthly Meeting.

5th da, 11th mo, 1778 - Jacob Downing to The Falls Monthly Meeting.

16th da, 12th mo, 1778 - Thomzine Thomas, wife of Richard Thomas, to the Falls Monthly Meeting.

6th da, 5th mo, 1778 - William Trimble to Concord with Wife, Grace and children: Richard, Susanna, Hannah, Lyddia and Ann. Thomas Richards to New Garden Monthly Meeting.

10th da, 6th mo, 1779 - Jonathan Hooper and Elizabeth, his wife to Goshen Monthly Meeting with children: Thamzen, William, Margaret, Jane and Israel. Sarah Helsby to Exeter Monthly Meeting.

6th da, 8th mo, 1779 - Jacob Thomas, Jr. to Exeter Monthly Meeting.

7th da, 10th mo, 1779 - Mahlon Haworth to Haverford Monthly Meeting.

4th da, 11th mo, 1779 - Jane Coates, a young woman to Abington Monthly Meeting.

7th da, 12th mo, 1779 - Hannah Richards, Wife of Thomas Richards to New Garden Monthly Meeting.

10th da, 2nd mo, 1780 - Rhoda Bolton to Northern District Philadelphia Monthly Meeting.

6th da, 4th mo, 1780 - Ann Coates, a youth, dau. of Benjamin Coates to Abington Monthly Meeting.

10th da, 6th mo, 1780 - Hannah Thomas to Concord Monthly Meeting.

4th da, 5th mo, 1780 - James Moore to Fairfax Monthly Meeting, VA.

6th da, 7th mo, 1780 - William Cotes to Abington Monthly Meeting. William Pearson to Bush River, SC Monthly Meeting to visit his family. Mary Wilson, Elizabeth Wilson and

UWCHLAN MONTHLY MEETING

Hannah Woodcraft, daus. of Elizabeth Jones to Nottingham Monthly Meeting.

10th da, 8th mo, 1780 - Amos and Anna Stall, children of John Stall to live with their mother's parents of the Gwynedd Meeting, at the request of their father and grandmother. Hannah Fisher, wife of William Fisher to Bradford Monthly Meeting.

7th da, 9th mo, 1780 - Ann Orrok, some time ago from Salem Monthly Meeting, MA to Uwchan Monthly Meeting, is returning to that meeting. Grace Taylor to Pipe Creek Monthly Meeting in Maryland.

5th da, 10th mo, 1780 - Thomas Moor and Elizabeth, his wife to Fairfax Monthly Meeting, VA.

7th da, 12th mo, 1780 - Hugh Judge, who was recommended as a Minister and Susanna, his wife and children, Thomas and Hannah to Concord Monthly Meeting. Hannah James to Haverford Monthly Meeting.

8th da, 2nd mo, 1781. Joel Davis to Kennett Monthly Meeting. Elizabeth Cadwalader to Goshen Monthly Meeting.

5th da, 4th mo, 1781. Peter Yarnall to Monthly Meeting of the Southern District of Philadelphia. Grace Davis to Kennett Monthly Meeting.

6th da, 7th mo, 1780 [sic], John Lewis, a minor, to Haverford Monthly Meeting.

7th da, 6th mo, 1781. Phebe Sharpless to Chester Monthly Meeting.

5th da, 7th mo, 1781. Benjamin Benson and Hannah, his wife to Pipe Creek Monthly Meeting, MD with their children: James, Abraham, Reuben, Elisabeth and Ann. Samuel Warner to Wilmington Monthly Meeting.

6th da, 9th mo, 1781. Sarah Rigg, who has recently married to Warrington Monthly Meeting. Sarah Ellis to Gwynedd Monthly Meeting. Elizabeth Bateman, wife of William Bateman, to Exeter Monthly Meeting.

4th da, 10th mo, 1781. Sarah Coates to [meeting not stated]. Sarah Daugherty to Chesterfield Monthly Meeting.

6th da, 12th mo, 1781. William Williams to Hopewell Monthly Meeting.

10th da, 1st mo, 1782. Rachel Valentine to Philadelphia Monthly Meeting. Phebe Valentine to Philadelphia Monthly Meeting.

7th da, 2nd mo, 1782 George Valentine to Bradford Monthly Meeting.

7th da, 3rd mo, 1782. Elizabeth Louden to Warrington Monthly Meeting.

6th da, 6th mo, 1782. Jonathan Coates, Jr. to Bradford Monthly Meeting. Jonathan Parke to Bradford Monthly Meeting.

Sarah Trimble to Bradford Monthly Meeting. Susanna Hatton is placed with her aunt, Susanna Judge and to Concord Monthly Meeting; in childhood was taken under the care friends at the request of her grandmother, Susanna Lightfoot. Elizabeth Coates to Bradford Monthly Meeting. James Rogers to Goshen Monthly Meeting with Priscilla, his wife and their children: Joseph, Jacob, William,
David, Hannah, Mahlan, Grace and Ann.

4th da, 7th mo, 1782. Aaron Dunkin and Wife, Susannah and children: Sarah, Ann and Susannah to Goshen Monthly Meeting. Jacob Lewis to Warrington Monthly Meeting.

8th da, 8th mo, 1782. Joshua Smith and Lydia, his wife to Concord Monthly Meeting with their children: Hannah, John, Thomas, Joshua, Elizabeth, Lydia, James, Samuel and Sarah.

5th da, 9th mo, 1782. Jacob Thomas and Rebekah, his wife to Exeter Monthly Meeting.

10th da, 10th mo, 1782. Elizabeth Ellis who was disowned for going out in marriage, but reinstated, to New Garden Monthly Meeting in NC.

7th da, 11th mo, 1782. Evan Owen and Jane, his wife to Abington Monthly Meeting with children: David, Elizabeth, Mordecai and Elisha. Ruth Roberts from Northern District Philadelphia Monthly Meeting to Southern District of Philadelphia Monthly Meeting. Mary Roberts to Philadelphia Monthly Meeting.

5th da, 12th mo, 1782. Sarah Starr, dau. of Joseph Starr to Horsham Monthly Meeting.

6th da, 2nd mo, 1783. Rebecca Embree, wife of James Embree to Exeter.

6th da, 3rd mo, 1783. Ann Maule, wife of Benjamin Maule, to Haverford Monthly Meeting.

10th da, 4th mo, 1783. Jesse Milhous to Kennett Monthly Meeting. Joseph Randal and Rachel, his wife, with children: John, Rachel, Ruth, Joseph, Mary, Jane and Charles to Fairfax Monthly Meeting, Va. Hannah Randal to Fairfax Monthly Meeting, VA. Rebekah Randal to Fairfax Monthly Meeting, VA. Elizabeth Randal to Fairfax Monthly Meeting, VA. Joseph Trimble to Concord Monthly Meeting.

8th da, 5th mo, 1783. Tacy Coates, dau. of Benjamin Coates, she bBeing placed with an uncle at Horsham Monthly Meeting.

5th da, 6th mo, 1783. Jonathan Coates and Jane, his wife and their minor children: Susanna, Phebe, Keziah, Grace, Isaac, Jane and Elizabeth to Kennett Meeting. James Coats to Kennett Monthly Meeting. Ann Coates with her parents to Kennett Meeting. Hannah Coates to Kennett Meeting with her parents. Rachel Sharpless to Concord Meeting. Isaac Whelen to Philadelphia Monthly

Meeting.
10th da, 7th mo, 1783. Rebecca Jones to Bradford Monthly Meeting.
7th da, 8th mo, 1783. Aaron Martin and Ann, his wife to
Bradford Monthly Meeting. Acquila Jones to Wilmington Monthly
Meeting. Thomas Martin to New Garden Monthly Meeting. Mary
Wiley, a youth, from Northern District of Philadelphia
Monthly Meeting in 1780 with her parents to Exeter Monthly
Meeting. John Williams and his dau., Catharine to Exeter Monthly
Meeting.
4th da, 9th mo, 1783. Moses Rese [Rose?] to Wilmington Monthly
Meeting.
4th da, 12th mo, 1783. Phebe Cadwalader to Bradford Monthly
Meeting. Hannah Cadwalader to Northern District of Philadelphia
Monthly Meeting. Hannah Edwards to Haverford Monthly Meeting.
8th da, 1st mo, 1784 - Jonathan Coope to Bradford Monthly Meeting.
Abner Coates, a youth, placed as an Apprentice to Goshen Monthly
Meeting.
4th da, 3rd mo, 1784 - Isaac Roberts to Richland Monthly Meeting. Job
Packer and Hannah, his wife with small children: Sarah, William
and Hannah to Kennett Monthly Meeting.
8th da, 4th mo, 1784 - Elizabeth Rea to Wilmington Monthly Meeting.
6th da, 5th mo, 1784 - Thomas Richards with Hannah, his wife to
Newgarden Monthly Meeting with their children, Sarah and Isaac.
William Thomas to Haverford Monthly Meeting.
10th da, 6th mo, 1784 - Joseph Jackson to Newgarden Monthly
Meeting.
8th da, 7th mo, 1784 - Lewis Maule to Haverford Monthly Meeting.
Hannah James to Concord Monthly Meeting. Rebecca, wife of
Joseph Smedley to Goshen Monthly Meeting.
9th da, 9th mo, 1784 - Thomas Hatton to Henrico Monthly Meeting, Va
with Sarah, his wife and their children: Edward, Mary, Susanna,
Thomas and Jesse.
4th da, 11th mo, 1784 - Elizabeth Yarnall to Goshen Monthly Meeting.
9th da, 12th mo, 1784 - Rachel Price, wife of Philip Price, Jr., to Darby
Monthly Meeting.
10th da, 2nd mo, 1785 - Joseph Whelen being placed by his parents to
Philadelphia Monthly Meeting.
7th da, 4th mo, 1785 - Edward Morris and wife, Hannah and children:
Jonathan, David and Elizabeth to Exeter Monthly Meeting.
5th da, 5th mo, 1785 - James Meredith and Rebecca, his wife to

Haverford Monthly Meeting. Nicholas Morris to Bradford Monthly Meeting. James Meredith and Rebecca, his wife to Haverford Meeting. Nicholas Morris to Bradford Monthly Meeting. Jane Morris, Jr. to Bradford Monthly Meeting.

5th da, 7th mo, 1785 - Daniel Thomas to Exeter Monthly Meeting.

7th da, 7th mo, 1785 - Moses Pimm to Bradford Monthly Meeting. Isaac Spackman and Susanna, his wife and their children: Ann, James, Isaac, Mary, Susannah and Thomas to Bradford Monthly Meeting. William Bennett to Newgarden Monthly Meeting.

8th da, 9th mo, 1785 - Isaac Jackson to Wilmington Monthly Meeting. Phebe Sharpless, wife of Abraham Sharpless to Concord Monthly Meeting. Jesse Davis, a minor, placed as an Apprentice at New Garden Monthly Meeting.

8th da, 12th mo, 1785 - Jesse Jones and wife, Mary to Bradford Monthly Meeting.

9th da, 2nd mo, 1786 - Sarah Rea, wife of Moses Rea to Wilmington Monthly Meeting.

4th da, 5th mo, 1786 - Joseph Grissel and Precilla, his wife to Westland Monthly Meeting with their children, Agnes and Thomas.

10th da, 5th mo, 1786 - Caleb Kimber and Wife, Deborah to Newgarden Monthly Meeting.

6th da, 7th mo, 1786 - John Martin to Chester Monthly Meeting. Rachel Johnson, and her husband to Concord Monthly Meeting and children: Isaac, Joshua and Rachel.

7th da, 12th mo, 1786 - Mary Bonsall to Exeter Monthly Meeting. Lydia Davis to Hopewell, VA Monthly Meeting.

4th da, 1st mo, 1787 - Susannah Crispin to Philadelphia Monthly Meeting.

8th da, 3rd mo, 1787 - Jonathan Hood from Northern District Monthly Meeting in Philadelphia to return there.

5th da, 4th mo, 1787 - Mary and Hannah Williams, daus. of Isaac Williams from Gwynedd Monthly Meeting to return there.

10th da, 5th mo, 1787 - Jane Morris from Exter Monthly Meeting to return there. Mary Sharpless to Goshen Monthly Meeting. William Kirk, disowned by Uwchlan Monthly Meeting for several years past, resides within Goose Creek Monthly Meeting, VA and is reinstated. James Meredeth, a minor placed as an Apprentice to Kennett Monthly Meeting. Nicholas Morris, to Exeter Monthly Meeting.

6th da, 9th mo, 1787 - Martha Scott and her husband to Goose Creek, VA Monthly Meeting. Sarah Jones, wife of Edward Jones to Warrington Monthly Meeting.

4th da, 10th mo, 1787 - Rebecca Harris to Exeter Monthly Meeting.
6th da, 12th mo, 1787 - Susanna Hatton, a minor from Uwchlan
Monthly Meeting by Wilmington Monthly Meeting to Goshen
Monthly Meeting. William Williams, a minor to Exeter Monthly
Meeting. Elizabeth Williams, dau. of Isaac to Gunpowder Monthly
Meeting, Md. Isaac Thomas and Eleanor, his wife and children:
Jane, Lydia, Rebecca, Elizabeth, Isaac and Ellen to Exeter Monthly
Meeting. Abraham Sharpless to Newgarden.
6th da, 3rd mo, 1788 - Esther Mathews, wife of John Mathews to
Fairfax Monthly Meeting, VA.
8th da, 5th mo, 1788 - Thomas Lloyd to Kennett Monthly Meeting.
Phinehaus Tibberd and Sarah, his wife to Goshen Monthly Meeting.
Hannah Dolby, wife of John Dolby to Goshen Monthly Meeting.
Abraham Rogers to Goshen Monthly Meeting. Mary Espin to
Haverford Monthly Meeting. Israel Espin to Haverford Monthly
Meeting. Jane Espin to Haverford Monthly Meeting. Lillah Espin to
Haveford Monthly Meeting.
7th da, 8th mo, 1788 - Rachel Valentine to Concord Monthly Meeting.
4th da, 9th mo, 1788 - Jesse Meredith, a minor placed as an apprentice
to Goshen Monthly Meeting.
6th da, 11th mo, 1788 - Jacob Wilson, from the Northern District of
Philadelphia Meeting is returning there.
9th da, 4th mo, 1789 - Isaac and Hannah Jacobs, and their children:
Mary, Phebe, William, Hannah, Elizabeth, Sarah, Isaac, Joseph and
Rachel to Gwynedd Monthly Meeting. Rachel Romans to
Philadelphia Monthly Meeting.
7th da, 5th mo, 1789 - Benejah Brown to Newgarden Monthly
Meeting.
4th da, 6th mo, 1789 - Abiah Parke, a minor placed as an Apprentice at
Bradford Monthly Meeting. Sarah Gibbons, wife of Joseph Gibbons,
with her husband to Northern District Philadelphia Monthly
Meeting. Elizabeth, wife of Eli Packer, and children: Moses, Rachel,
Ann, Eli and Aaron to Goshen Monthly Meeting.
9th da, 7th mo, 1789 - Ruth Price, wife of Benjamin Price to Monthly
Meeting of the Southern District Philadelphia.
7th da, 1st mo, 1790 - Hannah Atherton to Philadelphia Monthly
Meeting.
6th da, 5th mo, 1790 - Dinah Lewis to Goshen Monthly Meeting.
Hannah, wife of John Dolby to Haverford Monthly Meeting.
10th of 6th mo, 1790 - Hannah, wife of Jacob Humphries, from
Haverford Monthly Meeting returns there with her children:
Edward, Samuel, Rebeckah and Sarah, all minors.

8th da, 7th mo, 1790 - William Butler and Jane, his wife to Newgarden Monthly Meeting and their children: Amos, Ann, Rachel, Sarah and William. The two eldest, Amos and Ann are clear of marriage engagements. Phebe Coats to Gunpowder Monthly Meeting [Maryland].
9th da, 9th mo, 1790 - John Lloyd and Mercy, his wife and Joshua, his son to Exeter Monthly Meeting.
6th da, 1st mo, 1791. Mary Meredith to Bradford Monthly Meeting. Mary Gray with her husband to Bradford Monthly Meeting. Susana Spencer from Hopewell Monthly Meeting, VA to return there.
10th of 3rd mo, 1791. Samuel Bond to Hopewell Monthly Meeting, VA. Joseph Bond to Hopewell, VA Monthly Meeting. Sarah Bond to Monthly Meeting at Hopewell Monthly Meeting, VA.
7th da, 4th mo, 1791. Philip Price and Rachel, his wife to Concord Monthly Meeting with their children: Martha, Hannah, William and Sibbilla.
5th da, 5th mo, 1791. Isaiah Kirk and Elizabeth, his wife to Monthly Meeting of Northern District in Philadelphia with children, Samuel and Rachel. Frances Hope, a minor to Northern District in Philadelphia Monthly Meeting.
7th da, 7th mo, 1791. Charles [?] Atherton to Philadelphia Monthly Meeting. Sibbilla Kirk to Concord Monthly Meeting. Nicholas Morris to Robeson Monthly Meeting.
8th da, 4th mo, 1791. Thomas Edge, a minor, placed as an Apprentice at Philadelphia Monthly Meeting.
8th da, 9th mo, [Sic] 1791. Sarah Yarnall, wife of Moses Yarnall, to Goshen Monthly Meeting with two young children, Thomas and Enoch, 6th da, 10th mo, 1791. Elisha Davis to Haverford Monthly Meeting. Hannah, wife of John Hutchinson Coates to Gwynedd Monthly Meeting. Hannah Lewis, Jr. to Goshen Monthly Meeting. Hannah Garretson, wife of Cornelius Garretson, with her husband to Warrington Monthly Meeting. Henry Atherton to Darby Monthly Meeting with his wife, Hannah and children: George, Humphrey and Isaac. Ruth Atherton with her parents to Darby Monthly Meeting.
8th da, 12th mo, 1791. Joseph Barger to Evesham, West Jersey Monthly Meeting. Jonathan Roberts to Haverford Monthly Meeting.
5th da, 1st mo, 1792. Alice Woodward to Concord Monthly Meeting. Mary Jackson to Robison Monthly Meeting. Mary Bernard, wife of Joseph Bernard, with her husband to Bradford Monthly Meeting.
9th da, 2nd mo, 1792. Sarah Starr, wife of James Starr, with children: James, Joseph, Rebekah, Mary and John to Chester Monthly

UWCHLAN MONTHLY MEETING

Meeting. Ann and Sarah Starr with their parents to limits of Chester Monthly Meeting. Tacey Coate to Monthly Meeting of the Northern District of Philadelphia. Beulah Starr, a minor placed with a Friend at Goshen Monthly Meeting.

5th da, 4th mo, 1792. Robert Hawley to Bradford Monthly Meeting.

10th da, 5th mo, 1792. Hannah Philips with her husband and family to Exeter Monthly Meeting. Joshua John and Rachel, his wife, to Monthly Meeting at Warrington. Esther Pile attended meeting and produced an acknowledgment for her past misconduct, reinstated in membership and requested certificate of removal to Bradford Monthly Meeting. Gedeon John from Uwchlan Monthly Meeting to Westland Monthly Meeting in Redstone Settlement where he now resides. Isaiah John to Warrington Monthly Meeting. Rachel John and Ann John, daus. of Joshua John to live with their parents at Warrington Monthly Meeting.

7th da, 6th mo, 1792. Abel Lewis, a minor, placed as an Apprentice at Northern District Monthly Meeting in Philadelphia.

6th da, 7th mo, 1792. Isaac Jackson and Elizabeth, his wife, to Westland Monthly Meeting with their children: Sarah, Sidney, Mercy and Deborah.

4th da, 10th mo, 1792. Hannah, wife of John Rogers to Goshen Monthly Meeting.

2nd da, 11th mo, 1792. Elijah Butler to Goose Crick [Creek] Monthly Meeting, VA.

10th da, 1st mo, 1793. Abigail Davis to Bradford Monthly Meeting.

7th da, 2nd mo, 1793. Humphrey Lloyd sent an acknowledgment to our last meeting together with a few lines subscribed by a number of Friends at a Preparative Meting at Newgarden, NC.

4th da, 4th mo, 1793. Jacob Rogers to Gotion [Goshen] Monthly Meeting.

9th da, 5th mo, 1793. William Cooper and Mary, his wife with children: Mary, Rachel, Joshua, Samuel, Isaac and Sibilla to Haverford Monthly Meeting. Hannah James to Haverford Monthly Meeting. Richard Jacobs and Lydia, his wife to Concord Monthly Meeting with children, Phebe and Susannah.

6th da, 6th mo, 1793. Richard Trimble and Ann, his wife to Falls Monthly Meeting in Bucks County, Pa. Samuel Butler to London Grove Monthly Meeting. Ruth Hays to London Grove Monthly Meeting. Hugh Meredith placed as an Apprentice to Haverford Monthly Meeting.

4th da, 7th mo, 1793. Jane Maule to Haverford Monthly Meeting. Griffith John, Jr. and Sarah, his wife and their children: Emy, Abner and Rachel to Bradford Monthly Meeting.

8th da, 8th mo, 1793. Thomas Parke to Monthly Meeting of Springfield in West New Jersey.

10th da, 10th mo, 1793. John Starr, a youth placed as an Apprentice to Haverford Monthly Meeting.

7th da, 11th mo, 1793. Aquilla Starr to Chester Monthly Meeting.

6th da, 3rd mo, 1793. Ruben John and Lydia, his wife and their children: Ann, Sarah, Phebe, Townsend and Israel to Concord Monthly Meeting. Pameliah John, dau. of Ruben and Lydiah [Sic] to Concord Monthly Meeting.

8th da, 5th mo, 1794 - Anthony Gray and Mary, his wife to Bradford Monthly Meeting with children, John and Elizabeth.

10th da, 7th mo, 1794 - Sarah Martin to Gwynedd Monthly Meeting. Margaret Gill, wife of David Gill from Gwynedd Monthly Meeting, with their five children: Charles, Susannah, Ann, Francis and David to Gwynedd Monthly Meeting.

4th da, 9th mo, 1794 - Joannah John to Concord Monthly Meeting. John Meredith to Bradford Monthly Meeting, placed as an Apprentice.

9th da, 10th mo, 1794 - Sarah Jones, wife of John Jones to Philadelphia Monthly Meeting.

9th da, 4th mo, 1795 - Samuel Baldwin and Mary, his wife and their eight children: Joshua, Mercy, George, Israel, Lydia, Jane, Isaac and Samuel to the Cornwall Monthly Meeting, NY.

7th da, 5th mo, 1795 - Ruth Miller to Fairfax Monthly Meeting in VA. Jane Pearson to Philadelphia Monthly Meeting. Dorcas, wife of James Woolerton to Bradford Monthly Meeting. Rachel Coats to Bradford Monthly Meeting.

9th da, 7th mo, 1795 - Elijah Pearson, a minor placed as an Apprentice to Wilmington Monthly Meeting.

6th da, 8th mo, 1795 - William Hilles? and wife Rebecca and children: Hugh, Mary, Ann, Eli, David and Samuel to Monthly Meeting at Westland in Washington County. Nathan Yearsley to Chester Monthly Meeting.

10th of 9th mo, 1795 - Robert Hatten, his wife, Ann and children: Susanna, Eliza, Rachel, Jarves, Grace and Edward to Monthly Meeting at Monallen. Grace Meredeth to Exeter Monthly Meeting.

8th da, 10th mo, 1795 - Hannah Gibson, wife of Nathaniel Gibson to Redstone Monthly Meeting. Ann Starr to Abington Monthly Meeting [Md?].

7th da, 4th mo, 1796 - Sarah Williams to Goshen Monthly Meeting. Thomas Buchannan to New Concord Monthly Meeting, NY.

5th da, 5th mo, 1796 - Jane and Ann Edge with their parents to Bradford Monthly Meeting. John and Ann Edge from Bradford

Monthly Meeting; now returning with children: Fanny, George, John and Mary. Thomas Edge to Bradford Monthly Meeting. Josiah Wood to Abington Monthly Meeting. Susannah and Benjamin Lightfoot, placed by their guardians to Exeter Monthly Meeting.

7th da, 7th mo, 1796 - Thomzin Roberts to Northern District Monthly Meeting at Philadelphia.

4th da, 8th mo, 1796 - Phebe and Sarah Pierson to Philadelphia Monthly Meeting.

8th da, 9th mo, 1796 - Rebecca, wife of William Jones to Gwynedd Monthly Meeting. James Hibbert from Philadelphia Monthly Meeting where he was an Apprentice now returning.

8th da, 12th mo, 1796 - Tamzin Trimble to Falls Monthly Meeting.

5th da, 1st mo, 1797 - Mary Patton to Monthly Meeting at Catawissa.

9th da, 2nd mo, 1797 - Aaron Garrett to the Goshen Monthly Meeting.

3rd da, 6th mo, 1797 - William Ashbridge to Philadelphia Monthly Meeting with Mary, his wife and their dau. Lydia.

6th da, 7th mo, 1797 - Benjamin Starr to Catawissa Monthly Meeting.

9th da, 7th mo, 1797 - Mary Davis to Southern District Philadelphia Monthly Meeting.

10th of 8th mo, 1797 - Hugh Meredith to Nottingham Monthly Meeting.

4th da, 1st mo, 1798 - Jesse Meredith to Wilmington Monthly Meeting.

8th da, 3rd mo, 1798 - Joseph Longstretch to Philadelphia Monthly Meeting.

4th da, 5th mo, 1798 - Douglald Cameron to Southern District Philadelphia Monthly Meeting.

10th da, 5th mo, 1798 - Deborah Joyce to Radnor Monthly Meeting.

7th da, 6th mo, 1798 - Ames Bullet to Bradford Monthly Meeting.

9th da, 8th mo, 1798 - Rebecca Raubey/Haubey? wife of Joseph Raubey/Haubey to Bradford Monthly Meeting.

4th da, 10th mo, 1798 - Benjamin Coates to Bradford Monthly Meeting.

10th da, 1st mo, 1799 - John Meredeth to Concord Monthly Meeting.

4th da, 4th mo, 1799 - Mary Ingram to Bradford Monthly Meeting. Jesse Harry to Bradford Monthly Meeting with his wife, Catharine and their children: William, Hannah and Sarah.

9th da, 5th mo, 1799 - Mary Kenny to Bradford Monthly Meeting. Richard Kenney to Goshen Monthly Meeting.

6th da, 6th mo, 1799 - Elija Lewis/Lewes to Radnor Monthly Meeting.

Phineas Whitaker and Edith, his wife with children to Bradford Monthly Meeting.

10th da, 10th mo, 1799 - Ann, wife of John Hatton to Catawissa Monthly Meeting. *Jesse Bonsell recommended as a Minister. Signed in and on behalf of Uwchlan Monthly Meeting held by adjournment 17th da, 10th mo, 1799. Signed as Follows: Joseph Gibbons, Evan Jones, Reuben John, Geo. Valentine, William Trimble, William Milhous, Ruben John, Nathan Cadwallader, Abiah Parke, Daniel Kenney, Isaac Jacob, Jesse Kersey. By Request George Massey, Jehiu Roberts, Nathan Sharpless, John Lewis, John Meredith, John Mecham, Daniel Kenney, Jr., Bartholomew Fussell, David Lightfoot, Peter Smedly, John Gordon, Jesse Jones, John Baldwin, John Butler.*

9th da, 1st mo, 1800 - Rose, wife of James Packer of Bald Eagle Valley to Muncy Monthly Meeting. James and Lillah Packer, children of James and Rose Packer, now being of age to Muncy Monthly Meeting. Elizabeth, wife of Eli Packer, of Bald Eagle Valley, requested certificate for herself and five Minor children: Eli, Aaron, Amos, Amy and John to Muncy Monthly Meeting.

10th of 4th mo, 1800 - Dorothy Davison to Chester Monthly Meeting. William Davis to Chester Monthly Meeting. Samuel Baldwin, a minor to Goshen Monthly Meeting.

5th da, 6th mo, 1800 - Hannah Longstretch (a minor) to Philadelphia Monthly Meeting. Sarah Longstretch to Horsham Monthly Meeting. Samuel Longstretch, a minor to Philadelphia Monthly Meeting. Joseph Townsend to Chester Monthly Meeting.

5th da, 8th mo, 1800 - Mary, wife of Richard Kenny to Goshen Monthly Meeting.

9th da, 10th mo, 1800 - Abner Lewis, having returned to Radnor Monthly Meeting.

EAST VINCENT REFORMED CONGREGATION

Unless otherwise noted, the dates are assummed to be dates of baptism.

Dec 24, 1733 Barbara, dau. of Johannes Schönholtzer. Sponsor: Barbara Wittman and her husband.

July 13, 1736 Martin, son of Johannes Schönholtzer. Sponsor: Martin Kÿler and his wife.

June 30, 1739 Jacob, son of Johannes Schönholtzer. Sponsor: Father.

Jan 14, 1741 Christophorus, son of Michael Denÿ. Sponsor: parents themselves.

June 4 ?, Anna Maria, dau. of Simon Schunk. Sponsor: Anna Maria Schaümerin.

Aug 6, 1742 Catharina, dau. of Johannes Schönholtzer, Sponsor Catharina Ernstin.

Just at Easter, 1742 Catharina, dau. of Michael Denÿ. Sponsor: Mater.

Mar 21, 1744 Catharina Elisabetha, dau. of Simon Schunck, Sponsor Catharina Elisabetha Carlin.

Apr 11, 1744 Elisabeth, dau. of Sebastian Wagner, Sponsor Mater ipsa.

Feb 4, 1745 N. S., Johannes, son of Thomas Schneider. Sponsor: Johannes Schneider.

July 11, ___ Elizabeth, dau. of Johannes Schönholtzer. Sponsor: Elisabeth Carlin.

Feb 12, 1746 N. S., Anna Maria, dau. of Sebastian Wagner. Sponsor: Mater ipsa.

Oct 26, 1746 Conrad, son of Simon Schunck. Sponsor: Conrad Schaümer.

Apr 11, 1747 N.S., Catharina, dau. of Thomas Schneider, Sponsor Christiana Schaüderin.

Sep 15 born, Nov 3 baptized, Jacob, son of Peter Steyer, Sponsor Jacob Collman.

Dec 1748 born, May 27, 1758, baptized, Jacob, son of Caspar Schneider. Sponsor: Father.

Mar 11, 1748 Johannes, son of Johannes Schonhöltzer. Sponsor: Johannes Carl.

Jan 16, 1749 Anna Maria, dau. of Johannes Hippel. Sponsor: Ana Maria Schneiderin.

Apr 2, 1749 Anna Margaretha, dau. of Simon Schuncken. Sponsor: Ana Margaretha Schaümerin.

Mar 21, 1749 born, June 9, baptized, Elisabetha, dau. of Peter Steyer.

Sponsor: Elisabetha Spechtin.
Apr 10, 1749 Maria Elisabeth dau. of Michael Deny. Sponsor: Parentes ipsi.
Oct 11, 1750 Sebastian, son of Sebastian Wagner. Sponsor: Pater ipsi.
Apr 6, 1751 Simon, son of Simon Schuncken. Sponsor: Pater ipse.
On about the last of April Johannes, son of Johannes Wagner. Sponsor: Pater ipse.
Nov 15, 1751 born, Nov 24, baptized, Eva Elisabeth, dau. of Jacob Helwig. Sponsor: Eva Elisabeth Hägerin.
May 12, 1752 Johannes, son of Johannes Hippel. Sponsor: Johannes Hippel.
June 17, 1752 Anna Maria, dau. of Johannes Schneider. Sponsor: Anna Maria Schneiderin.
June 4, 1751 N.S., Jacob, son of Michael Seivert. Sponsor: Parents themselves (Parentes ipses).
Oct 29, 1752 Catharina, dau. of Michael Seivert. Sponsor: Catharina Carlin.
Jan 5, 1753 born, March 25 baptized, Henrich, son of Lorentz Hippel. Sponsor: Henrich Kÿle.
Apr 1, 1753 Peter, son of Johannes Schönholtzer. Sponsor: Peter Steger.
Apr 3, 1753 Margaretha, dau. of Michael Denÿ. Sponsor: Margaretha Eschentzellerin.
June 26, 1753 Henrich, son of Johannes Laubach. Sponsor: Pater.
Sep 7, 1753 born, Sep 14 baptized, Isaac, son of Isaac Schunck. Sponsor: Pater ipse.
Aug 9, 1753 born, Aug 20 baptized, Catharina, dau. of Jacob Helwig. Sponsor: Peter Steger's wife Eva Elisabeth.
Nov 18, 1753 born, Feb 24, 1754 baptized, Anna Maria, dau. of Thomas Schneider, Sponsor Anna Maria Jagerin.
Dec 17, 1753 Abraham, son of Michael Seivert, Sponsor Parentes ipses.
May 27, 1758 Sibilla, wife of Caspar Schneider, and Jacob, Magdalena, Margareth, Thomas - children of Caspar's former wife.
Feb 21, 1760 Evann, dau. of Caspar Schneider.
Aug 28, 1762 Catharina, dau. of Caspar Schneider.
1766 Daniel, son of Caspar Schneider.
Feb 7, 1754 Catharina, dau. of Johannes Schneider. Sponsor: Catherina Schneiderin.
May 13, 1754 Catharina, dau. of Sebastian Wagner. Sponsor: Mater ipsa.
Jan 14, 1754 born, Jan 25 baptized, Maria Catharina, dau. of Jacob

EAST VINCENT REFORMED CONGREGATION

Braun. Sponsor: Catharina Sälerin.
June 8, 1754 Lorentz, son of Henrich Hippel. Sponsor: Lorentz Hippel.
Feb 21, 1754 born, Feb 24 baptized, Anna Catharina, dau. of Peter Steger. Sponsor: Catharina and Peter Specht.
Feb 20, 1755 Peter, son of Simon Schunck. Sponsor: Peter du Vrain.
Apr 4, 1755 Elisabeth, dau. of Johannes Wagner. Sponsor: Mater ipsa.
Oct 8, 1755 born, Nov 2, 1755 baptized Johannes, son of Lorentz Hippel. Sponsor: Johannes Hippel.
Oct 2, 1755 born, Nov 2, 1755 baptized, Anna Maria, dau. of Görg Jäger. Sponsor: Parentes ipsi.
July 20, 1755 born and baptized, Isaac, son of Michael Seivert. Sponsor: Parentes ipsi.
Jan 3, 1756 Jacob, son of Henrich Hippel. Sponsor: Jacob Hippel.
May 14, 1756 Magdalena, dau. of Johannes Hippel, Parentes ipsi.
July 20, 1756 Anna Maria, dau. of Johannes Laübach. Sponsor: Pater.
Apr 3, 1756 Christina, dau. of Thomas Schneider. Sponsor: Christina Hängin.
Apr 5, 1756 Georg, son of Johannes Schneider. Sponsor: Georg Schneider.
June 17, 1756 Johannes, son of Jacob Müller. Sponsor: Johannes Schneider.
Apr 19, 1767 born, June 6, 1767 baptized, Susanna, dau. of Philip Andra.
Feb 6, 1767 born, June 6, 1767 baptized, Johannes, son of Elias Crescher.
Apr 5, 1767 Maria Chattharina, dau. of Adam Gondelt.
Apr 3, 1758 Peter, son of Peter Brunner. Sponsor: Peter Schümann Coelebs, Single.
May 28, 1758 born, Aug 6, 1758 baptized, Barbara, dau. of Paul Benner. Sponsor: Parentes ipsi.
July 6, 1758 born, Aug 6, 1758 baptized, Anna Margaretha, dau. of Johannes Laübach, Sponsor Anna Margaretha Schumann, Single.
Aug 24, 1758 born, October 1, 1758 baptized, Johannes, son of Johan Görg Jager.
Jan 24, 1758 Maria Magdalena, dau. of Adam Gondelt.
Feb 6, 1759 born, Feb 18, baptized, Georg Adam, son of Peter Steger. Sponsor: Georg Adam Hylman et Uxor.
Nov 24, 1759 Magdalena, dau. of Johannes Imhoftt.
Jun 10, 1754 Lorentz, son of Henrich Hippel.
Jan 3, 1756 born, Jacob, son of Henrich Hippel.
Mar 10, 1758 born, Anna Catharina, dau. of Henrich Hippel.

Feb 7, 1760 born, Anna Maria, dau. of Henrich Hippel.
Nov, 14, 1762 born, Anna Elisabeth, dau. of Henrich Hippel.
Feb 2, 1764 born, Anna Maria [Mar]gretha, dau. of Henrich Hippel.
Mar 7, 1766 born, Anna Marialisabetha, dau. of Henrich Hippel.
Nov 14, 1770 born, Anna Christina, dau. of Henrich Hippel.
Oct 26, 1760 born, Nov 21, 1760 baptized, Johann Jost, son of Lorentz Hippel, God parents: Joh. Jost Berger and Elizabeth Esch.
Jan 31, 1761 born, Apr 12, 1761 baptized, Jah. Jacob, son of Joh. Henge and Christina. Sponsor: Jacob Henge, Lediger [unmarried].
Nov 1, 1760 born, Apr 12, 1760 or 1761 baptized, Rosina, dau. of Joh. Georg. Schneider and Anna Elisabeth, his wife, Godparents, Jacob Miller and Rosina, his wife.
Feb 14, 1761 born, Apr 12, 1761 baptized, Caspar, son of Jacob Miller and Sibilla, Sponsor Caspar Bierbauer.
Jan 13, 1761? born, Apr 12, 1761? baptized, Elisabeth, dau. of Andreas Keller and Maria Catharina, Godmother, Elisabeth Shunk[in].
Feb 21, 1761? born, Apr 12, 1761? baptized, Johannes, son of Joh. Schneider and Maria Elisabetha, Godfather Joh. Mertz, single.
May 10, 1761 Sussannah, dau. of Catharina Stein, Widow.
Feb 1, 1761 Joh. Henrich, son of Georg Harts and Catharina, his wife, Godparents, Henrich Moser and Phillippina.
Jan 1, 1761 Adam son of Joh. Adam Gondel.
May 29, 1762 born, July 4, 1762? baptized, Christina, dau. of Johannes Laubach, Godmother, Christina Zeug.
Jan 10, 1762 born, April 11, 1762? baptized, Anna Catharina, dau. of Johan Görg Jager, Godmother, Cathrina Scheimmer.
July 14, 1762 Johan Jacob, son of Johannes Klein.
May 23, 1762 Philip, son of Adam Gondel.
May 3, 1762 Daniel, son of Joh. Daniel Benner.
Apr 22, 1762 John, son of Christian Stahl.
Apr 23, 1763 born, July 3, 1763? baptized, Gertraut, dau. of Martin Schönholtzer, God mother, Gertraut ---?.
Dec 11, 1762 Phillipps Heinrich, son of Adam De Frain [Du Vrain].
July 2, 1763 Frietrich, son of Lorentz Hippel.
Aug 15, 1764 Jacob, son of Daniel Benner.
Aug 14, 1764 Christina, dau. of Phillipp Lauderbach, Godparents: Joh. Hangan and Wife [Christina].
Dec 3, 1764 Sara, dau. of Jacob Conrat.
Jan 10, 1766 Johannes, son of Paul Henner, Godfather, Johannes -?.
Jan 27, 1765 Peter, son of Georg Jäger.
Feb 24, 1765 Johannes, son of Johannes Benner.

EAST VINCENT REFORMED CONGREGATION 41

May 8, 1765 Bernhart, son of Adam De Frain [Du Vrain].
Sep 10, 1765 Johann Peter, son of Henrich Carl, Sponsor Grandfather, Peter Hencke.
Apr 22, 1767 born, June 7, 1767 baptized, Henrich, son of Henrich Carl and Elisabeth.
Mar 17, 1766 born, June 21, 1766 baptized, Samuel, son of Jacob Conrad and Anna Margaretha.
Aug 2, 1767, baptized 9 months old, Anna Catharina, dau. of Joshannes Weely and Anna Catharina.
Jan 14, 1767 born, Aug 2, 1767 baptized, Ludwich, son of Friedrich Fraunfeltz and Eva.
Oct 13, [175-] born, Elisabeth, dau. of Valantine Schmid and Gertraut.
July 12, 1760, born, Jacob, son of Valantine Schmid and Gertraut.
Apr 18, 1763, born, Adam, son of Valantine and Catharina Schmid.
Apr 9, 1766, born, Johannes, son of Valantine Schmid and Catharina.
Aug 9, 1767 born, Sep 27, 1767? baptized, Catharina, dau. of Jacob Günter and Dorrothea.
Oct 11, 1767, baptized at the age of 15 months, Daniel, son of George Eristman and Sophia.
Aug 15, 1767 born, Oct 11, 1767? baptized, Margaretha, dau. of Caspar Bierbauer and Sara.
Apr 5, 1767 born, May 15, 1767 baptized, Johannes Henrich, son of Valantin Schmid and Catharina.
Nov 20, 1772 born, Dec 13, 1772? baptized, Eleanora, dau. of Vallantin Schmidt and Catharina.
Aug 3, ?? born, Oct 3, ? baptized, Abraham, son of Johann Michel Gründ and Ewa [Eva].
Sep 21, [1767] born, Oct 30 baptized, Susanna, dau. of Henrich Houck and Margaretha.
Feb 7, 1768 born, Mar 27, baptized, Elizabeth, dau. of Jost Schmid and Catharina.
Oct 20, 1768 born, Georg, son of Georg Jäger and Anna Maria.
Mar 3, 1768 born, April ---, baptized, Jacob, son of Phillip Wengard and Susanna.
Jan 14, 1768, born, June 5, baptized, Maria Elisabeth, dau. of Wilhelm Claus and Anna Cunigunda.
? weeks ago, yesterday, born, June 5, baptized, Johannes, son of Hieronimus Seiler and Maria Phillippina.

July 12, 176[7], born, June 5, 1768, baptized, Johannes, son of Benedict Bayrs and Margaretha Elisabeth.

Mar 9, 1768, born, June 5, baptized, Johannes, son of Caspar [Schneider] and Sibilla.

June 24, 1768, Saint John's Day, born, Sep 11, 1768, baptized, Johannes, son of Peter Schmehl and Elizabeth - Note: The literal translation seems to be "Ancient (old) John's Day.".

Aug 2, 1768, born, Sep 25, baptized, son of Johannes Mertz.

June 16, 1768, born, Sep 25, baptized, Magdalena, dau. of Hermann Bierbauer and Christina.

Sep 25, 1768, baptized, Thomas, son of Thomas Schneider and Barbara.

Born 5 weeks ago, Oct 23, 1768, baptized, Magdalena, dau. of (blank).

Dec 26, 1766, baptized, Anthony, son of ___ Acker.

Dec 26, 1766, baptized, Jacob, Maria, Magdalena, Catharina, Barbara, children of Anthony Acker and Anna Maria. Sponsor: Anthonay and Anna Maria Acker.

Oct 24, 1759, born, Sep 24, 1769, baptized, Johannes, son of Johannes Yungblut.

Dec 9, 1761 born, Sep 24, 1769 baptized, Michel, son of Johannes Yungblut.

May 17, 1764, born, Sep 24, 1769, baptized, Elisabeth, dau. of Johannes Jungblut.

Mar 22, 1767 born, Sep 24, 1769 baptized, Johann Henrich, son of Johannes Yungblut, [Mason].

July 3, 1769 born, Sep 24, 1769 baptized, Margareth, dau. of Johannes Yungblut, [Mason].

Aug 25, 1768 born, May 7, 1769 baptized, Catharina, dau. of Friedrich Brenholtz.

Feb 19, 1769 born, May 7, 1769 baptized, Johann Peter, son of Johann Henrich Hencken and Anna Margaretha.

Feb 3, 1769 born, May 7, baptized, Catharina, dau. of Lenhard Daubil and Apallon[i]a [Apollonia].

Dec 29, 1768 born, May 15, baptized [1769], Johann Phillip, son of Jacob Günther and Anna Dorothea.

Mar 29, 1769 born, May 21 baptized, Anna Maria, dau. of Jonah Heck and Sussanna.

Mar 1, 1769 born, June 4 baptized, Daniel, son of Johannes Klein and Henrietta.

May 9, 1769 born, July 2, baptized, Jacob, son of Phillip Stessan and Barbara.

EAST VINCENT REFORMED CONGREGATION

June 15, 1769 born, July 16, baptized, Peter, son of Lorentz Hippel and Anna Maria.

March 23, 1769 born, July 30, baptized, Johann Phillip, son of Johannes Arendorft and Eva Barbara.

May 30, 1769 born, July 30, baptized, Catharina, dau. of Henrich Karl and Elisabeth.

Jan 31, 1769 born, Aug 13, baptized, Jacob, son of Andreas Heck and Barbara.

Wednesday, 8 weeks ago, born, Aug 13, 1769 baptized, Maria Catharina, dau. of Paul Benner and Elisabeth.

Mar 2, 1769 born, Sep 10, baptized, Elisabeth, dau. of Georg Christmann and Sophia.

Aug 21, 1769 born, Oct 8, baptized, Reb-cka, dau. of Conrad Scheerer and Catharina Scheerer.

10 weeks ago, 1769, born, Oct 22, baptized, son of Thomas Eschenfelder and Anna [name almost obliterated by another hand].

Nov 14, 1769 born, Dec 25, baptized, Catharina, dau. of Melchior Shott and Catharina.

Feb 13, 1770 born, Mar 11 baptized, Anna Catharina, dau. of Philip Weyandt and Susanna. Godparents: Johannes Hippel and Catharina Schottin.

Jan 8, 1770 born, Apr 22 baptized, Elisabeth, dau. of Hans Jacob Hell and Maria Susanna.

Jan 29, 1770 born, Apr 22 baptized, Johannes, son of Johannes Grast and Julianna.

Mar 20, 1770 born, May 6, baptized, Maria, dau. of Jacob Hellwich and Dorrothea.

Apr 13, 1770 born, June 3 baptized, Joh. Georg, son of Jacob Stikel and Anna Maria.

Apr 13, 1770 born, July 29 baptized, Elisabeth, dau. of Joh. Nickel Grund and Eva.

Apr 24, 1770 born, July 1, 1770 baptized, Christina, dau. of Wilhelm Claus and Cunigunda.

May 1, 1770 born, July 1 baptized, Margaretha, dau. of Friedrich Hippel and Anna Maria.

Apr 15, 1769 born, July 1, 1770 baptized, Maria, dau. of Hugh Weay and Hanna.

Oct 24, [178-] born, July 1, 177? baptized, John, son of Hugh Way and Hanna.

June 14, 1770 born, Sep 19 or 23, 1770 baptized, Elisabeth, [son of]??]

Friedrich Brennholtz and Eva.

Nov 5, 1770 born, December 2, 1770 baptized, Philip Henrich, son of Henrich Hencken and Anna Margareth.

Oct 6, 1770 born, Dec 2, 1770 baptized, Maria Catharina, dau. of William Thomas and Christina.

Oct 19, 1770 born, Dec 2, 1770 baptized, Benjamin, son of Conrat Schünk and Maria.

Nov 7, 1770 born, Feb 24, 1771 baptized, Catharina, dau. of Johannes Mertz.

Mar 5, 1771 born, May 5, 1771 baptized, Joh. Georg, son of Leonharth Daübil and Appellona.

Jan 4, 1771 born, Apr 1, 1771 baptized, Johann Lüdwig, son of Johann Lübach and Catharina.

Feb 23, 1771 born, Apr 1, 1771 baptized, Johannes, son of Michel Geler and Margaretha.

Nov 16, 1770 born, Apr 1, 1771 baptized, Johann Georg, son of Johannes Reiss and Catharina.

Oct 4, 1770 born, Apr 1, 1771 baptized, Christian, son of Henrich Dritt and Elisabeth.

Feb 3, 1771 born, Apr 1, 1771 baptized, Christina Margaretha, dau. of Georg Jacob Elsaz and Christina.

Mar 20, 1771 born, May 19, 1771 baptized, Caspar, son of Caspar Schneider and Sybilla.

-- weeks ago yesterday, 1771 born (June 15, 1771), Aug 11, 1771 baptized, Elisabeth, dau. of Johannes Goetz and Anna Maria.

June 29, 1771 born, Aug 11, 1771 baptized, Elisabeth, dau. of Henrich Karl and Elisabeth.

July 5, 1771 born, Oct 6, 1771 baptized, Vallentin, son of Johannes Baart and Catharina.

Sep 28, 1771 born, Nov 3, 1771 baptized, Catharina, dau. of Wilhelm Claus and Anna Cunigünda.

July 3, 1771 born, Nov 3, 1771 baptized, Jacob, son of Jacob Günther and Dorothea.

Sep 6, 1771 born, Nov 3, 1771 baptized, Elisabeth, dau. of Christjan Hoff and Catharina.

Sep 26, 1771 born, Nov 3, 1771 baptized, Elisabeth, dau. of Friedrich Hippel and Anna Maria.

Aug 15, 1771 born, Oct 6, 1771 baptized, Margareda, dau. of Johannes Geitling, Schoolmaster, and Elisabeth. Godmother: Margareda Schurzdery, Single.

Sep 27, 1771 born, Nov 5, 1771 baptized, Jacob, son of Georg Jäger and Anna Maria. Witness: the Father.

Feb 8, 1771 born, Apr 5, 1771 baptized, Elisabeth, dau. of Lorentz Hippel and Anna Maria.

Dec 27, 1771 born, Mar 22, 1772 baptized, William, son of William Thomas and Sara [It is probable that the pastor, baptising this child in 1771, set down the year of his birth incorrectly. A later hand filled in 1772 as date of baptism.

Jan 6, 177[1] born, Mar 22, 177[1] baptized, Johannes, son of Johannes Klein and Margaretha.

Jan 9, 1772 born, May 31, 1772 baptized, David, son of Johannes Klein and Henrietta.

Mar 5, 1772 born, May 1[3], 1772 baptized, Magdalena, dau. of J. Nickel Grundt and Eliza.

-- ago today, 1772 (born April 13), June 8, 1772 baptized, Adam, son of Adam Geider and Magdalena.

Apr 7, 1772 born, June 8, 1772 baptized, Jacob, son of Henrich Drit and Elizabeth.

Oct 12, 1771 born, Dec 1, ---- [presumably 1772] baptized, Henrich, son of Melchoir Schott and Catharina.

June 28 born, July 26, baptized, Jacob, son of Peter Schönholtzer and Elisabetha.

Peter DeFrehn, [Du Vrain, De Frain], his children are here set down by name, with the dates of their birth:.

Anna Maria born July 30, 1754.

Catharina born Aug 6, 1756.

Peter born Apr 8, 1759.

Elizabeth born Mar --, 1761.

Margaretha born Nov 28, 1763.

Susanna born Dec 2, 1765.

Johannes born May 13, 1768.

Magdalena born Dec 20, 1771.

Jun 9, 177[2] born, Aug 23, 1772 baptized, Jacob, son of Jost Schmid and Catharina.

5 weeks ago born, Aug 23, 1772 baptized, Sophia, dau. of Jacob Achen and Maria.

Aug 15, 1772 born, Sep 20 1772 baptized, Georg, son of Henrich Hencken and Margaretha.

Apr 8, 1771 born, Maria, dau. of Joh. Jacob Hell and Maria Sussanna.

Sep 13, 1772 born, Conrath, son of Joh. Jacob Hell and Sussanna.

May 12, 1772 born, June 28, 1772 baptized, Magdalena, dau. of Conrad Scherer and Catharina.

Friday, 8 days ago, 1772 born, Dec 28, 1772 baptized, Anna Catharina, dau. of Peter Gehrich and Phillipina.

Dec 24, 1772 born, Apr 12, 1773 baptized, Elisabeth, dau. of Johannes Mertz and Catharina.

9 weeks ago on Friday, born, Apr 8 (presumably 1793) baptized, Catharina, dau. of Jacob Hauenstein and Catharina.

6 weeks ago today, born, June 27, 1773 baptized, Caspar, son of Bastian Wagener and Margareth.

May 19, 1773 born, June 27, [1773] baptized, Catharina, dau. of Phillip Stephan and Barbara.

May 8, 1773 born, Aug 22, [1773] baptized, Johannes, son of Henrich Karl and Elisabeth.

Sep 5, 1773 born, Oct 17, [1773] baptized, Elisabeth, dau. of Leonhart Daubil and Apellona.

Aug 21, 1773 born, Rebecka, dau. of Jacob Elsaz and Magdalena.

Of the deceased Schoolmaster Johannes Geitling and his wedded wife Elisabeth - [see p. 33,] was begotten and born in wedlock on the 23d of Nov [1773], a dau, and on the 9th of Jan she was brought to Holy Baptism, and the name given was Eliesabetha, the Pastor officiating. The godparents were Heinrich Schott and Eliesabetha Wünzin, both single persons.

Jan 6, 1774 born, Apr 3, baptized, Elisabeth, dau. of Jonas Heck and Susanna.

Dec 4, 1773 born, Apr 3, 1774 baptized, son of Conrad Carl and Maria.

Apr 2, 1774 born, May 15, [1774] baptized, Elisabeth, dau. of Peter Schöhnholtzer and Elisabeth.

Mar 31, 1774 born, May 15, 1774 baptized, Rebecca, dau. of Johannes Laubach and Catharina.

May 14, 1774 born, June 26, [1774] baptized, Magdalena, dau. of Jacob Hauerstein and Catharina.

Feb [Hornung] 27, 1774 born, June 26, 1774 baptized, Jacob, son of Johannes Carl and Catharina.

Jan 11, 1774 born, [Oct 2, 1774] baptized, Elisabeth, dau. of Anton Acker and Anna Maria.

Sep 1, 1774 born, Oct 2, 1774 baptized, Jacob, son of Jacob Jüng and Elisabeth.

Nov 24, 1774 born, Catharina, dau. of Lorentz Hippel and Catharina.

Oct 24, 1774 born, Jan 8, 1775 baptized, Johannes, son of Johannes Mertz and Catharina.

Dec 21, 1774 born, Feb 19, 1775 baptized, Catharina, dau. of Conrad Scherer and Catharina.

EAST VINCENT REFORMED CONGREGATION 47

Feb 3, 1775 born, Apr 2, 1775 baptized, Georg, son of Georg Jäger and Anna Maria. Sponsor Georg Jäger.

Jan 17, 1775 born, Apr 16, 1775 baptized, Magdalena, dau. of Johannes Hippel and Anna Maria. Sponsors, Jacob Schleÿter and Magdalena Hippel--both single persons.

Apr 28, 1775 born, June 25 baptized, Rebecka, dau. of Henrich Carl and Elisabeth.

May 21, 1775 born, July 23 baptized, Magdalena, dau. of Bastian Wagener and Margareth.

Sep 8, 1775 born, baptized, Johannes, son of Christoff Klaus and Catharina.

Nov 6, 1775 born, Jan 7, 1776 baptized, Henrich, son of Christopher Dony and Maria.

Nov 6, 1775 born, Jan 7, 1776 baptized, Margareth, dau. of Henrich Schererdin and Christina.

Jan 21, 1776 born, Apr 14, baptized, Catharina, dau. of Jacob Gruenstein and Catharina.

Oct 26, 1775 born, Apr 28, 1776 baptized, Catharina, dau. of John Carl and Catharina.

Mar 4, 1776 born, May 15, 1776 baptized, ----, ---- of Philip Seeller and Elisabetha.

Jan 21, 1776 born, May 12, baptized, Anna Catarina, dau. of Hennerch Laubach and Anna Maria.

Mar 24, 1776 born, June 9, baptized, Margareth, dau. of Hans Jacob Hell and Susanna.

May 13, 1776 born, June 9, 1776 baptized, Elisabeth, dau. of James Harry and Martha.

May 4, 1776 born, June 9, 1776 baptized, Elisabeth, dau. of Lorentz Hippel Junior and Margaretha.

May 4, 1776 born, June 28 baptized, Abraham, son of Conrad Carl and Maria.

[A year ago in] April, born, Aug 4, 1776 baptized, Anna Magdalena, dau. of Jacob Elsass and Anna Christina.

Feb 18 born, July 10, 1776 baptized, Barbara, dau. of Hannes Mertz and Catarina.

Feb 29, 1776 born, July 10, 1776 baptized, Margaretha, dau. of Leonhardt Daubel and Apollonia.

Oct 3, 1776 born, Nov 10, 1776 baptized, Catarina, dau. of Hannickel [Hans Nicholaus] Gründ and Eva.

July 9, 1776 born, Aug 9, 1776 baptized, Peter, son of Peter Schonholtzer and Elisabeth.

May 25, 1776 born, ---- baptized, Angelina, dau. of Vallantin Schmidt and Catharina.
Feb 2, 1777 born, Apr 27, [1777], Johan Jacob, son of Johannes Schmid and Anna Mar.
Oct 17, 1776 born, Apr 27, 1777 baptized, dau. of Jacob Acker and Maria(?).
Mar 28, 1777 born, May 11, 1777 baptized, Christoph, son of Christoph Klaus and Anna Catharina.
Mar 27, 1777 born, May 11, 1777 baptized, Catharina, dau. of Phillip Seeler and Elisabeth.
Oct --, 1776 born, [Aug 31, 1777] baptized, Christina, dau. of Friedrich Schmid and Catharina.
Mar 13, 1777 born, [Aug 31, 1777] baptized, Elisabeth, dau. of Herman Bierbauer and Christina.
Feb 28, 1777 born, Aug 31, 1777 baptized, Wilhelm, son of Friedrich Hippel and Anna Maria.
Sep 1, 1777 born, Oct 12, 1777 baptized, dau. of Johannes [Sestman] and Elisabeth.
Aug 10, 1777 born, Sep 14, baptized, Hannes, son of Hannes Hippel and Annamaria.
Sep 28, 1777 born, Oct 26, 1777 baptized, Borentz, son of Henrich Hippel and Catarina.
Nov 20, 1777 born, Dec 8, 1777 baptized, Elissabeta, dau. of Christian Ehmig and Maria Catarina. Godparents: Peter Schünholt and Elissabeta.
Nov 1, 1777 born, ----- baptized, Jacob, son of Conrad Scherer and Catharina.
May 17, 1777 born, Simon, son of Peter Schunck and Cathrina.
Nov 1, 1777 born, Apr 20, 1778 baptized, Peter, son of Johannes Schneider and Elisabeth.
Aug 8, 1778 born, [Aug 8, 1778] baptized, Johannes, son of Henrich Laubach and Anna Maria.
Feb 14, 1778 born, June 20, 1778 baptized, Michael (?), son of Christoph Denÿ and Maria.
Mar 15, 1778 born, [Mar 15, 1778], baptized, Philip, son of Jost Baedenbach and Magdalena.
Mar 24, 1778 born, ---- baptized, Johannes, son of Bastian Wagner and Margaretha.
Mar 29, 1780 born, June 5, 1780 baptized, Henrich, son of Johannes Sestman [Sastman] and Elisabeth.
July 12, [1778] born, Feb 14, 1779 baptized, Barbara, dau. of Peter

Schönfülter and Elissabetta.
May 5, 1779 born, baptized Abraham, son of Henrich Carl and Elisabeth.
Mar 10, 1779 born, baptized Johannes, son of Herman Bierbrauer and Christina.
Jan 30, 1779 born, baptized Johannes, son of Johannes Grund and Eva.
Jan 23, 1779 born, Peter and Johan Georg--twins no date of baptism, sons of Johannes Merz and Catrina.
Feb 5, 1779 born baptism Johannes, son of Henrich Schley[n] and Maria.
Apr 1, 1779 born, June 20, 1779 baptized, Sara, dau. of John Schmid and Barbara.
Feb 4, 1779 born, June 20, 1779 baptized, Abraham, son of Jacob Achen and Maria.
July 6, 1778 born, June 20, 1779 baptized, Susanna, dau. of John Hahlman and Esther (?).
Mar 22, 1779 born, baptized Vallentin, son of Vallentin Schmid and Cathrina.
July 17, 1779 born baptized, Cathrina, dau. of Jacob Nailor and Cathrina.
Dec 25, 1779 born, Mar 26, 1780 baptized, Sara, dau. of Conrad Scherer and Cathrina.
Feb 18, 1780 born, Mar 26, 1780 baptized, Jacob, son of Nicolaus Mack and Magdalena.
Dec 5, 1779 born, Mar 26, 1780 baptized, Magdalena, dau. of Peter Schmick and Cathrina.
Feb 8, 1780 born baptized Vallentin, son of Phillip Seeler and Elizebeth.
May 5, 1780 born, May 15, 1780 baptized, Maria Elizabeth, dau. of Henrich Hippel and Catharina.
Jan 1, 1780 born, baptized Abraham, son of Johannes Schneider and Elisabeth.
May 13, 1780 born, June 18, 1780 baptized, Jacob, son of Christophel Denÿ and Maria.
May 30, 1780 born, July 7, 1780 baptized, Johannes, son of Johannes Schmid and Barbara.
Dec 5, 1779 born, July 1, 1780 baptized, Susanna, dau. of Jacob [Schmick] and Elisabeth.
Mar 6, 1780 born, Aug 8, 1780 baptized, Maria Magdalena, dau. of Simon Schmid and Cathrina.
Sep 2, 1780 born, Nov 4, 1780 baptized, Elisabeth, dau. of Henrich

Laubach and Maria.

Feb 18, 1780 born, [ ] after, baptized, Elisabeth, dau. of Georg Schneider and Catharia. Godparents: Hannes Schneider and Elisabeth.

Feb 20, 1781 born, Apr 8, 1781, baptized Sophia, dau. of Christian Ehmich and Catarina.

Jan 12, 1781 born, Apr 16, 1781 baptized, Daniel, son of Sebastian Mayer and Margareth.

Sep 10, 1780 born, [July 15, 1781] baptized, Johannes, son of Johannes Hahlman and Est[h]er.

Mar 28, 1781 born, [July 15, 1781] baptized, Maria, dau. of Phillip Seeler and Elisabeth.

May 14, 1781 born, July 15, 1781 baptized, Maria Magdalena, dau. of Johannes Mertz and Cathrina.

Sep 18, 1781 born, Mar 24, 1782 baptized, Henrich, son of Conrath Schmick and Maria.

Dec 14, 1781 born [March 24, 1782], baptized, Mary, dau. of Jacob Neiler [Nailer] and Cathrina.

Oct 30, 1781 born, baptized, Margrith, dau. of Niklas Mack and Magdalena. Godparents: Conrad Filleman, Margrith Helwich.

Dec 14, 1781 born, baptized, Eva, dau. of Georg Schneider and Catharina. Godparents: Michel König and Eva, his wife.

Nov 2, 1781 born, Apr 1, 1782 baptized, Susanna, dau. of Johannes Deck and Catherina.

Dec 8, 1781 born, 1782 baptized Conrad, son of Phillip Filleman and Elisabeth.

Jan 17, 1782 born, May 5, 1782 baptized, Maria, dau. of Herman Bierbauer and Christina.

Dec 5, 1781 born, 1782 baptized, Magdalena, dau. of Henrich Hippel and Hanna.

Feb 11, 1782 born, 1782 baptized, Elisabeth, dau. of Johan Schneider and Susanna.

June 22, 1782 born, 1782, baptized, Elisabeth, dau. of John Schneider and Elisabeth.

Aug 7, 1782 born, 1782 baptized, Elisabeth, dau. of John Hallmann and Est[h]er.

Aug 22, 1782 born, 1782 baptized, Elisabeth, dau. of [Chri]stophel Denÿ and Anna Maria.

Dec 2, 1782 born, Feb 2, 1783 baptized, Lorentz, son of Lorentz Hippel and ----.

Oct 7, 1782 born, Jan 22 1783 baptized, Joh. Daniel, son of Johannes

[Gastman] and Maria Elisabeth.
Oct 30, 1782 born, Apr 20, 1783 baptized, Elisabeth, dau. of Phillip Seeler and Elisabeth.
Mar 22, 1783 born, May 18, 1783 baptized, Joh. Conrad, son of Johannes Mertz and Cathrina.
May 5, 1783 born, 1783 baptized, Catharina, dau. of Vallentin Schmid and Catharina.
June 7, 1783 born, July 27, 1783 baptized, Sebastian, son of Sebastian Wagener and Margreth.
May 16, 1783 born, July 27, 1783 baptized, Christina, dau. of Johannes Deck [Dick] and Catharina.
May 4, 1783 born, July 27, 1783 baptized, Adam, son of Jehu John and Barbara.
June 18, 1783 born, baptized, Joh. Nickel, son of Nicolaus Gründt and Eva.
Nov 25, 1782 born, 1783 baptized, Peter, son of Henrich La[u]bach and Anna Maria.
Apr 11, 1783 born, 1783 baptized, Rebecca, dau. of Conrad Kihly and Margreth. Godparents: Hanes Laubach and Catharina.
Aug 17, 1783 born, 1783 baptized, Johannes, son of Georg Schneider and Catharina. Godparents: Hannes Schneider and Elisabeth.

1784 - The Record of the Children who have received Holy Baptism at my hands. Friederich Dallicker, Minister of the Lord of God [Verbis Domini Minister].

Mar 12, 1784 born, Apr 18 1783 baptized, Conrad, son of Nicklas Mack and Magdalena. Godparents: Conrad Scherer and Catharina.
Jan 5, 1784 born, May 2, 1784 baptized, David, son of Stephen Zink and Susanna. Godparents: Parents.
May 2, 1784, baptized [1784] born, Henirich, son of Heinrich Grob and Barbara. Godparents: Parents.
Dec 3, 1783 born, May 16, 1784 baptized, Hannes, son of Jacob Hippel and Elisabeth. Godparents: Parents.
Apr 8, 1784 born, May 16, 1784 baptized, Margrith, dau. of Adam Stein and Catharina. Godparents: Lorentz Hippel Jr. and Margrith.
Feb 29, 1784 born, May 30, 1784 baptized, Elisabeth, dau. of Adam Andre and Catharina. Godparents: Parents.
Mar 05, 1784 born, June 25, 1784 baptized, Magdalena, dau. of Joh. Schneider and Elisabeth. Godparents: Parents.
Jan 9, 1784 born, June 27, 1784 baptized, Peter, son of Johannes Carl

and Catharina. Godparents: Parents.

Apr 29, 1784 born, June 27, 1784 baptized, Elisabeth, son of Johannes [Jeger] and Maria Magdalena. Godparents: Henrich Knerr and Elisabeth.

Mar 25, 1784 born, July 11, 1784 baptized, Elisabeth, dau. of Abraham Seifert and Eva. Godmother: Elisabeth Halman.

Aug 4, 1783 born, July 25, 1784 baptized, Elisabeth, dau. of Heinrich Scharitain and Christina. Godmother: Elisabeth [Henchen] Hench.

July 28, 1783 born, Sep 5, 1784 baptized, Peter, son of Jacob Carl and Christina. Godparents: His Parents.

July 21, 1784 born, Sep 5, 1784 baptized, Johannes, son of Heinrich Hippel and Hanna. Godparents: Hannes Walter and Catharina.

Dec 5, 1781 born, October 30, 1784 baptized, Sophia, dau. of Andreas Kihty and Maria. Godparents: Georg Christman and Sophia.

July 31, 1784 born, Oct 30, 1784 baptized, Jesajas [Isaias, Isaiah], son of Christoph Müller and Clara Elisabeth. Godparents: Jesayas [Isaias] and Ca --- Catharina.

Sep 12, born, Oct 30 baptized, Henna [Hanna], dau. of Herman Bierbauer and Christina. Godparents: Parents.

July 21, 1784 born, Oct 30, 1784 baptized, Catharina, dau. of David Seltenreich and Anna Maria. Godparents: Catharina Laubach.

Dec 18, 1783 born, Oct 30, 1784 baptized, Georg, son of Philip Se[e]ler and Elisabeth. Godparents: Parents.

Oct 20, 1784 born, Jan 2, 1785 baptized, Maria Barbara, dau. of Christophel Deny and Maria Barbara. Godmother: Maria-Barbara Shneider.

Nov 29, 1784 born, Feb 20, 1785 baptized, Verena, dau. of Jacob Grob and Elisabeth. Godparents: Heinrich Grob and Verena.

Mar 14, 1785 born, May 1, 1785 baptized, Mathias, son of Matthias Kiehly and Maria Margaretha. Godparents: Mathias Kiehly Sr. and Eva.

Mar 31, 1782 born, May 1, 1785 baptized, Barbara, dau. of Conrad Aker and Barbara. Godparents: Johan Mertz and Catharina.

Apr 25, 1784 born, May 1, 1785 baptized, Anna Maria, dau. of Conrad Aker and Barbara. Godparents: Heinrich Laubach and Maria.

May 9, 1784 born, May 1, 1785 baptized, Johannes, son of Georg Hainge and Maria Catharina. Godparents: Parents.

Oct 14, 1784 born, May 1, 1785 baptized, Elisabeth, dau. of Lorentz Hippel and Margrith. Godparents: Elisabeth Hippel.

---- 178-, born, May 5, 1785 baptized, Martin, son of Jacob Steger and

EAST VINCENT REFORMED CONGREGATION 53

Elisabeth. Godparents: Parents.
Mar 3, 1785 born, May 29, 1785 baptized, Magdalena, dau. of Conrad Carl and Maria. Godparents: Parents.
On May 30, 1785, a poor forsaken bound child was brought to baptism, and was named Maria. Her father was Jeremiah Gonn and his wife Barbara was her mother. The sponsors were Heinrich Brambach and his daughter Anna. The child at her baptism was 5 years, 1 month, 20 days.
July 8, 1785 born, Aug 7, 1785 baptized, Catharina, dau. of Johannes Schmid and Maria. Godparents: Conrad Scherer and Catharina.
Mar 19, 1785 born, Aug 21, 1785 baptized, Heinrich, son of Heinrich Essig and Anna. Godparents: Parents.
May 3, 1785 born, Oct 29, 1785 baptized, Johannes, son of Philip de Friderich and Elisabeth. Godparents: Parents.
Apr 26, 1785 born, Oct 29, 1785 baptized, Catharina, dau. of Jacob Zinck and Elisabeth. Godparents: Parents.
Born 3 months & a few days ago, Oct 30, 1785 baptized, Johannes, son of Samuel Hirsch and Susanna. Godparents: Parents.
Sep 10, 1785 born, Oct 30, 1785 baptized, Johannes, son of Johannes Zinck and Barbara. Godparents: Jacob Grob and Elisabeth.
Apr 14, 1785 born, Nov 27, 1785 baptized, Anna Barbara, dau. of Ludwig Eschenfelder and Maria. Godparents: Barbara Schneider.
Nov 20, 1785 born, Jan 7, 1786 baptized, Magdalena, dau. of Adam Andree and Catharina. Godparents: Parents.
Dec 20, 1785 born, Jan 7, 1786 baptized, Catharina, dau. of Johannes Hofmann and Elisabeth. Godparents: Parents.
July 16, 1785 born, Apr 16, 1786 baptized, Maria, dau. of Martin Schönholzer and Elisabeth. Godmother: Maria Hahlmann.
Mar 5, 1786 born, Apr 16, 1786 baptized, Elisabeth, dau. of Heinrich Gebel and Elisabeth. Godparents: Elisabeth Schot.
Nov 30, 1783 born, April 1784 baptized, Georg, son of Johannes Schneider and Susanna. Godparents: Joh. Georg Sohn and Anna Maria [der.
Jan 10, 1786 born, Apr 30, 1786 baptized, Catharina, dau. of Johannes Schneider and Susanna. Godmother: Catharina Emmeric.
Nov 1, 1784 born, May 5, 1785 baptized, Martin, son of Jacob Steger and Elisabeth. Godparents: Parents.
Dec 2, 1785 born, Apr 30, 1786 baptized, Jacob, son of Jacob Steger and Elisabeth. Godparents: Parents.
Apr 2, 1786 born, Apr 15, 1786 baptized, Joh. Georg, son of Lorentz Hippel and Rosina. Godparents: Joh. Georg Jeger and Anna

Maria.

Apr 16, 1786 born, June 2, 1786 baptized, Georg, son of Sebastian Wagner and Margrith. Godparents: Parents.

Mar 23, 1786 born, June 2, 1786 baptized, Rachel, dau. of Johannes Carl and Catharina. Godparents: Parents.

Nov 1, 1785 born, July 9, 1786 baptized, Zacharias, son of Jacob Hippel and Elisabeth. Godparents: Parents.

Mar 10, 1786 born, July 9, 1786 baptized, Magdalena, dau. of Georg Schneider and Catharina. Godparents: Hannes Moses and Magdalena.

May 3, 1786 born, July 24, 1786 baptized, Magdalena, dau. of Johannes Weber and Eva. Godparents: Parents.

Jan 26, 1786 born, Aug 6, 1786 baptized, Jacob, son of Stoffel Muller and Clara Elisabeth. Godparents: Johanes Carl and Catharina.

Mar 31, 1786 born, Sep 17, 1786 baptized, Anna Maria, dau. of Heinrich Bach and Elisabeth. Godparents: Friderich Hausm and Elisabeth.

June 1, 1786 born, Sep 30, 1786 baptized, Georg, son of Johannes Schneider and Elisabeth. Godparents: Parents.

Aug 28, 1786 born, Oct 15, 1786 baptized, Johannes, son of Adam Stein and Catharina. Godparents: Johannes Schnei and Susanna.

Dec 16, 1785 born, Oct 29, 1786 baptized, Johannes, son of Georg Hirsch and Magdalena. Godparents: Johannes Schönholz and Christina.

Apr 7, 1786 born, Oct 29, 1786 baptized, Jones [Jonas], son Jean Halmann and Esther. Godparents: Parents.

Sep 1, 1786 born, Oct 29, 1786 baptized, Susanna, dau. of Stephen Zinck and Susanna. Godparents: Parents.

Oct 23, 1786 born, Nov 12, 1786 baptized, Johannes, son of Philip Reffert and Ursula. Godparents: Johannes Haas and Maria.

Sep 27, 1786 born, Nov 12, 1786 baptized, Elisabeth, dau. of Hannes Schort and Elisabeth. Godparents: Hannes Mauser and Elisabeth.

July 2, 1786 born, 1786 baptized, David, son of David Seltenreich and Anna Maria. Godparents: Parents.

Nov 23, 1786 born, Apr 9, 1787 baptized, Johannes, son of Johannes Jeger and Magdalena. Godparents: Parents.

Jan 2, 1787 born, Apr 9, 1787 baptized, Catharina, dau. of Heinrich Hippel and Catharina. Godparents: Lorentz Hippel and Rosina.

Apr 8, 1787 born, Apr 15, 1787 baptized, Johannes, son of Christian Ehmich, Jr. and Elisabeth. Godparents: Christian Ehmich, Sr. and Catharina.

EAST VINCENT REFORMED CONGREGATION 55

Apr 20, 1786 born, Apr 15, 1787 baptized, Maria, dau. of Georg Henchy and Catharina. Godparents: Niclas Kercher and Maria.

Sep 20, 1786 born, Apr 15, 1787 baptized, ?ara, dau. of Johannes Henchy and Margrith. Godparents: Margrith Baling.

Oct 17, 1786 born, Apr 29, 1787 baptized, Magdalena, dau. of Philip Weÿand and Susanna. Godparents: Niclas Laar and Magdalena.

Mar 13, 1787 born, May 26, 1787 baptized, Abraham, son of Herman Bierbauer and Christina. Godparents: Parents.

Oct 14, 1785 born, May 27, 1787 baptized, Anna Maria, dau. of Christian Alsdorff and Anna Maria. Godmother: Anna Maria Hoffman.

Apr 5, 1787 born, June 24, 1787 baptized, Danjel [Daniel], son of Conrad Carl and Anna Maria. Godparents: Parents.

Apr 18, 1787 born, July 8, 1787 baptized, Johannes, son of Conrad Kihly and Margrith. Godparents: Johannes Labach and Catharina.

Apr 14, 1787 born, July 22, 1787 baptized, Jacob, son of Lorentz Hippel and Margrith. Godparents: Jacob Ludwig and Anna Maria.

Apr 1, 1787 born, Aug 5, 1787 baptized, Heinrich, son of Peter Jeger and Elisabeth. Godparents: Heinrich Christmann and Susanna.

Apr 19, 1787 born, Aug 5, 1787 baptized, Catharina, dau. of Heinrich Carl and Philippine. Godparents: Parents.

June 25, 1787 born, Aug 19, 1787 baptized, Anna Maria, dau. of Heinrich Laubach and Anna Maria. Godparents: Parents.

Dec 12, 1786 born, Sep 2, 1787 baptized, Samuel, son of Philip Himmelreich and Sara. Godparents: Parents.

July 6, 1787 born, Sep 2, 1787 baptized, Philip, son of Adam Andree and Catharina. Godparents: Parents.

June 8, 1787 born, Sep 2, 1787 baptized, Johannes, son of Heinrich Gebel and Elisabeth. Godparents: Johannes Hofmann and Elisabeth.

July 29, 1787 born, Sep 16, 1787 baptized, Magdalena, dau. of Samuel Hirsch and Susanna. Godparents: Parents.

Aug 28, 1787 born, Oct 14, 1787 baptized, Caspar, son of Heinrich Hippel and Anna. Godparents: Caspar Schneider and Sibilla.

Sep 13, 1787 born, Oct 28, 1787 baptized, Joseph, son of Johannes Schmid and Maria. Godfather: Conrad Scheier.

Sep 22, 1787 born, Nov 11, 1787 baptized, Maria Philippina, dau. of Borg Bechtel and Elisabeth. Godparents: Parents.

Dec 1, 1787 born, 1787 baptized, Heinrich, son of Christian Benner and Anna Maria. Godparents: Parents.

Dec 27, 1787 born, Mar 30, 1788 baptized, Elisabeth, dau. of David

Seltenreich and Anna Maria. Godparents: Elisabeth Seltenreich.
Dec 1, 1787 born, Apr 13, 1788 baptized, Johannes, son of Johannes Schneider and Susanna. Godparents: Johannes King and Anna Maria.
Mar 1, 1788 born, July 6, 1788 baptized, Maria Magdalena, dau. of Johannes Carl and Catharina. Godparents: Parents.
Jan 14, 1788 born, July 6, 1788 baptized, Catharina, dau. of Peter Jung [Young] and Catharina. Godparents: Catharina Schleier.
July 14, 1788 born, Aug 30, 1788 baptized, Jacob, son of Lorenz Hippel and Rosina. Godparents: Jacob Kihly and Maria.
Mar 10, 1788 born, Aug 20, 1788 baptized, Abraham, son of Christoph Deny and Anna Maria. Godparents: Abraham Scheridan and Anna Maria.
Apr 1, 1788 born, Aug 30, 1788 baptized, Margrith, dau. of Johannes Zink and Barbara. Godparents: Henrich Fulker and Margrith Schmid.
June 6, 1788 born, Sep 28, 1788 baptized, Elisabeth, dau. of Heinrich Carl and Philippine. Godparents: Stoffel Müller and Elisabeth.
June 14, 1788 born, Oct 25, 1788 baptized, Johannes, son of Friderich Geidling and Anna Maria. Godparents: Herman Bierbauer and Christina.
Jan 30, 1789 born, Apr 12, 1789 baptized, Heinrich, son of Heinrich Gebel and Elisabeth. Godparents: Parents.
Mar 2, 1789 born, Apr 12, 1789 baptized, Johannes, son of Conrad Scherer and Dorothea. Godparents: Parents.
Nov 17, 1788 born, Apr 12, 1789 baptized, Elisabeth, dau. of Sebastian Wagner and Margrith. Godmother: Elisabeth Steipen.
Oct 21, 1788 born, Apr 12, 1789 baptized, Margrith, dau. of Heinrich Laubach and Anna Maria. Godmother: Margrith Müller.
Jan 29, 1789 born, May 1, 1789 baptized, Anna Maria, dau. of Johannes Jeger and Magdalena. Godparents: Georg Jeger and Anna Maria.
Feb 22, 1789 born, May 1, 1789 baptized, Maria, dau. of Peter Jeger and Elisabeth. Godparents: Georg Jeger and Anna Maria.
Feb 17, 1789 born, May 10, 1789 baptized, Johannes, son of Adam Andree and Catharina. Godparents: Parents.
Dec 14, 1788 born, May 10, 1789 baptized, Catharina, dau. of Philip Himmelreich and Sophia. Godmother: Catharina Hartenstein.
Jan 22, 1789 born, June 6, 1789 baptized, Magdalena, dau. of Hannes Schott and Elisabeth. Godparents: Magdalena Schneider.
July 7, 1788 born, June 6, 1789 baptized, Maria, dau. of Philip

EAST VINCENT REFORMED CONGREGATION

Friderich and Elisabeth. Godparents: Parents.

May 22, 1788 born, June 6, 1789 baptized, Elisabeth, dau. of John Jungblut and Magdalena. Godparents: Parents.

Mar 5, 1789 born, June 7, 1789 baptized, Danjel [Daniel], son of Johannes Schneider and Elisabeth. Godparents: Parents.

Dec 4, 1788 born, June 7, 1789 baptized, Johannes, son of Herman Achy and Magdalena. Godparents: Johannes Fertig and Elisabeth.

Feb 10, 1789 born, June 7, 1789 baptized, Johannes, son of Georg Biery, and Barbara. Godparents: Johannes Bossart and Elisabeth Müller.

Feb 18, 1789 born, June 7, 1789 baptized, Sara, dau. of Heinrich Bach and Elisabeth. Godparents: Georg Biber and Susanna.

May 19, 1789 born, July 19, 1789 baptized, Jacob, son of Conrad Kihly and Margrith. Godparents: Mattheis Kihly and Eva.

Feb 24, 1788 born, Aug 16, 178?, ----, son of.

Jan 15, 1789 born, Aug 30, 1789 baptized, Catharina, dau. of Jacob Carl and Christina. Godparents: Parents.

July 4, 1789 born, Sep 13, 1789 baptized, Jesajas [Isaiah], son of Johanes Schmid and Maria. Godparents: Parents.

Mar 12, 1789 born, Sep 13, baptized, Elisabeth, dau. of Peter Steudler and Eva. Godparents: Parents.

Sep 29, 1788 born, Sep 13, 1789 baptized, Henna [Hanna], dau. of Conrad Aker and Barbara. Godparents: Parents.

July 12, 1789 born, Sep 13, 1789 baptized, Maria, dau. of Lorenz Hippel and Margrith. Godmother: Maria Hippel.

Aug 10, 1789 born, Sep 27, 1789 baptized, Christian, son of Christian Benner and Anna Maria. Godparents: Parents.

Aug 5, 1789 born, Oct 2, 1789 baptized, Henna [Hanna], dau. of Philip Eler and Maria. Godparents: Parents.

Sep 30, 1783 born, Oct 24, 1789 baptized, Danjel [Daniel], son of Jacob Schug and Elisabeth. Godparents: Parents.

Feb 6, 1786 born, Oct 24, 1789 baptized, Joseph, son of Jacob Schug and Elisabeth. Godparents: Parents.

Aug 28, 1787 born, Oct 24, 1789 baptized, Elisabeth, dau. of Jacob Schug and Elisabeth. Godparents: Parents.

Apr 9, 1789 born, Oct 24, 1789 baptized, Maria, dau. of Jacob Schug and Elisabeth. Godparents: Maria Werly.

Jan 10, 1789 born, Oct 24, 1789 baptized, Simon, son of Simon Schunck and Catharina. Godparents: Parents.

Mar 21, 1789 born, Oct 24, 1789 baptized, Susanna [Susanna], dau. of Caspar Schneider and Henna. Godparents: Parents.

Seven years old, Oct 24, 1789 baptized, Henna, dau. of Jeremias Conn and Barbara. Godparents: Caspar Schneider and Henna.

Oct 3, 1789 born, Oct 25, 1789 baptized, Danjel, son of Philip Wyand and Zusanna. Godparents: Danjel Preiser and Sophia.

Nov 23, 1787 born, Nov 15, 1789 baptized, Lorenz, son of Jacob Hippel and Elisabeth. Godparents: Lorenz Hippel and Margrith.

Sep 18, 1789 born, Nov 15, 1789 baptized, Joh. Georg, son of Jacob Hippel and Elisabeth. Godfather: Joh. Georg Reis.

Sep 20, 1789 born, Nov 15, 1789 baptized, Joh. Heinrich, son of Borg Bechtel and Elisabeth. Godfather: Heinrich Moses.

Mar 13, 1789 born, Nov 15, 1789 baptized, Johannes, son of Johannes Heid and Christina. Godparents: Parents.

Oct 13, 1789 born, Nov 15, 1789 baptized, Catharina, dau. of Adam Stein and Catharina. Godparents: Parents.

Feb 12, 1789 born, Nov 15, 1789 baptized, Maria, dau. of Johannes Ginter and Catharina. Godmother: Maria Bikerth.

Jan 1, 1790 born, Jan 31, 1790 baptized, Margrith, dau. of Johannes Schneider and Susanna. Godparents: Lorenz Hippel and Margrith.

Jan 2, 1790 born, Apr 24, 1790 baptized, Margrith, dau. of Christoph Theiss and Justina. Godmother: Margrith Worlhauser.

Apr 2, 1790 born, June 13, 1790 baptized, Elisabeth, dau. of Heinrich Hippel and Hanna. Godparents: Johannes Schneider and Elisabeth.

Mar 17, 1788 born, June 20, 1790 baptized, Samuel, son of Abraham Ohlweyn and Rebecca. Godfather: Christian Treed.

Apr 4, 1790 born, June 20, 1790 baptized, Heinrich, son of Abraham Ohlweyn and Rebecca. Godparents: Heinrich Labach and Maria.

May 1, 1790 born, June 20, 1790 baptized, Magdalena, dau. of Joh. Vander Weid and Magdalena. Godmother: Magdalena Scheumer.

Apr 6, 1790 born, June 20, 1790 baptized, Georg, son of Georg Schneider and Catharina. Godparents: Parents.

Mar 24, 1790 born, June 20, 1790 baptized, Rebecca, dau. of David Seltenreich and Anna Maria. Godparents: Johannes Labach and Catharina.

Mar 1, 1790 born, Aug 29, 1790 baptized, Jacob, son of Peter Steip and Elisabeth. Godparents: Parents.

June 21, 1790 born, Aug 29, 1790 baptized, Elisabeth, dau. of Bernhard Rapp and Esther. Godparents: Philip Rapp and Elisabeth.

June 12, 1790 born, Sep 26, 1790 baptized, Danjel [Daniel], son of Stephan Zink and Susanna. Godparents: Daniel Reusser and

EAST VINCENT REFORMED CONGREGATION

Sophia.
Aug 8, 1790 born, Sep 26, baptized, Susanna, dau. of Daniel Preusser and Sophia. Godparents: Stephen Zink and Susanna.
N.B. On October 20, with the consent of the Council and on Confession of faith were baptized:.
David Seltenreich - 34 years old.
Maria Cleer, wife of Philip Cleer, 23 years old.
Oct 22, 1790 born, Nov 29, 1790 baptized, Jesajas [Isaiah], son of Heinrich Carl and Philippina. Godparents: The father and Christina Carl.
Dec 7, 1790 born, Feb 25, 1791 baptized, Anna, dau. of Jacob Bender and Catharina. Godparents: John Boldin and Henna [Hanna, Anna].
Dec 26, 1790 born, Mar 12, 1791 baptized, Johannes, son of Johannes Hoffman and Elisabeth. Godparents: Johannes Heinrich and Magdalena.
Jan 1, 1791 born, Apr 10, 1791 baptized, Abraham, son of Laurens Hippel and Rosina. Godparents: Abraham Sheridan and Maria Barbara.
Sep 3, 1790 born, Apr 10, 1791 baptized, Magdalena, dau. of Johannes Carl and Catharina. Godparents: Parents.
Jan 14, 1791 born, Apr 18, 1791 baptized, Elisabeth, dau. of Philip Himelreich and Sophia. Godparents: Parents [probably].
Jan 30, 1791 born, May 8, 1791 baptized, Magdalena, dau. of Heinrich Gebel and Sophia. Godparents: Parents.
Jan 10, 1791 born, May 8, 1791 baptized, Zusanna [Susanna], dau. of Heinrich Benner and Elisabeth. Godparents: Parents.
Oct 5, 1790 born, May 22, 1791 baptized, Catharina, dau. of Peter Steidler and Eva. Godparents: Parents.
Feb 25, 1791 born, June 4, 1791 baptized, Hanna, dau. of Johannes Jeger and Magdalena. Godparents: Parents.
May 4, 1791 born, June 5, 1791 baptized, Maria, dau. of Johannes Schneider and Elisabeth. Godparents: Johannes Schmid and Maria.
Sep 12, 1790 born, June 13, 1791 baptized, Gertraud, dau. of Jacob Steyer and Elisabeth. Godparents: Parents.
Dec 28, 1790 born, June 19, 1791 baptized, Jacob, son of Heinrich Metz and Magdalena. Godparents: Borg Bechtel and Elizabeth.
Jan 31, 1791 born, June 19, 1791 baptized, Magdalena, dau. of Georg Hirsch and Magdalena. Godparents: Parents.
Apr 23, 1791 born, Aug 3, 1791 baptized, Georg, son of Samuel Hirsch

and Zusanna. Godparents: Parents.

Jan 23, 1791 born, Aug 3, 1791 baptized, Danjel [Daniel], son of Christoph Müller and Clar[a] Elis[abeth]. Godparents: Jacob Carl and Christina.

May 20, 1791 born, Aug 3, 1791 baptized, Elisabeth, dau. of Jacob Carl and Christina. Godparents: Carl Gerber and Elisabeth.

Jan 21, 1791 born, Aug 24, 1791 baptized, Heinrich, son of Johannes Brambach and Margrith. Godparents: Parents.

July 1, 1791 born, Aug 14, 1791 baptized, Catharina, dau. of Peter Schunk and Catharina. Godparents: Parents.

July 26, 1791 born, Aug 24, 1791 baptized, Johann Conrad, son of Conrad Scherer and Dorathea. Godparents: Parents.

June 19, 1791 born, Aug 14, 1791 baptized, Maria, dau. of Heinrich Hippel and Catharina. Godparents: Jacob Kihly and Maria.

July 9, 1791 born, Aug 14, 1791 baptized, Jacob, son of Heinrich Schleier and Elisabeth. Godparents: Parents.

July 9, 1791 born, Sep 11 baptized, Heinrich, son of Heinrich Labach and Anna Maria. Godparents: Parents.

July 17, 1791 born, Sep 11, baptized, Danjel [Daniel], son of Johannes Schmid and Maria. Godparents: Jacob Hartmann and Sara.

May 2, 1791 born, Sep 11, 1791 baptized, Magdalena, dau. of Conrad Kihly and Margrith. Godmother: Magdalena Labach.

Aug 8, 1791 born, Oct 22, 1791 baptized, Johannes, son of Philip Cleer and Maria. Godparents: Parents.

June 12, 1791 born, Oct 22, 1791 baptized, Elisabeth, dau. of Caspar Schneider and Hanna. Godparents: Parents.

Aug 25, 1791 born, Oct 23, 1791 baptized, Johannes, son of Christopher Deny and Maria. Godparents: Johannes Walter and Catharina.

Sep 29, 1791 born, Dec 4, 1791 baptized, Johannes, son of Lorenz Hippel and Margrith. Godparents: Philip Clinger and Barbara.

Oct 18, 1791 born, Dec 4, 1791 baptized, Elisabeth, dau. of Jacob Hippel and Elisabeth. Godmother: Elisabeth Hippel.

Sep 23, 1791 born, Dec 4, 1791 baptized, Abraham, son of Borg Bechtel and Elizabeth. Godparents: Parents.

Mar 27, 1792 born, May 13, 1792 baptized, Christina, dau. of David Seltenreich and Anna Maria. Godparents: Johannes Labach and Catharina.

Apr 7, 1792 born, May 27 or 28, 1792 baptized, Georg, son of Georg Hubener and Catharina. Godparents: Georg Heitzel and Catharina.

June 22, 1791 born, June 17, 1792 baptized, Philip, son of Philip

EAST VINCENT REFORMED CONGREGATION

Friderich and Elisabeth. Godparents: Parents.

May 15, 1792 born, June 17, 1792 baptized, Hannes, son of Peter Wagner and Maria. Godparents: Parents.

May 14, 1792 born, Sep 23, 1792 baptized, Georg, son of Peter Jeger and Elisabeth. Godparents: Parents.

Aug 1, 1792 born, Sep 23, 1792 baptized, Jos[h]ua, son of Christian Benner and Maria. Godparents: Parents.

July 1, 1792 born, Oct 20, 1792 baptized, Maria, dau. of Bernhard Rapp and Est[h]er. Godparents: Philip Rapp and Elisabeth.

Dec 31, 1791 born, July 1, 1792 baptized, Johannes, son of Johannes Ginter and Catharina. Godparent: Johannes Bikert.

June 16, 1792 born, Sep 12, 1792 baptized, Anna Maria, dau. of Georg Schneider and Catharina. Godparents: Parents.

June 17, 1792 born, Sep 12, 1792 baptized, Peter, son of Johannes Schneider and Susanna. Godfather: Peter Ludwig.

3 years old, Nov 4, 1792 baptized, Jacob, son of John King and Anna. Godparents: Conrad Stamm and Maria.

Nov 12, 1792 born, Nov 18, 1792 baptized, David, son of Conrad Carl and Anna Maria. Godparents: Parents.

Dec 2, 1792 born, Jan 1, 1793 baptized, Georg, son of Heinrich Gebel and Elisabeth. Godparents: Georg Hubener and Catharina.

Mar 7, 1793 born, Apr 1, 1793 baptized, Johannes, son of Jacob Weyand and Magdalena. Godparents: Parents.

Jan 14, 1793 born, Apr 7, 1793 baptized, Heinrich, son of Heinrich Hippel and Henna [Hanna, Anna]. Godparents: Parents.

Nov 8, 1792 born, May 19, 1793 baptized, Catharina, dau. of Heinrich Richtstein and Margrith [Margaret]. Godmother: Sophia Richstein.

Feb 22, 1793 born, June 2, 1793 baptized, Joseph, son of John Carl and Catharina. Godparents: Parents.

Feb 8, 1793 born, June 2, 1793 baptized, Henna [Hanna], dau. of Heinrich Benner and Elisabeth. Godparents: Parents.

N. B. On June 16 [1793] there was baptized a poor child, abandoned by his parents, yet legitimate, named Georg. His father, the ----, was named Georg Heinrich, and his mother is called Christel Hedricht. His sponsors were Michal Hartman and Elisabeth his wedded wife. The child is in his 9th year.

Jan 5, 1792 born, Aug 2, 1793 baptized, Elisabeth, dau. of Johannes Brambach and Margrith his wedded wife. Godparents: Johannes Schmid and Maria.

June 9, 1793 born, Sep 17, baptized, Goerg, son of Johannes Hofman

62 EARLY CHURCH RECORDS OF CHESTER CO.

and Elisabeth. Godparents: Parents.

Dec 8, 1792 born, Sep 22, 1793 baptized, Elisabeth, dau. of Philip Cleer [Kleer] and Maria. Godparents: Parents.

Oct 22, 1793 born, Oct 22, 1793 baptized, Johannes, son of John Jungblut and Magdalena. Godparents: The Doctor and the Mother.

Oct 2, 1789 born, Oct 22, 1793 baptized, Anna, dau. of John Jungblut and Magdalena. Godparents: The Doctor and the Mother.

July 16, 1791 born, Oct 22, 1793 baptized, Willy, son of John Jungblut and Magdalena. Godparents: The Doctor and the Mother.

July 9, 1793 born, Nov 3, 1793 baptized, Barbara, dau. of Peter Jung and Catharina. Godparents: Parents.

----, born, Nov 3, 1793 baptized, Samuel, son of Friderich Scholl and Philippine. Godparents: Jacob Hartman and Sara.

Oct 16, 1793 born, Nov 3, 1793 baptized, Adam, son of Adam Stein and Catharina. Godparents: Adam Muller and Elisabeth Hipp.

Apr 9, 1793 born, Nov 3, 1793 baptized, Isa[a]c, son of Peter Steidler and Eva. Godparents: Parents.

Oct 19, 1793 born, Dec 16, 1793 baptized, Maria, dau. of Lorenz Hippel and Rosina. Godparents: Johannes Schmid and Maria.

Apr 26, 179[3] born, Jan 25, baptized, Hanna, dau. of Jacob Carl and Christina. Godparents: Parents.

Nov 17, 1793 born, Mar 23, 1794 baptized, Heinrich, son of Peter Steip and Elisabeth. Godparents: Parents.

Dec 18, 1793 born, Apr 6, 1794 baptized, Johannes, son of Heinrich Diffendorffer and Juliana. Godparents: Parents.

Jan 1, 1794 born, Apr 22, 1794 baptized, Magdalena, dau. of Heinrich Schleier and Elisabeth. Godparents: Magdalena Schleier.

Feb 20, 1794 born, June 15, 1794 baptized, Jacob and Georg, Twin sons of Jacob Schmid and Maria. Godparents: George Schneider and Catharina.

Feb 12, 1794 born, June 15, 1794 baptized, Anna Maria, dau. of David Seltenreich and Anna Maria. Godparents: Parents.

Feb 26, 1794 born, June 15, baptized, Elisabeth, dau. of Samuel Hirsch and Susanna. Godparents: Parents.

Aug 18, 1793 born, June 15, 1794 baptized, Samuel, son of Georg Hirsch and Magdalena. Godparents: Samuel Hirsch and Susanna.

May 3, 1794 born, June 29, 1794 baptized, Sara, dau. of John Schmid and Maria. Godparents: Parents.

Oct 23, 1792 born, July 13, 1794 baptized, Elisabeth, dau. of Jacob Bauer and Anna. Godparent: Elisabeth Bauer.

EAST VINCENT REFORMED CONGREGATION 63

Apr 2, 1794 born, July 13, 1794 baptized, Rosina, dau. of Jacob Bauer and Anna. Godparents: Niclas Bauer and Rosina.
Dec 4, 1793 born, July 27, 1794 baptized, Hanna, dau. of Bernhard Rapp and Esther. Godparents: Elisabeth Rapp, the Grandmother.
Mar 25, 1794 born, July 27, 1794 baptized, Samuel, son of Jacob Haus and Elisabeth. Godparents: Parents.
Mar 19, 1794 born, Sep 3, 1794 baptized, Elisabeth, dau. of Christoph Knauer and Elisabeth. Godparents: Parents.
Apr 22, 1794 born, June 13, 1794 baptized, Wilhelm, son of Georg Hubener and Catharina. Godparents: Parents.
May 27, 1794 born, Sep 21, 1794 baptized, Wilhelm, son of Wilhelm Schmid and Elisabeth. Godparents: Parents.
June 27, 1794 born, Sep 21, 1794 baptized, Anna, dau. of Heinrich Fulkert and Margrith. Godparents: Parents.
Sep 16, 1794 born, Oct 5, 1794 baptized, Sophia, dau. of Wilhelm Schuler and Sara. Godmother: Sophia Schuler.
Apr 30, 1793 born, Oct 5, 1794 baptized, Sara, dau. of Peter Reis and Maria. Godparents: Valentine Fuch [Fues] and Rosina.
Aug 7, 1794 born, Oct 5, 1794 baptized, Peter, son of Georg Schneider and Catharina. Godparents: Peter Jung and Catharina.
July 19, 1794 born, Oct 19, 1794 baptized, Magdalena, dau. of Johannes Jeger and Magdalena. Godparents: Parents.
Aug 9, 1794 born, Oct 19, 1794 baptized, Benjamin, son of Philip Cleer [Kleer] and Maria. Godparents: Parents.
Dec 15, 1794 born, May 17, 1795 baptized, Maria, dau. of Jacob Hippel and Elisabeth. Godparents: Philip Muller and Maria.
Feb 14, 1795 born, May 17, 1795 baptized, Maria, dau. of Borg Bechtel and Margrith. Godparents: Maria Wallichin.
Nov 12, 1794 born, May 17, 1795 baptized, Elisabeth, dau. of Conrad Scherer and Dorothea. Godparents: Parents.
Dec 12, 1794 born, May 17, 1795 baptized, Adam, son of Johannes Schreider and Susanna. Godparents: Parents.
Mar 10, 1795 born, May 25, 1795 baptized, Philip, son of Peter Rap and Magdalena. Godparents: Parents.
Sep --, 1794 born, May 25, 1795 baptized, Samuel, son of John Zink and [Barbara]. Godparents: Parents.
Mar 22, 1795 born, May 31, 1795 baptized, Johannes, son of Jacob Steger and Elisabeth. Godparents: Hannes Schueman and Elisabeth.
Apr 2, 1795 born, June 28, 1795 baptized, Catharina, dau. of Heinrich

Apr 2, 1795 born, June 28, 1795 baptized, Catharina, dau. of Heinrich Benner and Elisabeth. Godparents: Parents.

Feb 12, 1795 born, July 12, 1795 baptized, Heinrich, son of Heinrich Metz and Magdalena. Godparents: Heinrich Hopf. N. B. Also were Heinrich Just, also Heinrich [Jay] baptized ---.

July 16, 1795 born, Sep 6, 1795 baptized, Johannes, son of Peter Steidler and Catharina. Godparents: Johannes Labach, Jr.

July 24, 1795 born, Sep 10, 1795 baptized, Daniel, son of Georg Hubner and Catharina. Godparents: Parents.

Mar 28, 1795 born, Sep 10, 1795 baptized, Hanna, dau. of Heinrich Hippel and Catharina. Godparents: Parents.

July 2, 1795 born, Sep 20, 1795, baptized, Elisabeth, dau. of Christian Benner and Maria. Godparents: Parents.

Apr 5, 1794 born, May 28, 1796 baptized, Elisabeth, dau. of Michel Colb and Elisabeth. Godparents: Parents.

Mar 6, 1796 born, May 28, 1796 baptized, Michel, son of Michel Colb and Elizabeth. Godparents: Parents.

July 30, 1795 born, July 10, 1796 baptized, Johannes, son of Philip Rapp and Catharina. Godparents: Parents.

Apr 29, 1796 born, July 10, 1796 baptized, Philip, son of Heinrich Diffendorfer and Juliana. Godparents: Philip Diffendorfer and Barbara Marison.

Feb 15, 1796 born, July 10, 1796 baptized, Maria Magdalena, dau. of Johannes Schmid and Maria. Godparents: Parents.

May 15, 1796 born, Aug 7, 1796 baptized, Heinrich, son of Hannes Hippel and Hanna. Godparents: Heinrich Hippel and Hanna.

Mar 27, 1796 born, Sep 4, 1796 baptized, Rebecca, dau. of John Carl and Catharina. Godparents: Parents.

Jan 12, 1796 born, Sep 4, 1796 baptized, Michael, son of Wilhelm Schmid and Elisabeth. Godparents: Michel Mertz and Catharina Prinz[in].

Dec 17, 1796 born, Sep 3, 1787 baptized, Benjamin, son of John Raseter and Elisabeth. Godparents: Benjamin Rapp.

May 27, 1797 born, Sep 3, 1797 baptized Regina, dau. of Peter Rapp and Maria. Godparents: Adam Renner and Regina.

Jan 28, 1797 born, Sep 3, 1797 baptized, Maria, dau. of Jacob Bauer and Anna. Godparents: Thomas Reims and Maria Bauer.

July 20, 1797 born, Oct 1, 1797 baptized, Nic[o]las, son of Conrad Schoer and Dorathea. Godparents: Parents.

July 17, 1797 born, Oct 21, 1797 baptized, Elisabeth, dau. of Peter Jeger and Elisabeth. Godmother: Elisabeth Bucher.

Aug 20, 1797 born, Oct 21, 1797 baptized, Elisabeth, dau. of Benjamin Rapp and Elisabeth. Godmother: Elisabeth Rapp[in].
July 13, 1797 born, Oct 21, 1797 baptized, Philip, son of Michel Munschauer and Catharina. Godparents: Philip Weyand and Est[h]er Munschauer.
Sep 2, 1797 born, Oct 21, 1797 baptized, Wilhelm, son of Jacob Wagner and Elisabeth. Godparents: Parents.
Feb 1, 1797 born, Oct 21, 1797 baptized, Heinrich, son of Casper Schneider and Susanna. Godparents: Heinrich Haas and Elisabeth Hippel.
Jan 22, 1797 born, Oct 21, 1797 baptized, Jacob, son of Jacob Moritz and Barbara. Godparents: Philip Dieffendorfer and Barbara.
Nov 1, 1796 born, Oct 21, 1797 baptized, Susanna, dau. of Samuel Hirsch and Susanna. Godparents: Parents.
Nov 18, 1797 born, Apr 15, 1798 baptized, Jesse, son of Johannes Schmid and Maria. Godparents: Parents.
Dec 31, 1797 born, Apr 15, 1798 baptized, Abraham, son of Georg Hubener and Catharina. Godparents: Parents.
Dec 2, 1797 born, May 23, 1798 baptized, Elisabeth, dau. of Philip Dieffendorfer and Barbara. Godparents: Peter Maurer and Elisabeth.
Jan 25, 1798 born, Aug 5, 1798 baptized, Johannes, son of Bernhard Rap and Est[h]er. Godparents: Parents.
Mar 5, 1798 born, Sep 2, 1798 baptized, Adam, son of Georg Hirsch and Magdalena. Godparents: Samuel Hirsch and Susanna.
Dec 29, 1794 born, Sep 2, 1798 baptized, Thomas, son of Heinrich Schneider and Margrith. Godparents: Parents.
May 24, 1797 born, Sep 2, 1798 baptized, Heinrich, son of Heinrich Schneider and Margrith. Godparents: Parents.
Aug 6, 1793 born, Sep 2, 1798 baptized, Thomas, son of Thomas Krebs and Violetta. Godparents: Parents.
July 10, 1798 born, Sep 2, 1796 baptized, Heinrich, son of Thomas Krebs and Violetta. Godparents: Parents.

EARLY CHURCH RECORDS OF CHESTER CO.

The Following Children were baptized in the Evangelical Reformed Church in Vincent (Township) by F[rederick] Herman, Minister of the Word of God.

June 10, 1798 born, June 9, 1799 baptized, Edward, son of Edward Brambach and Susanna. Godparents: Parents.

Dec 5, 1794 born, June 9, 1799 baptized, Edward, son of Adam Scheimer and Elisabeth. Godparents: Parents.

Dec 30, 1797 born, June 9, 1799 baptized, Anna Catharina, dau. of Adam Scheimer and Elisabeth. Godparents: Parents.

Jan 18, 1799 born, July, a. e. (same year) baptized, Elisabeth, dau. of Caspar Schneider and Susanna. Godparents: Henrich Miller and Elisabeth.

Oct 4, 1798 born, a. e. baptized, Catharina, dau. of Herich Hippel and Hanna. Godparents: John Walter and Catharina.

Oct 7, 1799 born, a. e. baptized, Johannes, son of Johannes Carl and Catharina. Godparents: Parents.

Sep 9, 1799 born, Oct 27, 1799 baptized, Johanes, son of Peter Yeager and Elisabeth. Godparents: Parents.

Sep 2, 1799 born, Oct 27, 1799 baptized, Jos[h]ua, son of Jacob Yeager and Catharina. Godparents: Parents.

Sep 8, 1799 born, (Oct 27, 1799) baptized, Dorothea, dau. of Conrad Schaerer and Dorothea. Godparents: Parents.

Dec 6, 1798 born, 1799 baptized, Elisabeth, dau. of Jacob Wagner and Elisabeth. Godparents: Parents.

Feb 4, 1798 born, May 11, [1799] baptized, An[n]a, dau. of George Michael Kolb and Elisabeth. Godparents: Parents.

Mar 22, 1800 born, [1800] baptized, Henrich, son of Peter Grundt and Elisabeth. Godparents: Parents.

Feb 28, 1800 born, [1800] baptized, Susanna, dau. of N. N. Wilson and Hanna. Godparents: Susana Strauss.

Aug 25, 1799 born, Jan 3, [1800] baptized, Maria, dau. of Benjamin Rap and Elisabeth. Godparents: Parents.

Aug 26, 1799 born, June 8, [1800] baptized, Jacob, son of Johan[n]es Rosetter and Elisabeth. Godparents: Parents.

Sep 24, 1799 born, June 8, [1800] baptized, Wilhelm, son of Thomas Rosetter and Elisabeth. Godparents: Parents.

May 23, 1800 born, Oct [20], 1800 baptized, Elisabeth, dau. of Peter Rap and Maria. Godparents: Parents.

Oct 11, 1800 born, Nov 23, 1800 baptized, Jesse, son of Johan Hippel and Hanna. Godparents: Parents.

Sep 20, 1800 born, Nov 23, 1800 baptized, Henrich, son of George Schneider and Elisabeth. Godparents: Parents.
Aug 24, 1800 born, Dec 21, 1800 baptized, Maria, dau. of Peter Kolb and Hanna. Godparents: Georg Hübener and Katharina.
1800 born, Dec 21, 1800 baptized, Johannes, son of John Sch[o]walter and Susanna. Godparents: John Thiel and --.
Jan 6, 1799 born, [1801] baptized, Elisabeth, dau. of Johan[n]es Schwaner and Susan[n]a. Godparents: Elizabeth Schwaner.
Oct 11, 1800 born, [Dec] 21, 1800 baptized, Johan(n)es, son of Johan[n]es Schwaner and Susanna. Godparents: Johan Diery and Susann Ludwig.
Feb 13, 1801 born, (1801) baptized, Susanna, dau. of Michal Mundschauer and Catharina. Godparents: Henrich Hoffman and Susann Wyand.
Oct 20, 1800 born, [1800] baptized, Catharina, dau. of Caspar and Susanna Schneider. Godparents: Jacob Faeger and Catharina.
May 30, 1800 born, July 20, [1800] baptized, Jacob, son of Henrick Diffendorfer and Juliana. Godparents: Parents.
Aug 23, 1800 born, Aug 30, 1801 baptized, Bernhard, son of Bernhard Rap and Est[h]er. Godparents: Parents.
Nov 5, 1776 born, May --, 1802 baptized Jacob, son of [---] Mundschauer and [----].
Nov 3, 1796 born, Oct 9, 1803 baptized, Samuel, son of John Evans and Catharina. Godparents: Peter Grund and Elisabeth.
Aug 30, 1781 born, [Oct 22, 1803] baptized, William, son of Edward Barker and Est[h]er. Godparents: Parents.
*Baptized in his 18th year--- 1786 born, Oct 22, 1803 baptized, Henrich, son of Edward Barker and Est(h)er. Godparents: Parents.

Marriages by Freiderich Dalliker.
Georg Hirsch well-born son of Philip Hirsch, Vincent Twp, and Anna Maria Andre, youngest dau. of Philip Andre, Pikeland Twp m. Apr 12, 1784, Chester Co.
Heinrich Zinck, youngest son of Michael Zinck, East Nentmil (Nantmeal) and Catharine Bender, well-born dau. of Friderich Bender, East Nentmil Twp, m. Nov 30, 1784, Chester Co.
Heinrich Fulkert, son of Christoph Fulkert, East Nentmil (Nantmeal) and Margrith Schmid dau. of Michael Schmid, East Nent Mil Twp. m. Oct 25, 1788, Chester Co.
Johannes Schneider, son of Casper Schneider, Vincent Twp. and

Elisabeth Hippel, dau. of Lorentz Hippel, Vincent Twp m. Apr 20, 1790, Chester Co.
Ludwig Labach, son of Johannes Labach and Maria Clinger, youngest dau. of Johannes Clinger m. Apr 10, 1792.
Peter Steidler, son of Peter Steidler, and Catharina Labach, dau. of Johannes Labach m. Oct 15, 1793.
Wilhelm Schuler, son of Wilhelm Schuler and Sara Groll, dau. of Michel Grol m. Oct 27, 1793.
Peter Rapp and Maria Rener, m. June 15, 1794.
Philip Rapp and Catharina Wurstler, m. Sep 30, 1794.
Hannes Hippel, youngest son of Hannes Hippel and Anna Schneider, youngest dau. of Andres Schneider, m. Dec 26, 1795.
Jacob Yeger, youngest son of George Jeger and Catharina Carl, dau. of Johannes Carl, m. Dec 6, 1797.
Sebastian Ruth, son of Joseph Ruth and Catharina Landes, youngest dau. of Carl Landes, m. May 13, 1798.

Register of the Children who this year in the simple Principles of the Christian Religion were instructed and on the first Sunday of the Easter Season were confrmed.
Name of child, Age, Name of Father.
Simon Schunck, 15, Simon Schunck.
Henrich Schott, 14, Henrich Schott the Elder.
Henrich Laubach, 13, John Laubach.
-- Christian Bauer, 13, Uhlrich Bauer.
Johannes Sahuger, 15, John Sauger.
Phillip Bierbauer, 14, Henrich Bierbauer.
Jacob Nagel, 14, Carl Nagel.
Vincent Bierbauer, 18, Henrich Bierbauer.
Matheiss Gristo, 20, Christoph Gristo.

Maidens.
Anna Margaret Kehr, 16, Jacob Kehr.
Elisabeth Steger, 17, Peter Steger.
Eva Elisabeth Solwig, 14, Jacob Solwig.
Magdalena Schneider, 14, Caspar Schneider.
Catharina Margaretha Bauer, 15, Uhlrich Bauer.
Anna Margaretha Schneider, 15, Johannes Schneider.
Barbara Andren, 13, Phillip Andren.
Catharina Andren, 15, Phillip Andren.
Maria Elisabeth Koenig, 14, Hannes Koenig the Elder.

EAST VINCENT REFORMED CONGREGATION 69

Elisabeth Schmid(t), 13, Vallentin Schmid(t).
Christina Hahugin (Haugen), 14, John Haugen.
Catharina Rattarin (Rader) 19, Melcher (Melchior) Rader.
Ida Elisabeth Stein, 14, Adam Stein.
Clara Elisabeth Carl, 17, Isaias Carl.

Children who were Confirmed in the Year 1768 are the following:.
Child, age, father.
Henrich Hippel, 15, Lorentz Hippel.
Jacob Seibert, 17, Michel Seibert.
Johannes Carl, 17, Ieseias (Isaias) Carl.
Bastian Wagener, 17, Bastian Wagner.
Johannes Hippel, 15, Johannes Hippel the Elder.
Conrad Spielmann, 15, Johannes Spielmann.
Adam Remy, 15, Jacob Remy.
Jacob Lehr, 14, Jacob Lehr.
Ludwig Arendorff, 16, Phillip Arendorff.
Jacob Schmid, 15, Fridrich Schmid the Elder.
Lorentz Hippel, 14, Henrich Hippel.
Johannes Nagel, 14, Carl Nagel.
Phillip Seiler, 14, Peter Seiler.

Maidens.
Catharina Siebert, 15, Michael Seibert.
Margareth Schünd, 19, Simon Schund.
Anna Maria Schneider, 15, Thomas Schneider.
Catharina Schott, 14, Henrich Schott the Elder.
Catharina Steger, 15, Peter Steger.
Elizabeth Stestan, 15, Philip Stestan.
Catharina Hellweis (Hellwich), 15, Jacob Hellwich.
Catharina Magever, 14, Bastian Magever.
Catharina Carl, 15, Iasaias Carl (Isaias).
Margareth Deny, 18, Michael Deny.
Margareth König, 18, Jacob König.
Maria Schmid (Smith), 16, Johannes Schmid(th).
Margareth Stein, 14, Adam Stein the Elder.
Catharina Schneider, 14, Johannes Schneider.
Catharina Husey (?), 14, Johannes Husey (?).
Christina Hertz (?), 15, Georg Hertz (?).

Children confirmed in the Year 1769 on the Sunday after Easter.

Wilhelm Christ, 28, Herman Christ.
Johannes Deny, 22, Johan(n)es Deny.
Jacob Deny, 20, Johannes Deny.
Catharina Claus, 15, Conrad Claus.
Friedrich Schmid, 15, S(ch)mid(t).
Jacob Hippel, 14, Henrich Hippel.
Adam Stein, 14, Adam Stein the Elder.
Georg Schneider, 14, Johannes Schneider.
Wilhelm Klein, 14, Johannes Klein.
Peter Fetter (Vetter), 16, Phillip Vetter.
Jacob Carl, 14, Isaias Carl.
Peter Heck, 16, Jonas Heck.
Johannes Hippel, 14, Lorentz Hippel.
Friedrich Jacob Bauer, 15, Uhlrich Bauer.

Maidens.
Christina Schneider, 14, Thomas Schneider.
Anna Margareth Ander, 14, The Widow Ander.
Anna Maria Labach, 14, Johannes Labach.
Margareth Schenider, 15, Caspar Schneider.
Anna Maria Jäger, 14, George Jäger.
Elisabeth Carl, 16, Johannes Carl.
Anna Maria Koenig*, 14, Jacob Koenig*.
Anna Maria Frehm,* 15, Peter Frehm*.
* Not too familiar with the names in this section and the chirography being temperamental, I am not at all sure of these two names. Köenig appeared earlier, but this may be a transition to an anglicized form.

Children confirmed 1772.
Henrich Carl, 16, Isaias Carl.
Henrich Scherardig, 18, Jacob Scherardig.
Abraham Scherardig, 16, Jacob Scherardig.
Christian Heck, 16, Jonas Heck.
Peter Schunck, 16, Simon Schunck.
Nicolaus Mack, 16, Nicolas Mack the Elder.
Johan Georg Hauge, 16, Johannes Hauge.
Johan Peter Hauge, 15, Johannes Hauge.
Johannes Schott, 17, Henrich Schott the Elder.
Catharina Frehn, 16, Peter Frehn.
Petronella Schmid, 15, Friedrich Schmid.

EAST VINCENT REFORMED CONGREGATION 71

Catharina Hippel, 15, Henrich Hippel.
Est(h)er Heck, 15, Jonas Heck.
Maria Barbara Schneider, 14, Thomas Schneider.
Catharina Stein, 14, Adam Stein the Elder.
Magdalena Stephan, 15, Phillip Stephen.
Susanna MacDanil ?, 21, "Is Wife of Henrich MadDanil"?.
Anna Maria Schner, 17, Wendel Schner.
Catharina Rohrbach, 18, Peter Rohrbach the Elder.
Maria Acker, 16, Antony Acker.
Magdalena Ander, 14, Phillip Ander the Elder.
Maria Scherard, 14, Jacob Scherard (Girard?).

Children Confirmed May 14, 1778.
Adam Schmid, 15, Vallentin Schmid Father.
Jacob Schmid, 17, Vallantin Schmid.
Peter Steger, --, Peter Steger Sr.
Martin Schonholtzer, 17, Martin Schönholtzer (Senior).
Conrad Stephan, 15, Phillip Stephan.
Jost Hippel, 18, Lorentz Hippel.
Friedrich Hippel, 15, Lorentz Hippel.
Jost Schmid, 18, Jost Schmid Sr.
Adam Steger, 18, Peter Steger Sr.

Girls.
Elisabeth Haugen, 15, Johannes Haugen.
Maria Elisabeth Haugen, 14, Johannes Haugen.
Maria Scherer, 14, Conrad Scherer.
Maria Hippel, 14, Henrich Hippel.
Magdalena Schleyer, 14, Henrich Schliyer (Schleyer).
Wilhelmina Emig, 18, Christian Emig.
Gerthraud Schonholtz, 15, Martin Schonholtz.
Christina Labuch (Cabuch), 15, Johannes Labuch.
Elisabeth Wagener, 18, Peter Wagener Sr.
Magdalena Werlich, 18, Johannes Werlich.
Maria Werlich, 19, Johannes Werlich.
Catharina Hoyt, 13, Christian Hoyt.
Catharine Schmid, 16, --.

Children who on the 17th of June, 1780 were Confirmed and on the 18th of the following January partook of their first Holy Evening Meal (Sacrament).

Boys.
Daniel Schneider, 14, Caspar Schneider.
Johne Heck, 16, Jonas Heck.
Johannes Schmid, 14, Jost Schmid Sr.
Peter Jäger, 14, Georg Jäger.
Phillip Himmelsreich, 16, Simon Himmelsreich.
Henrich Steger, 16, Peter Steger.

Girls.
Catharina Acker, 17, Anton Acker Sr.
Catharina Ache (Agy, Ege?), 18, Jacob Ache.
Margareth Ache, 15, Jacob Ache.
Susanna Mertz (Metz), 17, Johannes Metz.
Maria Hippel, 14, Henrich Hippel.
Elisabeth Labach, 15, Johannes Labach.
Christina Emig, 15, Christian Emig.
Catharina Mayer, 15, Peter Mayer Sr.
Susanna Koenig (Remy)?, 15, Jacob Remy ?.
Catharine DuFraine, 15, Jacob du Fraine.
Johannes Heilman who in this year also with the children submitted himself for confirmation.

Record of the Deaths and Burials under Friedrich Dällicher.
Sep 5, 1784, Peter, aged 1 year, 9 months, 7 days-Parents: Henry and Anna Maria Laubach.
Oct 3, 1784, Johannes Klinger, aged 57 years and Margaret (Margrith) his wife aged 47 years. Nota Bene: In this case man and wife (were laid) in one grave, and their children, since they were undivided in life, --a great rarity among human beings, (thought it) fitting. Both were of the Lutheran faith.
Mar 19, 1785, Abraham, aged 5 years, 2 months, 18 days. Parents: Johannes and Elisabeth Schneider.
May 4, 1785, Rebecca, aged 2 months, 2 weeks, 3 days. Parents: Georg and Magdalena Hirsch.
Apr 28, 1786, Catharina, aged 4 months, 4 days. Parents: Johannes Hoffman and Elisabeth, his wife.
Dec 4, 1788, Magdalena, aged 3 years, 9 months less 1 day. Parents: Conrad Carl and Maria -- Mother.
17 July, 1789, Simon Himelreich, 70 years old.
Apr 24, 1790, Justina, wife of Christoph Theis, aged 28 years, 8 months, 23 days.

June 4, 1790, Iesajas(Isaiah) Carl, age 7[3] years.
Aug 29, 1790, Georg Jeger (Yeager), age 72 years.
Nov 29, 1790, Phi ?????.
Feb 25, 1791, Catharina, wife of Jacob Bender, age 39 years, 5 months, 10 days.
Apr 18, 1791, Catharina, age 2 years, 4 months, 4 days. Parents: Philip Himelreich and Sophia, his wife.
July 13, 1791, Jacob, age 3 years, 3 months, 2 weeks, 4 days: Parents: William Posy and Susanna, his wife.
Aug 3, 1791, Clorliss(Ehefrau) wife of Christoph Muller, age 42 years, 6 months, 3 days.
Dec 27, 1791, Hanna, wife of Georg Heiny, age 78 years.
Dec 28, 1791, Johannes Ohlweyn, age 57 years.
Mar 3, 1792, Anna Maria, widow of George Yeger, the Elder.
Apr 7, 1793, Johannes, aged 1 month. Parents: Jacob Weyand and his wife, Magdalena.
Apr 21, 1793, Philip Rapp, age 68 years, 8 months, 3 days.
Oct 10, 1793, John Heinrich Benner, age 70 years, 4 months, 8 days.
Jan 25, 1794, Catharina, wife of Iesaias (Isaiah) Carl, Age 71 years.
Aug 20, 1794, Anna Maria, aged 6 years, 2 weeks, 4 days. Parents: Peter Sleip and Elisabeth, his wife.
Mar 11, 1795, Philip, age 11 years, 11 months, 3 weeks, 5 days. Parents: Samuel Hirsch and Susanna, his wife.
Mar 12, 1795, Johannes Wagner, age 76 years, 1 month, 2 days.
Aug 23, 1795, Heinrich, age 4 years, 1 month, 2 weeks. Parents: Heinrich Labach and Anna Maria, his wife.
Aug 25, 1795, Margrith, aged 6 years, 2 months, 9 days. Parents Heinrich Labach and Anna Maria.
Sep 5, 1795, Anna Maria, the wife of Heinrich Labach, age 46 years, 1 month, 4 days.
Oct 3, 1795, Laurentz Hippel, age 67 years, 8 months, 1 week.
May 15, 1796, Georg Yeger, 21 years old, his parents the deceased Georg Yeger and Anna Maria of happy memory.
Sep 3, 1797, Sara, age 3 years, 4 months, two days: Parents Johannes and Maria Schmid.
Oct 26, 1797, Sibilla, wife of Casper Schneider, age 67 years, 7 months, 5 days. N.B. 4 years, 9 days was she bereft of her senses oft in madness.

Marriages from the Memorandum Book of Rev. John E. Finley*.
* Rev. John Evans Finley, son of Rev. James and Hannah Evans

74   EARLY CHURCH RECORDS OF CHESTER CO.

Finley, was born in Cecil County, Maryland, July 26, 1753. He was pastor of Fagg's Manor, Chester County, Presbyterian Church from 1781 to 1793, when he removed to Mason County, Kentucky and thence to Ripley, Brown County, Ohio, where he died Jan 7, 1818, pastor of Red Oak Presbyterian Church. In 1782 he married Elizabeth, dau. of John Rutson of Faggs Manor, by whom he had seven children. Cf. *Torrence and Allied Families* by Robert M. Torrence, under Auspices of The Genealogical Society of Pennsylvania, Wickersham Press, 1939, p. 208.

Faggs Manor, Chester County, Pennsylavania, 1781-1787**.

**From The State Historical Society of Wisconsin, Draper Mss. 12ZZ, 386-391. Photostat copy of, in Collections of The Genealogical Society.

Courtesy of Miss Jessica C. Ferguson, Genealogical Librarian, State Library, Harrisburg.

Benj. Clap to Prudence Robison, Sep 20, 1781.
John Gardiner to Mary Stuart, Sep 25, 1781.
John Bailey to Phebe# Whitaker, Sep 25, 1781.
Alexander Andrews to Abigail Guthrie, Dec 4, 1781.
---- Stuart to Hannah Rodgers, Dec 6, 1781.
Alexander McCurdie to Lettice Cooper, Jan 3, 1782.
Isaac Sympson to Jane Henry, Jan 29, 1782.
Ebenezer Finley (Brother of the officiating clergyman) to Jane Kinkaid, Jan 31, 1782.
John Bird to Margaret Cooper, Feb 21, 1782.
David Conner and Elizabeth Daugherty, Mar 5, 1782.
Henry # Sanderson and Susanna Blair, Mar 14, 1782.
Edward Gavin to Sus. Woodrow, Mar 28, 1782.
John Patterson to Lettice Gardiner, April 9, 1782.
John Inner to Jane Withers, Apr 18, 1782.
David # Wallace to Elianor Alexander, May 29, 1782.
James Trimble to Ann Melony, June 6, 1782.
Joseph Welsh to Eliz. Logan, June 18, 1782.
Robert Currothers to ____ Ryin, Sep 17, 1782.
Alexander Russell to Esther Mathews, Sep 19, 1782.
James Walker to Jane Bunting, Oct 17, 1782.
William McKee to Susanna Grier, Oct 29, 1782.
Dennis Kelly to ---- Oar, Oct 31, 1782.
John Reynolds to Jane Wilson, Nov 4, [1782].
---- Bunton to ---- ----, Nov 6, [1782].

Jane Walton to John Miller, Dec 10 [1782].
John Boyd to Mary Cowen, Dec 10, 1782.

"Those marked thus are dead." J. E. F.

John Corsby to Sarah Ried, Jan 9, 1783.
Andrew Henning to Isbel Ramsey, a Tory, Jan 23, [1783].
George Welsh to Hannah White, Feb 11, ---.
John Bonlong to Jane Wilson, March.
Samuel Porter and Eliz. Farrin, March 20.
William Thompson and Jane Cochran, April 3.
George Luckie and Elizabeth Buchanan, Wed., Apr. 9, 1783.
Alexander Walker and Eleanor Calvon, Apr 10.
William Colmerry and Eliz. Hall, Apr 17, 1783.
Joseph Wherry to Rachel Mackey, Aug 21, 1783.
Charles Crisuri to I[s]bella Walker, Aug 24, 1783.
Daniel McAfee and I[s]bella McCorckle, Sep 4, 1783.
William Gleen to Marta Gray, Sep 25, 1783.
Abram Whiteside to I[sa]bel Rap, Sep 25, 1783.
James McCulloch and Mary Brynes, Oct 7, 1783.
Robert Evans and Margery Evans, Oct 9, 1783.
James McCulloch and Rebecca Hartshorn, Oct --, 1783.
Joseph McGahen to ----, Nov 26, 1783.
Robert Yumer to Nancy Carlisle, Dec 9, 1783.
Abram Smith to Isabel Currothers, published Jan 1, 1784.
David Corsby [Crosby?] to Isabel Walker, Jan 1, 1784.
Francis Armstrong to Sarah Pogue, Jan 13, 1784.
Robert Thompson, Dr. to Mary Withers, Feb 18 [1784].
James Lyet to Ann Logan, Mar 10, Published [1784].
Ebenezer Sword to Jane Melony, Mar 18, by license, per Alexander
    Mitchel.
John Jays and Mary Elliot, Apr 13, 1784.
William Beard and Ann Young. [No Date].
Robert Ewing and Isbel Jipy, May 27, 1784.
Robert Barr and Agnes Ferguson, May 27, 1784.
John Jackson and Mary Ewing, May 31, 1784.
James Mackey and Kathrine Mackey, June 3, 1784.
James Evans and Katharine Porter, July 1, 1784.
George Fleming and Eliz. Henderson, July 27, 1784.
Hugh Mehaffy and Mary Duff, Aug 12, 1784.
Aaron Work and ---- Yittal, Aug 23, 1784.

76 EARLY CHURCH RECORDS OF CHESTER CO.

Thomas McGiffen and Rachel Bolen, Aug 30, 1784.
Archibald McBride and Margaret Dearmin, Sep 6 [1784].
John Duglas Catorara and ---- Comiston, Oxford twp. Sep 27.
Shem Hill and Ann Low, both of Little Britain, Oct 7.
William Smith and Mary Liget, Oxford, Oct 7, 1784.
---- ---- and Margaret Wilson, Maryland, Oct 16, 1784.
James Mackey and Sarah Wallace, Elk, Oct 16, 1784.
---- Millir to ---- Mininch, Maryland, Oct 26, 1784.
Samuel Marquis and Rachel Touchstone, Maryland, Nov 4.
Timothy Collins, Maryland, to Margaret Cook, Nov 11, [1784].
James Galloway to Jane Baily, Jan 13, 1785.
David Cochran to Jane Boyd, Jan 28, 1785.
Greenbury Rawlings and Rebecca Taggert, Feb 22, [1785].
Andrew Lowry to Margaret Hood, Feb 24.
William Patten to Susanna Lewis, Jan 25, [1785].
William Cannon and Rebecca Sterrit, Apr 7, [1785].
---- Maxwil and Jane Lewis, Apr 17.
Samuel Harper and ---- Graham, Apr 21 [1785].
John Guthrie and ---- Holmes, May 26, [1785].
James Warfel [Harpel?] to Judith Rees, June 9.
David Jolly and ---- Rhea, Aug 26, 1785.
John Bailey to Hannah Criswel, Oct.
James Ewen to Mary Blackburn, Nov 1 [1785].
David Marchbanch to Jane Jones, Nov 8, published.
Joseph Wolliston and Mary Butterfield, Dec 1 [1785].
Walter Bunty and ---- Jacson, Dec 8, [1785].
Joseph Smith to ---- McCoy, Jan 5, 1786.
James Wild to Maary Knut [No date].
John Mahony to May Dysert.
Mat. Meek to Eliz. Dysert, Feb 21 [1786].
William Carlisle to Mary Taylor, Feb 23.
---- Simpson to ---- Walton, Mar 2, published.
---- Crawford to Sarah Camble, Apr 10, 1786.
---- ---- to ---- McMaster [1786].
Robert Cochran to Susanna Elton [1786].
John McBride, shoemaker, to Agnes Aitkeson, spinster, both of East
    Not. township, Pennsylvania, Mon, July 17, 1786.
Thomas Bacon to Mary Bigger, Lit. Brit.
John Tilford to Sarah Love, Oct 9, 1786.
James Gibson to Mary Kind, Oct 19.
James Neil to Kat. Mahony. [No Dates].

EAST VINCENT REFORMED CONGREGATION 77

Jacob Kind to Eliz. Trimble, Nov 26, 1786.

Marriages - Dr. John E. Finley.
John Evans to Jane Grubb, Feb 15, 1787.
David Hampton and Jane Falls, N. London township, Mar 20, 1787.
Samuel Martin and Mary Martin, Mar 27, 1787.
---- Wilkie and ---- ----.
Isaac Griffith and Nancy Eliot, May ----.
Thomas Mc leWhenny and Elianor Fries (could be intended for Thomas McIlhenny and Eleanor Jeriar) Londongrove, Dec 6, 1787.
John Whitcraft and Leah Gamble, New London township, Chester Co., Feb 28, 1788.
John Smith and Margaret Jordan, both of N. London township, Chester Co., Mar 13, 1788.
Robert Winters, Shoemaker, and Katharine Duvin, N. London township, Mar 20, 1788.
John Cooper of ---- township and county of York, farmer, and ---- Smith of E. Not. township and county of Chester, spinster, Apr 1, 1788.
William Criswell and Nancy Gibson, June 1788.
---- Hillis and Elizabeth Steel, June ----, ----.
James Rankin and Susanna Riddle, Aug 21, 1788.
William Russell of the borough of Wilmington and Ann M. Codden of Londonderry township, Sep 25, 1788.
William Clingan and Jane Black, both of ----, Sep 18, 1788.
William Keys and Violet Donaldson, Mon, Sep 21, 1788.
James Steele and Isabella Kind, May 24, 1789.

GOSHEN MONTHLY MEETING
Marriages, Births and Deaths
1722-1800

Allen, William of Londongrove m. 1779.12.1 Sarah Eldridge at Londongrove.

Ashbridge, George of Goshen, yeoman, m. 1729/30.1.6 Margaret Paschall of Goshen.

Ashbridge, George of Goshen, and his children: Mary m. 1727.8.18 Amos Yarnall at Goshen; Elizabeth m. 1729.4.6 John Sharpless at Goshen.

Ashbridge, George of Chester, yeoman and wife, Mary, and their children: George m. Margaret Paschall 1729.1.6 at Goshen; Hannah m. Joshua Hoopes; John m. Hannah Davis 1732.9.12; Aaron m. Sarah Davis 1737.2.21; Phebe m. Richard Thomas; Lydia m. Ellis Davies; Joseph m. Priscilla Davis 1749.4.8; Mary m. Jesse Jones, 1749.4.8.

Ashbridge, George and wife, Jane of Goshen, and their children: Mary, b. 1731.8.4, d. 1765.8.3; George, b. 1732.1.1, d. 1785.10.25; William, b. 1734/5.2.1; d. 1775.3/14; Susan, b. 1737.7.1, d. 1820.1.15; Phebe, b. 1739.7.19, d. 1774.11.27; Jane, b. 1742.8.10; Daniel, b. 1744.7.26; Joshua, d. 1746.9.17; Lydia, b. 1749.12.12, d. 1752.2.17 or 5.17. Phebe Ashbridge m. 1763.6.9 Isaac Massey at Goshen; Jane m. 1771.9.4 Jesse Maris at Goshen; Lydia m. 1776.10.31 Joseph Malin at Goshen; Mary m. 1779.5.27 Joseph Rhoads at Goshen; Susanna m. 1784.5.27 John Fairland at Goshen.

Ashbridge, John, son of George m. 1732.8.12 Hannah Davies at Goshen and their children: Jane, b. 1733.5.30; Jonathan, b. 1734.9.21; Elizabeth, b. 1736.8.22; John, b. 1738/9.11.8; Amos, b. 1741.6.25; Hannah, b. 1743.4.9, d. 1743.7.-; David, b. 1744.6.2; Aaron, b. 1747.5.29. Hannah Ashbridge, widow of John, d. 1771. John Ashbridge d. 1747.5-.

Ashbridge, Aaron, son of George of Chester Co. m. 1737.2.21 Sarah Davis at Goshen.

Ashbridge, Joseph of Chester Borough, son of George m. 1749.4.8 Priscilla Davis at Goshen.

Ashbridge, George Jr., son of George of Goshen m. 1754.12.5 to Rebecca Garrett at Goshen and their children: Lydia, b. 1755.11.6; Mary, b. 1758.9.13; Susanna, b. 1761.9.30; Jane, b. 1764.10.11; Phebe, b. 1767.9.8; George, b. 1770.8.17; William, b. 1773.8.2.

Ashbridge, Rebecca, aged 45 d. 1777.9.24. Ashbridge, George d. 1785.10.25.

Ashbridge, Mary, wife of George, Sr. d. 1728.2.-.

Ashbridge, George, aged near 70 d. 1773.3.6.

Ashbridge, Jonathan, son of John, dec'd, of Goshen, m. 1757.5.12 Sarah

James at Goshen.
Ashbridge, Mary, Wife of Joseph, of Goshen d. 1798.3.11.
Ashbridge, Rebecca d. 1799.1.13.
Ashton, Isaac, dec'd by 1767, of Makefield, Bucks Co., and his children: Lydia m. 1767.10.7 George Yarnell at Goshen; Susanna m. 1771.7.5 Jonathan Jones at Goshen.
Atherton, Henry, 2nd son of Henry, late of Whiteland m. 1731.8.14 Susannah Garrett at Goshen and their children: Henry, b. 1732.10.10; William, b. 1734.9.14; Caleb, b. 1736.12.12.
Atherton, Thomas, son of Henry, late of Chester Co. m. 1741.9.4 Abigail Marsh at Nantrall.
Baily, Joseph of Kennett, son of John and Hannah m. 1796.4.14 Elizabeth Hoopes at Goshen and Their Children: Jesse, b. 1797.7.5; Yarnall, b. 1799.8.19; Hoopes, b. 1801.7.18; Pennock, b. 1803.10.19.
Baker, Adam and wife, Margaret, and their children: Mary, b. 1714.11.17; Sarah, b. 1716.6.17.
Baker, Joshua and wife, Mercy, and their children: Ann, b. 1758.12.13; Mercy, b. 1761.1.15.
Baker, Joshua, son of John, dec'd, of Chester Borough m. 1744.4.7 Sarah Downing at Uwchlain and their child: Sarah, b. 1745.7.16.
Baker, Joshua and wife, Mercy, and their children: Hannah, b. 1748.11.4; John, b. 1751.10.11; Samuel, b. 1754.2.13; Rachel, b. 1756.7.13.
Baker, John and Sarah, his wife, dec'd, of Newtown, and their children: William m. 1791.4.14 Sidney Massey at Willistown; Mary m. 1790.12.22 Silas Green at Newtown.
Baker, John and wife, Ann, and their children: Mary, b. 1744.6.17; John, b. 1748.6.2; Caleb, b. 1749.6.31; Ann, b. 1752.6.20.
Baker, John and wife, Rebecca, and their children: John, b. 1780.7.8; Robert, b. 1782.2.15.
Bane, Alexander and wife, Jane, and their children: Jane, b. 1714.5.29; Mary, b. 1715.9.26; William, b. 1717.8.19; Catharine, b. 1719.8.5; Alexander, b. 1721.9.17; Daniel, b. 1723.11.15, d. 1723/4.11.-.
Bane, William and wife, Margaret, and their children: Alexander, b. 1747.3.18; Thomas, b. 1749.5.11; Elizabeth, b. 1751.5.1; William, b. 1753.4.3; Jesse, b. 1755.3.19; Nathan, b. 1757.5.11; Nathan, b. 1759.4.20; Abner, b. 1761.8.1; Jane, b. 1763.12.15; James, b. 1766.8.8.
Bane, Mordecai of Goshen, yeoman, and his children: Mordecai m. 1734.2.5 Mary Collins at Goshen; Mary m. 1730.7.11 James Burk at Goshen.
Bane, Nathan, dec'd by 1765, of Goshen, and his children: James m. 1765.4.25 Ruth Wall at Goshen; Amy m. 1758.12.7 Nathan Coope at Goshen; Elizabeth m. 1762.11.11 Daniel Hoopes, son of Nathan of

East Bradford at Goshen.
Bane, William, and his children: Jonathan d. 1765.4.-; Thomas d. 1769.6.-. Alexander d. 1770.7.
Batten, Richard of East Caln, son of John and Elizabeth m. 1746/7.1.4 Elizabeth James at Goshen and their child: Mary, b. 1747.9.15.
Beaumont, William of Goshen, batchelor m. 1730.3.6 Elizabeth Haines at Goshen.
Bembow, Gershon of Charlestown, yeoman m. 1727.11.6 Sarah Powell.
Bennett, William, son of William, dec'd, of Anne Arundel, MD m. 1790.4.22 Alice Hoopes, and their children: Juliet, b. 1791.6.15; Lewis, b. 1792.9.2; Malinda, b. 1794.7.6; Warner, b. 1796.6.2; Minveva, b. 1798.5.28; Imlah, b. 1800.4.26; Matilda, b. 1802.3.7; Titus, b. 1804.2.7; Harriet, b. 1806.7.29.
Bennett, James, son of William and Martha of Anne Arundel Co., MD m. 1794.4.17 Hannah Hoopes at Goshen.
Benson, Robert, son of Robert late of Uwchlan m. Jane Jones at Uwchlan and their children: John, b. 1714/15.12.19; James, b. 1717.6.22; Hannah, b. 1720.1.31; Ann, b. 1722.5.18; William, b. 1726.4.7.
Benson, William and wife, Jane, and their children: Robert, b. 1747.12.13; John, b. 1749.10.18; Margaret, b. --.6.13; William, b. --.1.11.
Benson, Robert of Uwchlan m. 1728.3.2 Catharine Richardson at Uwchlan.
Bond, Paul of Goshen, batchelor m. 1730.9.13 Hannah James at Goshen.
Bond, Samuel, son of Joseph, dec'd, of Bristol, Bucks Co. m. 1749.4.29 Thamzin Downing at Uwchlan.
Burk, James of Goshen, batchelor m. 1730.7.11 Mary Bane at Goshen.
Butler, Noble, of Kennett, yeoman m. 1727.8.18 Rachel Jones at Kennett.
Buzby, Joseph of Lower Dublin, yeoman m. 1728.3.28 Mary Rees at Newtown.
Buzby, Joseph and wife, Mary, child: Sarah, b. 1729.2.30.
Cadwalader, David of Uwchlan, son of David m. 1743.9.10 Hannah Davis at Uwchlan and their children: John, b. 1744.7.23; Mary, b. 1746.5.23; James, b. 1747/8.12.16; Hannah, b. 1749.11.2; Abigail, b. 1752.1.18; David, b. 1754.4.10; Dinah, b. 1756.7.30; Lydia, b. 1758.7.18.
Cadwalader, Nathan, son of David of Robinson, Lancaster Co. m. 1748.4.9 Elizabeth Gatliff at Uwchlan.
Cadwalader, Moses, son of John, dec'd, of Vincent, m. 1756.1.29

GOSHEN MONTHLY MEETING 81

Elizabeth Malin at Uwchlan.
Cadwalader, Sarah, wife of John d. 1737.8.-.
Cadwalader, John d. 1742.10.-.
Cadwalader, Mary, wife of David d. 1755.1.-.
Caer, John of Goshen m. 1751.3.3. Mary Wall at Goshen.
Camm, Henry, dec'd, by 1755 of Newtown, and his children: Esther m. 1761.11.18 Jonathan Thomas at Newtown; Sarah m. 1755.12.24 Hezekiah Thomas at Newtown.
Carleton, Thomas of Kennett m. 1795.4.24 Sarah Hoopes at Goshen.
Carpenter, Hannah, b. 1768.1.4 m. John Jefferis.
Childs, John, son of Francis of Birmingham, yeoman m. 1729.8.2 Elizabeth Richardson at Goshen.
Chamberlain, Jonas of Sadsbury, yeoman m. 1734.Oct.9 Jane Bane at Goshen.
Chamberlain, John of East Caln, son of John, dec'd, m. 1751.4.13 Jane Thompson at Uwchlan.
Chamberlain, John of Aston m. 1763.4.14 Mary Hoopes at Goshen.
Coates, Benjamin, son of Moses of Charlestown m. 1756.9.22 Ann Longstretch at Charlestown.
Collins, John, eldest son of Joseph, of Goshen m. 1731.9.19 Ann Garrett at Goshen.
Collins, Joseph, son of Joseph, of Goshen m. 1733.Oct.11 Elizabeth Garrett at Goshen.
Collins, Joseph, son of Joseph, dec'd, of Goshen m. 1771.5.22 Amey Jones at Goshen and their children: Elizabeth, b. 1773.3.22; William, b. 1775.4.12; Ann, b. 1777.8.18; Rebecca, b. 1780.2.27; Joseph, b. 1782.3.19; Amey, b. 1784.6.22.
Coope, Nathan, son of John of East Bradford m. 1758.12.7 Amy Bane at Goshen.
Cooper, John of Lancaster Co. m. 1793.5.23 Jane Yarnall at Willistown.
Cooper, Jeremiah m. Leah Morris at Newtown, dau of Lewis and Rachel Morris of Easttown.
Cox, John, son of Lawrence, of Upper Providence m. 1751.3.1 Mary Farr at Newtown.
Cox, Lawrence and Ellen, and their children: Mary, b. 1726.10.29; John, b. 1729.9.3.
Cox, Lawrence and Sarah, and their child: Jane, b. 1739.11.29.
Cox, Benjamin, son of Joseph and Catharine of Willistown m. 1780.5.10 Hannah Smedley at Goshen and their children born at Willistown; Catharine, b. 1782.3.8; Hannah, b. 1783.10.20; George, b. 1785.6.18; Jane, b. 1787.4.5; Joseph, b. 1789.5.17; Amy, b. 1791.2.10; William, b. 1792.7.5; Joshua, b. 1794.3.23; Margaret, b. 1795.12.5;

82 EARLY CHURCH RECORDS OF CHESTER CO.

Jeffery, b. 1797.6.17; Elizabeth, b. 1799.5.24; Benjamin, b. 1801.6.1.
Cox, William, son of Benjamin, dec'd, and Elizabeth of Providence, Philadelphia Co. m. 1780.6.15 Lydia Garrett at Goshen and their children: Hannah, b. 1781.4.29; Benjamin, b. 1782.10.12; John, b. 1786.3.12; Abner, b. 1788.5.16; Thomas, b. 1790.7.25; Elizabeth, b. 1793.4.20; Levi, b. 1795.11.8; Jonathan, b. 1799.3.16; Lydia, b. 1802.1.21; William, b. 1805.4.17.
David, Ellis of Goshen d. 1720.1.-.
David, Thomas d. 1722.5.-.
Davies, David and Jane of Goshen, and their children: Hannah, b. 1710.5.1; Richard, b. 1712.3.3, d. 1755; Ellis, b. 1713.10.24 m. 1741 Lydia Ashbridge at Goshen; Sarah, b. 1715.7.20; Jonathan, b. 1717.6.4 m. 1742.6.9 Esther Haines at Haddonfield; Amos., b. 1719.3.26 m. 1745.2.10 Ann Pratt at Newtown; Susanna, b. 1721.4.25.
Davies, Ellis and wife, Lydia, and their children: Sarah, b. 1741.7.12; Mary, b. 1743.6.6; Jane, b. 1745.6.23; Priscilla, b. 1747.6.23, d. 1752.4.-; Lydia, b. 1749.11.16; Elizabeth, b. 1753.1.20; Ellis, b. 1755.10.24; George, b. 1758.3.19; Israel, b. 1760.10.14; David, b. 176-.
Davis, Priscilla m. 1749.4.8 Joseph Ashbridge at Goshen.
Davis, David d. 1754.10.-. Jane, widow of David d. 1764.8.-.
Davis, Amos, son of John, dec'd, of Uwchlan m. 1757.5.5 Elizabeth Meredith at Uwchlan.
Davies, Amos and wife, Ann, and their children: Joseph, b. 1745.12.5; Hannah, b. 1747.11.5; Amos, b. 1751.6.9, d. 1752.10.-; Jesse, b. 1753.7.14; Phebe, b. 1756.4.11; Joseph, b. 1758.7.4; Sarah, b. 1760.9.12; Mary, b. 1762.9.24; Jane, b. 1764.9.5; Ann, b. 1766.11.14; Amos, b. 1769.7.6.
Davis, Isaac of Haverford, son of William, dec'd, of Darby m. 1768.6.2 Rachel Lewis at Haverford.
Davis, Hugh d. 1742.12.-.
Davis, Joseph and wife, Sarah, and their children: James, b. 1794.8.22; William, b. 1796.3.12; George, b. 1798.3.5; Joseph, b. 1800.4.13; Samuel, b. 1802.3.10; Sarah, b. 1804.12.16; Jesse, b. 1807.2.1; Susanna, b. 1810.9.3; Samuel, b. 1813.1.15; Mary, b. 1815.9.15; Martha Emily, b. 1819.12.26.
Davis, Amos, son of Amos and Ann of Edgmont m. 1793.10.7 Susanna Goodwin at Williston.
Deaves, Samuel of Pikeland m. 1744. 9.14 Mary Thomas at Goshen.
Deaves, Abraham, of Germantown m. 1747.8.14 Priscilla Thomas.
Dickes, Roger of Lower Providence, son of Peter and Sarah m. Rebecca Maris.

Dilworth, Caleb, son of James, dec'd, of Birmingham m. 1791.11.17 Ann Rankin at Goshen.
Downing, William of Uwchlan, son of Thomas m. 1741.10.10 Elen John at Uwchland.
Downing, Thomas of East Caln, and his children: Sarah m. 1744.4.7 Joshua Baldwin at Uwchlan; Thamzin m. 1749.4.29 Samuel Bond at Uwchlan; Thomas m. 1756.12.15 Jane Albin at Uwchlan.
Downing, Richard and Mary, wife of East Caln, and their children: Richard m. 1771.5.29 Elizabeth Rees at Newtown; Samuel m. 1790.10.28 Jane Ashbridge at Uwchlan.
Downing, Richard, and his children: John, d. 1748.5.20; Hannah, d. 1752.4.5; Thomas, d.1752.4.12; Jane, d. 1752.4.20; William, d. 1759.12.24.
Dunn, George, son of Philip, dec'd, and Susanna of Newtown m. 1779.12.8 Elizabeth Davies at Newtown.
Durborow, Daniel, son of Daniel, dec'd, of Philadelphia City m. 1757.5.5 Ann Parker at Goshen and their child: Daniel, b. 1758.1.27. Ann, wife of Daniel, d. 1758.2.-.
Durborow, Daniel and his wife, Phebe m. 1760.10.17 and their child: Hugh, b. 1761.12.25. Phebe Haines at Goshen, d. 1762.4.7.
Durborow, Daniel of Whiteland m. 1764.10.17 Margaret Betts at Goshen.
Eavenson, Richard and wife, Alice, and their children: Esther, b. 1740.2.14; Enoch, b. 1741.8.8; Hannah, b. 1742/3.12.11; Thomas, b. 1744.10.18; Isaac, b. 1746.9.27.
Eachus, John, son of Robert, dec'd, of Goshen m. 1734.9.22 Hannah Haines at Goshen.
Eachus, William of Goshen, son of Robert, dec'd, m. 1749.3.25 Sarah Peirce at Goshen.
Eachus, Phinehas, son of John of Goshen m. 1757.11.23 Sarah Trego at Goshen.
Edwards, John and wife, Priscilla, and their children: James, b. 1734.3.31; Dinah, b. 1736.4.7.
Edwards, John and wife, Sibbilla, and their child: Hannah, b. 1734.7.25.
Edwards, Joseph, son of Alexander, dec'd, of Gwynedd m. 1742.7.29 Ellin Rees at Newtown.
Edwards, William, son of James of Nether Providence m. 1754.9.11 Sarah Dunn at Newtown.
Edwards, Thomas of Easttown, son of Thomas, dec'd, of Bucks Co. m. 1763.4.6 Ann Yarnall at Newtown.
Eldridge, Jonathan of East Marlborough, son of Thomas, dec'd, m. 1771.10.3 Sarah Davis at Goshen.
England, William, son of William, dec'd, of Willistown, blacksmith m. 1771.1.6 Susanna Hall at Goshen.

Eleman, John and wife, Mary, and their children: Thomas, b. 1725.10.31; Dorcas, b. 1728.5.19; Margaret, b. 1731.1.31; Esther, b. 1732.12.20; Enos, b. 1734.5.8; Sarah, b. 1737.12.17.

Evan, Thomas of Goshen m. 1751.4.27 Mary Lewis of Whiteland at Goshen.

Evan, Thomas d. 1738.10.-, aged 87. Hannah, widow of Thomas d. 1741.9.-, Aged 85.

Evans, John of Goshen, son of Evan and Catharine of Newtown m. 1799.6.14 Phebe Lewis, dau of Eli, dec'd, and Hannah of Brandywine Hundred at Goshen.

Evans, John and wife, Mary, and their child: Josiah [Joshua], b. 1721.9.16.

Evans, John and wife, Margaret, and their children: Ruth, b. 1729.12.21; John, b. 1737.8.5.

Evans, Hannah d. 1741.9.

Evans, Thomas and wife, Elizabeth, and their children: Hannah, b. 1721.2.22; Margaret, b. 1723.1.5; David, b. 1726.2.16.

Farquhar, Samuel, son of William and Ann of Pipe Creek, MD m. 1773.4.15 Phebe Yarnall at Goshen.

Farr, Edward of Goshen m. 1732.10.15 Jane Serrill at Goshen and their children: Mary, b. 1733.11.13; Richard, b. 1735.6.30; John, b. 1737.4.2; James, b. 1739.3.31; Isaac, b. 1741.3.22; Jane, b. 1743.8.18; Phebe, b. 1745.11.24; William, b. 1747.1.18; Abraham, b. 1749.3.13; Phebe, b. 1754.10.7.

Farr, Edward of Edgmont, and his children: Mary m. 1751.3.1 John Cox at Newtown; Phebe m. 1775.6.21 Gideon Vernon at Newtown.

Fawkes, Richard of Newtown, and his children: Ann m. 1768.11.3 Caleb Maris at Newtown; Mary m. 177-.6.8 Joseph Hood at Newtown.

Fawkes, Samuel of Newtown, son of John and Sarah m. 1801.3.25 Rachel Morris at Newtown.

Garrett, William, son of Thomas, dec'd, and Rebecca of Willistown m. 1728.Dec.5 Lydia Lewis at Newtown.

Garrett, James of Goshen d. 1797.6.3.

Garrett, Thomas, son of George, dec'd, and Ann of Whiteland m. 1741.4.5 Jabez Lewis at Newtown.

Garrett, George and wife, Ann, and their children: Ann, b. 1710.8.21 m. John Collins; Ellen, b. 1713.1.25 m. David Meredith; Elizabeth, b. 1715.3.10 m. Joseph Collins; Alice, b. 1717.1.26 m. James Serrill; Thomas, b. 1719.1.31 m. Mary Williams; George, b. 1720.9.15 m. Hannah Rees; William, b. 1722.10.16; Mary, b. 1726.6.9; John, b. 1730.11.22.

Garrett, Amos and wife, Rachel, and their child: Davis, b. 1777.4.27.

Garrett, Josiah, son of Samuel, dec'd, of Willistown m. 1753.11.29

Mary Yarnall at Goshen and their children: Amos, b. 1754.1.11, d. 1770.9.21; Sarah, b. 1758.4.7; Ezra, b. 1762.3.15, d. 1764.9.30; Mary, b. 1765.5.20; Jane, b. 1767.11.24; Amey, b. 1770.7.29; Josiah, b. 1776.1.3.

Garrett, William of Willistown, and his children: Rebecca m. 1754.12.5 George Ashbridge at Goshen; Susanna m. 1756.10.27 Joshua Hoopes at Goshen.

Garrett, George of Edgmont, son of George, dec'd, m. 1754.6.6 Hannah Rees at Newtown and their children: Reese, b. 1755.4.26, d. 1786.9.10; Peter, b. 1756.6.17, d. 1786.10.7; David, b. 1758.6.26; Lydia, b. 1759.12.11; Joel, b. 1762.11.21.

Garrett, George d. 1786.9.4.

Garrett, Isaac of Willistown, son of William and Mary, dec'd, of Darby m. 1757.1.13 Agnes Lewis at Newtown.

Garrett, Isaac and wife, Elizabeth, and their children: Edith, b. 1784.1.17; Sarah, b. 1785.4.24; Isaac, b. 1787.4.3, d. 1796.10.21; William, b. 1789.6.1, d. 1796.10.21; Mary, b. 1791.3.12; Amos, b. 1794.8.22; Isaac, b. 1797.10.9; William, b. 1800.2.1.

Garrett, Thomas, son of William and Lydia of Willistown m. 1759.11.22 Hannah Yarnall at Goshen and their children: Ann, b. 1760.12.29; Lydia, b. 1762.7.29; Abigail, b. 1765.2.22; Margaret, b. 1767.8.1; Abner, b. 1770.3.19; Hannah, b. 1772.9.9.

Garrett, Jesse, son of Samuel and Sarah, dec'd, of Willistown m. 1759.11.29 Abigail Yarnall at Goshen.

Garrett, William of Willistown, and his children: Mary m. 1761.4.16 Joshua Hoopes at Goshen; Lydia m. 1763.4.13 Abraham Gissons at Goshen; William m. 1769.10.26 Debby Lewis at Newtown.

Garrett, Samuel, son of Samuel, dec'd, of Willistown m. 1764.11.29 Susanna Lewis at Newtown.

Garrett, Isaac of Willistown, and his children: Mary m. 1769.10.19 Benjamin Hibberd at Willistown; Amos m. 1776.5.23 Rachel Davies at Goshen and their child: Davis, b. 1777.4.27. Rachel, wife of Amos Garrett d. 1784.10.11.

Garrett, Samuel and wife, Sarah, and their children: Josiah, b. 1733.1.25; Jesse, b. 1735.6.18; Samuel, b. 1743.12.2; Aaron, b. 1746.12.27.

Garrett, Aaron and Rachel his wife, and their children: Levi, b. 1770.8.26; Amos, b. 1772.9.2, d. 1774.7.22; Aaron, b. 1775.8.22; Sarah, b. 1778.12.13; Robert, b. 1782.10.27; Mary, b. 1789.6.29; d. 1789.6.29.

Garrett, Samuel, son of Jesse of Willistown m. 1787.5.23 Elizabeth Williamson at Newtown of East Goshen and their children: Abraham, b. 1788.3.12; Sarah, b. 1790.2.15; Abigail, b. 1796.5.5. Elizabeth W., b. 1803.12.28. Elizabeth, wife of Samuel, b. 1764.1.13.

Garrett, Samuel, son of Samuel d. 1747.1.-.
Garrett, Gideon, son of Samuel of Willistown m. 1791.9.22 Abigail Garrett, dau of Thomas of Willistown at Goshen.
Garrett, Jonah, son of Jesse of Willistown m. 1792.3.28 Esther Williamson.
Garrett, Jeru, son of Samuel of Willistown m. 1792.11.22 Unity Lewis and their children: Susanna, b. 1795.2.22; Unity, b. 1797.5.26; Martha, b. 1807.5.8.
Garrett, Benjamin, son of Joseph, dec'd, of Goshen m. 1793.10.31 Debbye Lewis and their children: Lydia, b. 1795.9.16; Nathan, b. 1799.12.3; Enos, b. 1805.6.15; Debby, b. 1808.2.26, d. 1808.7.31.
Garrett, Abner, son of Thomas of Willistown m. 1793.10.31 Rebecca Maris and their children: George, b. 1794.11.20; Thomas, b. 1796.8.18. Jane, b. 1799.9.29; Lydia, b. 1801.12.6.
Garrett, Nathan, son of Nathan and Ann of Upper Darby m. 1789.6.26 Elizabeth Davis, dau of Ellis and Lydia Davis.
Garrett, Nathan and wife, Rebecca: children: Eli, b. 1798.3.28, d. 1799.1.4; Debby L., b. 1800.9.13; Hannah, b. 1803.9.6, d. 1806.10.29; Nathan, b. 1809.2.27.
Garrett, Samuel, son of Samuel d. 1747.1; Rachel, wife of Amos Garrett d. 1784.10.11.
Garrett, David d. 1759.8.18.
Garrett, Joel d. 1762.11.21.
Garrett, Reece d. 1786.9.10.
Garrett, George d. 1786.9.14.
Garrett, Peter d. 1786.10.7.
Garrett, Hannah d. 1763.7.15.
Garrett, Unity, wife of Jehu d. 1797.6.3.
Garrett, James, of Goshen d. 1793.12.25.
Gatliff, Charles of Uwchlan, dec'd by 1748, and his children: Elizabeth m. 1748.4.9 Nathan Cadwalader at Uwchlan; Mary m. 1750.2.5 Cadwalader Jones at Uwchlan.
Gilbert, Joseph of Byberry, Philadelphia Co., yeoman m. 1744.9.16 Sarah James at Goshen.
Gleave, John of Springfield, yeoman m. 1728/9.1.13 Elizabeth Eachus at Goshen.
Goodwin, John and Naomy, his wife, and their children: Jesse, b. 1760.7.16; Ann, b. 1762.2.5. Naomy, wife of John d. 1764.8.-.
Goodwin, John and Mary, his wife, and their children: Hannah, b. 1793.3.29; Thomas, b. 1794.8.5.
Goodwin, Richard and Lydia, and their children: Isaac, b. 1760.8.30; Enoch, b. 1766.1.15.
Goodwin, Thomas of Edgmond, yeoman m. 1729.9.12 Ann Jones at Newtown and their children: John, b. 1731.3.14; Thomas, b.

1733.4.26; Richard, b. 1735.8.18; Jane, b. 1737.11.9 m. 1774.12.22 Thomas Massey at Willistown; Isaac, b. 1741.12.12; Elizabeth, b. 1743.4.1; Sarah, b. 1746.2.1 m. 1774.5.5 Jesse Williams.

Goodwin, Thomas, son of Thomas of Goshen m. 1759.5.25 Mary Hall at Goshen and their children: Elizabeth, b. 1760.5.23; Ezra, b. 1762.9.12; John, b. 1764.2.- m. 1792.5.3 Mary Starr at Willistown; Susanna, b. 1766.1.9 m. 1793.10.7 Amos Davis at Willistown; George, b. 1767.7.-; Gideon, b. 1769.3.-; Jane, b. 1772.4.10; Sarah, b. 1775.6.22.

Green, Silas, son of Robert, dec'd, and Hannah of Birmingham m. 1790.12.22 Mary Baldwin at Newtown.

Gregg, William, son of Michael and Sarah of Chester Co. m. 1782.6.20 Mary Yarnall at Bradford.

Griffith, Benoni and wife, Catharine, and their children: Elizabeth, b. 1720.7.6; Nathan, b. 1722.7.21.

Griffith, John of Uwchlan m. 1734.8.31 Mary John at Uwchlan and their children: William, b. 1736.3.28; John, b. 1737.6.13.

Griffith, William, son of William of Edgmont m. 1757.4.13 Hannah Yarnall at Newtown.

Griffith, Abner, son of Nathan, dec'd, of Edgmont m. 1792.10.18 Phebe Griffith, dau of William, dec'd, of Ashtown at Goshen.

Griffith, Abner of Willistown, son of Nathan and Rachel, dec'd, m. 1799.10.24 Amy Garratt at Goshen.

Grubb, Nathaniel, Dec'd by 1771, of Willistown, and his children: Ann m. 1752.12.7 George Sinkler at Newtown; Phebe m. 1759.5.3 William Worrall at Newtown; Nathaniel m. 1771.12.18 Sarah Reece at Newtown.

Haines, Isaac and wife, Catharine of Goshen, and their children: Esther, b. 1715.6.13; Hannah, b. 1717.1.4; Isaac, b. 1718.8.10 m. 1744.8.5 Mary Cox at Goshen; Mary, b. 1720.6.2 m. 1741.Sept. 25 William Wall at Goshen; Jane, b. 1721.2.18 m. 1743.8.7 Joseph Yarnall at Goshen; Ellis b. no date; Josiah, b. no date.

Haines, Lydia m. 1748.2.1 Ellis Williams at Goshen.

Haines, Phebe m. 1760.10.17 Daniel Durborow at Goshen.

Haines, Isaac and wife, Lydia of West Goshen, and their children: David, b. 1773.6.18; Ezra, b. 1774.2.12; Mary, b. 1776.2.22; Isaac, b. 1779.11.21; Lydia, b. 1784.7.17; George, b. 1788.7.10; William D., b. 1790.4.18.

Hall, John and wife, Susanna m. 1793.11.21 and their children: Maris, b. 1794.9.20; Mary Ann, b. 1799.3.3; Caleb, b. 1801.9.28; Phebe, b. 1805.11.3.

Hall, Thomas and wife, Mary, and their children: Seth, b. 1763.5.21; Sarah, b. 1764.7.6; John, b. 1700.10.28; Mary, b. 1772.3.29; Thomas, b. 1777.5.29; Phebe, b. 1782.6.24.

Hall, Thomas of Willistown, and his children: Samuel m. 1750.9.9 Sarah

Warner at Goshen; Sarah m. 1753.11.2 Thomas Townsend at Goshen; Mary m. 1759.5.25 Thomas Goodwin.

Hall, Thomas of Willistown, yeoman m. 1763.6.17 Sarah Holland.

Hammans, William of Upper Providence, widower m. 1732.10.27 Lowry Lewis at Newtown.

Harlan, Joel of Newlin, son of Joel and Hannah m. 1798.5.3 Lydia Smedley at Williston.

Harrison, John, son of Caleb and Hannah of Chester Co. m. 1745.9.14 Mary Thomas at Uwchlan.

Harvard, David, son of John, dec'd, of Tredyffrin m. 1774.12.8 Susanna Malin at Goshen.

Hawley, William of Westtown, son of Benjamin, dec'd, m. 1791.8.18 Phebe Hoopes at Goshen.

Haycock, Joseph, son of Jonathan and Ann of Springfield m. 1752.10.25 Hannah Massey at Newtown.

Helsby, Joseph and wife, Jane of Uwchlan, and their child: Mary, b. 1713.3.6. Joseph Phipps d. 1719.2.-.

Hibbard, John, son of Joshua of Darby m. 1729.10.25 Deborah Lewis at Newtown and their children: Abraham, b. 1731.5.11; Ann, b. 1733.5.21; Phinehas, b. 1736.5.13 m. 1765.10.31 Sarah Pike at Goshen; John, b. 1739.8.2; Samuel, b. 174-.3.23; Deborah, wife of John, d. 1744.6.-.

Hibbard, John, son of Joshua, dec'd, m. 1745/6.11.30 Mary Mendenhall at Goshen and their children: Deborah, b. 1747.4.2; Lydia, b. 1749.4.1; Mary, b. 1750.9.18, d. 1798; Jacob, b. 1752.10.3; Martha, b. 1754.7.6; Amos, b. 1756.8.12, d. 1760.7.-; Abraham, b. 1758.12.31. Mary, wife of John, d. 1760.3.

Hibbard, John d. 1766.9.-.

Hibbard, Benjamin of Willistown and wife, Phebe, and his children: Josiah, b. 1733.2.22; Jane, b. 1734.12.23 m. 1753.5.17 Amos Yarnall at Goshen; Hannah, b. 1737.1.31 m. 1757.10.6 Caleb Sheward at Goshen; Joseph, b. 1738/9.12.19 m. 1767.4.30 Jane James at Goshen; Benjamin, b. 1740.8.25; Caleb, b. 1742.12.1 m. 1767.11.18 Phebe Thomas at Willistown; Phebe, b. 1745.2.16 m. 1765.4.11 Allen Farquhar at Goshen. Phebe, wife of Benjamin, d. 1772.3.29.

Hibbard, Caleb m. Phebe Thomas 1767.11.18, and their children: Mary, b. 1768.11.18 m. 1801.11.19 Thomas Hall at Willistown; William, b. 1770.10.19 m. 1796.11.2 Jane Williamson at Newtown; Phebe, b. 1772.8.12; Elizabeth, b. 1774.10.4, d. 1791.12.11; Hannah, b. 1777.3.28; Rhoda, b. 1779.7.13; Caleb, b. 1781.11.19; Isaac, b. 1784.6.21; Martha, b. 1787.12.21; Samuel, b. 1792.8.29; Esther, b. 1789.7.1.

Hibbard, William and wife, Jane Williamson m. 1796.11.2 at Newtown of East Goshen and their children: Elizabeth, b. 1798.4.2;

John, b. 1800.10.8; Preston, b. 1802.9.15; Walter, b. 1804.12.30; Thomas, b. 1806.12.8; Esther, b. 1808.12.28; Phebe, b. 1811.2.19; William, b. 1813.1.21; Sarah, b. 1815.8.12, d. 1815.10.2; Mary, b. 1817.1.17.

Hibbard, Benjamin, b. 1740, son of Benjamin of Willistown m. 1769.10.19 Mary Garrett at Willistown and their children: Amos, b. 1770.11.1 m. 1797.12.14 Hannah Garrett at Goshen; Enos, b. 1773.11.5, d. 1790.4.3; Benjamin, b. 1775.10.29; Lydia, b. 1777.10.2 m. 1804.11.15 Josiah Garrett at Willistown; Orpah, b. 1782.2.18.

Hibbard, Joseph and wife, Jane, and their children: Hannah, b. 1768.3.26; Aaron, b. 1769.10.22; Allen, b. 1771.7.29; Jane, b. 1775.1.5; Sarah, b. 1777.6.28; Joseph, b. 1779.4.18; Silas, 1782.3.3; Phebe, b. 1784.6.21.

Hibbard, Amos and wife, Hannah Garrett m. 1797.12.14, and their children: Philena, b. 1798.9.5; Enos, b. 1800.7.5.

Hibbard, John, dec'd, of Willistown, and his children: Samuel m. 1770.5.3 Mary Tomlinson at Goshen. Abraham m. 1786.5.17 Susanna Griffith at Newtown.

Hibbard, Abraham m. Susanna Griffith m. 1786.5.17 and their children: Naomi, b. 1788.8.21; Hannah, b. 1790.11.9; Edith, b. 1792.6.6; Rebecca, b. 1793.8.30; Mary, b. 1794.12.221; Abraham, b. 1796.7.21; Susanna, b. 1798.1.21; Sidney, b. 1799.7.1; Isaac, b. 1803.3.20.

Hibbard, Joseph and wife, Jane, and their children: Hannah, b. 1768.3.26; Aaron, b. 1769.10.22; Allen, b. 1771.7.29; Jane, b. 1775.1.5; Sarah, b. 1777.6.28; Joseph, b. 1779.4.18; Silas, b. 1782.3.3; Phebe, b. 1784.6.21.

Hibbard, Josiah and wife, Susanna, and their children: Owen, b. 1765.7.26; Rebecca, b. 1767.3.30, d. 1771.10.27; Josiah, b. 1769.3.4 m. 1805.10.30 Alice Hunter at Newtown; George, b. 1771.1.13, d. 1773.2.12; Susanna, b. 1772.10.1; James, b. 1775.1.24.

Hibbard, Samuel and wife, Mary Tomlinson m. 1770.5.3, and their children: Anna, b. 1771.3.21; Martha, b. 1772.9.3; Deborah, b. 1774.2.14; Elizabeth, b. 1775.9.30; Sarah, b. 1777.11.9; Rachel, b. 1779.2.16 m. 1801.4.22 James Hood at Newtown; Mary, b. 1780.12.17.

Hibbard, Samuel d. 1792.1.13.

Holland, John of Whiteland m. 1752.5.7 Sarah Boake at Goshen.

Holland, John and wife, Mary, and their children: John, b. 1714.4.7; Samuel, b. 1717.6.15; Hannah, b. 1721.4.10.

Hood, Joseph of Philadelphia, son of Thomas, dec'd, m. 1774.6.8 Mary Fawkes at Newtown and their children: Richard, b. 1775.10.9; Jonathan, b. 1777.9.17; James, b. 1779.6.26 of Newtown m. 1801.4.22 Rachel Hibbard at Newtown; Thomas, b. 1781.12.15; Joseph, b. 1783.8.4; Rebecca, b. 1786.12.15; William, b. 1788.11.10.

Hoopes, Daniel of Westtown, yeoman, and his children: Joshua m. 1731.2.8 Hannah Ashbridge at Goshen. Joshua Hoopes d. 1769.10.4. Abraham m. 1732/3.12.28 Mary Williamson at Newtown.

Hoopes, Daniel and wife, Elizabeth, and their children: Mary, b. 1763.9.13; Nathan, b. 1765.5.6; Eli, b. 1766.12.12; William, b. 1768.9.30; George, b. 1770.9.6; James, b. 1772.10.1; Joseph, b. 1775.2.5, d. 1775.3.14.

Hoopes, Jesse and wife, Rachel, and their children: Elizabeth, b. 1776.1.16; Albinah, b. 1779.4.24; Jane, b. 1781.7.25; David, b. 1785.2.9; Susanna, b. 1792.3.2; Thomas, b. 1794.7.27; Benjamin, b.1797.12.15, d. 1802.3.17; Amy C., b. 1801.10.4. Rachel, wife of Jesse, d. 1787.11.26.

Hoopes, Hannah d. 1787.11.16.

Hoopes, Susanna d. 1772.10.23.

Hoopes, Joshua and wife, Hannah Ashbridge, and their children: Jane, b. 1732.7.12; George, b. 1734.5.8; Joshua, b. 1736.7.15; Mary, b. 1739.4.4; Phebe, b. 1741.9.13; Amos, b. 1745.6.9; Joseph, b. 1748.3.10; Israel, b. 1750.6.1, d. 1751.2.13; Ezra, b. 1751.7.31.

Hoopes, Ezra and wife, Ann, and their children: Moses, b. 1774.2.6; Lydia, b. 1775.12.7; Caleb, b. 1777.11.29; Sarah, b. 1780.4.5; Ann, b. 1782.5.14; Phebe, b. 1784.3.11; Curtis, b. 1786.2.20 m. Sarah Roberts; Ezra, b. 1788.4.15; Hannah, b. 1790.2.22; Lavinah, b. 1792.4.10; Elizabeth, b. 1794.12.6.

Hoopes, Ann, wife of Ezra Hoopes, b. 1753.4.8.

Hoopes, Caleb and MARY, child: Amy, b. 1799.11.4.

Hoopes, Thomas of Goshen, son of Daniel and Jane, his late wife m. 1741.9.13 Susanna Davies at Goshen and their children: David, b. 1743.7.29; Jesse, b. 1749.3.29.

Hoopes, Thomas and wife, Sarah, and their children: Margaret, b. 1765.2.16; Amy, b. 1767.3.11; Caleb, b. 1769.4.19; Thomas, b. 1770.10.7; Sarah, b. 1772.11.1; Lydia, b. 1775.3.19; Abner, b. 1777.1.13; Mary, b. 1781.3.16.

Hoopes, Abner and wife, Sarah, and their children: Caleb, b. 1792.4.4; Marshall, b. 1793.11.26; Mary, b. 1800.10.1; Garrett, b. 1803.8.5.

Hoopes, Thomas and wife, Ann, and their child: Samuel G., b. 1797.2.4.

Hoopes, George, son of Joshua of Westtown m. 1756.4.8 Elizabeth James at Goshen.

Hoopes, Joshua, son of Daniel and Alice, of Goshen m. 1756.10.27 Susanna Garrett at Goshen.

Hoopes, Joshua of Westtown, and his children: Jane m. 1757.11.3 William Starr at Goshen; Joshua m. 1761.4.16 Mary Garrett at Goshen.

Hoopes, Joshua and wife, Mary Garrett, and their children:

William, b. 1762.4.26; Abner, b. 1764.4.24; Joel, b. 1765.9.12; Hannah, b. 1767.9.29.
Hoopes, Joshua and wife, Hannah, and their children: Mary, b. 1786.2.20; Joshua, b. 1788.2.12; Rebecca, b. 1790.9.12; Martin, b. 1792.8.10, d. 1795.8.13; George M., b. 1794.9.1, d. 1798.6.-; Hannah, b. 1797.5.3. Hannah, wife of Joshua, d. 1799.11.18.
Hoopes, Nathan, son of Nathan of East Bradford m. 1764.12.6 Ann Speakman at Goshen and their children: Elisha, b. 1765.10.12; Elijah, b. 1767.4.5; Moses, b. 1769.3.15; Susanna, b. 1771.4.23; Amos, b. 1773.3.12; Enos, b. 1774.10.4; Lewis, b. 1777.2.9, d. 1777.11.26; Elizabeth, b. 1778.10.3; Ann, b. 1781.4.14; Margaret, b. 1783.9.29; Lydia, b. 1785.6.26, d. 1785.7.3; Elizabeth, b. 1776.1.16.
Hoopes, David, son of Thomas of Goshen m. 1766.4.17 Esther Townsend at Goshen and their children: Thomas, b. 1767.2.16; Susanna, b. 1768.9.12; Joseph, b. no date; Jesse, b. no date; Lydia, b. no date.
Hoopes, Nathan of East Bradford and wife, Margaret, and their children: Daniel, b. 1738.7.8; Thomas, b. 1739.11.13, d. 1791.1.8; Nathan, b. 1741/2.12.9; Aaron, b. 1743.10.10 m. 1767.11.26 Ann Collins at Goshen; Ann, b. 1745/6.12.12, d. 1752.5.-; Jonathan, b. 1747.10.21 m. 1769.11.23 Elizabeth Bane at Goshen; William, b. 1749.7.21; Margaret, b. 1752.4.20, d. 1753.5.-; James, b. 1754.5.20, d. 1783.7.19; Susanna, b. 1756.10.11.
Hoopes, John and wife, Christian of Goshen, and their children: John, b. 1745.6.7 m. 1772.5.20 Jane Pratt at Newtown; Henry, b. 1747.3.12; Elizabeth, b. 1748.8.31, d. 1751.10.-; James, b. 1750.5.25, d. 1752.5.-; Francis, b. 1752.4.3; Jane, b. 1754.2.9; Lydia, b. 1755.11.24; Christian, b. 1757.7.17. John Hoopes d. 1795.3.1; Christian d. 1800.8.10.
Hoopes, Henry and wife, Hannah, and their children: William Lewis, b. 1793.10.5.
Hoopes, James, son of Nathan of East Bradford m. 1777.6.19 Phebe Davis at Goshen and their children: David, b. 1778.3.15; James, b. 1780.1.10, d. 1782.5.27; Susanna, b. 1781.7.2.2.
Hoopes, John of Goshen, and his children: Francis m. 1777.10.23 Mary Pratt at Goshen; Lydia m. 1777.11.13 Davis Pratt at Goshen.
Hoopes, Samuel, dec'd by 1790, of Goshen, and his children: Alice m. 1790.4.22 William Bennett at Goshen.
Hoopes, Hannah, dau of Samuel and Rebecca m. 1794.4.17 James Bennett at Goshen.
Hoopes, Gimlah of East Bradford, son of Joshua and Susanna m. 1801.10.22 Edith Garrett at Willistown.
Hoopes, Hannah d. 1793.9.28
Hoopes, Susanna d. 1772.10.23.
Hoopes, Henry and Hannah, his wife, and their child: William, b.

1793.10.5.

Howell, Jonathan of Edgmont m. 1750.4.28 Elizabeth Thomas at Uwchlan.

Howell, Rees d. 1734.

Howell, David d. 1736.

Humphrey, Richard of Derby, son of Solomon, dec'd, m. 1787.1.24 Margaret Lewis at Newtown.

Jacobs, Israel, son of John of New Providence, Philadelphia Co. m. 1753.11.28 Sarah Massey at Newtown.

Jacobs, John and wife, Elizabeth, and their children: Benjamin, b. 1754.1.1; Sarah, b. 1756.2.22; John, b. 1757.4.12.

Jacobs, Thomas and wife, Mary, and their children: John, b. 1713.7.16; Thomas, b. 1715.12.14; Joseph, b. 1717.9.9; Benjamin, b. 1720.10.11; Isaac, b. 1725.5.19.

James, Ezekiel and wife, Keziah, and their children: Ann, b. 1775.12.9; Hannah, b. 1778.1.7; John, b. 1779.8.20; Ezekiel, b. 1782.6.6.

James, Samuel, son of Joseph and Elizabeth of Willistown m. 1746.4.1 Joanna Paschall at Goshen.

James, John and wife, Ann, and their children: Ezekiel, b. 1736.10.24; Hannah, b. 1740.1.23.

James, Joseph of Willistown, and his children: Elizabeth m. 1756.4.8 George Hoopes at Goshen; Sarah m. 1757.5.12 Jonathan Ashbridge at Goshen; Hannah of Westtown m. 1760.11.27 John Marshall at Goshen.

James, Joseph and wife, Hannah, and their children: Caleb, b. 1736.5.4; Mary, b. 1737.7.25; Hannah, b. 1739.8.1; Ann, b. 1741.6.3; Joseph, b. 1743.3.21; Elizabeth, b. 1744.11.25; Sarah, b. 1746/7.12.22; Susanna, b. 1749.2.20; Ruth, b. 1750.11.7; Moses, b. 1752.12.20; Aaron, b. 1754.10.11; Jesse, b. 1756.3.112; Esther, b. 1757.9.6; Rebeckah, b. 1759.5.3.

James, Thomas, jr., son of Thomas, of Willistown m. 1737.8.12 Elizabeth Baker at Goshen and their child: Mary, b. 1738.1.11.

James, Aaron and wife, Hannah, and their children: Jane, b. 1742.6.1; Jacob, b. 1744.4.4; Isaac, b. 1745.10.13.

James, Elizabeth, wife of Aaron of Westtown d. 1751.9.-.

James, Aaron, jr. of Westtown d. 1750.9.-; Aaron, Sr. of Westtown d. 1752.2.-.

James, Thomas and wife, Hannah, and their children: Phebe, b. 1733.2.3; Robert, b. 1734.3.14; Joseph, b. 1736.5.11; Aaron, b. 1738.7.20, d. 1758.5.-; Thomas, b. 1740.6.14; Sarah, b. 1743/4.12.2; Lydia, b. 1746.8.14; Ruth, b. 1749.2.2, d. 1750.6.-; Mary, b. 1751.10.4, d. 1754.8.-.

James, Sarah, dau of Thomas d. 1724.9.-.

James, Gainor, wife of Mordecai d. 1728.9.-.

Jefferis, Evan and wife, Elizabeth, and their children: Gainer, b. 1744/5.1.23; Evan, b. 1746.9.8.
Jefferis, Samuel and wife, Mary, and their child: John, b. 1763.1.28 m. Hannah Carpenter, b. 1768.1.4 and d. 1799.7.30, dau of John.
Jefferis, John and wife, Hannah Carpenter, and their children: Minerva, b. 1787.12.17, d. 1795.8.23; Townsend, b. 1789.6.22; Carpenter, b. 1790.12.1; Malinda, b. 1792.9.9; Phebe Baily, b. 1794.8.29; William Walter, b. 1796.12.5.
Jenkins, Evan of Uwchlan, and his children: Mary m. 1730.8.7 John Pugh at Uwchlan; Anne m. 1737.10.14 Samuel John at Uwchlan.
Jenkins, Sarah, wife of Evan Jenkins d. 1748.10.-.
John, Samuel of Uwchlan and Margaret, his wife, and their children: Mary, b. 1709.12.19 m. 1734.8.31 John Griffith at Uwchlan; Samuel, b. 1711.11.22 m. 1737.10.14 Anne Jenkin[s] at Uwchlan; Margaret, b. 1713.1.2 m. 1733.10.6 John Evans at Uwchlan; David, b. 1715.11.30, d. 1723/4; Ellen, b. 1718.2.26; Daniel, b. 1720.2.12.
John, Owen, son of William m. 1738.3.30 Sarah Jones at Uwchlan.
John, Samuel of Uwchlan, and his children: Elen m. 1741.10.10 William Downing at Uwchlan; Daniel m. 1742/3 Elizabeth Rees at Uwchlan.
John, Griffith and wife, Ann of Uwchlan, and their children: Joshua, b. 1720.6.31; Hannah, b. 1723.1.19; Jane, b. 1725.2.5; Abel, b. 1727.7.22; Griffith, b. 1729.8.26 m. 1752.5.13 Sarah Lloyd at Uwchland; Esther, b. 1731.1.3; Robert, b. 1734.7.22; Sarah, b. 1736.8.31.
John, Griffith and his wife, Sarah, and their children: Hannah, b. 1757.6.28 and a son Asa who d. 1758.
John, Abel of Uwchlan m. 1755.10.8 Mary Fisher at Uwchlan, and their children: Joseph, b. 1756.9.20; Ann, b. 1758.3.2.
John, Joshua and wife, Rachel, and their children: Sarah, b. 1747.5.13; Elizabeth, b. 1749.8.15; Sibilla, b. 1753.8.3; Griffith, b. 1755.5.2; Abner, b. 1757.8.2.
John, Thomas, son of Owen, dec'd, of Uwchlan m. 1765.5.1 Elizabeth Hoopes at Goshen.
John, Thomas and wife, Gwen, and their child: Thomas, b. 1721.10.2.
John, Thomas d. 1731.3.-.
Jones, Cadwalader and wife, Elenor of Uwchlan, and their children: John, b. 1711.8.19; Mary, b. 1712/13.12.20 m. 1733.10.6 Hugh Pugh at Uwchlan; Sarah, b. 1715.2.6 m. 1738.3.30 Owen John at Uwchlan; Rebecca, b. 1718.8.31 m. 1747.2.30 John Thomas at Uwchlan; Evan, b. 1721.10.15; Cadwalader, b. 1724.1.8. Elinor, wife of Cadwalader Jones d. 1756.4.-.
Jones, Elisha, son of Robert of Merion, miller m. 1759.11.14 Gwen Lewis at Newtown.

Jones, Jonathan of Philadelphia County m. 1771.7.5 Susanna Ashton at Goshen.
Jones, Joseph and wife, Hannah, and their children: William, b. 1766.9.14; Benjamin, b. 1767.7.9.
Jones, Evan, son of Rees, dec'd, of Goshen m. 1780.5.18 Jane Williams at Goshen.
Jones, Reese and wife, Ann (or Amy), and their child: Henry, b. 1733.4.22.
Jones, Joseph d. 1768.5.-.
Jones, Richard and wife, Rebecca, and their children: Rebecca, b. 1719.7.21; Deborah, b. 1721.7.13; Nehemiah, b. 1723.7.21. Rebecca, wife of Richard Jones d. 1748.12.-; Richard c. 1771.7.-, Aged 92.
Jones, Nehemiah and wife, Mary, and their child: Rebecca, b. 1753.1.14.
Jones, Elinor, wife of Cadwaller d. 1756.4.
Jones, Joseph, son of Reese d. 1758.
Kenney, Thomas, son of Daniel of Charlestown m. 1797.12.22 Betty Mendenhall at Goshen and their children: Hannah, b. 1799.3.30; Edith, b. 1800.11.21; Samuel, b. 1803.12.24.
Kirk, Timothy of Nantmel, yeoman, son of Alfancy m. 1734.3.2 Sarah Williams at Goshen and their children: Jacob, b. 1735/6.12.19; Alphonsus, b. 1736/7.12.16; Rachel, b. 1738.12.18; Adam, b. 1740.12.16, d. 1740.4.-; Joseph, b. 1742.3.5; Thomas, b. 1744.9.26; William, b. 1746.12.21; Timothy, b. 1749.1.8; Sarah, b. 1751.10.10, d. 1753.3.-; Ezekiel, b. 1753.12.19, d. 1754.7.-.
Kirk, William of East Nantmel m. 1754.3.27 Sibbila Williams at Uwchlan.
Kirk, William and wife, Mary, and their children: Caleb, b. 1734.5.4; Ruth, b. 1736.7.16; Tamar, b. 1738.8.25; Hannah, b. 1740.10.21; Rebecca, b. 1744.3.31; Rachel, b. 1746.6.24; Lydia, b. 1748/9.12.11; Mary, b. 1751.1.1.
Kirk, William and wife, Sibbila and their child: Sarah, b. 1751.1.1.
Lambert, Matthew of Easttown, weaver m. 1740.2.9 Mary Norbury at Newtown.
Larkin, John, son of Joseph and Ann of Bethel m. 1789.3.18 Martha Thomas at Newtown.
Lewis, Lewis and Mary of Newtown, and their children: Lydia m. 1728 Dec. 25 William Garrett at Newtown; Deborah m. 1729.10.25 John Hibberd, son of Joshua of Darby at Newtown.
Lewis, Jabez of Newtown, tanner, son of Lewis m. 1738.4.15, Hannah Garrett at Newtown and their children: Lydia, b. 1739.1.31; Phinehas, b. 1741.11.23; Rebecca, b. 1742.12.27; Gabriel, b. 1744.12.1, d. 1757.8.-; Thomas, b. 1747.5.17, d. 1747.6.-; James, b. 1748.5.21; David, b. 1750.11.8; Jonathan, b. 1750.11.8; Elizabeth, b.

1753.5.6; Gideon, b. 1755.7.23. Jabez Lewis of Newtown d. 1757.8.-.
Lewis, Lewis and wife, Mary of Newtown, and their children: Lewis m. 1740.4.5 Rose Pratt at Newtown; Elizabeth m. 1745.6.8 Amos Evans at Newtown; Mary m. 1746.6.14 Jasher Roberts at Newtown.
Lewis, Lewis d. 1800.7.9, aged 47.5.-.
Lewis, Griffith, dec'd by 1747 and wife, Mary, and their children: William, b. 1724.2.23 m. 1747.8.9 Elizabeth Thomas at Goshen; Samuel, b. 1726.8.5; Abigail, b. 1734.11.7.
Lewis, Joseph, son of Nathan of Newtown m. 1751.9.7 Sarah Buzby at Newtown and their child: Nathan, b. 1755.8.18.
Lewis, Samuel of Whiteland m. 1756.11.4 Margaret Trotter at Goshen.
Lewis, Samuel and wife, Margaret, and their child: Hannah, b. 1747.9.12.
Lewis, Margaret d. 1789.10.13.
Lewis, Nathan of Newtown, and his children: Azariah m. 1769.11.29 Hannah Scott; Deby m. 1769.10.26 William Garrett.
Lewis, Nathan and wife, Margaret, and their children: Joseph, b. 1732.1.20; Levi, b. 1734/5.12.3; Tamar, b. 1735.13.23, d. 1742/3.11.8; Leah, b. 1739.7.16, d. 1742/3.11.3; Miles, b. 1742.2.1, d. 1742/3.11.4; Azariah, b. 1743.8.29; Ambrose, b. 1745.1.9, d. 1746.7.5; Didymus, b. 1747.11.16; Debe, b. 1750.5.15; Peter, b. 1753.1.26 at the Home of Robert Peters in West Street in the County of Gloucester near the City of Bristol in Great Britain.
Lewis, Nathan d. 1788.2.5, Aged 83.
Lewis, Azariah and Hannah, his wife, and their children: Unity, b. 1770.10.22; James, b. 1773.5.17, d. 1785.1.7, Aged 12; Sarah, b. 1775.4.4; Margaret, b. 1778.8.27; Nathan, b. 1780.11.29, d. 1782.8.8, Aged 2; Hannah, b. 1782.4.1; Robert, b. 1786.2.27.
Lewis, Evan, son of John and Katharine of Radnor m. 1770.10.31 Esther Massey.
Lewis, Evan and wife, Sarah, and their child: Jonathan, b. 1726.7.24.
Lewis, Evan d. 1735.5.-.
Lewis, Margaret, b. 1712.5.18 d. 1789.10.13.
Lewis, Ruth d. 1785.5.28, Age 77.
Lewis, Mary d. 1765.12.28, Age 44.
Lewis, Mary d. 1740.10.-.
Lewis, Esther, dau of Evan d. 1726.11.-.
Lewis, Henry, Son of David of Radnor m. 1783.11.21 Mary Davis.
Lewis Henry and wife, Mary, and their children: Esther, b. 1785.3.16; Enos, b. 1787.5.15; Henry, b. 1790.4.25; Mary, b. 1792.4.4.
Lewis, John, son of William, dec'd, of Newtown m. 1795.1.21 Tamar Lewis, dau of Didymus of Newtown at Newtown.
Lewis, Joseph, son of Evan and Susanna of Newtown m. 1798.6.21

Elizabeth Yarnall at Willistown.

Lewis, Didymus and Phebe, his wife and their children: Debbe, b. 1771.7.22; Lamar, b. 1774.7.15; Phebe, b. 1777.9.27; Mary, b. 1779.12.19; Nathan, b. 1782.7.18 m. 1810.12.131 Jane Massey at Willistown; Eli, b. 1784.7.18,; Thomas, b. 1786.9.23; Margaret, b. 1789.2.14; Tacy, b. 1793.1.22.

Lewis, Ruth d. 1785.5.28, Aged 44.

Lewis, William and wife, Gwen, and their children: Nathan, b. 1705.9.21; William, b. 1708.8.23; Jephthah, b. 1711.3.27, d. 1731.6.-; Enos, b. 1714.6.19.

Lewis, William and Lowry, his wife, and their children: Joseph, b. 1719.3.4, d. 1731.6.-; Benjamin, b. 1721.7.18, d. 1731.6.-; Gideon, b. 1723.5.26, d. 1731.6.-; Ann, b. 1725.6.21, d. 1731.6.-; Ambrose, b. 1728.8.13.

Lewis, William d. 1731.5.-.

Lewis, William d. 1784.10.8, Aged 48.

Lewis, David of Newtown d. 1794.11.12, Aged 89 Years 4 Mos.

Lobb, Benjamin of Darby, and his children: Abraham m. 1757.11.9; Dinah Thomas at Newtown; Jacob m. 1762.8.15 Sarah Randall at Pikeland.

Lownes, Benanuel, son of George, dec'd, of Springfield m. 1744.6.29 Alice Williamson at Newtown.

Lloyd, Humphrey of Uwchlan and his wife, Hannah, and their children: Sarah, b. 1729.11.25 m. 1752.5.13 Griffith John at Uwchlan; Margaret, b. 1731.1.31 m. 1751.3.30 Robert Williamson at Uwchlan; Grace, b. 1733.11.23; Rebecca, b. 1735.11.12 m. 1759.5.9 William Orven at Uwchlan; Hannah, b. 1737.11.24; David, b. 1741.1.29; Jones, b. 1742.9.7; Humphrey, b. 1745.2.10; John, b. 1749.9.27.

Mcmillian, William, son of Thomas, dec'd, of Warrington, York Co. m. 1760.2.20 Deborah Holland at Nantiel.

Malin, Isaac of Whiteland, and his children: Isaac m. 1729.10.12 Lydia Booth at Goshen; Thomas m. 1729.11.8 Sarah Collins at Goshen; Elizabeth m. 1731.2.15 John Rhoads at Goshen; Alice m. 1731.2.15 Jesse Pugh at Goshen; Randal m. 1743.3.1 Alice Pratt at Newtown.

Malin, John and wife, Sophia, and their children: James, b. 1774.6.22; Alice, b. 1775.10.22; Susanna, b. 1777.5.4; Sarah, b. 1779.5.8; Elizabeth, b. 1781.12.25; John, b. 1787.9.22; John Malin d. 1800.10.13.

Malin, Elizabeth, dau of Thomas m. Moses Cadwallader.

Malin, Sarah, dau of Thomas m. Thomas White.

Malin, Joseph and wife, Lydia, and their children: George, b. 1777.8.21; Rebecca, b. 1779.9.15; Mary, b. 1781.12.30; Joseph, b. 1784.2.10; Jane, b. 1786.5.7; Ezra, b. 1788.8.31, d. 1788.9.2; Randal, b.

1790.11.13. Lydia, wife of Joseph, d. 1796.1.7.
Malin, Randal of East Whiteland wife, Alice, and their children: Mary, b. 1744.2.19; John, b. 1746.3.28; Sarah, b. 1748.2.25, d. 1772.11.24; Randall, b. 1750.8.23 m. 1776.6.27 Jane Hoopes at Goshen, d. 1793.4.6; Susanna b, 1751.12.14 m. 1774.12.8 David Havard [Harvard] at Goshen; Joseph, b. 1753.6.21 m. 1776.10.31 Lydia Ashbridge at Goshen. Jane, b. 1755.3.-, d. 1769.8.15. Alice, wife of Randal, d. 1770.3.17.
Malin, Randal and wife, Jane, and their child: John, b. 1780.1.17.
Malin, Thomas and wife, Mary, and their children: Elisha, b. 1757.7.31; Lucy, b. 1759.11.13; Thomas, b. 1762.3.14.
Malin, Alice d. 1770.3.17, wife of Randal.
Malin, Randall, SR. d. 1793.4.6, husband of Alice.
Malin, Lydia d. 1796.1.17, wife of Joseph.
Maris, George, son of John of Springfield m. 1730.7.24 Mary Buzby at Springfield.
Maris, Caleb and wife, Ann of Willistown, and their children: Rebecca, b. 1769.8.28, m. 1797.5.25 Roger Dicks at Willistown; Susanna, b. 1771.7.22 m. 1793.11.21 John Hall at Willistown; Mary, b. 1774.1.28; George, b. 1775.8.25 m. 1802.5.20 Elizabeth Jones at Uwchlan; Ann, b. 1777.5.26; Hannah, b. 1783.10.31; Phebe, b. 1785.12.22; Caleb, b. 1788.2.25; Richard, b. 1790.1.20; Jonathan, b. 1791.9.12 m. 1822.11.14 Mary Garrett at Goshen.
Marshall, John, son of Thomas, dec'd, of Birmingham m. 1760.11.27 Hannah James at Goshen.
Martin, Thomas, son of John, dec'd, of Chichester m. 1750.4.7 Sarah John at Uwchlan, and their children: Eleanor, b. 1751.1.29; Hannah, b. 1752.12.4; Susanna, b. 1753.11.23; Aaron, b. 1755.2.5.
Massey, James, son of Thomas, dec'd, of Marple m. 1723.2.2 Ann Lewis at Newtown and their children: Thomas, b. 1724.1.19; Lewis, b. 1726.9.4; Abram, b. 1729.2.6; James, b. 1731.11.2; Mary, b. 1734.4.12; William, b. 1736.12.7; Phinehas, b. 1739.10.13; Mordecai, b. 1747.1.24; Lydia, b. ----.10.25.
Massey, Thomas and Sarah of Willistown, and their children: Sarah, b. 1725.5.9 m. 1753.11.28 Israel Jacobs at Newtown; Mordecai, b. 1726.9.2, d. 1746.9.-; Phebe, b. 1728.2.13 m. 1765.3.6 George Miller at Newtown; Hannah, b. 1729.6.10 m. 1752.10.25 Joseph Haycock at Newtown; Mary, b. 1730.8.30; Isaac, b. 1732.2.5 m. 1763.6.9 at Goshen, d. 1774.11.27; Elizabeth, b. 1734.1.31; Thomas, b. 1735.2.7 m. Jane Goodwin 1774.12.22 at Willistown; Jane, b. 1736.10.18, d. 1744.3.-; Joseph, b. 1738.4.26; Esther, b. 1740/1.12.15 m. 1770.10.31 Evan Lewis at Newtown; Levi, b. 1742.3.23; Rebecca, b. 1743.8.1; Aaron, b. 1745.10.0, d. 1746.0. . Thomas d. 1785.6.13; Thomas, Jr. d. 1784.10.23; Sarah, widow of Thomas, d. 1786.9.28. Jane, widow of Thomas, Jr. d. 1813.5.26.

Massey, Thomas and wife, Jane, and their child: Esther, b. 1777.5.
Massey, Joseph and wife, Ann, and their children: Phebe, b. 1767.8.5, d. 1790.7.2; Israel, b. 1769.6.7; Sarah, b. 1771.2.22, d. 1771.12.8; Susannah, b. 1773.2.2, d. 1773.12.28; Sarah, b. 1774.11.22, d. 1791.12.26; Mary, b. 1778.5.21, d. 1778.9.20; Joseph, b. 1780.9.5; Isaac, b. 1782.8.22; Jane, b. 1786.11.21.
Massey, Levi and wife, Catharine, and their child: Phebe, b. 1794.3.14. Catharine, wife of Levi d. 1794.9.20.
Massey, Thomas d. 1784.6.13; Thomas Jr. d. 1784.10.23.
Massey, Isaac d. 1792.2.6.
Massey, Levi and wife, Esther, and their children: George, b. 1775.8.11; Thomas, b. 1777.6.15; Sarah, b. 1778.9.26; Mary, b. 1781.12.17; John, b. 1783.3.11; William, b. 1785.11.28.
Matlock [Matlack], Joseph of Goshen and Rebecca, and their children: Jemima, b. 1722.4.20 m. 1741.8.15 James Pennell at Goshen; Isaiah, b. 1725.2.25; Nathan, b. 1727.3.16; Ruth, b. 1729.12.23 m. 1748.9.10 Thomas Sherward at Goshen; Esther, b. 1733.6.23; Jesse, b. 1735.10.2; Jonathan, b. 1737.3.16; Joseph, b. no date; Amos, b. no date.
Matlock [Matlack], Nathan and wife, Mary of Radnor, and their children: Phebe, b. 1750.9.12; Rebecca, b. 1752.1.21; William, b. 1753.6.21; Simeon, b. 1755.12.10 m. 1782.11.21 Elizabeth Yarnall; Hannah, b. 1757.12.26.
Matson, Alice, dau of John d. 1748.3.-.
Matson, John d. 1748.3.-.
Matson, Rebecca, dau of Joseph d. 1748.3.-.
Mc Cord, John and wife, Hannah, and their children: Hannah, b. 1742.8.11; John, b. 1744.11.23; Mary, b. 1746.12.28.
Mechem, Francis, son of John of Goshen m. 1791.9.29 Naomi Goodwin.
Mendenhal, James, son of Aaron of E. Caln m. Hannah Thomas 1743.9.10 at Uhwland.
Mendenhall, Benjamin of Concord, dec'd by 1745, and his children: Samuel m. 1745.2.24 Esther Williamson at Newtown; Mary m. 1745/6.11.30 John Hibbard at Goshen.
Mendenhall, Moses of East Bradford, son of John and Elizabeth, dec'd, m. 1785.11.24 Christian Hoopes at Goshen.
Mendenhall, Robert and wife, Mary, and their children: Daniel, b. 1784.8.31; Martha, b. 1788.9.12; Alice, b. 1790.12.15; Mary, b. 1792.12.7; Jane Newlin, b. 1794.3.18.
Mercer, Caleb, son of Robert of Birmingham m. 1770.11.16 Mary Peirce at Goshen.
Meredith, John of Vincent and his wife, Grace, and his children: Enoch, b. 1728.1.18; Simon, b. 1729.10.12 m. 1755.4.30 Dinah Pugh at Nantmel; James, b. 1731.10.11; Jane, b. 1734/5.11.30; Elizabeth, b.

1736.9.18 m. 1757.5.5 Amos Davies at Uwchlan; Ann, b. 1738.6.6;
Hannah, b. 1741.5.1; Jane, b. 1742/3.1.12; Grace, b. 1744.11.13; John,
b. 1747.4.29; Ruth, b. 1750.3.17.

Meredith, Enoch and wife, Jane, and their children: James, b.
1753.10.1; Elizabeth, b. 1755.4.30; John, b. 1757.3.21; Hannah, b.
1759.1.2; Ezra, b. 1760.11.5.

Milhouse, Thomas of Pikeland, and his children: John m. 1749.2.7
Margaret Paschall at Goshen; Thomas m. 1751.9.7 Elizabeth
Paschall at Uwchlan; Sarah m. 1762.9.16 Thompson Parker at
Uwchlan.

Miller, George, son of Henry and Sarah, of Upper Providence m.
1765.3.6 Phebe Massey at Newtown.

Moore, Thomas Jr. of Newtown, weaver m. 1741.3.27 Sarah Pratt at
Newtown.

Moore, William of Newtown m. 1763.9.21 Susanna Warner at
Newtown.

Moore, Mordecai of Marple m. 1736.12.10 Rebecca Reece at Newtown.

Moore, John and wife, Ann of Easttown, and their children: Ruth m.
1769.4.13 Benjamin Walker at Newtown; Lewis m. 1769.4.13 Rachel
Walker at Newtown.

Moore, James and his wife, Phebe, and their children: Abner, b.
1754.4.25; James d. 1784.6.8; Phebe d. 1795.

Moore, Abner and his wife, Leah, and their children: Benjamin, b.
1783.10.24; Isaac, b. 1785.7.13; Sarah, b. 1787.5.16; Phebe, b.
1790.4.28; Walker, b. 1792.5.27; Leah, b. 1795.9.10.

Moore, Lewis and his wife, Rachel of Easttown, and their children:
John m. 1797.3.22 Hannah Rogers at Newtown; Rachel m. 1801.3.25
Samuel Fawkes at Newtown; Leah m. 1803.11.23 Jeremiah Cooper
at Newtown; Phebe m. 1806.11.19 Joseph Dickinson at Newtown.

Morgan, John of Uwchlan, son of Thomas m. 1723 Hannah Williams at
Uwchlan and their children: Ruth, b. 1724.8.18, d. 1741.6.-; Sarah,
b. 1729.3.28; Elizabeth, b. 1732.4.19, d. 1741.6.-; Jacob, b. 1735.2.15;
Rebuen, b. 1738.3.16, d. 1741.8.-; Hannah, wife of John, d. 1741..7.-.

Morgan, Rees, son of Thomas, dec'd, of Goshen m. 1746 June 26 Sarah
Griffith at Goshen.

Morris, Lewis and wife, Rachel, and their children: John, b. 1769.12.17,
d. 1801.4.19; Isaac, b. 1771.-.2, d. 1797.12.18; Sarah, b. 1772.11.12,
d. 1773.10.10; Hannah, b. 1774.4.18, d. 1803.3.27; Leah, b.
1776.5.14; Rachel, b. 1778.6.7; Ann, b. 1782.2.27; Sarah, b.
1782.2.27, d. 1801.3.20; Phebe, b. 1784.6.8; Lewis, b. 1786.9.22;
Joseph, b. 1790.4.10.

Morris, John and wife, Hannah, and their children: Mary, b. 1798.7.10;
Priscilla, b. 1800.1.20.

Osborne, Peter of Whiteland, batchelor m. 1734.4.6 Hannah Paschall at Goshen.
Owen, William, son of William late of Vincent, yeoman m. 1759.5.9 Rebecca Lloyd at Uwchlan.
Parker, Thompson of Philadelphia, saddler, son of Alexander m. 1762.9.16 Sarah Milhouse at Uwchlan.
Paschall, William and Grace, and their child: Grace, b. 1721.4.26.
Paschall, Hannah, b. 1723.10.3.
Passmore, Richard and wife, Deborah, and their children: Everatt, b. 1787.11.9; Hannah, b. 1789.6.8; Mary, b. 1791.2.11; Beulah, b. 1792.7.7; Abigail, b. 1794.1.6; Richard, b. 1795.10.29, d. 1796.5.27; Abijah, b. 1796.11.12; Deborah, b. 1799.2.18; Rachel, b. 1801.1.7.
Paynter, Richard, son of Richard, dec'd, of Philadelphia m. 1787.12.14 Ann Taylor at Goshen.
Pearson, Lawrence and wife, Esther, and their children: Benjamin, b. 1710.1.22; Hannah, b. 1712.3.25; Thomas, b. 1714.17.9 m. 1744.3.2 Elizabeth Morris at Newtown; Sibilla, b. 1717.8.24 m. Thomas Wright; Phebe, b. 1719.10.2; Benjamin, b. 1721/2.1.10; Esther, b. 1724.10.31; Margery, b. 1726.5.14; Charity, b. 1730.9.17; Lydia, b. 1733/4.1.8.
Pearson, William of East Caln m. 1762.3.25 Elizabeth Everington at Uwchlan.
Peirce, Gainer, dec'd by 1748, and wife, Sarah, and their children: George, b. 1720.8.10 m. 1748.9.3 Mary Moore at Goshen, d. at Goshen 1756; Elizabeth, b. 1722.1.24; Ann, b. 1725.8.7; Sarah, b. 1727.11.27 m. 1758.1.4 Andrew Steel at Goshen; Susanna, b. 1730.6.24; Mary, b. 1733.3.10, d. 1741.6.-; James, b. 1737.8.31; Gainer, 1740.1.7.
Peirce, Hannah, b. 1727.1.11.
Peirce, James of Goshen m. 1749.3.11 Mary Rees at Goshen.
Pennell, Joshua, late of Ashton, son of John m. 1726.2.20 Hannah Lewis at Newtown.
Pennell, James, son of William and Mary of Middletown m. 1741.8.15 Jemima Matlock at Goshen.
Phipps, Joseph of Uwchlan, yeoman m. 1742.4.3 Mary Helsby at Uwchlan.
Pratt, Joseph and wife, Jane of Edgmont, and their children: Abraham, b. 1746.12.19 m. 1773.4.28 Sarah Williamston at Newtown; Sarah, b. 1748.5.13; Jane, b. 1751.5.30 m. 1772.5.28 John Hoopes at Newtown; Joseph, b. 1753.9.12; David, b. 1756.6.12 m. 1777.11.13 Lydia Hoopes at Goshen; Mary, b. 1759.5.8, b. 1759.5.8 m. 1777.10.23 Francis Hoopes at Goshen; Priscilla, b. 1761.9.3; Thomas, b. 1764.1.13. m. 1786.11.30 Hannah Massey at Willistown.
Pratt, Joseph and wife, Sarah, and their child: Elizabeth, b. 1774.6.2.

Pratt, Thomas d. 1743.8.-; Hannah Pratt, widow of Thomas d. 1743.8.-; Jane Pratt, wife of Joseph d. 1772.6.15; Joseph Pratt, d. 1775.8.19.
Pratt, David and Lydia his wife, and their children: John, b. 1779.1.6; David, b. 1780.12.9; Joseph, b. 1783.2.18; Jane, b. 1785.3.5; Abraham, b. 1787.2.24; Jeromia, b. 1789.4.18; Henry, b. 1791.9.1.
Pratt, David and wife, Lydia of Newtown, and their children: Lydia, b. 1794.5.28; Christian, b. 1796.8.30; Orpah, b. 1798.12.4; Randal, b. 1801.9.30.
Pratt, Thomas and wife, Hannah, and their children: Ann, b. 1788.6.2; Susanna, b. 1790.10.3; Mary, b. 1793.5.5; Phinehas, b. 1795.10.20; Jane, b. 1797.10.8; Massey, b. 1800.1.13; Priscilla, b. 1802.11.7.
Pugh, John of Uwchlan, son of James, dec'd, m. 1730.8.7 Mary Jenkins at Uwchlan and their children: Sarah, b. 1731.5.31; Joshua, b. 1733.5.19, d. 1733.8.-; Jonathan, b. 1734.9.21; James, b. 1736.11.31; Mary, b. 1739.3.28; Evan, b. 1743.12.17.
Pugh, Jesse, son of Thomas late of Dolgelle in Co. of Philadelphia m. 1731.2.15 Alice Malin at Goshen.
Pugh, Hugh, son of James, dec'd, of Uwchlan m. 1733.10.6 Mary Jones at Uwchlan and their children: Dinah, b. 1734.7.20; Hannah, b. 1736.5.6; John, b. 1738.8.8; Joseph, b. 1740.7.27; Rebecca, b. 1745.7.10.
Pugh, Margaret, dau of James d. 1719.
Pugh, James d. 1724.4.-.
Pugh, Hannah, dau of John d. 1737.8.-.
Pugh, John, son of John d. 1739.10.-.
Pugh, John d. 1743.7.-.
Pugh, Joseph, son of John d. 1745.4.-.
Pugh, Sarah, dau of John d. 1748.
Randall, Joseph, son of Joseph of Blockley m. 1757.5.11 Rachel Griffith at Goshen.
Rattew, William and wife, Rebecca, and their children: Mary, b. 1743.1.23; Hannah, b. 1744.8.24; Abigail, b. 1746.11.24; William, b. 1748.6.9; John, b. 1751.4.24; Edith, b. 1754.8.16; Jesse, b. 1756.6.12.
Rea, Samuel, son of John, dec'd, of Bradford m. 1774.4.14 Deborah Bane at Goshen.
Reed, William of Chester Co., son of James and Ruth of New Castle Co. m. 1804.9.13 Mary Branson at Kennett.
Rees, Thomas and wife, Margaret, and their children: Elizabeth, b. 1709.7.18; Rachel, b. 1711.2.11, d. 1722.9.-; David, b. 1713.5.8, d. 1745.7.-; Caleb, b. 1716.1.28; Joshua, b. 1716.1.28; Ann, b. 1718.2.20; Thomas, b. 1721.2.24; Rachel, b. 1724.7.4; Lewis, b. 1727.3.9.

Rees, Caleb of Newtown, carpenter m. 1731.2.15 Hannah Yarnall at Newtown.

Rees, Lewis of Newtown, and his children: Hannah m. 1754.6.6 George Garrett at Newtown; David m. 1762.2.17 Sarah Cox at Newtown. Lewis Reece d. 1775.11.10, aged 91.

Reese, David. m. 1736.1.25 Jane Yarnall, dau of Traver of Willistown.

Reese, Grace, wife of Lewis, d. 1740.9.-.

Rees, David and wife, Mary, dec'd, of Newtown and their children: William m. 1765.12.4 Mary Lewis at Newtown; Elizabeth m. 1771.5.29 Richard Downing at Newtown; Sarah, dau. of David of Newtown m. 1771.12.18 Nathaniel Grub at Newtown.

Reece, William and wife, Mary, and their children: Sidney, b. 1766.10.29; Mordecai, b. 1769.1.16, d. 1792.3.8; Orpha, b. 1772.7.12; William d. 1790.2.10.

Regester, Robert, son of David and Lydia of Edgemont m. 1743.9.9 Jane Williamson at Newtown.

Regester, David and wife, Catherine, and their children: Lydia, b. 1787.8.7; Daniel, b. 1789.11.30; William, b. 1792.3.3; Elizabeth, b. 1794.9.1; Abigail, b. 1797.5.1; Mary, b. 1800.6.15; David, b. 1803.7.10.

Reynolds, Henry of Easttown, son of Richard, dec'd, of New Castle Co. m. 1757.9.28 Rebecca Ellis at Newtown.

Rhoads, John, son of Joseph of Marple, yeoman m. 1731.2.15 Elizabeth Malin at Goshen.

Rhoads, Adam of Philadelphia, carpenter, son of John, dec'd, m. 1738.4.7 Ann Lewis at Newtown.

Rhoads, Benjamin, son of Joseph, dec'd, of Marple m. 1739.9.8 Catharine Pugh at Springfield.

Rhoads, Joseph, son of James, dec'd, of Marple m. 1779.5.27 Mary Ashbridge at Goshen.

Richards, Isaac, son of Richard, dec'd, of Radnor m. 1767.10.28 Phebe Yarnall at Newtown.

Richardson, Isaac and wife, Catharine, and their children: Elinor, b. 1714.10.28; Martha, b. 1719.3.25; John, b. 1721.4.21.

Roberts, Nicholas of Gwynedd, widower m. 1728.9.7 Gaynor Bowen at Gwynedd.

Roberts, Aubrly, son of Owen, dec'd, of Philadelphia m. 1732.4.4 Ruth Jones at Nantiel.

Roberts, John, son of John, dec'd, of Merion m. 1743.4.1 Jane Downing at Uwchlan.

Roberts, Mordecai m. 1745.9.1 Mary Pugh at Nantchel.

Roberts, Jasher, son of Evan, dec'd, of Radnor m. 1746.6.14 Mary Lewis at Newtown.

Roberts, John, son of Thomas of Blockley m. 1764.12.14 Sarah Williamson at Goshen.
Roberts, Robert of Goshen, son of Robert and Ellen of Merion m. 1799.4.24 Elizabeth Pratt at Goshen and their children: Abraham P., b. 1800.1.24, d. 1801.2.12; Sarah, b. 1801.2.10; George, b. 1803.4.1; Pratt, b. 1805.2.15.
Roberts, William and wife, Jane, and their children: Margaret, b. 1714/5.2.27; Jacob, b. 1719.11.13.
Rogers, Robert, son of Owen of Plimouth m. 1751.8.31 Ann Hibberd at Goshen.
Rogers, Jonathan, son of Joseph, dec'd, of Vincent m. 1780.5.11 Ann Jones at Pikeland.
Rogers, James, Dec'd by 1797, and wife, Priscilla of Goshen, and their children: Jacob m. 1797.2.22 Esther Smedley at Goshen; Hannah m. 1797.3.22 John Morris at Newtown.
Rogers, Abner and wife, Sarah, and their children: John, b. 1786.3.29; Thomas, b. 1787.10.6.
Rogers, Sarah d. 1788.4.8.
Rogers, Abner and wife, Alice, and their children: Ann, b. 1794.4.28; Jacob, b. 1795.9.12; Joseph, b. 1797.3.12; Benjamin, b. 1797.3.12; Abner, b. 1799.8.10; Phebe, b. 1800.11.15; Samuel, b. 1802.3.10; Abraham, b. 1804.1.24; Isaac, b. 1806.1.21; Sarah, b. 1808.1.11.
Russell, William, son of William of Edgmont m. 1763.5.25 Susanna Griffith at Newtown.
Samuel, John of Radnor m. 1727.10.12 Magdalen Howell at Newtown.
Sanders, John, son of John and Ann of Mill Creek, DE m. 1792.11.21 Sarah Evans at Newtown.
Scott, James d. 1775.8.18, Aged 55.
Scott, John d. 1775.8.26, Aged 26.
Serrill, James and wife, Jane of Goshen, and their children: John, b. 1707.6.4; Jane, b. 1709.7.23; Mary, b. 1710.11.2; James, b. 1714.5.9 m. 1741.4.5 Alice Garrett at Goshen; Isaac, b. 1717.11.12; Jacob, b. 1721.4.6.
Sharpless, John of Nether Providence, Yeoman m. 1729.4.6 Elizabeth Ashbridge at Goshen.
Sharpless, Joseph, son of Joseph, dec'd, of Middletown m. 1769.5.18 Mary Hibberd at Middletown.
Sharpless, Daniel, son of Daniel, dec'd, of Nether Providence m. 1775.11.22 Hannah Thomas at Newtown.
Sheward, Thomas, son of John. dec.'d, of West Bradford m. 1748.9.10 Ruth Matlack at Goshen.
Sheward, Caleb, son of Moses of Redditch, Worcestershire, England m. 1707.10.6 Hannah Hibberd at Goshen.

Sinkler, George, son of William of West Clan m. 1752.12.7 Ann Grubb at Newtown.
Smedley, Thomas and Sarah of Willistown, and their children: Mary m. 1737.11.12 Samuel Taylor at Goshen; Sarah m. 1739.11.9 John Minshall at Goshen; Thomas m. 1749.11.11 Lydia James at Goshen.
Smedley, Thomas and wife, Abigail, and their children: Sarah, b. 1792.8.31; Thomas, b. 1797.12.13; Joel, b. 1799.11.4.
Smedley, Thomas and wife, Abigail, and their children: Mary, b. 1792.2.25; Elizabeth, b. 1793.4.22; Bennett, b. 1795.1.16; Thomas, b. 1796.11-, d. 1796.11.16; Edith, b. 1798.1.1.
Smedley, George, Jr. of Willistown m. 1757.12.22 Hannah Mattison; Children: Hannah, b. 1758.10.2.
Smedley, Thomas, son of George of Willistown m. 1779.10.14 Susanna Hoopes.
Smedley, Thomas and wife, Sarah, and their children: Francis, b. 1712.7.12; John, b. 1714.11.22; Sarah, b. 1717.5.2.
Smedley, Jeffrey, son of George, dec'd and Hannah of Willistown m. 1787.4.20 Amy Hoopes at Goshen.
Smedley, Ambrose, son of George and Mary, dec'd, of Middletown m. 1789.12.24 Elizabeth Yarnall at Willistown.
Smedley, Francis, son of George, dec'd, and Hannah of Willistown m. 1793.3.22 Dinah Lewis at Goshen and their children: George, b. 1794.1.5, d. 1794.3.30; Samuel, b. 1795.11.28.
Smedley, John, dec'd by 1796 and wife, Susanna of Willistown, and their children: Elizabeth, b. 1773.7.4; Thomas, b. 1774.10.24 m. 1796.3.17 Lydia Hoopes at Willistown; Esther, b. 1776.1.18 m. 1797.2.2 Jacob Rogers at Goshen; John, b. 1777.9.7; Susanna, b. 1779.11.11; Benjamin, b. 1782.1.13; Mary, b. 1783.11.7; Isaac, b. 1786.12.4; Jacob, b. 1789.12.27.
Smedley, Susanna d. 1774.1.2.
Smedley, Joseph and wife, Rebecca, and their children: Lewis, b. 1785.3.14; Eli, b. 1786.12.4; Joseph, b. 1787.3.27; Lydia, b. 1790.7.11; Sarah, b. 1792.8.31; Thomas, b. 1797.12.13; Joll, b. 1799.11.4.
Smith, William, son of George of Goshen m. 1776.6.20 Jane Davies at Goshen.
Spencer, Timothy and wife, Phebe, and their children: Susannah, b. 1730/1.10.28; John, b. 1732.9.25; Sarah, b. 1734.7.20.
Stalker, Thomas, son of Hugh of East Caln m. 1749.4.1 Grace Thomas at Uwchlan.
Starr, Joseph, son of James and Rachel of Charlestown m. 1739.3.16 Rebecca Lewis at Goshen.
Starr, Isaac, dec'd by 1754 of Goshen, yeoman, and his children: Thomas m. 1754.10.3 Jane Ashbridge at Goshen; William m.

1757.11.3 Jane Hoopes at Goshen; Isaac m. 1762.5.13 Elizabeth Ashbridge at Goshen.
Starr, John, son of Jeremiah, dec'd, of Maiden Creek m. 1787.4.23 Phebe Massey at Goshen.
Steel, Andrew of Goshen m. 1758.1.4 Sarah Peirce at Goshen and their children: Jane, b. 1759.4.17.
Stemple, John, son of Leonard and Rebecca of Horsham, Montgomery Co. m. 1786.4.20 Jane Garrett at Willistown.
Taylor, Samuel, son of Abijah and Deborah of Bradford m. 1737.11.12 Mary Smedley at Goshen.
Taylor, James of Goshen m. 1747.1.27 Elizabeth Parker at Goshen.
Taylor, Samuel and Ann, and their children: Jonathan, b. 1721.10.10; Joseph, b. 1723.1.5; James, b. 1726.2.16.
Taylor, Peter d. 1720.9.-.
Taylor, John d. 1720.8-.
Taylor, Isaac and wife, Sarah of East Goshen, and their children: David, b. 1784.11.15, d. 1791.11.5; John, b. 1788.6.15, d. 1795.6.30; Ann, b. 1792.6.13; Jane, b. 1796.1.21; Isaac, b. 1798.9.6.
Thomas, Watkin of Easttown, batchelor, son of Evan and Gwen m. 1728.11.2 Elizabeth Bevan at Newtown.
Thomas, Richard and wife, Grace, of Whiteland, yeoman, and their children: Richard, b. 1713.2.22 m. 1739.2.10 Phebe Ashbridge at Goshen; Hannah, b. 1715.3.16 m. 1743.9.10 James Mendenhall at Uwchlan; Hananh, b. 1716.11.14; Mary, b. 1719.5.14; Grace, b. 1722.7.9.
Thomas, Joseph and wife, Jemima, and their children: Lydia, b. 1719.8.5; Mathau, b. 1721.2.16; Dina, b. 1724.5.20; Joseph, b. 1726.9.29; Priscilla, b. 1727.5.25; Abraham, b. 1729.9.21, d. 1766.9.-, aged 37; James, b. 1732.3.26; Samuel, b. 1741.1.7.
Thomas, Peter and wife, Elizabeth of Willistown, and their children: Jacob, b. 1711.11.12; Sarah, b. 1713.7.2; Peter, b. 1715.9.19; John, b. 1717.8.7 m. 1747.2.30 Rebecca Jones at Uwchlan; Thomas, b. 1719.8.13, d. 1719.11.-; Isaac, b. 1721.4.21; Elizabeth, b. 1723.1.11 m. 1747.8.9 William Lewis at Goshen; Mary, b. 1724.9.23; Rachel, b. 1726.8.13; James, b. 1727.10.29; Lydia, b. 1730.6.15. Elizabeth, wife of Peter d. 1730.6.-.
Thomas, Richard, dec'd by 1749 and wife, Phebe of Whiteland, and their children: Lydia, b. 1740/1.12.4; Grace, b. 1742.11.3 m. 1749.4.1 Thomas Stalker at Uwchlan; Richard, b. 1744.10.30; George, b. 1746/6.12.21; Hannah, b. 1749.5.5; Elizabeth m. 1750.4.28 Jonathan Howell at Uwchlan.
Thomas, Hezekiah, son of Thomas, dec'd, of Newtown m. 1755.12.24 Sarah Camm at Newtown.
Thomas, Jonathan, son of William of Lower Merion m. 1761.11.18 Esther Camm at Newtown.

Thomas, Joseph and wife, Jemima, and their children: Lydia, b.
1719.8.5; Nathan, b. 1721.2.16; Dina, b. 1724.5.20; Joseph, b.
1726.9.29; Priscilla, b. 1727.5.25; Abraham, b. 1729.9.21; James, b.
1738.3.26; Samuel, b. 1741.1.7.
Thomas, Joseph, son of Joseph and Jemima of Willistown m.
1762.12.22 Mary Yarnall at Newtown.
Thomas, Isaac of Willistown, and his children: Nathan m. 1773.11.25
Sarah Scott at Willistown; Hannah m. 1775.11.22 Daniel Sharpless
at Newtown; Enos m. 1778.4.23 Sarah Garrett at Goshen.
Thomas, Enos and wife, Sarah Garrett, and their children: Mary, b.
1779.8.8; Eli, b. 1782.2.12; Isaac, b. 1786.6.7; Enos, b. 1790.8.30.
Thomas, Peter d. 1722.4
Thomas, Elizabeth d. 1730.6.
Thomas, Jacob of Newtown and Sarah, and their children: Thomas, b.
1748.4.12; Philip, b. 1750.10.13 m. 1784.12.2 Hannah Yarnall at
Willistown; Joseph, b. 1754.4.5 m. 1783.10.24 Ann Currey at
Goshen; Jacob, b. 1757.6.9.
Thomas, Philip and wife, Hannah Yarnall, and their children: Jane, b.
1786.10.2; Jehu, b. 1789.3.9; Jesse, b. 1791.10.8; Sarah, b.
1794.11.21; Hannah, b. 1797.12.26; Amos Yarnall, b. 1800.7.25.
Thomas, Isaac and wife, Mary of Willistown and their children: Phebe,
b. 1746.11.12; Enos, b. 1747.11.121; Nathan, b. 1749.10.20; Hannah,
b. 1751.10.31; Isaac, b. 1754.5.12; Mary, b. 1756.8.23, d. 1759.5.-;
Jonathan, b. 1759.10.21, d. 1759.5.-; Townsend, b. 1760.6.4; Thomas,
b. 1763.6.3; Martha, b. 1765.2.22 m. 1789.3.18 John Larkin at
Newtown; Mordecai, b. 1767.7.21 m. 1796.10.20 Lydia Hoopes at
Goshen.
Thomas, Mordecai and wife, Lydia Hoopes, and their children: Isaac, b.
1797.9.16; Ezra, b. 1799.5.17; Emmor, b. 1800.9.13; George, b.
1802.5.25; Jesse, b. 1804.10.27; Hooper?, b. 1806.5.27; Mary Ann, b.
1809.10.30; Lydia, b. 1811.11.23; Eliza, b. 1813.8.7; Mordecai H., b.
1817.12.4.
Thomas, Isaac, Jr. and wife, Hannah, and their children: Beulah, b.
1784.9.13; Mary, b. 1787.13.13; Hannah, b. 1790.1.19; William, b.
1792.6.16.
Thomas, Joseph, son of Joseph and Mary of Willistown m. 1799.5.16
Susanna Yarnall at Willistown.
Thomas, Joseph and wife, Mary, and their children: Nathan, b.
1763.11.18; Dinah, b. 1766.3.3; Francis, b. 1766.3.3; Phebe, b.
1770.7.23; Joseph, b. 1773.4.29; Mary, b. 1776.10.28; Jemima, b.
1780.1.9.
Thomas, Gideon and wife, Phebe, and their children: Sarah, b.
1793.5.2; Robert M., b. 1794.12.10; Ann, b. 1797.1.10.
Thomas, Richard of West Whiteland, son of Richard and Thamzin m.
1799.10.25 Rebecca Malin at Goshen.

Thomas, Sarah d. 1789.10.28,aged 53.
Thomas, Henry d. 1797.9.17, Aged 31.
Thomas, Jemima d. 1766.9.20.
Thomas, Tamer d. 1766.9.21, Aged 34.
Thompson, Moses, son of Peter, dec'd, carpenter m. 1764.6.23 Grace Hoopes at Goshen.
Townsend, Amos, dec'd by 1753 and wife, Mary, and their children: Thomas, b. 1730.16.10 m. 1753.11.2 Sarah Hall at Goshen; Amos, b. 1732.10.9.
Townsend, John, son of John, dec'd, of Westtown m. 1755.6.5 Deborah Jones at Goshen.
Townsend, Samuel, son of Francis and Rachel, dec'd, of Washington Co., Pa., m. 1787.3.22 Priscilla Yarnall at Goshen.
Trego, William and wife, Margaret of Goshen, and their children: Hannah, b. 1724.3.19; William, b. 1725/6.11.8; Margaret, b. 1728.1.28; Benjamin, b. 1730.4.2 m. 1767.7.13 Mary Rattew at Goshen.
Trimble, William of Concord m. 1757.9.15 Phebe Thomas at Uwchlan.
Turner, George of Middletown m. 1750.1.27 Sarah Heayes at Newtown.
Underwood, Joseph of Christianity Hundred, DE, m. 1751.8.30 Elizabeth Vance at Nantmel.
Valentine, Robert, son of Thomas and Mary of New Providence, Philadelphia Co. m. 1747.4.4 Rachel Edge at Caln and their children: Thomas, b. 1748.3.28, d. 1752.3.-; Mary, b. 1750.7.26, d. 1752.3.-; Robert, b. 1752.6.24; Rachel, b. 1754.10.14; Jane, b. 1756,10.25, d. 1757.2.-; Sarah, b. 1757.11.14, d. 1758.4.-; Phebe, b. 1758.6.5.
Vernon, Isaac and wife, Hannah, and their children: Catharine, b. 1737/8.11.28; Mary, b. 1739.6.4; Phebe, b. 1741.2.17; Isaac, b. 1742.1.21; Amos, b. 1745.2.17.
Vernon, Isaac and wife, Hannah, and their children: Susannah, b. 1711.4.8; Rachel, b. 1715.12.20; Isaac, b. 1715.12.19; Hannah, b. 1717.6.16; Nehemiah, b. 1719.10.19; Lydia, b. 1721.2.11; Rebecca, b. 1724.1.1.
Vernon, Hannah, wife of Isaac d. 1729.4.-.
Vernon, Aaron, son of Aaron and Margaret of Newtown m. 1758.10.11 Rachel Evans at Newtown.
Vernon, Gideon of Lower Providence, son of Moses, dec'd, m. 1775.6.21 Phebe Farr at Newtown.
Vore, Christian of Willistown m. 1736/7.1.2 Sarah Thomas at Newtown.
Walker, Isaac and wife, Sarah of Tredyffrin, and their children: Benjamin m. 1769.4.13 Ruth Morris at Newtown; Rachel m. 1769.4.13 Lewis Morris at Newtown; Leah m. 1782.5.22 Abner

Moore at Newtown.

Wall, William, son of John and Mary of Goshen m. 1741 Sept. 25 Mary Haines at Goshen.

Waln, Richard of Philadelphia Co., yeoman m. 1739.2.26 Mary Lewis, widow of Newtown at Springfield.

Waln, Samuel of Goshen m. 1747.9.13 Ann Rushton at Goshen and their children: Jane, b. 1748.7.20; William, b. 1750.3.10; Susanna, b. 1751.10.19; Hannah, b. 1754.3.24; Samuel, b. 1756.9.25; Mary, b. 1760.1.9; Ann, b. 1762.4.13; Joseph, b. 1764.4.4.

Waln, Samuel of Goshen, widower m. 1767.6.11 Sarah Steel at Goshen.

White, Uriah of Willistown m. 1742.10.10 Elizabeth Griffith at Goshen.

Whalen, Dennis and wife, Ann, and their children: Mary, b. 1740.1.28; John, b. 1742.6.19; Catharine, b. 1744.9.23; Phebe, b. 1746.8.21.

Whalen, Dennis and wife, Sarah, and their children: Ann, b. 1750.8.13; Israel, b. 1752.12.13; Isaac, b. 1754.8.3; Sarah, b. 1756.11.20.

White, Thomas, son of Nicholas and Jane of Goshen m. 1751.11.5 Sarah Garrett at Goshen.

White, Thomas of Willistown m. 1764.4.26 Sarah Malin at Goshen.

White, Thomas d. 1784.8.6.

White, Sarah d. 1791.3.10.

White, Nathaniel, son of Nathaniel of Frederick Co., VA m. 1784.3.11 Phebe Smedley at Wallistown.

Williamson, Francis of Londongrove, widower m. 1797.5.30 Mary Hoopes at Londongrove.

Williams, Robert of Uwchlan, and his children: Hannah m. 1723.-.-; John Morgan at Uwchlan; William m. 1723.10.3 Joan Pugh at Uwchlan.

Williams, Ellis and Mary of Goshen, and their children: Ellis m. 1748.2.1 Lydia Haines at Goshen; Mary m. 1744.8.13 Thomas Garrett at Goshen.

Williams, Robert, son of William, dec'd, of Vincent m. 1751.3.30 Margaret Lloyd at Uwchlan.

Williams, Jacob of Uwchlan m. 1756.10.7 Ruth Davies at Uwchlan.

Williams, Isaac of Goshen, m. 1762.4.15 Esther Davies at Goshen.

Williams, Lewis, son of Lewis of Willistown m. 1763.1.13 Miriam Lewis at Goshen.

Williams, Lewis and wife, Ann, and their children: Mary, b. 1721.2.15, d. 1722.8.-; Nathan, b. 1722.8.19.

Williams, Jesse of Goshen, son of Ellis, dec'd, m. 1774.5.5 Sarah Goodwin.

Williams, Ellis and wife, Mary, and their children: Robert, b. 1715.6.29;

GOSHEN MONTHLY MEETING

Esther, b. 1718.11.11; Mary, b. 1720.1.3; Mary, wife of Ellis d. 1753.3.-.
Williams, William and wife, Joann: Robert, b. 1724.1.31; John, b. 1725.9.9; Adino, b. 1727.9.5; Abner, b. 1729.10.19; Rehoboth, b. 1731.9.3.
Williams, John and wife, Jane, and their children: Edward, b. 1718.8.30; Enoch, b. 1723.6.21.
Williams, Ellis, dec'd, and wife, Lydia of Goshen, and their children: Ellis m. 1789.11.19 Jane Garrett at Goshen; Lydia m. 1789.12.9 Griffith Lewis at Goshen.
Williams, Ellis and wife, Jane Garrett, and their children: Lydia, b. 1790.8.19; Mary, b. 1792.9.9; Jesse, b. 1794.11.19; Ellis, b. 1797.11.24.
Williams, William of Vincent d. 1744.7.
Williamson, John and Sarah of Newtown, and their children: Mary, b. 1715.10.11 m. 1732/3.12.28 Abraham Hoopes at Newtown; Sarah, b. 1718.5.28; Margaret, b. 1719.10.17; Alice, b. 1721.4.22 m. 1744.6.29 Bennuel Lownes at Newtown; Esther, b. 1723.2.2. m. 1745.2.24 Samuel Mendenhall at Newtown; Jane, b. 1725.6.30 m. 1743.9.9 Robert Regester at Newtown; John, b. 1726/7.1.21; Daniel, b. 1732.9.10.
Williamson, Abraham, son of William of Thornbury m. 1777.9.18 Esther James at her father's.
Williamson, John and wife, Elizabeth, and their children: Sarah, b. 1753.7.21; John, b. 1755.9.21; Anne, b. 1757.6.15; Hannah, b. 1759.1.5, d. 1761.12.2; Walter, b. 1761.8.3; Elizabeth, b. 1764.1.13; George, b. 1766.4.15, d. 1792.7.5; Enos, b. 1768.6.4; Esther, b. 1770.6.18; Jane, b. 1772.5.24.
Williamson, Walter and wife, of Rebecca, and their children: John, b. 1795.5.16; Rebecca, b. 1796.12.9.
Williamson, John of Newtown, and his children: Elizabeth m. 1787.5.23 Samuel Garrett at Newtown; Esther m. 1787.5.23 Jonah Garrett at Newtown; Jane m. 1796.11.2 William Hibbard at Newtown; Enos m. 1796.12.4 Sarah Lewis at Newtown.
Williamson, Enos and wife, Sarah Lewis, and their children: Hannah, b. 1799.12.27; Adam Buckley, b. 1800.3.31; Azariah Lewis, b. 1802.12.23; Sarah, b. 1805.11.13; Enos, b. 1808.3.16; Walter, b. 1811.1.4; Elizabeth, b. 1813.6.22; Mary, b. 1816.2.17.
Williamson, George, son of John d. 1738.9.-.
Willamson, Sarah d. 1789.5.29.
Williamson, John d. 1794.11.1.
Woodward, Edward of Middletown, widower m. 1722.3.23 Alice Allen, of Newtown, widow at Providence.
Woodward, William of West Bradford, yeoman m. 1762.5.13 Hannah Lewis at Bradford.

Woodward, William, son of William of West Bradford m. 1765.11.28 Lydia Lewis at Bradford.
Wooley, John of Springfield, son of Thomas, dec'd, m. 1773.4.22 Phebe Hoopes at Springfield.
Worrall, William of Marple m. 1759.5.3 Phebe Grubb at Newtown.
Worral, Maris, son of Elisha of Springfield m. 1793.4.11 Rebecca Garrett at Willestown.
Yarnall, Francis, dec'd by 1722 of Willistown, and his children: John m. 1722.9.21 Ann Cropfrock?; Amos m. 1727.3.18 Mary; Moses m. 1726 Oct. 28 Dowse(?); John m. 1728.8.31 Jane Thomas at Newtown; Joseph m. 1736.1.25 Mary Townsend at Springfield; Jane m. 1740.3.7 David Reese, in Newtown.
Yarnall, Peter and wife, Alice, and their children: Francis, b. 1719.7.27; Ann, b. 1721.7.11.
Yarnall, John and wife, Ann, and their children: Sarah, b. 1723/4.1.31; Amos, b. 1725.5.31; John, b. 1725.10.18; Ann, b. 1726/7.12.15.
Yarnall, Moses and wife, Dowse, and their children: David, b. 1728.7.23; Hannah, b. 1730.8.11; Rebecca, b. 1732.5.20; Susanna, b. 1734.2.13, d. 1755.6.-; Moses, b. 1735.8.19, d. 1755.5.-; Phebe, b. 1737.10.6; Enoch, b. 1742.5.5.
Yarnall, Mordecai and wife, Catharine, and their children: Sarah, b. 1734.8.27; Ellin, b. 1736.8.7; Hannah, b. 1738.6.26; Catharine, b. 1741.11.1; Catharine, wife of Mordecai, d. 1741.8.-.
Yarnall, Francis and Mary his wife, and their children: Joseph, b. 1724.12.25; Jane, b. 1725.6.7; Hannah, b. 1718.4.15; Aaron, b. 1726.6.22, d. 1726.11.-. Mary, wife of Francis, d. 1728.11.
Yarnall, Moses and wife, Sarah, and their children: Thomas, b. 1789.6.5; Enoch, b. 1791.2.1, d. 1792; Enos, b. 1795.5.3; Allen, b. 1803.12.3.
Yarnall, Francis d. 1721.
Yarnall, Daniel d. 1726.10.-.
Yarnall, Joseph, son of Francis and Mary Willistown m. 1743.8.7 Jane Haines at Goshen.
Yarnall, Daniel, son of Amos of Willistown m. 1747.10.10 Ann James at Goshen and their children: Joseph, b. 1748/9.11.22; Mary, b. 1750.3.27; Elizabeth, b. 1751.8.6; Sarah, b. 1753.6.7; Amos, b. 1754.11.19; Lydia, b. 1756.5.19; Jonathan, b. 1757.11.13, d. 1759.3.19; Ann, b. 1759.2.21; Susanna, b. 1761.1.7; Aaron, b. 1762.8.23; Rebecca, b. 1764.3.23; Samuel, b. 1765.10.19; James, b. 1769.4.6.
Yarnall, John, son of John of Willistown m. 1749.8.4 Sarah Ellis at Newtown.
Yarnall, Joseph, son of Francis of Willistown m. 1750.3.9

GOSHEN MONTHLY MEETING

Elizabeth Richard at Newtown.
Yarnall, Amos of Willistown m. 1750.12.28 Sarah Garrett at Goshen.
Yarnall, Amos of Willistown and wife, Mary, and their children: Daniel, b. 1727/8.12.15; Amos, b. 1730.8.28 m. 1753.5.17 Jane Hibberd at Goshen; Mary, b. 1734.1.28 m. 1753.11.29 Josiah Garrett at Goshen; Aaron, b. 1738.2.20; George, b. 1745/6.11.12. Mary, wife of Amos Yarnall, d. 1745.11.-.
Yarnell, David m. 1752.10.11 Sarah Moore at Newtown.
Yarnell, Hannah m. 1757.4.13 William Griffith at Newtown;
Yarnall, Amos, jr. and wife, Jane, and their children: Phebe, b. 1754.5.19; Ezra, b. 1756.1.13, d. 1758.9.-; Caleb, b. 1759.1.25; Benjamin, b. 1760.11.20; Hannah, b. 1762.10.5; Amos, b. 1768.3.17; Jane, b. 1769.8.29; Jesse, b. 1774.9.27.
Yarnall, John and Abigail, both dec'd, by 1759 of Wilmington, and their children: Hannah m. 1759.11.22 Thomas Garrett at Goshen; Abigail m. 1759.11.29 Jesse Garrett at Goshen.
Yarnall, Benjamin and wife, Susanna, and their children: Rachel, b. 1796.3.24; Jane, b. 1799.1.22; Truman, b. 1802.3.9; Reuben, b. 1805.9.25; Amos, b. 1809.3.26; Rebecca, b. 1812.4.17.
Yarnall, George, son of Amos of Willistown m. 1767.10.7 Lydia Ashton at Goshen.
Yarnall, Moses, son of Enoch and Susanna of Willistown m. 1788.4.24 Sarah Hall at Willistown.
Yarnall, Amos m. 1727.3.18 Mary Ashbridge, dau of George of Goshen at Goshen.
Yarnall, Sarah d. 1795.2.24.

NEW GARDEN MONTHLY MEETING
Births and Deaths

Bailey, John m. Lydia Wickersham 1753.11.22.
Bailey, John and his children by first wife, unknown: Susanna, b. 1735, d. 1767.6.26, m. Ellis Pusey, 1755.5.31; William, b. no date, m. Mary Musgrove, 1769.10.18; Betty, b. 1741 m. John Ferree 1765.9.18; Hannah, b. 1754.6.16 m. Caleb Pusey 1778.4.8; Sarah, b. no date, m. Aaron Clayton 1779.6.9; Mary, b. no date m. William Farqnhar 1780.10.11; Elisha, b. no date m. Hannah Starr 1785.3.31; Ann, b. no date m. Richard Jones.
Bailey, Thomas and Sarah and their children: Isaac m. Mary Jones 1758.3.9, then Hannah Scarlet 1765.4.17; Mary m. Caleb Hayes; John m. Hannah Pennock 1766.3.8; Thomas, removed to Redstone mm; Jemima m. William Leonard; Ann m. James Powell, removed to Redstone mm; Hannah, m. Isaac Powell; Sarah m. William McNeil. Thomas disowned 1734.28.10 for going out in marriage.
Bailey, Josiah and Sarah and their children: Joel m. Hannah Wickersham 1757.11.24; Lydia m. Jesse Harlan 1774.5.11; Josiah; Sarah.
Bailey, John and Hannah, their children: Alice, b. 1767.2.16 m. Daniel Mercer 1790.11.25 removed to Ohio; Sarah, b. 1768.10.30 m. Francis Carpenter 1795.10.15; Joseph b. 1770.12.27; Moses, b. 1773.5.19 m. Elizabeth Parker; Thomas b. 1777.8.4; Isarel, b. 1780.7.5; John, b. 1783.1.13, d. 1800.8.6; Mary b. 1784.12.8; Hannah, b. 1787.2.25, d. 1808.3.14 m. Caleb Mercer 1807.11.12; Ann, b. 1789.7.5 m. Thomas Galbraith 1822.10.17.
Bailey, Joshua, son of Joel and Betty Bailey, b. 1747.4.20, m. Ann Jackson, dau of John and Sarah Jackson, b. 1755.6.16 m. 1778.5.13 and their children: Lewis, b. 1779.3.20; Phebe, b. 1780.11.29; Sarah, b. 1782.8.8; Reuben, b. 1784.1.22; Joshua, b. 1787.3.14; Joel, b. 1789.7.8; Judith, b. 1791.9.12, d. 1792.6.30.
Ailes, Stephen and his wife, Mary and their children: Hannah, b. 1712.4.3, d. 1725.8.23; William, b. 1714.8.2; Stephen, b. 1717.4.9.
Allen, John, b. 1720.8.2, d. 1754.10.1, son of John and Amy ALLEN of Londongrove and his wife, Hannah, b. 1722.11.4, dau of Shadrach and Phebe Scarlet of Londongrove, and their children: Hannah, b. 1741.7.10 at Londongrove; Emey, b. 1743.12.18 at Londongrove; Ann, b. 1744 or 1746.5.10 at Londongrove; John, b. 1749.3.22 at Londongrove; Samuel, b. 1751.10.21 at Londongrove; Thomas b. 1754.8.25, d. 1754.9 buried at Londongrove.
Bailey, Joel and his wife, Betty b. 1727/8.1.8 of W. Marlborough.
Bailey, John and his wife Mary of W. Marlborough and their child: Susanna, b. 1735.8.17, d. 1767.6.26.
Balderson, John and his wife, Hannah, and their child: Mordecai, b.

1755.1.31.
Balderson, Mordecai and his wife Sarah Michener and their child: Deborah, b. 1757.4.23.
Balderson, Mordecai and his wife, Deborah and their children: Sarah, b. 1778.3.5; Jacob, b. 1779.10.20, d. 1784.6.14; Mordecai, b. 1781.3.3, d. 1784.6.14; Hannah, b. 1782.9.19; Isaiah, b. 1784.3.16, d. 1784.3.17; Jacob, b. 1785.3.12; Deborah, b. 1787.4.29; Mary, b. 1789.1.9; Mordecai, b. 1791.4.18; Katherine, b. 1793.5.10; Joseph, b. 1795.4.9; Jonathan, b. 1797.4.28. The family all moved to Ohio.
Baldwin, Thomas and his wife, Sarah, and their child: Hannah m. Jesse Pennock.
Bernard, Thomas and his wife, Sarah, dau of James and Ann Miller of Newgarden, b. 1727.10.10 and their children: Joshua, b. 1751.12.17; John, b. 1754.2.23; Ann, b. 1756.2.11; Hannah, b. 1757.12.24; Lydia, b. 1758.10.1; Jonathan, b. 1760.10.9; Rachel, b. 1762.12.23; Abner, b. 1765.4.27; Deborah, b. 1768.10.25.
Bassett, Arthur and his wife, Lydia and their children: John, b. 1707.10.28; Arthur, b. 1709.11.7; Thomas, b. 1711.1.16; William, b. 1713.2.13; Richard, b. 1717.10.20.
Beals, John and his wife, Mary, and their children: John, b. 1685.1.20; William, b. 1687.2.1; Jacob, b. 1689.7.28; Mary, b. 1692.4.24; Patience, b. 1695.4.15.
Beals, John, Jr. and his wife, Sarah and their children: Sarah, b. 1713.5.29; John, b. 1717.2.17; Thomas, b. 1719.20.1.14.
Beals, William and his wife, Rebecca and their child: Lydia, b. 1719.6.1.
Beals, Jacob and his wife, Mary and their children: John, b. 1715.7.11; Jacob, b. 1717.7.18; Mary, b. 1719.9.15; William, b. 1721.9.16.
Bennett, William and his wife, Grace and their children: Amos, b. 1790.8.5; Isaac, b. 1791.9.8; Elizabeth, b. 1793.4.27; Jane, b. 1794.9.24; Rachel, b. 1796.4.10; James, b. 1798.2.28; William, b. 1800.10.3; Elizabeth, b. 1805.11.5.
Brooks, David and his wife, Eleanor and their children: Isaac, b. 1726.10.13; David, b. 1726.7.25.
Brown, William and his wife, Dorothy from England and their child: Joseph, b. 1682.4.12, d. 1715.10.30
Brown, William and his wife, Ann of PA and their children: Messer, b. 1685.12.27; Ann, b. 1687.10.1; William, b. 1689.7.21; John, b. 1691.5.3; Richard, b. 1693.1.31; Thomas, b. 1694.11.17.
Brown, William and his wife, Catharine and their children: Samuel, b. 1700.8.12; Samuel. b. 1700.8.12; Mary, b. 1705.4.29.
Brown, Joseph and his wife, Margaret and their children: William, b. 1712.5.18; Joseph, b. 1714.12.16; John, b. 1716.2.30.
Brown, Messer and his wife, Jane and their children: Ann, b. 1711.3.28;

Catherine, b. 1712.10.20; Hannah, b. 1714/5.12.27; Messer, b. 1717.11.11; Jane, b. 1720.4.11; Mary, b. 1722.6.14.
Brown, William, Jr. and his wife, Elizabeth and their children: John, b. 1717.2.27, d. 1723.7.12; Elizabeth, b. 1718.12.16.
Brown, William, Jr. and his wife, Margaret, and their children: William, b. 1722.10.14; Jacob, b. 1724.7.15.
Brown, Richard and his wife, Hannah, and their children: Richard, b. 1718.1.1, d. 1725.3.26; Henry, b. 1720.3.8; William, b. 1722.9.16; John, b. 1724.5.7.
Brown, Jeremiah and Mary, his wife and their children: Jeremiah, b. 1714.12.2; Joshua, b. 1717.3.5; Isaac, b. 1720.3.20.
Brown, Thomas and his wife, Elinor and their children: Nathan, b. 1720.3.24; Thomas, b. 1722/3.1.12.
Brown, Daniel and his wife, Elizabeth and their children: Elizabeth, b. 1718.1.22; Rachel, b. 17--.12.18.
Brown, Thomas and Elinor and their child: Rachel, b. 1727.11.23.
Brown, Hannah, wife of Richard d. 1726.3.14.
Brown, Joseph and his wife, Elizabeth and their children: Sarah, b. 1784.6.25; Mary, b. 1786.3.16; Benjamin, b. 1788.5.7; Hannah, b. 1788.5.7; Elizabeth, b. 1790.6.7; Rebecca, b. 1792.7.7, d. 1792.7.14; Deborah, b. 1793.10.9; Joseph, b. 1796.1.25; Esther, b. 1798.4.9; Rebecca, b. 1800.9.10; Tabitha, b. 1803.6.15; Rachel, b. 1805.11.14.
Brown, Thomas and wife, Mary, and their child: John, b. 1741.5.28.
Buller, Richard and wife, Jane, and their child: Hannah, b. 1732.10.22; John, b. 1734.11.14; Jane, b. 1737.5.22; Richard, b. 1740.12.9, d. 1743.8.12; Elizabeth, b. 1742.9.13; Mary, b. 1744/5.12.28; Lydia, b. 1747.2.27; Sarah, b. 1749.4.29; Susanna, b. 1752.7.29.
Cain, Ann, dau of John and Ann Cain, b. in Cochrdnich, Ireland m. at Newgarden 1722.3.24 James Miller.
Cain, John, son of John and Ruth Cain, b. 1753.12.2 and his wife, Sarah, dau of Nehemiah and Ann Hutton, and their children:Hannah, b. 1783.5.20; Sarah, b. 1785.3.19; John, b. 1787.8.28; Ann, b. 1789.12.26; Robert, b. 1792.5.8, d. 1793.9.16; Ruth, b. 1794.4.23; Robert, b. 1799.3.10.
Canby, Hannah, b. 1753.3.31, widow of Joseph Canby m. Joshua Pusey 1782.11.6.
Carson, Dinah, b. 1744.4.21 at Wilmington.
Carson, George and wife, Hannah, and their children:George, b. 1751.5.23 m. Lydia James, and their children: Hannah, b. 1776.11.22; Sarah, b. 1779.2.3, d. 1779.2.10; George, b. 1780.6.21.
Chalfant, Henry, son of John of W. Marlborough m. Elizabeth Jackson, dau of Thomas of W. Marlborough 1740.8.15, and their children: Jonathan, b. 1743.4.8; Thomas, b. 1745.11.20; Henry, b. 1748.5.1; Ann, b. 1750/1.12.12; Elizabeth, b. 1754.2.2; Jacob, b. 1758.1.11;

NEW GARDEN MONTHLY MEETING 115

Mary, b. 1760.8.8; Abner, b. 1762.11.16; Caleb, b. 1766.2.7.
Chalfant, Henry and his wife, Phebe and their child: Mary, b, 1782.12.6.
Chambers, William, b. 1692.1.17, d. 1761.3.30, son of John and Elizabeth in Yorkshire m. Elizabeth Miller, b. 1704.1.-, d. 1783.2.18 in Ireland, dau of John and Mary Miller on 1729.8.22 at Newgarden, and their children: William, b. 1731.6.8, d. 1735.3.11; Mary, b. 1732.11.27 m. James Woolston 1752.11.16 and Robert Johnson; Deborah, b. 1734.9.6, d. 1760.3.12; Joseph, b. 1735.4.25, d. 1742.6.5; William, b. 1736.4.25, d. 1760.9.27; John, b. 1738.1.4 m. Rebecca Johnson; Hannah, b. 1741.8.14, d. 1747.6.7; Elizabeth, b. 1743.5.14; child, b. 1744.1.23.
Chambers, John and wife, Rebecca and their children: William, b. 1764.1.11; Joshua, b. 1765.12.8; Elisabeth, b. 1768.4.18; Caleb, b. 1770.3.21; Mary, b. 1772.6.29; Sarah, b. 1774.3.24; David, b. 1777.10.5; Phebe, b. 1780.9.26. Rebecca Chambers d. 1790.8.12.
Chambers, Joseph and his wife, Rebecca, and their children: Isaac, b. 1797.5.7; David, b. 1799.2.12; Reuben, b. 1801.7.19; John, b. 1802.12.22; Leah, b. 1804.12.20; Patience, b. 1807.12.26; Jesse, b. 1809.7.7; Joseph, b. 1811.11.1; Joshua, b. 1815.4.12; Rebecca, b. 1815.4.12.
Chandler, William and wife, Ann and their children: Jane, b. 1713.3.1; Lydia, b. 1714.8.2; Samuel, b. 1716.3.7; William, b. 1718.2.20; John, b. 1719.20.1.20; Ann, b. 1721.12.27; Thomas, b. 1724.6.11.
Churchman, John and wife, Hannah, and their children: George, b. 1697.7.13; Dinah, b. 1699.6.7; Susanna, b. 1701.7.13; John, b. 1705.6.4; Thomas, b. 1707.11.16; Miriam, b. 1710.8.25; Edward, b. 1713.9.4; Sarah, b. 1716.3.17; William, b. 1720.11.29.
Clendenon, Isaac, b. 1720/1.11.28 and his wife, Phebe, b. 1731.4.5, d. 1757.5.7 and their children: Robert, b. 1756.1.15; Phebe, b. 1757.4.29.
Coles, William and wife, Mary and their children: William, b. 1705.5.9; Mary, b. 1708.3.4.
Cole, Lydia, dau of Joseph Pusey, wife of Samuel Cole, b. 1758.7.1.
Comfort, Robert, b. 1797.4.25 near Richmond, Indiana and Mary.
Commons, John and his wife, Sarah, and their children: Isaac, b. 1779.11.12; Mary, b. 1781.7.12. Sarah, wife of John d. 1784.9.17.
Cook, Stephen and his wife, Margaret, m. 1759.3.31, and their children: Isaac, b. 1762.6.28; Peter, b. 1764.10.26; John, b. 1767.3.26; Stephen, b. 1769.12.12; Ennion, b. 1773.1.1; Job, b. 1775.7.7; Hannah, b. 1777.9.27.
Curle, John and wife, Deborah, and their children: Benjamin, b. 1749.3.12, d. 1766.9; Mary, b. 1759.1.24; John, b. 1761.5.3.

Darlington, Elizabeth, dau of Abraham and Elizabeth m. Isaac Pyle.
Davis, Elisha and wife, Alice, and their children: John, b. 1785.7.15; Mary, b. 1786.11.15, d. 1786.12.1; Margaret, b. 1790.6.1; Joseph, b. 1790.6.1; Nathan, b. 1792.4.12.
Dixon, Sarah, b. 1732.5.3 m. David Pusey.
Dixon, William, son of Joseph and Sarah Dixon, m. Rebecca, dau of Thomas and Elizabeth Woodward, and their children: Susanna, b. 1767.11.12; Joseph, b. 1769.10.7; Thomas, b. 1771.8.31, d. 1771.9.21; William, b. 1773.3.22; Sarah, b. 1775.4.8, d. 1776.4.30.
Douglas, Jeremiah and wife, Elizabeth and their children: Mary, b. 1742.2.17; Joseph, b. 1743/4.12.4.
Dutton, Robert and wife, Ann and their children: Mary, b. 1708.8.15; Ann, b, 1711.10.10; Robert, 1713.8.26; Elizabeth, 1722.1.25.
Edwards, Jonathan and wife, Isabel and their children: Lydia, b. 1719.6.17; Jane, b. 1721.1.9.
Edwards, John and wife, Mary, b. in Middletown and their children: Moses, b. 1721.2.2.
Edwards, Robert m. Elinor Plummer, and their child: Esther, b. 1724.-.-
Edwards, Moses and wife, Esther and their children: Sarah, b. 1743.12.19; Esther, b. 1745.4.11; Joshua, b. 1746.9.4; Caleb, b. 1748.9.7; Hannah, b. 1750.7.13; Moses, b. 1752.3.10; Mary, b. 1755.5.15; John, b. 1757.12.12; Thomas, b. 1760.3.20; Phebe, b. 1763.6.15; Nathan, b. 1766.2.24.
Elliott, John and wife, Sarah, and their children: Eli, b. 1773.11.1; Hannah, b. 1776.9.7, removed to Pike Creek Monthly Meeting.
Emlen, George and wife, Hannah and their child: Ann, b. 1705.3.19.
England, David, b. 1737.7.19, son of John and Elizabeth England of New Castle, Co., and his wife, Mary, b. 1738.3.17, and their children: John, b. 1764.3.24; Elizabeth, b. 1766.5.30; Isaac, b. 1768.9.12; Israel, b. 1771.2.10; Sarah, b. 1773.3.22.
England, Elizabeth, widow of John England m. Joshua Johnson.
Fairlamb, Hannah, dau of Nicholas and Katharine of Chester b. 1711.9 m. John Hurford.
Farlow, William and his wife, Margaret, and their children: James, b. 1736.1.6 in Londongrove, d. 1745.7.18; Ann, b. 1737.11.30 in Londongrove; Rebecca, b. 1739.10.30 in Londongrove; William, b. 1743.8.31 in Londongrove; Isaac, b. 1745/6.11.11 in Kennett; Margaret, b. 1748.10.27 in Kennett; Jemima, b. 1751.7.30 in Kennett; Elizabeth, b. 1754.4.19 in Londongrove.
Fell, Thomas, b. 1759.5.14 and his wife, Elizabeth, b. 1760.8.5, and their children: Alice, b. 1783.1.14; Letitia, b. 1784.3.27; Sarah, b.

1786.1.8; Cynthia, b. 1789.3.7; Elizabeth, b. 1791.4.27; Joseph, b. 1793.2.25; Thomas, b. 1795.4.2; Lewis, b. 1797.4.7; Rebecca, b. 1800.12.23; Esther, b. 1804.1.20.

Fell, David and his wife, Sarah of New London, and their children: David, b. 1792.11.9; Hannah, b, 1794.8.10.

Fell, Sarah, wife of John d. 1796.3.15 buried at West Grove.

Fisher, Sarah, dau of John and Elizabeth b. 1722.2.11 m. Mordecai Michner.

Flower, Richard, son of Richard and Mary, b. in Lestershire, England m. 1724.12 at Kennett to Abigail, dau of Michael and Dinah Harlan, b. at Center, New Castle Co., DE, and their children: Thomas, b. 1725.10.27, d. 1738.8; Mary, b. 1727.10.14; Richard, b. 1730.7.3; Dinah, b. 1732.10.27, d. 1738.11.

Fred, Joseph, b. 1727.11.27, son of Nicholas and Ann in Birmingham m. 1732.11 to Sarah Holley, dau of Joshua and Mary Holley, of Mill Creek, DE, and their children: Mary, b. 1754.10.10; Ann, b. 1755.11.18; Benjamin, b. 1757.11.13; Joseph, b. 1759.3.23; Joshua, b. 1761.11.25; Thomas, b. 1763.3.13; Nicholas, b. 1765.8.9, d. 1765.12.8.

Gilpin, Thomas and his wife, Mary, and their children: Sarah, b. 1795.2.25; John, b. 1799.4.29.

Good, Thomas, b. 1735.8.14.

Good, Charles and his wife, Jane and their children: Evan, b. 1724.1.23; Charles, b. 1731.3.11.

Grey, Joseph and his wife, Ann and their children: Sarah, b. 1773.12.26, d. 1774.3.18; Elizabeth b. 1776.7.15; Hannah, b. 1779.11.18; William, b. 1782.5.31, d. 1782.6.18; Jacob, b. 1783.10.19; William, b. 1785.11.7, d. 1795.5.28; Ann, b. 1788.7.17; Margaret, b. 1791.6.19; Joseph, b. 1792.8.5.

Grey, Enoch, son of Enoch and Margery GREY and Sarah, dau of Samuel and Hannah SWAYNE, b. 1769.11.8 and their children: Samuel, b. 1794.11.25; Hannah, b. 1796.9.18; Matilda, b. 1798.9.5; Edwin, b. 1800.10.226; Enoch Sewell, b. 1803.11.25; Ezra, b. 1806.9.1; Michajah b. 1808.9.6.

Greenfield, Amos, and his wife, Margaret and their children: Elizabeth, b. 1797.10.17; Benjamin, b. 1799.2.17; Betsy, b. 1801.1.17; Mary Ann, b. 1803.12.11; Margaret, b. 1807.2.22.

Headley, Simon and his wife, Ruth, and their children: Joseph, b. 1698.8.25; Deborah, b. 1710.2.25; Joshua, b. 1703.3.6; Hannah, b. 1709/10.11.16; Simon, b. 1704.12.23, d. 1730/1.11.4; Ruth, b. 1711.12.6; Katharine, b. 1715.2.25; Anna, b. 1717.12.7. All born in Ireland. Ruth Headly, wife of Simon, d. 1750.12.18, buried at New Garden.

Headley, Sarah, dau of Joshua and Mary of Mill Creek b. 1730.8.16.

Headley, John, b. 1724.2.2 and his wife, Margaret, dau of Samuel and Elizabeth Morton and their children: Elizabeth, b. 1751.8.27; Simon, b. 1754.2.6; Emey, b. 1756.1.11; Mary, b. 1759.7.12; Hannah, b. 1762.2.24; Samuel, b. 1767.6.14.

Haines, Joseph and his wife, Dorothy and their children: William, b. 1703.1.3; Sarah, b. 1706.6.24, d. 1716.4.30; Ruth, b. 1709.8.23; Meriam, b. 1711.7.24; Solomon, b. 1713.9.22, d. 1726.9.16; Patience, b. 1715.1.24; Dorothy, b. 1718.11.24, d. 1718/9.7.5.

Halliday, William and his wife, Deborah and their children: Robert, b. 1702.7.16; Rachel, b. 1704.10.25; Jacob, b. 1706.8.18, d. 1721.5.24; Marget, b. 1709.11.13; Sarah, b. 1713.1.24; Deborah, b. 1716.2.28. All born in Ireland.

Hallowell, John and his wife, Lydia and their children: Grace, b. 1780.12.11; Thomas, b. 1782.9.26; John, b. 1787.3.11; Elizabeth, b. 1789.3.14; Joseph, b. 1791.1.7; Lydia, b. 1795.12.5; Jesse, b. 1797.9.1; Margaret, b. 1800.12.29.

Hambleton, John and his wife, Rachel, b. 1762.8.2 and their children: Sarah, b. 1795.7.16; William, b. 1797.6.18; Thomas, b. 1798.6.23; Rachel, b. 1800.12.3; Hannah, b. 1802.7.23; Charles, b. 1800.3.5; Eli, b. 1806.2.9.

Hanbe, William and his wife, Mary and their child: Elizabeth, b. 1721.9.26.

Harlan, George, b. 1724.11.10, in Newlin, d. 1786.9.3 and his wife, Hannah, b. 1723.5.5, dau of Thomas and Abigail Wickersham, E. Marlborough m. at Kennett 1746.10.16 and their children: Dinah, b. 1747.7.16; Ruth, b. 1750.11.31; Mary, b. 1753.3.5; Caleb, b. 1755.5.9; Joshua, b. 1757.7.7; Joel, b. 1764.8.16; Abigail, no date.

Harris, Evan and his wife, Elizabeth and their child: Elizabeth, b. 1719.9.27.

Harrold, Richard and his wife, Mary and their child: Elizabeth, b. 1711.3.10; Mary, b. 1713.1.28; John, b. 1714.10.21; Jonathan, b. 1717.11.20; Mary, b. 1718.9.19; Rachel, b. 1721.2.9.

Harrold, Samuel and his wife, Levinia and their children: Jonathan, b. 1723.3.13.

Harley, Samuel and his wife, Levinia and their children: William, b. 1782.2.18; Sidney, b. 1784.2.5; Ruth, b. 1736.5.19; Thomas, b. 1789.2.23; Levi, b. 1798.1.26; Samuel, b. 1794.9.25.

Harvey, Susanna, dau. of Joshua Pusey, b. 1745.5.11, d. 1768.7.11, buried at Londongrove.

Harvey, Hannah, dau. Of Joshua Pusey, b. 1752.4.21, d. 1807.3.31.

Hayes, Henry and his wife, Elizabeth and their children: Elizabeth, b. 1769.10.13; Phebe, no date.

Hayes, Hannah, dau of William and Jane Hayes, b. 1736.1.1, d. 1799.9.13.

Hiett, Thomas and his wife, Elizabeth and their children:

NEW GARDEN MONTHLY MEETING 119

Katharine, b. 1726.2.26; Ann, b. 1728.1.7, born in Ireland.
Hobson, Joseph, b. 1768.2.14, son of Joseph and Elizabeth and his wife, Ann and their children: Elizabeth, b. 1799.3.17; Martha, b. 1800.11.20; Benjamin, b. 1803.4.17; Joseph, b. 1805.12.22; Francis, b. 1807.12.20; Jacob, b. 1810.6.23; Thomas, b. 1814.1.8; Margaret, b. 1818.11.6.
Hobson, Francis and his wife, Martha of Newgarden and their children: Francis, b. 1720.9.12, d. 1792.9.29; Mary, b. 1724.12.19; John, b. 1726.7.7; Joseph, b. 1731.10.23, d. 1797.12.11; Martha, b. 1738.2.19.
Hobson, Francis d. 1766.9.29 in his 80th year. Martha Hobson d. 1775.11.25 aged 83.
Hobson, Joseph and his wife, Elizabeth and their children: Francis, b. 1768.2.14; Thomas, b. 1769.7.6; Hannah, b. 1772.12.16, d. 1796.7.23; Joseph, b. 1775.3.8; Phebe, b. 1777.11.18.
Holland, Thomas and his wife, Margaret and their child: Margaret, b. Prince George's Co, MD 1730.5.18 m. at Londongrove 1749.10.6 to William Wood, d. 1775.10.29 buried at Londongrove.
Hoopes, Benjamin, son of Jonathan and Elizabeth Hoopes and Elizabeth, his wife, dau of James and Margaret Marshall, b. 1784.10.12. Benjamin Hoopes remarried to Phebe Pennock, b. 1783.7.21, dau of Caleb and Ann Pennock.
Hoopes, Jonathan and his wife, Elizabeth, b. 1751.7.8, dau of William and Margaret Bane and their children: Tomzin, b. 1771.9.10 m. Isaac Richards; William, b. 1773.4.21 m. Ann Alford; Margaret, b. 1774.12.25 Amos Greenfield; Jane, b. 1777.1.17; Israel, b. 1778.10.30 m. Mabel (Jackson) Hadley; Elizabeth, b. 1780.11.27 Reuben Greenfield; Benjamin, b. 1782.8.15 Elizabeth Marshall and Phebe Pennock; James, b. 1784.10.3 Ann Greenfield; Phebe, b. 1788.11.24 William West and Lewis Lamborn; Joel, b. 1788.11.15 Rebecca Thompson; Thomas, b. 1791.3.25 Mary Moore; Susanna, b. 1793.2.2.
Hurford, John, son of John and Elizabeth Hurford, b. 1712.5.14 and his wife, Hannah, b. 1711.9 dau of Nicholas and Katherine Fairlamb of Chester and their children: Samuel, b. 1732.12.28; John, b. 1733/4.11.8, d. 1740.3.7; Joseph, b. 1737.2.12; Isaac, b. 1739.8.4; Elizabeth, b. 1740.10.25; Hannah, b. 1743.12.15; Caleb, b. 1745.12.4; Katherine, b. 1748.1.25, d. 1766.7.6; Eli, b. 1749.12.18, d. 1750.4.19; Sarah, b. 1751.10.18; Nicholas, b. 1754.3.14.
Hurford, Caleb and his wife, Martha and their child: John, b. 1774.8.9.
Hurford, Samuel and his wife, Rachel and their children: John, b. 1760.9.8; Sarah, b. 1763.3.9; Joseph, b. 1765.6.12; Hannah, b. 1768.2.24; Catharine, b. 1770.8.26; Rachel, b. 1773.1.1; Elizabeth, b. 1775.8.5; Samuel, b. 1778.4.23; Ruth, b. 1780.9.3; William, b. 1783.3.2, d. 1783.5.20.

Hurford, Joseph and his wife, Naomi and their children: Hannah, b. 1765.3.5; John, b. 1766.9.3; Ann, b. 1768.9.24; William, b. 1770.8.14; Nathan, b. 1772.12.12; Joseph, b. 1774.12.29; Benjamin, b. 1777.1.22; Thomas, b. 1779.7.26; Samuel, b. 1781.10.5. The family moved to Virginia.

Hutton, Joseph and his wife, Mary and their children: John, b. 1715.6.31; Thomas, b. 1716.12.20; Joseph, b. 1720.5.28; Susanna, b. 1722.3.10; Samuel, b. 1724.2.15; William, b. 1725.12.14; Benjamin, b. 1728/9.12.1; Nehemiah, b. 1731.6.27; Ephraim, no date.

Hutton, Nehemiah and his wife, Sarah and their children: Susanna, b. 1724.11.20; John, b. 1727.2.7.

Hutton, Joseph and his wife, Mary and their children: Benjamin, b. 1723/4.12.1, d. 1797.5.16.

Hutton, William and his wife, Hannah Temple and their child: Elizabeth, b. 1725.1.27, d. 1764.12.15 in Kennett, buried in Newgarden.

Hutton, Henry and his wife, Sarah Nayle and their child: Ann, b. 1740.8.8.

Hutton, Benjamin, d. 1797.5.15 and his wife, Elizabeth Temple, dau of William and Hannah, b. 1735.1.21 and their children: William, b. 1759.7.1; Joseph, b. 1761.9.9.; Mary, b. 1768.2.8.

Hutton, Benjamin and his wife, Ann, dau of Henry and Sarah Nayle, b. 1740.6.6 and their children: Sarah, b. 1767.3.3; Isaac, b. 1769.6.13; Elizabeth, b. 1771.8.28; Hannah, b. 1774.11.17; Caleb, b. 1776.8.12, d. 1777.11.20; Rachel, b. 1778.8.25; Ann, b. 1781.7.9; Lydia, b. 1784.6.4.

Hutton, Nehemiah and his wife, Ann and their children: Sarah, b. 1755.11.18; Elizabeth, b. 1758.1.29.

Hutton, Joseph and his wife, Mary and their child: Thomas, b. 1715.12.20, d. 1786.

Hutton, Evan and his wife, Elizabeth Harris of E. Marlborough and their child: Elizabeth, b. 1719.9.27.

Hutton, Thomas and his wife, Elizabeth Hiett and their child: Katharine, b. 17226.2.26.

Hutton, Thomas and his wife, Elizabeth and their children: Mary, b. 1739.12.14; Joseph, b. 1742.2.29; Ebenezer, b. 1744.4.4, d. 1747.12.26; Thomas, b. 1746.11.11, d. 1746.11.17.

Hutton, Thomas and his wife, Katharine and their children: Hannah, b. 1749/50.1.7; Jesse, b. 1752.7.4; Isaac, b. 1754.9.21, d. 1755.4.23; Hiett, b. 1756.2.12; Thomas, b. 1758.3.9; John, b. 1760.12.19; Samuel, b. 1763.6.25.

Hutton, Hiett and his wife, Sarah at Nottingham and their children: Joshua, b. 1793.3.26; Hannah, b. 1795.1.10; Mary, b. 1797.9.8; Sidnee, b. 1800.5.30; Martha, b. 1802.5.17; Sarah, b. 1804.6.5; Joseph, b. 1706.10.8; Lydia, b. 1808.6.22; Emmer,

b. 1810.11.7.
Jackson, Joseph and his wife, Hannah and their children: Ephraim, b. 1723.6.19, d. 1733.12.16; Alice, b. 1728.3.26, d. 1740.10.21; Rachel, b. 1726.10.11; Joseph, no date.
Jackson, Joseph and his wife, Susanna and their children: Ephraim, b. 1735.3.27; John, b. 1736.7.11; Mary, b. 1738.3.27; Josiah, b. 1739.11.8; Hannah, b. 1741.7.27; Susanna, b. 1743.7.7; Alice, b. 1745.12.1; Sarah, b. 1748.2.6; Samuel, b. 1749.1.15.
Jackson, Samuel and his wife, Mary and their children: Sarah, b. 1728.7.9; Deborah, b. 1730.11.21; Ruth, b. 1733.4.27; Samuel, b. 1739.5.11; Mary, b. 1742.1.31; Jesse, b. 1744.8.10.
Jackson, Isaac of Old Castle, and Ann Evans, dau of Roland Evans of Balling, in the county of Wicklow m. 1696.11.29 at Ballenderry and their children: Rebekah, b. 1697.1.23 at Old Castle; Thomas, b. 1696.11.9 In Ireland; Isaac, b. 1701.7.1, d. 1701.12.15 at Old Castle; Alice, b. 1703.8.29 at Gilbon; William, b. 1705.2.24 at Clonerany; Mary, b. 1705.2.24 at Clonerany; Jarries, b. 1708.2.10 at Baltimore; Isaac, b. 1710.3.15 at Baltimore; John, b. 1712.10.16 at Baltimore; Isaac, b. 1715.1.13 at Baltimore.
Jackson, James and his wife, Mary and their children: Joshua, b. 1776.3.81; Rachel, b. 1778.2.20; Sarah, b. 1779.7.2; Ann, b. 1782.2.2; Mary, b. 1784.2.3; Thomas, b. 1786.10.4; Mary, b. 1769.1.16.
Jackson, Mary, wife of James d. 1789.1.20 aged 31.
Jackson, John and his wife, Mary and their child: Elizabeth, b. 1720.2.25.
Jackson, Thomas, JR. and his wife, Lydia and their children: Ann, b. 1738.12.19; Caleb, b. 1740.7.2; Mary, b. 1742.2.27; John, no date.
Jackson, John and his wife, Sarah and their children: Rachell, b. 1740.11.2; Isaac, b. 1741.10.29.
Jackson, Thomas d. 1727.6.9.
Jackson, Hannah, wife of Joseph d. 1728.6.21.
Jackson, Samuel of Marlborough d. 1745.6.9.
Jackson, Mary, formerly widow of Samuel Jackson d. 1757.10.4 buried at Newgarden.
Jackson, Isaac and his wife, Mary and their children: Thomas, b. 1731.4.22; James, b. 1733.12.4; Katharine, b. 1736.2.6; William, b. 1738.5.6; Isaac, b. 1740.12.4; Nathaniel, b. 1743.12.27; Elizabeth, b. 1745.8.10; Ruth, b. 1748.12.25.
Jackson, William, b. 1705.2.24, son of ISAAC and Ann Jackson at Clonerany, Ireland, d. 1785.11.24 m. 1732.9.9. at Newgarden to Katharine, dau of James and Catharine Miller, b. 1713.1.30 in Ireland, d. 1786.4.2, buried at Newgarden and their children: Isaac, b. 1734.7.2; James, b. 1700.11.0; Ann, b. 1739.5.19; Elizabeth, b. 1741.11.19, d. 1742.2; Thomas, b. 1743.6.8, d. 1745.6.12; William, b. 1746.5.14; John, b. 1748.11.9; Catharine, b. 1752.4.10, d. 1754.5.16;

Catharine, b. 1754.10.12; Hannah, b. 1757.5.15.

Jackson, John, son of Isaac and Ann, b. 1712.10.16 at Ballastore, d. 1791.5.31 m. 1740.2.17 to Sarah, dau of James and Rachel Miller of Kennett, b. 1723.4.30 and their children: Rachel, b. 1741.11.28, d. 1765.2.24; Isaac, b. 1742.10.29; Hannah, b. 1745.1.16; John, b. 1746.11.16, d. 1794.1.1; Sarah, b. 1750.3.4, d. 1791.10.14; James, b. 1752.8.1; Ann, b. 1755.6.17; Thomas, b. 1757.11.4.

Jackson, Isaac, b. 1734.7.2 son of William and Katherine and Hannah, b. 1741.7.27 m. 1762.5.13 and their children: Joseph, b. 1763.2.13; William, b. 1764.3.1; Mary, b. 1766.2.8; Hannah, b. 1767.12.13; Katherine, b. 1769.12.27, d. 1771.7.24; Katherine, b. 1771.8.22; Susannah, b. 1773.10.23; Isaac, b. 1775, 10.1; Phebe, b. 1777.7.7; Alice, b. 1779.6.23; Rebecca, b. 1781.12.13; Samuel, b. 1783.8.3.

Jackson, John, son of William and Katherine, b. 1748.11.9 and Mary, dau of Joel and Hannah Herlin, b. 1733.3.5 and their children: Joel, b. 1776.10.20; Israel, b. 1779.7.4; Isaiah, b. 1781.12.3; Hannah, b. 1784.7.17; Lydia, b. 1787.7.6; William, b. 1789.11.7; Katherine, b. 1792.1.27.

Jackson, John, son of John and Sarah, b. 1746.11.16 and his wife, Susanna, b. 1743.7.7, dau of Joseph and Susanna (Miller) Jackson and their children: Rachel, b. 1769.9.15; Sarah, b. 1771.4.3; Alice, b. 1773.9.3, d. 1776.6.30; Susanna, b. 1775.7.27; John, b. 1777.11.13; Joseph, b. 1779.3.25; Samuel, b. 1782.6.20; Thomas, b. 1788.5.15.

Jackson, Caleb, son of Thomas and Lydia, b. 1740.7.2 and his wife, Hannah, dau of Joseph and Deborah Bennett m. 1765.10.3 and their children: Lydia, b. 1765.6.25; Deborah, b. 1767.10.1, d. 1767.10; Joseph, b. 1768.9.13, d. 1770.10; Mary, b. 1770.7.2, d. 1770.10; Thomas, b. 1771.8.13, d. 1771.9; Jacob, b. 1772.10.1; Ann, b. 1774.7.31; Esther, b. 1776.5.20; Caleb, b. 1778.4.8; Joshua, b. 1780.3.14; Thomas, b. 1782.3.18, d. 1783.10; William, b. 1784.4.14.

Job, Andrew and his wife, Elizabeth and their children: Jacob, b. 1694.5.3; Thomas, b. 1695.9.15; Mary, b. 1698.1.27; Enoch, b. 1700.11.7; Abraham, b. 1702.6.14; Caleb, b. 1704.5.26; Joshua, b. 1706/7.1.2; Hannah, b. 1708.8.24; Patience, b. 1710.7.2. Andrew Job d. 1722.4.5.

Johnson, James and his wife, Mary and their child: Abigail, b. 1724.5.1.

Johnson, Robert and his wife, Katharine and their children: Hannah, b. 1735.6.22; Simon, b. 1737.10.14; Caleb, b. 1740.3.22; Lydia, b. 1742.5.4; Stephen, b. 1744.8.28; Jonathan, b. 1748.1.6; Isaac, b. 1750.4.14.

Johnson, Sarah, dau of Robert d. 1718.5.22.

Johnson, Joshua, son of Robert and Margaret (Berthwaite) Johnson, b.

NEW GARDEN MONTHLY MEETING 123

1696.7.9 at Coleboy in county of Wicklow, Ireland and his wife, Sarah, dau of Gayen and Margaret Miller, b. 1704.9.1 at Kennett, d. 1749.6 and their children: James, b. 1725.3.17; Lydia, b. 1727.1.1; Margaret, b. 1729.5.10, d. 1733.9; William, b. 1731.7.23; Sarah, b. 1733.9.11; Joshua, b. 1735.10.22; Hannah, b. 1738.2.9; Robert, b. 1740.4.5; Dinah, b. 1742.5.22, d. 1760.2.8; Rebecca, b. 1744.12.18, d. 1791.4.24; David, b. 1747.7.23.

Johnson, Joshua and his wife, Elizabeth, widow of John England m. 1751.2.10 and their children: Joseph, b. 1752.4.4; Elizabeth, b. 1755.4.5.

Johnson, Joseph, son of Joshua and Elizabeth Johnson m. 1774.11.24 to Rachel, dau of Robert and Ruth Miller and their children: Isaac, b. 1775.6.5; Ruth, b. 1778.5.4, d. 1778.8.10; Joshua, b. 1779.8.13; Rachel, b. 1781.8.1; William, b. 1782.11.10.

Johnson, Jonathan and his wife, Elizabeth and their children: William, b. 1772.11.10; Jonathan, b. 1775.11.10; Joanna, b. 1778.5.20, d. 1795.9.6; Hannah, b. 1780.8.18; Hadly, b. 1782.7.6; Isaac, b. 1784.11.4; Lewis, b. 1788.3.29; Joshua, b. 1791.6.10, d. 1795.12.28; Robert, b. 1792.12.17; Richard, b. 1796.9.8.

Johnson, Joseph and his wife, Sarah and their children: Rachel, b. 1798.10.23; Ruth, b. 1800.7.12; Rebecca, b. 1802.1.9; Mary, b. 1804.4.17; Benjamin, b. 1806.8.11; William, b. 1808.8.9; Joseph, b. 1810.8.11; Davies, b. 1812.11.5; Sarah, b. 1814.12.11; Jane, b. 1817.10.16.

Johnson, Isaac and his wife, Lydia and their children: Katharine, b. 1772.10.3; Reuben, b. 1775.12.13; Isaac, b. 1778.6.22; Hadley, b. 1780.5.24; Lydia, b. 1782.9.24; Ruel, b. 1784.8.7; Zillah, b. 1786.4.23.

Jones, Joseph and his wife, Patience and their children: Judith, b. 1718.5.1; Mary, b. 1720.4.2; Charity, b. 1725.8.27.

Jones, Henry and his wife, Eleanor, widow of James Lindley and their child: Sarah, b. 1732.11.6.

Jones, Joseph, d. 1783.8.10 and his wife, Rachel and their children: William, b. 1776.12.6; Lydia, b. 1780.5.5; Mary, b. 1783.1.26.

Jones, John and his wife, Hannah of Marlborough and their children: Joel, b. 1786; William, b. 1787.10.11, d. 1789.5.6.

King, James and his wife, Isabel and their children: Mary, b. 1710.12.19; Margaret, b. 1712.10.20; Michael, b. 1714.10.30; Thomas, b. 1716.7.28; Jane, b. 1718.9.19; Vincent, b. 1720.5.5; Hannah, b. 1722.7.3.

Lamborn, Robert, son of Josiah and Ann, b. in Berkshire, Old England and his wife, Sarah, dau of Francis and Elizabeth Swayne, b. in Berkshire, Old England, m. E. Marlborough, Chester Co, 1722.8.5 and their children: Robert, b. 1723.6.3; William, b. 1725.10.31; Ann, b. 1728.8.8; Elizabeth, b. 1730.11.8; Francis, b. 1733.1.8; John, b. 1736.12.15; Thomas, b. 1738.3.9; Josiah, b. 1738.3.9;

Sarah, b. 1741.2.21.
Lamborn, Thomas, son of Robert m. 1762.4.1 to Dinah, b. 1744.4.21 dau of Richard and Martha Carson at Wilmington and their children: Richard, b. 1763.12.10; Parmena, b. 1766.8.4; Levi, b. 1769.7.21; Isaac, b. 1772.8.17, d. 1773.3.2; Thomas, b. 1774.7.22; Miriam, b. 1776.8.18; Jonathan, b. 1778.8.7; Jacob, b. 1782.10.19; Ezra, b. 1786.7.14.
Lamborn, Josiah and his wife, Sarah and their children: Joseph, b. 1767.9.24; Samuel, b. 1769.4.4; Susanna, b. 1771.1.22; Josiah, b. 1773.1.2; Isaac, b. 1775.12.8; John, b. 1778.2.14; Alice, b. 1780.8.19; Sarah, b. 1782.11.25; Ephraim, b. 1784.11.15; Hannah, b. 1789.3.1.
Lewis, Mary, b. 1715/6, d. 1760.8.22 dau of Ellis and Elizabeth, m. Joshua Pusey, buried at Londongrove.
Lewis, Alice, b. 1779.6.23 dau of Isaac and Hannah Jackson.
Lightfoot, Michael and his wife, Mary and their children: Sarah, b. 1707.4.30; Elinor, b. 1708.10.16; Mary, b. 1710/11.1.20; Katharine, b. 1714.6.12; Thomas, b. 1717.5.16; William, b. 1720.3.22. All born in Ireland.
Lindley, James and his wife, Eleanor and their children: Thomas, b. 1706.2.25; Rachel, b. 1707.5.11; James, b. 1709.4.30; Robert, b. 1712.4.30; Margery, b. 1712.4.30; William, b. 1714.12.20, d. 1726.10.26; Alice, b. 1716.2.25; Mary, b. 1717.9.4; Jonathan, b. 1719.3.11; Elizabeth, b. 1720.8.4; Hannah, b. 1723.1.11; Elinor, b. 1727.8.1.11. All born in Ireland.
Lindley, Thomas and his wife, Ruth and their children: Katharine, b. 1732.9.22; James, b. 1735.9.22; Simon, b. 1738/9.1.5; Thomas, b. 1740.8.7; William, b. 1742.12.27.
Lindley, Jonathan and his wife, Deborah and their children: Jacob, b. 1744.9.18; James, b. 1746.10.18; Jonathan, b. 1750.9.18; Deborah, b. 1753.12.26.
Lindley, James, Sr. d. 1726.10.13 at Newgarden.
Littler, Samuel and his wife, Rachel and their children: John, b. 1708.3.28; Joshua, b. 1710/1.1.10; Samuel, b. 1712/3.12.7; Rachel, b. 1715.8.21, d. 1726.1.12; Minshall, b. 1718.2.2; Sarah, b. 1721.6.24.
Maris, Katharine, dau of John and Susanna b. 1708, d. 1773.10.23 m. John Pusey 1734.
Maris, Martha, dau. of John and Katharine, b. 1750.6.8.
Marshall, Elizabeth, dau of James and Margaret b. 1784.10.5 m. Benjamin Hoopes.
Mason, Benjamin and his wife, Sarah and their children: George, b. 1783.5.17; Benjamin, b. 1785.6.19; Jane, b. 1788.9.3; Mary, b. 1791.1.3; Sarah, b. 1793.3.9.
Mason, George and his wife, Susanna and their children: William, b. 1779.9.27; George, b. 1782.1.21; Rachel, b. 1782.10.16; Susanna, b. 1785.5.18.

Mickle, Robert and his wife, Mary and their children: Ann, b. 1724.8.7; John, b. 1736.8.12; Sarah, b. 1739.3.17; Jane, b. 1741.9.29.

Milhener, Mordecai, son of William and Mary Milhener m. Sarah, his wife, b. 1722.2.11, dau of John and Elizabeth Fisher and their children: Barak, b. 1754.3.17; Deborah, b. 1757.4.23; Mordecai, b. 1759.1.28.

Milhener, Barak and his wife, Jane, b. 1748.11.13, dau of John and Ann Wilson and their children: Alice, b. 1781.2.25; John, b. 1785.9.15; Hannah, b. 1788.6.9; Ann, b. 1789.10.24; Sarah, b. 1791.11.27.

Milhener, William, b. 1788.7.13, son of Joseph and Anna m. Hannah, and his wife, b. 1783.5.20, dau of John and Sarah Cain.

Milhener, Joseph and his wife, Ann and their children: Martha, b. 1783.6.13; b. Abie, b. 1785.8.10; William, b. 1788.9.13; Joseph, b. 1791.8.22, d. 1793.3.18; Jesse, b. 1796.9.26.

Milhener, Jesse, son of Joseph and Anna b. 1795.9.26 m. Rebecca Fell, dau of Thomas and Elizabeth Fell.

Milhener, Mordecai and his wife, Alice, dau of Ralph and Anne Dunn, b. 1762.7.7 and their children: Robert, b. 1787.3.3; Lydia, b. 1788.11.13; Phebe, b. 1790.12.18; Ezra, b. 1794.11.24; Joseph, b. no date; Anna, b. no date, d. 1796.7.29.

Miller, Joseph and his wife, Ann and their children: John, b. 1725.10.30; Isaac, b. 1727.3.2.

Miller, James and his wife, Rachel and their children: Sarah, b. 1723.4.30; Deborah, b. 1725.9.14; James, b. 1728.10.30; Jesse, b. 1730.11.30.

Miller, James and his 2nd wife, Rachel and their children: Thomas, b. 1734.3.28; Benjamin, b. 1736.6.10; Katharine, b. 1738/9.1.24.

Miller, Joseph and his wife, Jane and their children: Samuel, b. 1738/9.1.11.

Miller, Joseph d. 1727.7.30.

Miller, Rachel, wife of James Miller d. 1748.12.23.

Miller, James, son of John and Mary, b. 1693.1 near Charlemont in county of Ardimah, Ireland m. 1722.3.24 at Newgarden to Ann, dau of John and Ann Caras, b. in county of Ardimah and their children: Mary, b. 1724.3.17; Ann, b. 1726.1.3; Sarah, b. 1727.10.10; John, b. 1730.2.20; Joseph, b. 1732.3.17; Susannah, b. 1734/5.1.11; Hannah, b. 1737.2.20; William, b. 1739.10.10; James, b. 1745.5.28.

Miller, William, b. 1698.2, son of John and Mary of Grange Monthly Meeting, Terone Co., Ireland and Ann, dau of George and Hannah Emelen, b. 1705.3.19 at Philadelphia m. 1732.4.15 at Philadelphia and their children: John, b. 1732/3.1.24, d. 1755.6.19; Hannah, b. 1734.10.19, d. 1759.3.6; William, b. 1737.8.5, d. 1791.1.16; Mary, b. 1741.7.19, d. 1776.10.17; Ann, b. 1743.2.25; Joshua, b. 1746.2.3, d. 1748.7.3; Ann, b. 1775.12.18, d. 1777.7.1;

Mary, b. 1778.8.12; Rebecca, b. 1780.6.24.
Miller, Isaac and his wife, Hannah and their children: Lydia, b. 1751.11.4; Ann, b. 1753.10.10; William, b. 1755.8.13; Thomas, b. 1757.3.8; Hannah, b. 1759.7.2; Isaac, b. 1761.10.18; Sarah, b. 1764.2.30, d. 1761.6.5; Joseph, b. 1765.4.8; John, 1766.8.8; Caleb, b. 1770.6.7.
Miller, Elizabeth, b. 1704.1, dau of John and Mary in Ireland, d. 1783.2.78.
Miller, Sarah, b. 1714.9, dau of Grifen and Margaret, d. 1749.6.
Miller, Katharine, dau of James and Catharine, b. at Timakoe in Kildare, Co., Ireland 1713.1.30, d. 1781.4.2, m. William Jackson 1723.9.9.
Millhouse, Thomas and his wife, Sarah and their children: John, b. 1722.1.8; James, b. 1727.7.21; Thomas, b. 1731.2.27; Robert, b. 1733.11.26; Sarah, b. 1736.4.3; William, b. 1738.6.12. All born in Ireland.
Millhouse, Phebe d. 1785.8.18, dau of Thomas and Elizabeth.
Moode, Hannah d. 1791.9.23, dau of Alexander and Rebecca E. Fellowfield.
Moore, David and his wife, Martha and their children: David, b. 1769.11.10; Mary, b. 1771.9.1; Joseph, b. 1773.7.16; Hannah, b. 1777.3.15; Rachel, b. 1778.5.14; Jacob, b. 1781.7.14; Caleb, b. 1785.12.26; Joshua, b. 1785.12.26; Jesse, b. 1789.3.24; Sarah, b. 1792.1.26
Moore, David, JR. and his wife, Martha Sharpless and their children: Mary, b. 1792.10.13; Lydia, b. 1795.2.7; William, b. 1796.7.22; Sidney, b. 1798.1.29; Zeba, 1800.1.16; Esther, b. 1801.9.11; Sarah, b. 1803.9.13; Hibberd, b. 1806.3.10; Hannah, b. 1808.9.14; Sharpless, b. 1809.8.23, Isaac, b. 1811.11.14.
Moore, Joseph and his wife, Jane and their children: Ann, b. 1757.8.29; Rachel, b. 1759.7.10; Phebe, b. 1761.5.24; Ruth, b. 1763.1.23; Jane, b. 1764.2.17; Joseph, b. 1767.4.11; Mary, b. 1769.6.3; William, b. 1771.2.24; Joshua, b. 1774.3.15; David, b. 1776.5.30; Dinah, b. 1778.4.5. Jane Moore, wife of Joseph Moore d. 1779.11.15.
Morton, Samuel, son of William and Elinor, b. in parish of Kilmore, County of Ardimah, Ireland m. at Bellshagan Monthly Meeting 1728.2.6 to Eliza, dau of John and Mary Blackburn, b. county of Ardimah, Ireland and their children: Margaret, b. 1727/8.10.1; John, b. 1729.4.28, d. 1741.9; Samuel, b. 1732.7.27; William, b. 1734/5.1.9; Mary, b. 1737.9.9.; Thomas, b. 1740.7.6. Samuel Morton d. 1766.3.20. Eliza, his wife d. 1763.6.12.
Morton, Samuel, b. 1732.7.27 and his wife, Hannnah, and their children: Benjamin, b. 1765.9.26; Samuel, b. 1766.12.11; Thomas, b. 1768.10.12; William, b. 1770.3.11; Hannah, b. 1771.6.13; Elizabeth,

b. 1773.2.3; Sarah, b. 1775.2.25; Ann, b. 1776.11.11; Mary, b. 1779.4.7.
Kneel, Henry and his wife, Sarah and their child: Ann, b. 1740.8.8 m. 1766.5.22 to Benjamin Hutton.
Pain, Josiah and his wife, Martha and their children: Josiah, b. 1716.8.3; Maray, b. 1718.2.7; Mathew, b. 1719.3.20; Alice, b. 1720.10.22; Martha, b. 1722.10.10; Elizabeth, b. 1724.12.5; Ruth, b. 1724.2.27 [sic]; George, b. 1728.10.4.
Parker, Thompson, b. 1737.3.10 in Philadelphia, son of Alexander and Sarah, m. Sarah, b. 1736.4.3, dau of Thomas and Sarah Mathews at Newgarden 1762.9.16 and their children: George, b. 1763.11.2; Alexander, b. 1772.3.30 Thomas, b. 1774.5.10.
Parsons, Henry, son of Henry and Margaret, b. 1721.12.7.
Passmore, George, son of John and Mary, b. 1719.2.23 in Berkshire, England and Margaret, dau of John and Magdalen Stroud, b. 1723.9.18 at W. Marlborough m. 1742.7.10 at Londongrove and their children: John, b. 1743.7.2, d. 1791.3.12; George, b. 1748.7.28; Margaret, b. 1751.3.11; Mary, b. 1753.12.18; Thomas, b. 1756.3.7; Elizabeth, b. 1759.3.13; Margery, b. 1762.2.24; Ann, b. 1764.6.6.
Passmore, John and his wife, Phebe and their children: Mary, b. 1766.1.7, d. 1767.1.1; Margaret, b. 1767.4.26; Susanna, b. 1768.12.16, d. 1769.12.17; Susanna, b. 1771.12.9, d. 1777.8.27; Ellis, b. 1771.3.1; Margery, b. 1772.10.23; Hannah, b. 1774.6.16; Mary, b. 1776.11.9; Lydia, b. 1778.6.18; Phebe, b. 1780.2.2; Sarah, b. 1781.12.52; George, b. 1783.7.20; Elizabeth, b. 1785.10.14.
Passmore, George, b. 1748.7.28, son of George and Margaret and his wife, Mary, dau of Levis and Ruth Pennock and their children: Levis, b. 1777.2.17; Margaret, b. 1778.4.26; Abram, b. 1779.11.14; John, b. 1781.9.20; William Pennock, b. 1784.1.21; Rachel, b. 1785.9.3; George S., b. 1788.3.22; Pennock, b 1790.8.2; Joseph, b. 1794.2.8; Mary, b. 1795.11.21; Thomas, b. 1799.7.4; Imlah, b. 1802.8.26.
Pennock, Joseph, b. 1715.9.15, son of Joseph and Mary of W. Marlborough and his wife, Sarah, b. 1725.8.11, d. 1775.11.22, dau of Joseph and Mary Taylor, E. Marlborough and their children: Mary, b. 1743.12.23, d. 1744; Jesse, b. 1745.5.15; Hannah, b. 1747.5.15; Hannah, b. 1747.9.9; Joseph, b. 1750.6.7, d. 1770.4.16; Jacob, b. 1753.2.9; d. 1768.7.31; Levis, b. 1756.1.20, d. 1760.4.6; Isaac, b. 1761.6.3, d. 1765.9.9; George, b. 1762.5.25; Sarah, b. 1765.10.23, d. 1776.5.23; Isaac, b. 1767.1.16.
Pennock, Levis and his wife, Ruth and their children: John, b. 1754.10.26; Mary, b. 1756.12.11; Hannah, b. 1759.6.14; Abraham, b. 1761.7.30; William, b. 1763.11.27, d. 1784.1.26; Sarah, b. 1766.4.10, d. 1789.5.19; Ann, b. 1768.4.10; Joseph, b. 1770.6.21; Elizabeth, b.

1772.7.6.

Pennock, Caleb and his wife, Ann and their children: Phebe, b. 1773.7.21; Grace, b. 1777.5.17; Alice, b. 1778.5.23; Elizabeth, b. 1779.12.3.

Pennock, Caleb, son of William and Alice of E. Marlborough and his wife, Ann, dau of James and Elizabeth Thompson, Mill Creek, DE and their child: Samuel, b. 1754.11.23.

Pennock, Samuel, son of William and Alice and his wife, Mary, b. 1759.7.12, dau of John and Margaret Hadley and their children: Margaret, b. 1780.3.15; Simon, b. 1781.9.27.

Pennock, Jesse, b. 1745.5.15, son of Joseph and Sarah Pennock and his wife, Hannah, dau of Thomas and Sarah Baldwin and their children: Joseph, b. 1773.1.27; Sarah, b. 1774.9.20; Hannah, b. 1776.10.14; Thomas, b. 1779.7.4; Mary, b. 1783.4.21.

Phillips, John and his wife, Lydia and their children: Mahlon, b. 1780.7.27; William, b. 1785.10.25; Deborah, b. 1789.2.10; Sarah, b. 1791.6.5, d. 1792.1.10; Isaac, b. 1794.2.6; Jediah, b. 1796.3.17, d. 1798.6.2; John J., b. 1802.11.2.

Piggott, John and his wife, Rebecca and their children: Mary, b. 1706.6.2; Rebecca, b. 1707.10.1; Hannah, b. 1709.8.14; Margery, b. 1715.6.30; John, b. 1717.2.18; Samuel, b. 1718.6.11; Elizabeth, b. 1720.1.10.

Piggott, Henry, b. 1738.7.13, son of John and Rachel in Cecil Co., MD to Hannah, b. 1742.8.25 in Newlin, dau of Thomas and Mary Pife m. 1760.4.10 and their children: Rachel, b. 1761.3.27 at E. Nottingham; Hannah, b. 1763.3.29 at Newgarden; Moses, b. 1765.2.18 at Newark.

Plummer, Robert and his wife, Elinor born at the Hook, m. 1743.3.4 at Londongrove and their child: Esther, b. 1744.

Powell, Evan and his wife, Mary and their child: Sarah, b. 1714.6.1. Mary Powell, wife of Evan, d. 1731.2.2.17.

Preston, David and his wife, Judith and their children: Isaac Hollingsworth, b. 1798.1.10; Eliza, b. 1799.11.29; Hannah, b. 1801.11.3; Sylvester Bills, b. 1804.8.23.

Preston, Joseph, b. 1748.1.11., son of William and Deborah and his wife, Rebecca, b. 1744.11.30, d. 1790.3.7 and their children: William, b. 1770.11.6; Jonas, b. 1772.10.22; David, b. 1774.9.20; Rachel, b. 1776.9.1; Joseph, b. 1779.3.8, d. 1786.1.20; Mahlon, b. 1781.2.8; Deborah, b. 1783.8.4; Sarah, b. 1783.8.4, d. 1786.1.25; Amos, b. 1786.7.15.

Preston, Joseph and his wife, Anna, dau of Nathaniel Samms.

Pugh, Jesse and his wife, Catharine and their children: Isaac, b. 1794.11.5, d. 1797.8.24; Hannah, b. 1796.10.1, d. 1796.11.6; Mary, b. 1798.1.21, d. 1798.7.6; Isaac, b. 1799.10.24, Sarah, b. 1800.10.6; David, b. 1803.1.14, d. 1803.9.13.

NEW GARDEN MONTHLY MEETING

Pugh, Ann, wife of Cabel, Sr. d. 1725.12.5 buried at Londongrove.
Pusey, Cabel, d. 1736.4.14, husband of Prudence.
Pusey, William and his wife, Elizabeth and their children: Elizabeth, b. 1716.11.14; Jane, b. 1719.10.2. Other children listed in Chester records.
Pusey, Caleb, son of Caleb and Prudence, E. Marlborough and their children: Caleb, b. 1713.9.30; Robert, b. 1715.10.16; Thomas, b. 1718.6.24; Margaret, b. 1720.8.16; Ann, b. 1723.4.2; David, b. 1726.4.19.
Pusey, John, b. 1708, d. 1766.4.17, son of William and Elizabeth of Chester Co., and his wife, Katharine, b. 1708, d. 1773.10.13, dau of John and Susanna Maris of Chester Co., and their children: James, b. 1735.5.3; Lydia, b. 1736.11.13; John, b. 1738.11.1, d. 1783.9.24; Samuel, b. 1741.1.27, d. 1754.3.1; George, b. 1743.3.12; Jane, b. 1746.3.30; Nathan, b. 1748.5.17; Susanna, b. 1750.10.16.
Pusey, Joshua, b. 1714.11.9, d. 1760.8.16, son of William and Elizabeth of Chester Co., and his wife, Mary, b. 1715.1.6, d. 1760.8.22, dau of Ellis and Elizabeth Lewis of Concord m. 1734.8.39 at Kennett and their children: Ellis, b. 1735.6.21; William, b. 1736.8.26, d. 1786.9.18 at Philadelphia; Joshua, b. 1738.9.19; Elizabeth, b. 1740.5.17, d. 1783.9.30; Mary, b. 1742.6.8; Susanna, b. 1745.5.11, d. 1768.7.1; Robert, b. 1746/7.12.15, d. 1747.6.12; Phebe, b. 1748/9.12.7, d. 1785.11.21; Hannah, b. 1752.4.31; Lewis, b. 1754.3.4; Lydia, b. 1755.7.2,
Pusey, James and his wife, Rachel and their children: John, b. 1762.10.28; Isaac, b. 1765.2.3.
Pusey, Thomas, son of Caleb and Prudence, b. 1718.6.24 and Mary, his wife, b. 1728.3.29, dau of William and Elizabeth Swayre m. 1748.4.15 and their children: Prudence, b. 1749.1.29; Caleb, b. 1750.10.21; Jesse, b. 1754.1.24; Mary, b. 1756.4.13; Thomas, b. 1758.5.3; Elizabeth, b. 1760.8.9; Abner, b. 1763.2.19; Ruth, b. 1766.6.14.
Pusey, John, b. 1738.11.1, d. 1783.9.24, son of John and Katherine of Londongrove and his wife, Elizabeth, dau of Thomas and Grace Painter, m. 1763 at Birmingham and their children: Lydia, b. 1764.5.8; Thomas, b. 1767.1.10; James, b. 1768.6.26, d. 1790.10.6; Susanna, b. 1771.3.29; Nathan, b. 1774.3.10.
Pusey, Joshua, b. 1738.9.19, son of Joshua and Mary of Londongrove and Mary, b. 1741.7.19, d. 1776.10.17, dau of William and Ann Miller of Newgarden and their children: William, b. 1762.6.1; Joshua, b. 1763.10.22; Ann, b. 1765.2.14; Mary, b. 1767.7.23; Caleb, b. 1769.2.12; Hannah, b. 1771.2.8; Samuel, b. 1773.1.29; Miller, b. 1775.4.10, Susanna, b. 1770.10.17.
Pusey, Joshua and his wife, Lydia, widow of John Trimble of Concord, d. 1780.11.15 and their children: Lydia, b. 1780.2.9.

Pusey, Joshua and his wife, Hannah, b. 1753.3.31, widow of Joseph
  Canby m. 1782.11.16 and their children: Joseph, b. 1783.8.22; Lea,
  b. 1785.6.8; Edith, b. 1787.1.22; Jonas, b. 1789.7.23, d. 1790.3.21;
  Jonas, b. 1791.1.12; Jacob, b. 1792.9.10; Mary Ann, b. 1794.3.26.
Pusey, Lewis, b. 1754.3.4, son of Joshua and Mary and his wife,
  Rebecca, dau of Isaac and Hannah Taylor m. 1777.10.9 and their
  children: Isaac, b. 1778.7.18; Sarah, b. 1780.7.17; Ellis, b. 1782.11.7;
  Hannah, b. 1787.4.4, d. 1794.7.30.
Pusey, David, b. 1726.4.19, son of Caleb and Prudence and his wife,
  Sarah, b. 1732.5.3, dau of John Dixon and their children: Ann, b.
  1757.5.4; Sarah, b. 1759.7.27; Solomon, b. 1761.3.2; David, b.
  1765.4.13; John, b. 1768.9.23; Lydia, b. 1772.11.6; Mary, b.
  1776.1.31.
Pusey, William, son of William and Elizabeth and his wife, Mary, dau of
  John and Mary Passmore and their children: Betty, b. 1743.10.11;
  Elenor, b. 1746.5.21; William, b. 1754.12.9; Mary, b. 1758.3.31;
  Enoch, b. 1761.9.20; Jane, b. 1765.8.26.
Pusey, William, son of Joshua and Mary, b. 1762.6.1 and his wife,
  Elizabeth, b. 1761.11.28, dau of Isaac and Hannah Taylor and their
  children: Benjamin, b. 1787.4.1; William, b. 1789.4.15; Mary, b.
  1792.4.21; Jonathan, b. 1793.13.18; Ann, b. 1796.3.10.
Pusey, Ellis, b. 1735.6.21, son of Joshua and Mary and his wife,
  Susanna, b. 1735.8.17, d. 1767.6.36, dau of John and Mary Bailey,
  W. Marlborough and their children: Abigail, 1751.12.14; Mary, b.
  1756.3.12; Joshua, b. 1759.5.12; Elizabeth, b. 1761.9.3; John, b.
  1764.7.24.
Pusey, Ellis, and his wife, Abigail and their children: Susanna, b.
  1778.8.17; Elinor, b. 1781.12.18; Abigail, b. 1784.4.16; Phebe, b.
  1786.9.9; Ellis, b. 1789.1.2, d. 1790.2.22; Ellis, b. 1791.7.24; Philema,
  b. 1794.5.224.
Pyle, Isaac and his wife, Elizabeth, dau of Abraham and Elizabeth
  Darlington and their children: Job, b. 1751.7.28; Thomas, b.
  1754.12.24; John, b. 1756.9.14; Mary, b. 1758.4.5; Elizabeth, b.
  1760.8.27; Olive, b. 1762.5.10.
Pyle, Hannah, dau of Moses and Mary Newlin, b. 1742.8.25.
Rees, Morris and Sarah, and their children: John, b. 1720.3.24; Morris,
  b. 1721.9.1.
Reynolds, Henry and his wife, Hannah and their children: Rachel, b.
  1718.11.6; William, b. 1721/2.1.22; Samuel, b. 1723.8.26; Henry, b.
  1725.2.1; Jacob, 1728.9.14.
Reynolds, William and his wife, Mary and their children: Jeremiah, b.
  1727.11.23; David, b. 1728/9.1.1.
Richards, Isaac, son of Isaac and Mary, b. 1759.4.15 and Ann, his wife,
  b. 1765.2.14, d. 1796.6.5, dau of Joshua and Mary Pusey and their
  children: Joshua, b. 1788.6.20; Samuel Emlen, b. 1791.8.30;

NEW GARDEN MONTHLY MEETING 131

William, b. 1796.9.27.
Richards, Thomas and his wife, Hannah and their children: Sarah, b. 1781.2.18; Isaac, b. 1783.1.8; Hannah, b. 1785.9.19; Thomas, b. 1787.11.11; Mary, b. 1790.5.7; Jacob, b. 1793.9.4.
Richardson, Joseph and his wife, Dinah and their children: Joel, no date; Samuel, no date; Hannah, b. 1773.8.2; John, b. 1775.12.22; Joseph, b. 1776.4.22; Mary, b. 1780.2.22; Lydia, b. 1785.5.16; Isaac, b. 1788.4.6; Caleb, b. 1792.12.5.
Ross, Alexander and his wife, Katherine and their children: Mary, b. 1706.12.13; Lydia, b. 1708.7.7; Rebecca, b. 1711.3.3; John, b. 1713.2.18; George, b. 1716.3.23; Albinah, b. 1720.11.10.
Scarlet, Shadrach and his wife, Phebe of Londongrove and their child: Phebe, b. 1729.11.4.
Sharp, Joseph and his wife, Mary and their children: Abigail, b. 1714.5.26, d. 1726.9.27; Elizabeth, b. 1717.5.25, d. 1719.10; Mary, b. 1719.7.7, d. 1719.10; Elizabeth, b. 1720.12.19; Sarah, b. 1723.6.5, d. 1723.10.22; Joseph, b. 1724.8.19; George, b. 1726.9.4; Abigail, b. 1729.2.28; Mary, b. 1731.6.21, d. 1731.6.30; Samuel, b. 1734.8.30.
Sharp, John and his wife, Ann and their children: John, b. 1730.5.19; Elizabeth, b. 1732.4.23; George, b. 1735.2.27; Benjamin, b. 1738.7.25; Mary, b. 1740.8.26; Thomas, b. 1747.11.12.
Sharp, Joseph, Jr. and his wife, Deborah and their child: Mary, b. 1744.5.16.
Sharpless, Joshua and his wife, Edith and their children: Benjamin, 1769.8.24; Rachel, b. 1771.5.3; Nathan, b. 1772.12.18; Martha, b. 1775.4.27; Edith, b. 177.6.15.
Shortledge, John and his wife, Phebe and their children: James, b. 1769.7.12; Hannah, b. 1770.12.24; Swithin, b. 1772.10.6; Isaac, b. 1774.6.30; Samuel, b. 1777.1.8; Enoch, b. 1779.2.26; Jacob, b. 1781.7.7; John,. b. 1783.6.10; Joshua, b. 1785.7.14; Samuel, b. 1790.11.27, d. 1791.12.5.
Simmons, Henry, b. 1768.9.16, son of Henry and Mary m. Rachel, b. 1776.9.1, dau of Joseph and Rebecca Preston.
Sinclair, Samuel and his wife, Mary and their children: Samuel, b. 1795.4.8; Ann Grubb, b. 1798.4.4; Bery Berry, b. 1800.9.17; Sarah, b. 1803.5.25; Thomas Lightfoot, b. 1805.5.16; William, b. 1808.5.12.
Smith, John and his wife, Ann and their children: Lydia, b. 1719.1.3.
Smith, John and his wife, Dorothy and their children: Anne, b. 1730.6.12; John, b. 1732.9.27; Ruth, b. 1734.11.6; Thomas, b. 1737.11.1; Sarah, b. 1741.9.17.
Smith, Mary, wife of Joseph Smith, d. 1786.1.2.
Spencer, Samuel and his wife, Mary and their children: Joseph, b. 1776.3.7; Jonathan, b. 1778.2.20; Asa, b. 1780.0.20, Aaron, b. 1780.8.20; Elizabeth, b. 1782.10, d. 1784.12.31; Hannah, b. 1786.8.2; Sarah, b. 1789.1.24.

Starr, James and his wife, Rachel, born in Ireland and their children: Mary, b. 1707.2.25 in Ireland; Joseph, b. 1710.10.19 in Ireland; John, b. 1713.7.29; James, b. 1715.10.3; Rachel, b. 1718.4.16; Moses, b. 1720.12.21; Samuel, b. 1723.12.19; Susanna, b. 1726.5.14.

Starr, Isaac and his wife, Margaret and their child: Thomas, b. 1724.10.25.

Starr, Moses and his wife, Deborah and their children: Merrick, b. 1717.7.17; John, b. 1722/3.1.16; James, b. 1724/5.12.13; Moses, b. 1726.9.25; Moses, b. 1728.10.6; Jeremiah, b. 1731.2.6; Deborah, b. 1733.2.19; Abraham, b. 1735.2.22.

Stroud, Margaret, b. 1723.9.18, dau of John and Magdalena of W. Marlborough.

Swayne, William and his wife, Elizabeth and their children: William, b. 1721.4.11, d. 1785.9.8; Francis, b. 1722.12.18; John, b. 1724.8.27, d. 1755.2.28; Thomas, b. 1729.9.19, d. 1792.12.23; Mary, b. 1728.3.29; Elizabeth, b. 1729.8.22, d. 1757.4.29; Samuel, b. 1730.12.13; Joseph, b. 1732.6.22; Ann, b. 1735.2.

Swayne, William and his wife, Ann and their children: William, b. 1744.7.11; David, b. 1746.9.19; Caleb, b. 1749.8.28; Margaret, b. 1752.6.16..

Swayne, Francis d. 1721.9.30.

Swayne, William, b. 1721.4.11, son of William and Elizabeth of E. Marlborough and his wife, Ann, b. 1723.4.2, dau of Caleb and Prudence Pusey and their children: William, b. 1744.7.11, d. 1772.1.23; David, b. 1746.9.19, d. 1760.9.23; Caleb, b. 1749.8.28; Margaret, b. 1752.6.16; Mary, b. 1754.12.20; Ruth, b. 1757.10.7; Elizabeth, b. 1760.4.17; Benjamin, b. 1763.11.1.

Swayne, Francis, b. 1722.12.18, son of William and Elizabeth of E. Marlborough and his wife, Betty, b. 1727/8.1.8, dau of Joel and Betty Bailey and their children: Lydia, b. 1750.12.11; Hannah, b. 1753.8.11; John,. b. 1755.11.26; Betty, b. 1758.8.1; Phebe, b. 1762.1.29; Orpha, b. 1765.3.25; Ruth, b. 1767.9.7; Joshua, b. 1770.5.8; Joel, b. 1775.3.13.

Swayne, Francis and his wife, Elizabeth, b. in Berkshire, Old England, m. 1722.8.5 and their child: Sarah, no date.

Swayne, Isaac son of Edward and Sarah and his wife, Susanna, dau of John and Katharine Maris and their children: Rachel, b. 1769.8.16; Sarah, b. 1771.4.13; Isaac, b. 1772.8.23, d. 1772.8.30.

Swayne, Caleb, b. 1749.8.28, son of William and Ann and Mary, b. 1753.7.22, dau of William and Margaret Wood m. 1774.4.13 and their children: Ann, b. 1775.1.3; Rest, b. 1778.4.7; Caleb, b. 1781.12.27, d. 1785.9.14; William, b. 1786.12.30.

Swayne, Jonathan, b. 1731.2.3, son of Edward and Sarah of E. Marlborough and his wife, Mary, b. 17--.3.28, dau of William and

Elizabeth White of Kennett and their children: Sarah, b. 1756.7.13; Elizabeth, b. 1758.4.16.

Swayne, James, son of Caleb and Lydia and Hannah, b. 1753.8.11, dau of Francis and Betty m. 1773.11.17 at Londongrove and their children: Francis, b. 1774.12.8; Caleb, b. 1776.10.4.

Swayne, Samuel, b. 1730/1.12.13, son of William and Elizabeth and Hannah, b. 1736.1.1, d. 1799.9.13, dau of William and Jane Hayes and their children: Jacob, b. 1757.3.29; Stephen, b. 1758.10.9, d. 1759.8.31; Joshua, b. 1760.9.21, d. 1765.8.18; David, b. 1762.10.17, d. 1765.8.12; Rachel, b. 1765.1.2; Samuel, b. 1767.7.11; Sarah, b. 1769.11.8; Hannah, b. 1772.7.31; William, b. 1775.4.30; Nathan, b. 1778.2.4; Lydia, b. 1780.9.3.

Swayne, Jacob, son of Samuel and Hannah, b. 1737.3.29 and his wife, Phebe, dau of Thomas and Elizabeth Milhous and their children: Deborah, b. 1782.2.9; David, b. 1783.4.31; Thomas, b. 1785.2.17. Phebe Swayne, wife of Jacob d. 1785.8.18.

Taylor, Thomas and his wife, Rachel and their children: Thomas, b. 1701.10.16, d. 1726.10.14; Simon, b. 1704.3.5.

Taylor, Joseph, son of Jesse and Ann and Jane, b. 1750.7.7, d. 1795.11.8, dau of James and Lydia Walter and their children: Jesse, b. 1777.1.14, d. 1798.9.20; James, b. 1779.1.14; Joseph, b. 1780.12.31; Israel, b. 1782.10.27; Sarah, b. 1784.9.18; Ann, b. 1791.2.21; Joel, b. 1792.10.8; Lydia, b. 1794.8.3.

Taylor, Lydia, dau of Isaac and Hannah m. Lewis Pusey.

Taylor, Elizabeth, b. 1761.11.28 m. William Pusey.

Taylor, Joseph and his wife, Mary and their children: Sarah, b. 1725.8.11, d. 1775.1.22, m. Joseph Pennock; Rebecca m. William Jackson.

Temple, William and his wife, Hannah of Kennett and their children: Elizabeth, b. 1735.1.27, d. 1764.12.15 m. Benjamin Hutton.

Temple, Mary w., b. 1798.3.14, dau of Samuel and Elizabeth.

Thompson, William, b. 1765.8.22, son of Daniel and Elizabeth and his wife, Hannah, b. 1762.2.24, dau of John and Margaret Hadley and their child: Rebecca, b. 1789.1.16.

Thompson, William, b. 1765.8.22, son of Daniel and Elizabeth and his wife, Mary and their children: Joseph, b. 1792.11.13; Elizabeth, b. 1794.7.4; Lydia, b. 1795.12.28; Richard, b. 1798.5.1; Daniel, b. 1800.2.14; Hannah, b. 1801.12.25; Lettice, b. 1804.2.16; William, b. 1806.9.20.

Thompson, Eli, b. 1770.10.14, son of Daniel and Elizabeth and his wife, Elizabeth and their children: Joel, b. 1799.6.2; Daniel, b. 1801.3.1.

Thompson, William and his wife, Katharine of Londongrove and their children: Levi, b. 1792.8.23; Hannah, b. 1793.11.4; John, b. 1795.5.15; Ann, b. 1797.1.19; Esther, b. 1798.7.12; Barak, b.

1799.11.27; George, b. 1801.6.5; Joseph, b. 1803.1.23; David, b. 1804.11.16; Robert, b. 1807.1.24.

Trimble, Lydia d. 1780.11.15, widow of John of Concord.

Vancourt, Mary d. 1787.10.4, formerly widow of Samuel Jackson, now wife of Daniel Vancourt.

Walter, Jane, b. 1755.7.7, d. 1795.11.8.

Walton, Abigail, b. 1794.12.4, d. 1799.10.29, dau of Joshua and Hannah.

Warner, John and his wife, Lydia and their children: Mary, b. 1767.5.31; William, b. 1769.3.9; Isaac, b. 1769.3.9; Simeon, b. 1771.3.11; Lydia, b. 1773.3.26; Rachel, b. 1775.5.4; Joseph, b. 1777.11.19; Levi, b. 1779.12.12; Nancy, b. 1782.3.15.

Way, William and his wife, Elizabeth and their children: Thomas, b. 1792.3.18; Jacob, b. 1793.8.2; Isaac, b. 1794.9.15; Joshua, b. 1796..3.3; William, b. 1797.9.22; Mary Miller, b. 1799.4.11; Moses, b. 1801.2.25; Deborah B., 1803.10.31; Paschall, b. 1804.10.13; Elizabeth, b. 1809.12.24.

Way, James, son of Jacob and Hannah of Kennett and Hannah, b. 1749.11.25, dau of John and Hannah Marshall and their children: Ann, b. 1774.10.29; John, b. 1776.8.17; Marshall, b. 1778.7.10, d. 1780.7.16; Joseph, b. 1779.4.17, d. 1779.6.19; James, b. 1780.6.17, d. 1789.4.19; Joseph, b. 1782.9.29; Jesse, b. 1784.11.29; Hannah, b. 1787.1.22; James, b. 1789.4.18, d. 1790.7.1; Lydia C., b. 1791.7.19.

Webster, William and his wife, Sarah and their children: John, b. 1722.2.29; William, 1723/4.12.12; Rebecca, b. 1725.5.11.

Webster, William d. 1754.7.21 aged near 71.

Webster, Thomas, son of William d. 1770.6.5.

Wells, John and his wife, Katherine and their children: Mary, b. 1784.7.24; Josiah, b. 1786.12.11; Elizabeth, b. 1788.9.15; Susannah, b. 1790.10.12; Thomas, b. 1793.9.16; Sarah, b. 1796.3.27, d. 1716; Sarah, b. 1798.11.5.

White, John and his wife, Mary and their children: William, b. 1717/8.5.21; John, b. 1719.10.13; Mary, b. 1721.5.20; Samuel, b. 1722.11.28; Mary, b. 17--.3.28.

Wickersham, Hannah, dau of Thomas and Abigail b. in E. Marlborough 1723.5.5.

Wiley, Joseph and his wife, Abigail and their children: Sarah, b. 1716.11.6; Ann, b. 1718.9.6; John, b. 1721.11.19.

Wilkinson, Francis, b. 1741.12.15, son of Joseph and Elizabeth and his wife, Hannah, b. 1750.4.18, d. 1791.9.23, dau of Alexander and Rebecca Moode of E. Fallowfield and their children: Rebecca, b. 1771.1.6; Elizabeth, b. 1772.8.28; Joseph, b. 1774.3.8; Hannah, b. 1776.6.20; Francis, b. 1778.3.5; Susanna, b. 1780.9.4; Moode, b. 1783.1.3, d. 1783.7.8; Emey, b. 1785.2.5; William, b. 1787.9.28; Ruth, b. 1789.12.26.

Wilson, John and his wife, Ann and their children: Jane, b. 1774.11.13; Sarah, b. 1778.7.16; Edward, b. 1779.10.7; Isaac, 1781.8.25; Hugh, b. 1783.9.28; Samuel, b. 1786.1.18.

Wilson, Isaac and his wife, Rebecca and their children: Martha, b. 1788.2.25; Hannah, b. 1790.9.3; Stephen, b. 1793.7.20.

Wilson, Ephraim and his wife, Elizabeth and their children: Elizabeth, b. 1777.7.16; Phebe, b. 1779.10.11; Rachel, b. 1781.10.22; Joel, b. 1784.2.23; Rebecca, b. 1786.10.24; Mary, b. 1789.3.18; Ephraim, b. 1791.11.25.

Wilson, David, son of Samuel and Rebecca (Canby) and his wife, Margaret and their children: Hannah, b. 1779.12.10; Amos, b. 1781.2.28; a son, 1782.11.7; Margaret, b. 1784.2.7; Sarah, b. 1786.12.9; Rebecca, b. 1789.3.9; Oliver, b. 1791.12.9; Amos, b. 1794.9.16. Margaret Wilson d. 1796.7.31.

Windle, David and his wife, Abigail and their children: Joseph Kirk, b. 1787.11.2; Benjamin, b. 1789.9.12; Cabel, b. 1792.1.8. WINDLE, FRANCIS, father of David d. 1788.9.26 aged about 87.

Wollaston, Thomas and his wife, Elinor and their children: Martha, b. 1714.6.3; Mary, b. 1715.1.23, d. 1721.3.17; Prissilla, b. 1717.10.30; Sarah, b. 1719.6.14; Thomas, b. 1726.2.23; Mary, b. 1722.10.16.

Wood, William, b. 1723.6.22, d. 1775.4.20, son of Thomas and Mary of Warwishshire, England and Margaret, b. 1730.5.18, d. 1775.10.29, dau of Thomas and Margaret Holland, b. Prince George's Co., MD and their children: Thomas, b. 1750.11.17; George, b. 1751.12.18; Mary, b. 1753.7.22; Joseph, b. 1755.3.20; Cassandrew, b. 1756.9.26; William, b. 1758.4.11; Elizabeth, b. 1760.1.8; Margaret, b. 1761.8.7; Joshua, b. 1763.7.5; Ruth, b. 1765.10.14.

Wood, Thomas, b. 1750.11.17, son of William and Margaret and his wife, Susanna, b. 1750.10.16, dau of John and Katherine Pusey and their children: Joel, b. 1774.8.28, d. 1776.5.22; William, b. 1775.12.30; John, b. 1777.11.5; Lydia, b. 1779.10.3; Nathan, b. 1781.2.7; Margaret, b. 1783.4.11; Thomas, b. 1785.9.27.

Woodward, Thomas, b. 1722.11.7, d. 1785.6.15 and his wife, Elizabeth, dau of Roger and Elizabeth Kirk, b. 1721/2.1.5 and their children: Rebeca, b. 1746.9.24; Elizabeth, b. 1748.6.12; Samuel, b. 1750.8.9; Thomas, b. 1753.3.17; Deborah, b. 1755.3.19, d. 1765.8.28; Mary, b. 1756.1.26, d. 1786.1.2; Timothy, b. 1759.10.22, d. 1760.5; Susanna, b. 1761.8.7, d. 1765.9.6.

Woodward, Samuel, b. 1750.8.9, son of Thomas and Elizabeth and his wife, Sarah, b. 1755.3.4, d. 1791.10.14, dau of John and Sarah Jackson m. 1773.5.11 at Londongrove and their children: Susanna, b. 1773.8.5; John, b. 1775.5.22; Samuel, b. 1777.3.18; Sarah, b. 1779.2.11; William,. b. 1782.1.23; Thomas, b. 1784.2.15; Levi, b. 1786.1.29; Rachel, b. 1787.11.25; Rebecca, b. 1790.4.4.

Worsley, Sarah, dau of Daniel and Sarah b. 1717.4.3.
Wright, James and his wife, Mary and their children: Mary, b. 1708.6.3; Hannah, b. 1709/10.1.24; Martha, b. 1713.2.14; Elizabeth, b. 1714.11.23; John, b. 1716.11.4; James, b. 1718.11.8; Thomas, b. 1720.1.14; Isaac, b. 1723.3.25.
Wright, Fismore and his wife, Margaret born in Ireland and their children: Isaac, b. 1718.12.4; Thomas, b. 1719.12.4; Margaret, b. 1720.10.18; Ann, b. 1723.4.31.
Wright, Jacob d. 1786.9.1.
Wright, Mary, b. 1708.2, d. 1784.2.21, dau of Thomas and Ann Jackson.

NEW GARDEN MONTHLY MEETING MARRIAGES

Stephen Ades, son of Stephen of Londongrove and Ann Underwood 1742.9.3 at Londongrove.
William Ades, son of Stephen of Londongrove and Elizabeth Underwood, dau of Alexander of Londongrove 1738.8.18 at Londongrove.
Benjamin Allen, son of John of Londongrove and Hannah Greenfield, dau of James of Londongrove 1764.12.20 at Newgarden.
John Allen, son of John of Londongrove and Phebe Scarlet, dau of Shadrack 1740.9.12 at Londongrove.
Joseph Allen, son of John of Londongrove and Deborah Hill, dau of Samuel 1755.11.13 at Newgarden.
William Atkinson of Talbot Co., MD., son of Aaron and Miriam Good, dau of Thomas and Esther of Londonberry 1798.5.9 at West Grove.
Thomas Atmore of Philadelphia, son of William and Mary and Mary Jackson, dau of Isaac and Sarah, dec'd, of Kings Co., Ireland 1785.1.6 at Newgarden.
Jacob Baels, son of John Baels of Nottingham and Mary Brooksley, dau of John, dec'd, of MD. 1714.4.25 at Nottingham.
John Baels, son of John Baels of Nottingham and Sarah Bowater, dau of Thomas of Chester Creek 1711.9.14 at Chester.
Isaac Bailey, son of Thomas of W. Marlborough and Hannah Scarlet, dau of Nathaniel of Newgarden 1765.4.17 at Londongrove.
Joel Bailey, son of Isaac and Abigail, dec'd, of Newton and Lydia Pusey, dau of John and Katharine of Londgrove 1759.11.14 at Londongrove.
John Bailey and Lydia Wickersham, dau of William of Newlin.
Joshua Bailey and Ann Jackson, dau of John and Sarah of E. Marlborough.
William Bailey, of Sadsbury, son of Edward and Ann, and

Margaret Passmore at West Grove.

Emmor Baily, son of Joel and Elizabeth of W. Bradford and Elizabeth Hayes, dau of Henry and Elizabeth of Londongrove 1791.4.27 at Londongrove.

Isaac Baily, son of Isaac of E. Marlborough and Sarah Jackson, dau of Samuel, dec'd, of E. Marlborough 1749.9.8 at Londongrove.

Joel Baily, son of Josiah of W. Marlborough and Hannah Wickersham, dau of William of Newlin 1757.11.24 at Londongrove.

John Baily of Marlborough and Mary Mash 1732.4.8 at Sadsbury.

John Baily, son of John of Marlborough and Lydia Wickersham 1753.11.22 at Londongrove.

John Baily, son of Joel of Marlborough and Lydia Pusey, dau of William of Londongrove 1729.3.29 at Londongrove.

Joshua Baily of W. Marlborough, son of Joel and Betty Baily and Ann Jackson 1778.5.13 at Londongrove.

Josiah Baily of Marlborough and Sarah Marsh 1734.3.9 at Sadsbury.

William Baily, son of Daniel of E. Marlborough and Hannah Taylor, widow of Joseph 1762.12.16 at Londongrove.

William Baily, son of John and Mary of W. Marlborough and Mary Musgrove 1759.10.18 at Newgarden.

Arron Baker, son of Aaron and Mary of W. Marlborough and Hannah Harlan of Marlborough, dau of Michael and Susanna 1790.2.10 at Londongrove.

John Baker, son of Aaron and Mary of W. Marlborough and Hannah Pennock, dau of Joseph and Sarah of E. Marlborough 1767.6.24 at Londongrove.

Joshua Baker of Senter, New Castle, Co. and Mary Hill 1740.9.5 at Londongrove.

Levi Baker, son of Aaron and Mary of W. Marlborough and Ann Pyle, dau of Joseph and Alice of W. Marlborough 1791.4.13 at Londongrove.

Thomas Baker, son of Richard and Rachel of W. Bradford and Sarah Woodward, dau of Neal and Lydia of E. Marlborough 1785.4.7 at Bradford.

John Baldwin of Kennett, son of William of Bristol, Bucks Co., and Elizabeth Pusey, dau of William, dec'd, of Londongrove 1734.9.13 at Londongrove.

William Baels, son of John of Nottingham and Rebecca Chambers, dau of John of Chichester 1712.4.26 at Nottingham.

Henry Ballinger of the Salem Monthly Meeting, son of Henry of West Jersy and Hannah Wright, dau of James 1726.6.18 at Nottingham.

Josiah Ballinger of Potomack, son of Henry of Burlington Co., NJ and Mary Wright, dau of James 1727.6.31 at Nottingham.

Jeremiah Barnard, son of Richard and Susanna, dec'd, of Newlin and Elizabeth Passmore, dau of George and Margaret 1780.10.25 at Londongrove.
Jeremiah Barnard, widower of W. Marlborough and Mary Passmore of W. Marlborough, dau of George and Margaret 1787.6.6 at Londongrove.
Thomas Barnard, son of Richard and Ann of Newlin and Sarah Miller, dau of James of Newgardn 1750.9.8 at Newgarden.
John Bartlett of Talbot Co., Md, son of Joseph and Martha and Susanna Thatcher, dau of Richard and Abigail of Kennett 1781.5.10.
John Beeson of Leacock, son of Richard and Mary Varman 1733.10.7 at Leacock.
Samuel Beverly and Ruth Jackson, dau of Samuel, dec'd, of E. Marlborough.
Newton Black of Newgarden, son of David, dec'd, and Rachel and Sarah Rowen, dau of William, dec'd, and Elizabeth of Newgarden 1764.6.7 at Newgarden.
Robert Boyce and Mary Hobson of Newgarden, dau of Francis 1747.4.18.
David Brooks of Newgarden and Elinor Edmundson of Newgarden 1725.6.1.3.
David Brown and Lydia Hutton, dau of Benjamin and Ann of Newgarden
Isaac Brown and Margaretta Kinsey, dau of Samuel and Rachel of Londongrove.
Jacob Brown, son of William, dec'd, and Phebe of W. Nottingham and Elizabeth Cook, dau of John and Rebecca of Londongrove 1772.11.25 at Londongrove.
Joseph Brown, Cordwainer, son of William of Nottingham and Margaret Sinkler of Ridley 1710.9.30 at Chester.
Messer Brown of Nottingham and Dinah Churchman of Nottingham 1728.11.2 at Nottingham.
Thomas Brown and Mary Shaw, dau of Moses of Londongrove 1740.8.16 at Newgarden.
William Brown, Jr. of Nottingham, farmer, and Margaret Davis of Nottingham.
William Brown of Nottingham, son of William, dec'd, and Susannah Churchman of Nottingham 1728.11.2.
James Buckingham of Christiana Hundred, son of John, dec'd, and Mary Chambers, dau of Richard of White Clay Creek 1755.6.12 at Newgarden.
John Cain, son of Robert and Ruth of Londongrove and Sarah Hutton, dau of Nehemiah and Ann of Newgarden 1782.9.19.
Robert Cain and Ruth Shaw, dau of Moses near Wilmington 1750.11.10 at Newgarden.

Thomas Carrington of E. Marlborough, son of Thomas and Mary, dec'd, and Mary Baker, dau of Aaron and Mary of W. Marlborough 1762.6.16 at Londongrove.
George Carson of E. Marlborough and Elinor Pasemore of W. Marlborough 1736.4.16 at Londongrove.
George Carson of E. Marlborough and Hannah Pusey, dau of William, dec'd, of W. Marlborough 1750.7.5 at Londongrove.
Henry Chalfant and Susanna Swayne, widow, dau of John and Katherine Maris.
Jonathan Chalfant, of W. Marlborough, son of Henry and Elizabeth and Ann Barnard, dau of Thomas and Sarah 1777.12.24 at Londongrove.
Thomas Chalfant and Phebe Hayes, dau of David and Ann of W. Marlborough.
Henry Chalfant, son of John of W. Marlborough and Elizabeth Jackson, dau of Thomas of W. Marlborough 1740.8.15 at Londongrove.
James Chalfont, son of John of W. Marlborough and Hannah Harris 1744.2.18 at Londongrove.
Thomas Chalfont, son of Henry and Elizabeth of W. Marlborough and Phebe Hayes 1775.4.5 at Londongrove.
John Chambers of White Clay Creek, son of William, dec'd, and Rebecca Johnson, dau of Joshua of Londongrove 1762.2.15.
Joseph Chambers of Mill Creek, son of William of White Creek and Emey Thompson, dau of James of Mill Creek 1767.5.21 at Newgarden.
Joseph Chambers and Deborah Phillips, dau of John and Lydia of Newgarden.
Richard Chambers, son of John of New Castle Co. and Elener Miller, dau of John, dec'd, of Newgarden 1729.4.19.
Samuel Chambers, son of Richard of White Clay Creek and Sarah Thompson, dau of James of Mill Creek 1766.5.22 at Newgarden.
William Chambers of Lampeter, son of John and Rebecca and Susanna Pusey, dau of John and Elizabeth 1790.11.7 at Londongrove.
William Chambers, son of John of New Castle Co. and Elizabeth Miller, dau of John, dec'd of Newgarden 1729.8.22.
William Chambers and Hannah Mitchell of Mill Creek, dau of Thomas and Lucy.
Allen Chandler of Londongrove, son of William and Rebecca and Sarah Pyle of Marlborough, dau of Joseph and Alice 1789.5.13.
John Chandler, son of William of Londongrove and Susanna Parks, 1741.2.8 at Londongrove.
John Chandler and Patience Painter, dau of Thomas and Hannah,

dec'd, of Concord.

John Churchman, of Nottingham, son of John, dec'd, and Margaret Brown, dau of William, dec'd, 1729.11.17 at Nottingham.

Samuel Clark, of Marlborough, son of Walter of the Grange Co of Antrim and Mary Lightfoot, dau of Michael of Newgarden 1737.8.6 at Newgarden.

Samuel Clark, of E. Caln, son of John, dec'd, and Hannah and Ruth Wilkinson of Londongrove, dau of Joseph and Elizabeth 1779.5.5 at Londongrove.

Aaron Clayton, son of Joshua and Martha of W. Bradford and Sarah Bailey, dau of John and Mary of W. Marlborough 1779.6.9 at Londongrove.

Joshua Clayton, son of Edward and Ann of W. Bradford and Martha Baker, dau of Aaron and Mary of W. Marlborough 1753.5.16 at Londongrove.

Samuel Clayton, son of Joshua and Martha of W. Bradford and Ann Speakman, dau of Hugh and Mary of Londongrove 1781.11.7 at Londongrove.

Isaac Clendenon, widower, son of Robert, dec'd, of E. Marlborough and Elizabeth Barger, dau of John, dec'd, of Berk Co. 1761.4.8 at Londongrove.

Joshua Cloud, son of William and Mary of W. Marlborough and Ruth Jackson, dau of Jonathan and Mary of E. Marlborough 1774.4.20 at Londongrove.

Mordecai Cloud, son of Mordecai, dec'd, of E. Marlborough and Ann Jackson, dau of Thomas, dec'd, of E. Marlborough 1757.10.13 at Londongrove.

Thomas Cloud of E. Marlborough, son of Mordecai and Ann and Jane Allen, dau of William and Sarah, dec'd, 1783.6.18 at Londongrove.

Seymour Coates and Deborah Preston of Londongrove, dau of Joseph and Rebecca.

Thomas Cock and Elizabeth Fincher, dau of John of Newgarden 1722.9.2 at Marlborough.

John Cocks, son of John of Londongrove and Mary Harlan, dau of Moses of Londongrove 1735.8.9 at Newgarden.

Thomas Cocks of Newgarden and Elizabeth Fincher 1722.9.2 at Marlborough.

William Coles of Nottingham, son of William, dec'd, and Prudence Shaw, dau of Thomas, dec'd, of Duck Creek 1730.4.16 of Nottingham.

Thomas Colins, son of Joseph and Mary of W. Nottingham and Sarah Johnson, dau of Joshua of Londongrove 1755.18.10.

Isaac Common and Hannah Sharp, dau of Benjamin of Kennet, dec'd.

Robert Common, son of William and Sarah of New London and Ruth
  Hayes, dau of Isaac and Hannah of W. Marlborough 1780.11.16 at
  Newgarden.
Jesse Conard and Ann Pennington of Londongrove, dau of Thomas and
  Susanna dec'd.
Isaac Conrad, of New London, son of Evard and Margaret and Mary
  Evans of Londongrove, dau of Isaac and Ann 1787.5.10 at
  Newgarden.
John Cook, son of John and Rebecca of Londongrove and Elizabeth
  Davis, dau of Caleb and Margaret of Newgarden 1784.12.2 at
  Newgarden.
Peter Cook of Londongrove, son of Stephen and Margaret and Hannah
  Starr, of Newgarden, dau of Thomas and Sarah 1794.4.10 at
  Newgarden.
Samuel Cook, son of Peter and Sarah of Warrington, York Co., and
  Ruth Moode, dau of Alexander, dec'd, 1772.11.11 at Londongrove.
Samuel Cookson, of W. Nottingham, MD, don of Samuel and Jane and
  Olive Pyle, dau of Isaac and Elizabeth of W. Marlborough 1788.5.7.
William Cooper of Kennett and Mary Miller, dau of Samuel and
  Margaret of Sadsbury 1732.8.18.
Aaron Coppock of Aston and Miriam White of Aston, a widow
  1704.9.30 at Chichester.
Job Cowperthwaite and Asenath Roman, dau of Joshua and Rebecca of
  E. Caln.
John Cox of Mill Creek, son of William and Mary Scarlett, dau of
  Nathaniel of Newgarden 1755.5.12 of Londongrove.
John Curle, son of Richard of Mill Creek and Deborah Hadley, dau of
  Joseph of Mill Creek 1746.7.25 at Newgarden.
John Curle, son of John and Deborah of Newgarden and Elizabeth
  Fotter, dau of Francis and Elizabeth, dec'd, 1792.12.13 at
  Newgarden.
Joseph Davis, son of Joseph and Hannah of Birmingham and Margaret
  Passmore, dau of George and Margaret of Londongrove 1773.10.13
  at Londongrove.
James Dawson, son of Benjamin and Elizabeth of Talbot Co., MD and
  Ann Lamborn 1790.9.6.
Thomas Dennis, son of Thomas of E. Fallowfield and Elizabeth Webb,
  dau of Joseph of Lancaster Co 1757.6.15 at Londongrove.
Joseph Dickinson, of Sadsbury, son of Joseph and Elizabeth and
  Elizabeth Chalfont, dau of Henry and Elizabeth of W. Marlborough
  1777.4.16.
Thomas Dickson and Hannah Hadley of Mill Creek Hundred, dau of
  Simon 1727.8.25 at Newgarden.
Joseph Dickson and Mary Pusey, dau of William, dec'd, of

EARLY CHURCH RECORDS OF CHESTER CO.

Londongrove.

Henry Dixon of Newgarden, son of John and Rebecca and Elizabeth Hadley, dau of John and Margaret of Mill Creek 1771.5.9 at Newgarden.

Isaac Dixon of Mill Creek, son of Isaac and Emey Hadley, dau of John of Mill Creek 1776.5.7 at Newgarden.

Joseph Dixon of Londongrove and Sarah Powell, dau of Evan of Newgarden 1733.10.13 at Newgarden.

Joseph Dixon, son of Henry, dec'd, of Mill Creek and Mary Pusey 1742.9.25 at Newgarden.

Simon Dixon of Cane Creek, NC, son of Thomas, dec'd, and Elizabeth Allen, dau of John of Londongrove 1752.11.8 at Newgarden.

William Dixon, son of Joseph and Sarah, dec'd, of Newgarden and Rebecca Woodward, dau of Thomas and Elizabeth of E. Marlborough 1766.12.26 at Londongrove.

Samuel Dobson of Newgarden, son of John, dec'd, and Sarah Black of Newgarden, widow of Newton Black, dau of William and Elizabeth Rowen 1772.12.10 at Newgarden.

William Downing, son of William and Ellen of Bart and Phebe Bicket, dau of Samuel and Mary, dec'd, of VA 1781.12.20 at Newgarden.

William Downing of Bart, widower and Margaret Miller, widow of Samuel of Newgarden 1765.12.19 at Newgarden.

Joshua E. Maule and Rebecca Johnson, dau of Caleb and Martha of Newgarden.

John Edmundson of Kent Co., MD, son of Thomas and Sophia and Lydia Miller 1788.9.11 at Newgarden.

Jonathan Edwards of Nottingham, a Cooper, son of Ahab, ship carpenter and Isabella Lewis 1718.3.22 at Nottingham.

Moses Edwards of Londongrove, son of John of Middletown and Esther Plummer of Londongrove, dau of Robert, dec'd, 1743.3.4 at Londongrove.

Thomas Ellicott and Mary Miller, dau of William, dec'd, and Hannah of Newgarden.

John Elliot, son of William and Mary of Newgarden and Sarah Milhous, dau of John and Margaret of Newgarden 1772.10.12 at Newgarden.

Samuel Embree, son of James and Phebe of W. Bradford and Hannah Richardson, dau of Joseph and Dinah of Londongrove 1796.5.11 at West Grove.

David England, son of John of Chester Co. and Mary Keelar, dau of Owen of Chester Co 1763.2.26 at Londongrove.

John England, son of John and Mary of Chester Co. and Sarah Swayne, dau of Edward and Sarah of Chester Co. 1768.11.16 at Londongrove.

Isaac Evans, son of William of Lampeter and Alice Pennock, dau of Joseph and Mary of W. Marlborough 1756.5.5 at Londongrove.
William Farquar, son of Allen of Pipe Creek, Md and Ann Miller, dau of James of Newgarden 1733.2.17 at Newgarden.
William Farquar, son of William and Ann of Pipe Creek, MD and Mary Baily, dau of John and Mary of W. Marlborough 1780.10.11 at Londongrove.
Mark Fell and Mary Jones of Londongrove, dau of Joseph and Rachel, dec'd.
Robert Fell and Hannah Roman, dau of Joshua and Rebecca of E. Caln.
John Ferree, son of John of Sadsbury, Lancaster Co. and Betty Baily, dau of John of W. Marlborough 1765.9.18 at Londongrove.
Francis Fincher, son of John of Londongrove and Hannah Shewin, dau of William of Kennett 1731.4.30 at Londongrove.
Jonathan Fincher, son of John of Londongrove and Deborah Dicks 1726.4.29 at Londongrove.
Francis Fisher, son of Thomas, dec'd, of E. Caln and Rachel Wickersham, dau of William of Newlin 1753.1.25 of Londongrove.
Samuel Fisher, son of Thomas, dec'd, of E. Caln and Ann Lamborn, dau of Robert of Londongrove 1749.12.22 at Londongrove.
Thomas Fisher, son of Thomas, dec'd, of E. Caln and Elizabeth Lamborn, dau of Robert of Londongrove 1752.10.26 at Londongrove.
George Fitzwater and Caroline Chambers of New Castle Co., dau of Richard and Susanna.
Richard Flower, son of Richard, dec'd, of Londongrove and Alice Harlan, dau of William of W. Marlborough 1754.9.25 at Londongrove.
Moses Frazier, of Kennett, son of Alexander, dec'd, and Mary Allen, dau of John of Londongrove 1754.1.17 at Newgarden.
Benjamin Fred, of Newgarden, son of John, dec'd, of Birmingham and Deborah Hadley, dau of Simon of New Castle Co., 1721.4.20 at Newgarden.
Joseph Fred, of Newgarden, son of Nicholas, dec'd, and Sarah Hadley, dau of Joshua of VA. 1753.10.18 at Newgarden.
John G. Griffith and Abigail Kinsey, dau of John and Margaret of Mill Creek.
Joseph Galloway of W. River, MD and Susana Paca of Bush River, Baltimore Co., MD 1722.8.18 at Bush River, Baltimore Co.
Richard Galloway, of Cumberstone, Anne Arundel Co., MD and Mary Paca, of Bush River, Baltimore Co., MD 1728/9.11.2.
Joseph Gamble, son of Samuel and Catharine of Gwynedd and Elizabeth Milton 1781.12.6 at Newgarden.
Garrett Garretson, widower of Newlin and Margaret Wood, dau of William and Margaret of Londongrove 1785.3.17 at Bradford.

Garrett Garretson, son of Eliakim and Lydia of New Castle Co., and Phebe Webster, dau of John and Jane of Chester Co. 1782.5.15 at Londongrove.

Thomas Gawthrop and Elizabeth Thompson of Mill Creek, dau of Daniel and Elizabeth.

Jacob Giles of Patapsco River and Hannah Webster of Bush River, dau of John 1728/9.11.3 at Bush River.

William Goodson and Ann Johnson, dau of Caleb and Martha of Newgarden.

John Greacy of Haverford, widower and Dorothy Smith, widow 1772.4.16 at Newgarden.

Elijah Gray of Newgarden, son of Enoch and Margery and Mary Moore of Londongrove, dau of David and Martha 1796.10.13 at Newgarden.

Enoch Gray, of E. Bradford, widower and Rachel Starr, widow of Newgarden 1793.4.18 at Newgarden.

John Gray and Dorothy Smith, widow of John.

Samuel Gray and Hannah Colgan of E. Fallowfield, dau of William and Grace.

John Greacy of Londongrove and Katherine Matthews of Londongrove 1733/4.12.14 at Newgarden.

John Greacy of Chester and Ruth Miller of Londongrove 1741.3.8 at Newgarden.

William Greacy of Christiana Hundred and Emey Mode of Londongrove 1767.9.23 at Londongrove.

James Greenfield, son of James of Londongrove and Ann Ailes, dau of Stephen of Londongrove 1771.12.19 at Newgarden.

Benjamin Gregg, son of Joseph of Kennett and Sarah Chambers, dau of Richard of White Clay 1763.11.15 at Newgarden.

George Gregg and Hannah Baily, dau of William and Hannah of Marlborough.

John Gregg, a dumb Man, son of George of New Castle Co., and Susanna Curle, dau of Richard of New Castle Co 1737.8.13 at Newgarden.

John Gregg, son of Thomas, dec'd, of Kennett and Ruth Sheward, Widow of Samuel of Kennett 17565.9.29 at Londongrove.

Michael Gregg, son of Thomas, dec'd, and Dinah of Kennett and Sarah Carpenter, dau of William, dec'd, and Margaret of Newgarden 1755.12.11 at Newgarden.

Richard Gregg, son of George of New Castle Co., and Anne Hadley, dau of Simon of Newcastle Co. 1735.4.12 at Newgarden.

Thomas Gregg and Dinah Harlan, dau of Michael of Londongrove 1729.2.10 at Newgarden.

John Griffith of Sadsbury and Esther Musgrove of Sadsbury, dau of John 1728.5.18 at Sadsbury.

Joseph Griffith of Birmingham, Del Co., son of William and Hannah of
Aston and Sarah Conard, dau of Evard and Margaret of New
London 1798.3.14 at West Grove.
John Hadley, of Mill Creek, son of Joseph and Margaret Morton, dau
of Samuel of Londongrove 1750.6.16 at Londongrove.
Thomas Hadley, son of Joshua of August Co., Va and Mary Thompson,
dau of John of Londonberry 1750.4.13 at Londongrove.
Isaac Haines, son of Joseph and Elizabeth of W. Nottingham and Mary
England, dau of John, dec'd, and Elizabeth 1762.11.24 at
Londongrove.
Jacob Haines of Goshen, widower and Mary Hoopes, a widow of
Londongrove 1797.4.6 at Newgarden.
Jacob Haines of Nottingham, son of William of Burlington, NJ and
Mary Coles 1725.2.22 at Nottingham.
Joseph Haines of Nottingham and Elizabeth Thomas, dau of James of
Whiteland 1721/2.1.1 at Nottingham.
William Haines, son of Joseph of W. Nottingham and Lydia Johnson,
dau of Joshua of Londongrove 1750.8.10 at Londongrove.
Samuel Hadley, son of John and Margaret of Mill Creek and Mable
Jackson, dau of Isaac and Phebe of Newgarden 1791.5.17.
Jacob Halliday, son of Robert and Mable, dec'd, of Newgarden and
Phebe Painter 1768.4.13 at Londongrove.
Robert Halliday of Newgarden, son of William and Miriam Haines of
Newgarden, dau of Joseph of Nottingham 1730.4.3 at Nottingham.
Samuel Hambleton and Hannah Brown, dau of Joseph and Elizabeth of
Londonberry.
Eli Hampton and Rachel Speakman, dau of Enoch and Mary of
Londongrove.
Caleb Harlan of Newlin, son of Joel and Hannah and Hannah Edwards,
dau of William and Martha of Lower Milford, Bucks Co 1781.11.8 at
Newgarden.
Caleb Harlan, son of Michael and Hannah of Londongrove and Ann
Jackson 1760.10.23 at Newgarden.
David Harlan of Londongrove, son of Michael and Alice Starr, dau of
Jeremiah of Londongrove 1756.12.16 at Newgarden.
Elwood Harlan and Rachel Paxson of Newgarden, dau of Henry and
Matilda.
George Harlan, son of George, dec'd, of Newlin and Susanna Harlan,
dau of Ezekiel of W. Marlborough 1750.9.14 at Londongrove.
Jesse Harlan, son of William, Jr. and Abigail of W. Marlborough and
Lydia Baily 1774.5.11 at Londongrove.
Solomon Harlan, son of James and Susanna of Londongrove and Mary
Marshall of W. Marlborough, dau of John and Hannah 1766.11.26 at

Londongrove.

Stephen Harlan, son of Michael of Bradford and Hannah Carter, dau of Robert 1723.7.26 at Marlborough.

Thomas Harlan, son of Thomas of Kennett and Mary Baily, dau of Joel of W. Marlborough 1757.10.12 at Londongrove.

Jesse Harlan and Lydia Baily, son of Josiah and Sarah of W. Marlborough.

George Harry, son of Amos and Phebe Carrington, dau of Thomas, dec'd, of E. Marlborough 1786.5.10 at Londongrove.

William Harvey, son of William and Ann of Kennett and Susanna Pusey, dau of Joshua and Mary of Londongrove 1767.5.27 at Londongrove.

David Hayes, son of William of E. Marlborough and Ann Baily, dau of Joel of W. Marlborough 1752.5.12 at Londongrove.

Henry Hayes, son of Richard, dec'd, of W. Marlborough and Ann Stode, dau of John, dec'd, of W. Marlborough 1748.9.17 at Londongrove.

HENRY HAYES of Newlin, widower and Jane Todd, dau of John and Margaret, dec'd, of New London 1773.6.10 at Newgarden.

Isaac Hayes, son of Joseph, dec'd, of E. Marlborough and Hannah, dau of Ezekiel Harlan of W. Marlborough 1750.10.5 at Londongrove.

John Hayes, son of William of E. Marlborough and Hannah Kirk, dau of Alphonsus of New Castle Co 1749.8.11 at Londongrove.

William Hayes of Marlborough, son of Henry and Jane Jones 1725.6.11.19 at Londongrove.

Joshua Hadley of New Castle Co. and Mary Rowland of Newgarden 1725.7.2 at Newgarden.

Robert Hill of Newgarden and Violeta Linus, of Newgarden, dau of Thomas of New Providence, Philadelphia Co 1741.9.12 at Newgarden.

Francis Hobson, son of Joseph and Elizabeth of Newgarden and Ann Johnson 1767.4.15 at Londongrove.

Francis Hobson, son of Francis of Newgarden and Martha Shaw, dau of Moses of Londongrove 1744.8.17 at Londongrove.

Joseph Hobson, son of Francis of Newgarden and Elizabeth Foster, dau of Francis, dec'd, of Londongrove.

Benjamin Hoopes and Elizabeth Marshall of Londongrove, dau of James and Margaret.

Israel Hoopes and Mable Hadley, of Newgarden, widow.

Thomes Hoopes, son of David and Esther of Newgarden and Mary Richardson, dau of Isaac and Mary of Newgarden 1788.10.16 at Newgarden.

William Hoopes, of Kent Co., MC, son of Joshua and Mary and Rebecca Wilkinson, dau of Francis and Hannah 1790.11.15 at

Londongrove.
William Hoopes, son of Nathan and Margaret of E. Bradford and Phebe Woodward, dau of Neal and Lydia of Marlborough 1780.11.16 at Goshen.
Nathaniel Houlton of Newgarden and Martha Jordan, widow of John, dau of John Miller 1732.6.10 at Newgarden.
Amos House of Pennsbury, son of James and Mary and Mary Swayne, dau of William and Ann of Marlborough 1790.11.24.
Jacob Howell, Sr. of Chester and Deborah Fred of Newgarden, widow of Benjamin Fred 1753.10.4 at Newgarden.
Stephen Howell of E. Marlborough, son of Jacob and Elizabeth, dec'd, and Sarah Pusey of E. Marlborough, dau of David and Sarah 1779.11.24 at Londongrove.
Samuel Hughes and Mary Ann Harvey of PA, dau of Samuel and Esther.
Jesse Hughes, of Frederick Co., MD, son of Samuel and Elizabeth and Elizabeth Swayne 1788.6.11 at Londongrove.
Thomas Hughes of Nottingham and Elizabeth Gatchel, dau of Elisha of Nottingham 1726.9.35 at Nottingham.
Caleb Hurford and Martha Maris, dau of John and Catherine of W. Marlborough.
Nicholas Hurford of Newgarden, son of John and Hannah of Newgarden and Mary Hutton, dau of Benjamin and Sarah of Newgarden 1788.5.15 at Newgarden.
Samuel Hurford, son of John and Hannah and Rachel Dixon of Newgarden, dau of Joseph and Sarah 1760.2.21 at Newgarden.
Joseph Husband, son of William and Mary of Cecil Co. and Mary Pusey, dau of Joshua and Mary of Londongrove 1768.4.14.
John Hutton, son of Thomas and Catharine of Newgarden and Rachel Foreman, dau of Alexander and Esther of E. Caln 1782.5.9 at Newgarden.
Benjamin Hutton, widower, of Newgarden, son of Joseph and Mary, dec'd, and Ann Neal/Noyle, dau of Henry and Sarah, dec'd, of E. Marlborough 1766.5.22 at Londongrove.
John Hutton of Newgarden and Sarah Lightfoot 1724.4.25 at Newgarden.
John Hutton of Newgarden, son of Joseph, dec'd, and Ann Harry 1741.3.6 at Londongrove.
Joseph Hutton of Newgarden, son of Joseph, dec'd, and Betty Willis 1747.9.5 at Newgarden.
Joseph Hutton and Hannah Halliday, widow of Robert of Newgarden.
Nehemiah Hutton of Newgarden and Sarah Miller, dau of John, dec'd, of Nottingham 1723.5.25 at Newgarden.
Nehemiah Hutton of Newgarden, son of Joseph, dec'd, and Ann

Hiett 1753.11.8.
Seph Hutton, of Newgarden, son of Thomas and Elizabeth and Hannah Wilkins 1768.5.26 at Newgarden.
Thomas Hutton of Newgarden, son of Joseph, dec'd, and Katharine Hiett 1749.2.13 at Newgarden.
Thomas Hutton of Newgarden, son of Joseph, dec'd, and Elizabeth Harry 1739.3.9 at Londongrove.
William Hutton of Newgarden, son of Joseph, dec'd, and Deborah Todd 1750.9.15 at Newgarden.
Caleb Jackson and Hannah Bennett, dau of Joseph and Deborah of Wilmington.
Caleb Jackson, son of Thomas and Lydia of E. Marlborough and Hannah Bennett 1765.10.3 at Londongrove.
Ephraim Jackson, son of Susanna of Londongrove and Tacy Thompson, dau of Jane of Londonderry 1760.11.26 at Londongrove.
Isaac Jackson of Marlborough and Mary Miller, dau of James of Newgarden 1730.4.11.
Isaac Jackson, son of William and Katharine of Londongrove and Hannah Jackson, dau of Joseph and Susanna 1762.5.18 at Newgarden.
Isaac Jackson of E. Marlborough, son of John and Sarah, dec'd, and Phebe Halliday, dau of Robert and Mable, dec'd, of Newgarden 1765.10.24 at Newgarden.
Isaac Jackson, of Newgarden, widower and Sarah Jackson, dau of Jonathan and Mary of E. Marlborough 1786.2.16 at Londongrove.
James Jackson, son of William of Londongrove and Mary Jackson, dau of Joseph of Londongrove 1760.6.19 at Newgarden.
Joel Jackson and Alice Morris of Londongrove, dau of Jonathan and Alice.
John Jackson, son of Isaac of Londongrove and Sarah Miller 1740.2.17 at Newgarden.
John Jackson, son of Thomas of Marlborough and Mary Garnett, dau of Theodia of Md 1734.3.30 at Newgarden.
John Jackson, Widower of E. Marlborough and Margaret Starr, widow 1769.11.15 at Londongrove.
John Jackson, son of John, dec'd, of E. Marlborough and Susanna Jackson, dau of Joseph and Susanna of Londongrove 1768.12.22 at Newgarden.
John Jackson and Jane Swaine, dau of Francis and Elizabeth of Marlborough.
Joseph Jackson of Londongrove and Susanna Miller of Newgarden 1734.2.18 at Newgarden.
Samuel Jackson of Marlborough, son of Thomas, dec'd, and Mary Chambers of Hoopyard, New Castle Co., dau of John 1727.9.16 at Newgarden.

Samuel Jackson, son of Ephraim and Rachel of Edgmont and Jane Swaine 1719.4.3 at Newgarden.
Samuel Jackson and Ann Johnson, dau of Robert and Margaret of Newgarden.
Thomas Jackson of E. Marlborough, son of Jonathan and Mary and Sarah Taggart of E. Marlborough, dau of Jacob and Ann 1772.4.15 at Londongrove.
Thomas Jackson, son of Thomas of Marlborough and Lydia Smith, dau of John of Marlborough 1738.3.17 at Londongrove.
Thomas Jackson of Marlborough and Mary Willy 1718.11.25 at Newgarden.
William Jackson, son of Isaac of Londongrove and Katharine Miller, dau of James of Newgarden 1733.9.9 at Newgarden.
Abraham Jobe, son of Andrew, dec'd, of Nottingham and Sarah Gatchell, dau of Elisha of Nottingham 1726.9.24 at Nottingham.
Thomas Jobe, son of Andrew of Nottingham and Elizabeth Maxwell 1725.8.28 at Nottingham.
Hadley Johnson, son of Robert and Katherine of Wilmington and Joanna Richards, dau of William and Joanna of Newgarden 1776.11.14 at Newgarden.
James Johnson, son of Joshua of Londongrove and Margaret Cook, dau of John of Londongrove 1748.2.20 at Londongrove.
James Johnson and Ruth Mickle of Newgarden.
Joshua Johnson, son of Robert and Mary of Mill Creek and Ann Pennock 1792.9.12 at Londongrove.
Robert Johnson and Katherine Hadley, dau of Simon of New Castle Co.
Henry Jones of Leacock, formerly of Jersey and Eleanor Lindley of Londongrove, widow 1730.10.17 at Newgarden.
John Jones of E. Marlborough, son of John and Lydia and Hannah Baily of E. Marlborough, dau of Joel and Lydia 1785.12.14 at Londongrove.
Joseph Jones and Elizabeth Brown of Londongrove, dau of Joseph and Elizabeth.
Joseph Jones of Nottingham, don of John of Worchestershire and Patience Baels, fau of John of Nottingham 1717.4.20 at Nottingham.
Richard Jones of Nottingham and Miriam Coppock, dau of Aaron, dec'd, of Nottingham 1727.8.12 at Nottingham.
John Jordan of Maiden Creek, son of John, dec'd, and Rachel Jackson, dau of Joseph of Londongrove 1747.4.18 at Newgarden.
Caleb Kimber of Coventry, son of Predy and Gertrude and Deborah Milhous, dau of Thomas and Elizabeth 1785.5.12 at Newgarden.
Thomas Kinsey and Elizabeth Cook of Londongrove, dau of Thomas and Hannah.

Alphonsus Kirk, son of Timothy of Pikeland and Mary Pryor, dau of James and Elizabeth of Kennett 1762.7.6 at Pikeland.

Roger Kirk, son of Alphonsus of New Castle Co. and Jane Bowen, dau of Henry of Cecil Co. 1726.12.9 at Nottingham.

William Kirk of Nottingham, son of Samuel and Margaret Brown, widow of William Brown 1781.3.6 at Nottingham.

Hobson Lamborn and Rebecca L. Hayes, dau of Israel, dec'd, and Lydia of Fallowfield.

Josiah Lamborn, son of Robert and Sarah of Londongrove and Sarah Jackson, dau of Joseph, dec'd, and Susanna of Londongrove 1766.12.18 at Newgarden.

Richard Lamborn and Phebe Empson of Newgarden, widow.

Richard Lamborn and Alice Owens of Newgarden, dau of George and Mary dec'd.

Robert Lamborn of Marlborough and Sarah Swayne, dau of Francis, dec'd, of Marlborough 1722.8.5 at Marlborough.

Robert Lamborn, son of Robert of Londongrove and Ann Bourne, dau of Jesse, dec'd, late of MD 1746.9.19 at Londongrove.

Samuel Lamborn, son of Josiah and Sarah of Londongrove and Ann Chalfant, dau of John, dec'd, and Ann of Londongrove 1791.3.28 at Londongrove.

Thomas Lamborn and Phebe Hobson, dau of Joseph and Elizabeth of Newgarden.

William Lamborn, son of Robert and Sarah of Londongrove and Sarah Hayes, dau of William and Jane of E. Marlborough 1753.6.20 at Londongrove.

Eli Lewis of Newberry, York Co. and Pamela Webster of E. Marlborough 1779.11.10 at Londongrove.

Ellis Lewis, Jr., son of Robert and Mary of Wilmington and Hannah Miller, dau of William and Ann of Newgarden 1755.2.20 at Newgarden.

Enoch Lewis, of Delaware Co., son of Evan and Jane and Alice Jackson 1799.5.9 at Newgarden.

Samuel Lightfoot, of Newgarden, son of Thomas and Mary Head 1725.7.30 at Newgarden.

Jonathan Lindley, son of James, dec'd, of Londongrove and Deborah Halliday, dau of William of Newgarden 1741.2.15 at Newgarden.

Thomas Lindley and Jane Hoopes, dau of Francis and Mary of Londongrove.

Thomas Lindley, son of James, dec'd, of Londongrove and Ruth Hadley, dau of Simon of New Castle Co 1731.10.31 at Londongrove.

William Lindley, son of Thomas and Ruth of Cane Creek, Orange Co., NC and Mary Morton, dau of Samuel and Eliza of Londongrove 1766.11.5 at Londongrove.

Jacob Lindley and Hannah Miller, widow of William of Newgarden.
John Edmundson and Lydia Miller, dau of Jesse and Lydia of Newgarden.
Christian Linerd and John Musgrove, son of John 1727.1.16 at Sadsbury.
John Littler, son of Samuel, dec'd, of Nottingham and Mary Ross, dau of Alexander of Nottingham 1728.4.5 of Nottingham.
Richard Lowden of Chester and Patience Wright 1728.4.5 at Samuel Blumston's.
John Marsh, son of William, dec'd, of Sadsbury and Ruth Wickersham, dau of William of Newlin 1758.5.18 at Londongrove.
Humphrey Marshall, son of Abraham and Mary of W. Bradford and Sarah Pennock, dau of Joseph of W. Marlborough 1748.9.16 at Londongrove.
Jacob Marshall, son of Abraham and Mary of W. Bradford and Hannah Pennock, dau of Joseph of W. Marlborough 1748.9.16 at Londongrove.
John Marshall and Mary Miller, dau of James and Rebecca of Newgarden.
John Marshall of W. Bradford and Sarah Miller 1773.12.15 at Kennett.
John Marshall of Newgarden, son of Jacob, Jr., dec'd, of North of Ireland and Ruth Hadley, dau of Joshua of Mill Creek Hundred 1742.8.14 at Newgarden.
Joshua Mason of Little Brittain, son of Samuel and Hannah and Rebecca Jackson 1797.9.7 at Newgarden.
Thomas Mcconnell, son of Matthew and Mary, dec'd, of Newgarden and Rebecca Day, dau of John and Ann, dec'd, of Londongrove 1763.1.5 at Londongrove.
James Mcfadgen and Rebecca Brown of New London, dau of Joseph and Elizabeth, dec'd.
John Mcilvain of Ridley, son of John and Lydia and Ann Pennock, dau of Nathaniel and Sarah of W. Marlborough about 1788 at Londongrove.
George Mcmillan, Jr., son of George and Ann of Warrington, York Co. and Rebecca Cutler, dau of Benjamin and Susanna of Londongrove 1792.11.6 at Londongrove.
Thomas Mcmillan, son of John and Jane, dec'd, of Warrington, York Co. and Ruth Moore, dau of Joseph and Jane, dec'd, of Londongrove 1791.10.11 at West Grove.
Abraham Medcalf and Mary Pyle, dau of Moses and Mary of New Castle Co.
John Mead, son of William and Mary of Cecil Co. and Mary Abrell, dau of Richard Abrell of Cecil Co. 1726.12.2 at Nottingham.
Abraham Medcalf, son of James, dec'd, and Margaret of Little Brittan

1767.6.18 at Newgarden.

Aaron Mendenhall and Deborah Brown, dau of Joseph and Elizabeth of Londonberry.

Griffith Mendenhall, son of James and Martha of E. Caln and Sarah Lamborn 1769.4.29 at Londongrove.

Jacob Mendenhall and Beulah Thomas of Newgarden.

Mordecai Mendenhall, son of John of Earl Twp and Charity Beeson, dau of Richard of Leacock 1735.3.21 at Leacock.

William Mendenhall of Alexandria, Va, son of Aaron and Mary of Mill Creek and Martha Beeson, dau of John and Mary of Mill Creek 1772.9.13 at Newgarden.

Jesse Mercer of Westtown, son of Thomas and Jane and Betty Baily, of Marlborough, dau of Isaac and Lydia 1790.11.18 at Londongrove.

Barak Michener and Lydia R. Cook of Londongrove, dau of Thomas and Hannah.

Joseph Michener of Londongrove, widower and Rebecca Good, dau of Thomas and Esther of Londonberry 1798.10.10 at West Grove.

Mordecai Michener, son of Mordecai and Sarah of Londongrove and Alice Dunn, dau of Ralph and Anne of Londongrove 1786.4.20 at Newgarden.

William Michener and Hannah Cain of Londongrove, dau of John and Sarah.

Robert Mickle of Newgarden and Mary Beverly, dau of Samuel of Marlborough 1733.10.19 at Londongrove.

James Miller Sr. of Newgarden and Ruth Seaton 1734.2.10 at Londongrove.

James Miller of Newgarden, son of John, dec'd, and Ann Cain, dau of John, dec'd, 1722.3.24 at Newgarden.

James Miller, son of Gayen of Kennett and Rachel Fred, dau of John, dec'd, of Birmingham 1721.4.20 at Nottingham.

John Miller of Newgarden and Elizabeth Hill, dau of Samuel 1747.5.24 of Londongrove.

Reuben Miller of Newgarden, son of Samuel, dec'd, and Hannah Wilson of Londongrove, dau of David and Margaret, dec'd, 1798.9.13 at Newgarden.

Samuel Miller, son of Gayen of Kennett and Margaret Halliday, dau of William of Newgarden 1732.4.23 of Newgarden.

Samuel Miller, Jr., son of Joseph, dec'd, of Newgarden and Martha Hobson, dau of Francis of Newgarden 1759.6.17 at Newgarden.

William Miller of Newgarden, son of William and Ann, dec'd, and Hannah Miller of Newgarden, dau of James and Rebecca 1774.11.10 at Newgarden.

William Miller, son of Gayen of Kennett and Ruth Rowland, dau of Thomas, dec'd, of Newgarden 1724.7.30 at Newgarden.
Thomas Mills, son of John of Monoquisy near Potomack and Elizabeth Harold 1730.4.18.
William Millson, of W. Marlborough, son of James and Grace and Elizabeth Allen 1791.4.6 at Londongrove.
Alexander Mode of Fallowfield and Rebecca Allen, dau of John of Londongrove 1741.4.18 at Newgarden.
James Mode of Londongrove, son of John and Elizabeth, dec'd, and Elizabeth Hartley 1795.10.24 at West Grove.
William Mode, son of Alexander and Rebecca of E. Fallowfield and Phebe Taylor, dau of Joseph and Mary of W. Marlborough 1764.11.14 at Londongrove.
James Money of Sadsbury, son of Neal and Mary Linnard 1733.4.13 at Sadsbury.
Andrew Moore of Sadsbury, son of Andrew, dec'd, and Rebecca Starr, dau of Jeremiah of Londongrove 1754.9.26 at Newgarden.
Andrew Moore of Sadsbury and Rachel Holliday of Newgarden, dau of William 1725.4.24 at Newgarden.
David Moore, son of David and Martha of Londongrove and Martha Sharpless, dau of Joseph and Mary of Newgarden 1791.11.17 at West Grove.
Isaac Moore and Rachel Bibs, dau of Charles and Rachel of New London.
Isaac Moore of Newgarden, son of Andrew and Rebecca and Lydia Wilson, dau of James and Amy of Mill Creek 1786.4.6 at Newgarden.
James Moore, son of Andrew and Rebecca and Lydia Sharpless of W. Sadsbury 1785.4.6 at Sadsbury.
James Moore, son of Andrew of Sadsbury and Ann Starr, dau of Jeremiah 1741.2.16 at Newgarden.
John Moore, son of David, dec'd, of W. Caln and Rachel Hayes, dau of Joseph of E. Marlborough 1747.4.17 at Londongrove.
Joseph Moore and Mercy Cutler, dau of Benjamin and Susanna of Londongrove.
Joseph Moore, son of Joseph and Jane, dec'd, of Londongrove 1791.10.27 and Mercy Cutter at West Grove.
Joshua Moore and Jane Bane, dau of Nathan and Margaret of Londongrove.
Robert Moore and Elizabeth Bailey, dau of William and Tacy, dec'd, of Londongrove.
William Moore of Newgarden, son of Joseph and Jane and Sarah Richards of Newgarden, dau of Thomas and Hannah 1797.5.18 at Newgarden.
William Moore of Fallowfield, son of David, dec'd, and Mary

Harlan, dau of William 1742.8.20 at Londongrove.
John Morton, son of John of Kennett and Mary Todd, dau of John of New London 1747.10.11 at Newgarden.
James Musgrove, son of John of Sadsbury, Lancaster Co. and Hannah Cox, dau of Thomas of Londongrove 1739.4.13 at Londongrove.
Ellis Newlin, son of Joseph and Phebe of Wilmington and Jane Mason, dau of George and Jane of Newgarden 1771.6.6. at Newgarden.
Nathaniel Newlin of Concord and Esther Medcalf of Sadsbury, Lancaster Co 1735.3.15 at Sadsbury.
James Nichols and Elizabeth Sharp, dau of John, dec'd, of Newgarden.
John Nichols of Kennett and Ann Sharp 1751.3.30 at Newgarden.
Samuel Nichols of Mill Creek, son of Thomas, dec'd, and Elizabeth Jordan of W. Marlborough, dau of John, dec'd, 1754.5.2 at Newgarden.
Thomas Nichols of Christian Hundred and Lydia Hayes, dau of Henry of E. Marlborough 1741.12.3 at Kennett.
Thomas Oldham of Nottingham and Rachel Little of Nottingham 1728.5.3 at Nottingham.
John Packson and Sarah Miller, dau of James of Kennett.
Charles Parson and Sarah Chambers, dau of Joseph and Deborah of Chester Co.
Joseph Parson and Sarah Dutton of Kennett, widow, dau of James and Sarah Walter.
Francis Parvin, late of Chester and Eleanor Lightfoot, dau of Michael of Newgarden 1734.3.2 at Newgarden.
Caleb Passmore, son of William and Alice, dec'd, of E. Marlborough and Ann Tomson 1776.5.9 at Newgarden.
George Passmore of Londongrove, son of George and Margaret and Mary Pennock, dau of Levis and Ruth of W. Marlborough 1776.4.24 at Londongrove.
George Passmore, son of John of W. Marlborough and Margaret Stroud 1742.9.10 of Londongrove.
John Passmore, Jr. of Kennett and Elizabeth Harris of Mill Creek Hundred, dau of Roger, dec'd, and Sarah 1727.3.18 at Newgarden.
John Passmore, son of George and Margaret of W. Marlborough 1765.4.24 at Londongrove.
John Passmore and Phebe Pusey, dau of Joshua and Mary of Londongrove.
John Passmore of Christiana Hundred, son of Joseph and Hannah, dec'd, and Rachel Starr 1786.2.15 at Londongrove.
Samuel Passmore, son of William and Alice of E. Marlborough and Mary Hadly 1779.5.6 at Newgarden.

Thomas Pennington and Sarah Cain of Londonberry, dau of John and Sarah.
Thomas Pennington, of Newgarden, widower and Rachel Jones of E. Marlborough, widow of Joseph 1785.12.7 at Londongrove.
Thomas Pennington of Londongrove, widower and Katharine Jackson, dau of William and Katharine 1795.4.8 at West Grove.
Caleb Pennock and Ann Thompson, dau of James and Elizabeth of Mill Creek.
Jesse Pennock, son of Joseph and Sarah Pennock of E. Marlborough and Hannah Baldwin, dau of Thomas and Sarah of Newgarden 1772.4.7 at Londongrove.
John Pennock and Rachel Starr of W. Marlborough, dau of Thomas and Sarah.
Joseph Pennock, son of Joseph of W. Marlborough and Sarah Taylor, dau of Joseph of Marlborough 1743.3.18 at Londongrove.
Moses Pennock, son of William of E. Marlborough and Grace Thompson, dau of James of Mill Creek 1765.1.1.17 at Newgarden.
Nathaniel Pennock, son of Joseph of W. Marlborough and Jane Pusey, dau of William, dec'd, of Marlborough 1738.4.22 at Londongrove.
Samuel Pennock and Mary Hadley, dau of John and Margaret of Mill Creek.
William Pennock of E. Marlborough and Hannah Chamberlain of Sadsbury 1736.10.15 at Londongrove.
John Perry of Marlborough and Margaret Pusey, dau of Caleb 1737.9.16 at Londongrove.
Henry Persons, son of John of Bristol, England and Margaret Brown of Nottingham, widow of Joseph Brown.
Henry Piggott, son of John, Jr., dec'd of E. Nottingham and Hannah Pyle, dau of Moses of E. Marlborough 1761.4.14 of Londongrove.
Eli Plummer of Newgarden, son of Thomas and Phebe and Alice Smith, dau of James and Rachel, dec'd, 1798.12.6 of Newgarden.
Thomas Plummer, son of Robert, dec'd, of W. Marlborough and Phebe Cook, dau of John of Londongrove 1758.11.15 at Londongrove.
Evan Powell of Nottingham and Mary Rowland of Newgarden, widow of Thomas 1713.8.30 at Newgarden.
John Powell, son of Thomas of Huntingdon, York Co. and Ann Todd, dau of John of New London 1750.3.1 at Newgarden.
William Preston, son of Joseph and Rebecca of Londongrove and Mary Moore 1791.10.11 at West Grove.
Jesse Pugh, son of Joshua and Hannah of E. Nottingham and Catharine Jackson, dau of Isaac and Hannah 1793.11.14 at Newgarden.

Lewis Pugh and Mary Hutton, dau of Hiatt and Sarah of Newgarden.
Nicholas Purtle, son of Samuel of New London and Eliza Thompson, dau of John of Londonderry 1755.6.18 at Londongrove.
Caleb Pusey and Eliza Ogle, dau of William and Maria of Cecil Co.
Caleb Pusey of E. Marlborough, son of Thomas and Mary and Hannah Baily, dau of John and Mary 1778.4.8 at Londongrove.
Ellis Pusey, son of Joshua and Mary of Londongrove and Susanna Baily, dau of John and Mary of W. Marlborough 1755.5.21 at Londongrove.
James Pusey, son of John and Katharine of Londongrove and Rachel Jackson, dau of John and Rachel, dec'd, of E. Marlbrough 1761.10.28 at Londongrove.
Jesse Pusey of E. Marlborough, son of Thomas and Mary and Elizabeth Chambers of Londongrove, dau of John and Rebecca 1786.2.13 at Londongrove.
Jonathan Pusey and Sarah Hughes of Londongrove, dau of Samuel and Lydia.
Joshua Pusey, son of Joshua and Mary of Londongrove and Mary Miller, dau of William and Ann of Newgarden 1761.6.25 at Newgarden.
Thomas Pusey son of Caleb of E. Marlborough and Mary Swayne, dau of William, dec'd, of Marlborough 1748.4.15 at Londongrove.
James Pyle and Hannah Neal/Noyle of E. Marlborough, dau of Henry and Sarah, dec'd, 1775.3.27 at Londongrove.
John Pyle and Ann Passmore of W. Marlborough, dau of George and Margaret.
Jesse Hughes and Mary Passmore, dau of George and Mary.
Moses Pyle of Newlin, son of John of Thornbury and Mary Cooke, dau of John of Londongrove 1741.10.9.
Robert Pyle of E. Marlborough, son of Joseph and Deborah Jackson, dau of Samuel of E. Marlborough 1748.10.7 at Londongrove.
William Pyle, son of John and Rachel of Kennett and Sarah Hutton, dau of Benjamin and Ann of Newgarden 1784.11.11 at Newgarden.
John Rakestraw and Mary Ann Passmore, dau of Jesse and Hannah of Londongrove.
William Reynolds, son of William of Orange Co. Nc and Dinah Jackson, dau of John, dec'd, of E. Marlborough 1764.10.10 at Londongrove.
William Reynolds, son of Henry of Chichester and Mary Brown, dau of William, Sr. of Nottingham 1723.11.23 at Nottingham.
Isaac Richards of Newgarden, son of Isaac and Mary and Ann Pusey, dau of Joshua and Mary of Londongrove 1785.12.21 at

Londongrove.
Isaac Richards, widower and Rebecca Miller of Newgarden, widow of James, dau of Jacob Kirk, dec'd.
Lawrence Richards of Leacock, Lancaster Co. and Mary Jones 1732.2.21 at Leacock.
William Richards, son of Nathaniel, dec'd, of Newgarden and Jane Miller, Widow of Joseph 1759.5.10 at Newgarden.
William Richards, son of Nathaniel, dec'd, of Newgarden and Joanna Jenkins 1751.4.13 at Newgarden.
Lawrence Richardson and Mary Jones of Leacock, Lancaster Co.
Benjamin Ring, son of Nathaniel and Rachel Jones 1758.12.6 at Concord.
George Robinson of Cecil Co., son of George of Newark and Mary Mackay 1726.2.14 at Nottingham.
James Robinson of Nottingham, carpenter and Elizabeth Davis 1721.3.18 at Nottingham.
John Robinson of Newgarden from Abington Monthly Meeting and Eunice Conely 1734.11.30 at Newgarden.
Lacey Roules of Nottingham and Mary Oldham, dau of Thomas of Nottingham 1724.3.21.
Moses Rowen, son of William and Elizabeth of Newgarden and Hannah Jackson, dau of John and Sarah Jackson of E. Marlborough 1770.10.17 at Londongrove.
John Russell of Marlborough, son of Thomas and Sarah and Hannah Fincher, dau of John and Jane, dec'd, Fincher 1767.11.11 at Londongrove.
John Scarlet, son of Nathaniel and Hannah and Mary Dixon, dau of Joseph and Sarah, dec'd, of Newgarden 1765.10.31 at Newgarden.
Joseph Seal and Sarah Gawthrope, dau of Thomas and Elizabeth of Londongrove.
Joshua Seal, son of Caleb of Wilmington and Lydia Richards 1783.6.11 at Newgarden.
John Sharp of Newgarden and Ann Bryan 1726.12.16 at Newgarden.
Abraham Sharpless of Londongrove, son of Abraham and Ann and Dinah, dau of Richard and Alice Flower 1788.11.13 at West Grove.
William Shepherd and Pishmonday Wood of Londongrove, dau of Thomas 1749.3.33 at Londongrove.
Solomon Sheppard of Newgarden and Jane Wilson 1733.9.15 at Newgarden.
William Sheppard of Monallen, son of Solomon, dec'd, of Ireland and Rebecca Wood 1749.5.21 at Londongrove.
Samuel Sheward, son of James, dec'd, of W. Bradford and Ruth

Smith, dau of John of E. Marlborough 1754.6.10 at Londongrove.
Swithin Shortledge of Newgarden, son of John and Phebe and Hannah, dau of George and Jane Gawthorp of Londongrove 1799.12.19 at Newgarden.
Elisha Sidwell of E. Nottingham, son of Richard and Ann and Mary Jackson 1791.5.11 at Londongrove.
Nathan Sidwell of W. Nottingham, son of Hugh and Anne and Elinor Cook of Londgrove, dau of John and Rebecca 1779.5.5 at Londongrove.
Henry Simmons and Rachel Preston of Londongrove, dau of Joseph and Rebecca.
Robert Sinclair of Nottingham and Mary Coppock, dau of Aaron of Nottingham 1721.12.15 at Nottingham.
Thomas Smedley and Rachel G. Preston, dau of Isaac, dec'd, and Mary of Frankford, Phila co.
Ephraim Smith, son of Ephraim and Rachel of West Sadsbury and Elizabeth Harry, dau of Jesse and Mary of E. Marlborough 1799.2.6 at Londongrove.
James Smith, son of John, dec'd, and Margaret of Lampeter and Mary Pyle, dau of James and Elizabeth of W. Marlborough 1779.4.7 at Londongrove.
James Smith, son of James of Lampeter and Rachel Musgrove, dau of Aaron of Kennet 1757.5.19 at Newgarden.
John Smith of Marlborough and Dorithy Windle 1728.6.6 of Londongrove.
John Smith, jr., son of John of E. Marlborough and Elizabeth Pusey, dau of Joshua of Londongrove 1756.9.15.
Joseph Smith of Londongrove, son of John, dec'd, and Margaret of Lampeter and Mary Woodward, dau of Thomas and Elizabeth of E. Marlborough 1784.10.20 at Londongrove.
Ebenezer Speakman, son of Thomas, dec'd, of Londongrove and Mary Hayes, dau of Richard, dec'd, of W. Marlborough 1744.9.7 at Londongrove.
Enoch Speakman, son of Hugh and Mary of Londongrove and Mary Clayton, dau of Joshua and Martha of W. Bradford 1782.1.9 at Londongrove.
Joseph Spencer and Rebecca Good of New London, dau of Francis, dec'd, and Sarah.
Isaac Starr of Newgarden and Margaret Lightfoot 1723.12.20 at Newgarden.
Jeremiah Starr of Londongrove and Rachel Moore, dau of Joseph and Jane of Londongrove 1787.12.6 at West Grove.
Jeremiah Starr of Londongrove and Margaret Hayes of W. Marlborough, dau of Richard, dec'd, 1746.10.11 at Londongrove.
Jeremiah Starr, son of Jeremiah of Londongrove and Elizabeth

Hiett 1756.7.1 at Newgarden.
Moses Starr, son of Jeremiah of Londongrove and Sarah Harlan, dau of Michael of Londongrove 1760.3.19 at Londongrove.
John Steer of Leacock, Lancaster Co. and Rachel Evans of Leacock, Lancaster Co. 1732.1.21 at Leacock.
Isaac Stephens, late of Newton, Gloucester Co. and Rachel Jones, dau of Samuel of Leacock 1735/6.1.3 at Leacock.
Jonathan Stephens of Robinson, Berk Co., widower and Margaret Wilson of W. Marlborough, widow 1791.9.7 at Londongrove.
Edward Swaine, son of Francis, dec'd, of Marlborough and Sarah Fincher 1728.2.25 at Londongrove.
Caleb Swayne, son of William. and Ann of E. Marlborough and Mary Wood, dau of William and Margaret of Londongrove 1774.4.13 at Londongrove.
Edward Swayne, son of Edward and Sarah of E. Marlborough and Catherine Haydon 1753.4.26 at Londongrove.
Francis Swayne of E. Marlborough, son of William, dec'd, and Betty Baily, dau of Joel of W. Marlborough 1748.3.18 at Londongrove.
Isaac Swayne, son of Edward and Sarah of E. Marlborough and Susanna Maris, dau of John and Catherine of W. Marlborough 1768.10.21 at Londongrove.
Jacob Swayne of E. Marlborough, son of Samuel and Hannah and Phebe Milhous, dau of Thomas and Elizabeth of Londongrove 1781.5.17 at Newgarden.
James Swayne of E. Marlborough, son of Caleb and Lydia and Hannah Swayne, dau of Francis and Betty of Kennett 1773.11.17 at Londongrove.
Samuel Swayne, son of William, dec'd, of E. Marlborough and Hannah Hayes, dau of William of E. Marlborough 1756.6.16 at Londongrove.
William Swayne of E. Marlborough, son of William., dec'd, and Eliz and Ann Pusey, dau of Caleb and Prudence of E. Marlborough 1743.10.1 at Londongrove.
Gasper Sybolt, of W. Marlborough and Rebeka Clendenon of W. Marlborough, dau of Robert, dec'd, 1748/9.1.15 at Londongrove.
Edward Tatnall, of Marlborough from Philadelphia Monthly Meeting and Elizabeth Pennock, dau of Joseph of Marlborough 1735.4.11 at Londongrove.
Isaac Taylor and Lydia Edmundson of Kennett, Widow.
John Taylor, son of Richard, dec'd, and Elinor of Kennett and Mary Jackson, dau of Samuel, dec'd, and Mary of Marlborough 1762.5.13 at Birmingham.
Joseph Taylor, son of Joseph of W. Marlborough and Hannah

Johnson, dau of Robert of E. Marlborough 1753.10.17 at Londongrove.
Samuel Taylor of Tinicum and Elizabeth Wright 1728.3.8.
Nicholas W. Taylor and Elizabeth Gawthrope, dau of George and Jane of Londongrove.
Isaac Thomas, son of Isaac and Mary of Willistown and Hannah Jackson, dau of William and Katharine of Londongrove 1781.11.8 at Newgarden.
Daniel Thompson and Jane Gawthrope, dau of George and Jane of Londongrove.
Daniel Thompson and Beulah C. Hughes of Londongrove, dau of Mark and Lydia.
Daniel Thompson of Mill Creek, son of James and Elizabeth Chambers of White Clay Creek 1764.10.25 at Newgarden.
James Thompson, son of James of Mill Creek and Martha Chambers of White Clay Creek, dau of Richard 1766.11.6 at Newgarden.
James Thompson of Leacock, son of James of Ellinborough, Salem Co. and Sarah Worsley 1735.3.22 at Newgarden.
James Thompson of Mill Creek Hundred, son of James of Elinborough and Elizabeth Hadley 1742.4.10 at Newgarden.
James Thompson of Mill Creek, son of Daniel and Elizabeth and Mary Scarlet of Newgarden, dau of John and Mary 1798.4.19 at Newgarden.
John Thompson, of Newgarden, Cordwainer, son of William of Dublin, Ireland and Jane Davis 1725.4.24 at Nottingham.
Joseph Thompson and Hannah Hutton, dau of Thomas and Katharine of Newgarden.
Joseph Thompson and Elizabeth Seal, dau of Benjamin and Phebe of Newgarden.
William Thompson, son of Daniel and Elizabeth of Mill Creek and Hannah Hadley, dau of John and Margaret of Mill Creek 1787.11.15 at Newgarden.
James Thomson and Elizabeth Hadley of Mill Creek Hundred, dau of Joseph.
Joseph Thompson, son of James and Elizabeth of Mill Creek and Hannah Hutton 1778.3.19 at Newgarden.
John Todd of New London and Martha Wilson of Londongrove 1749.8.12 at Newgarden.
John Todd of Newgarden and Margaret Cain 1720.8.20 at Newgarden.
William Townsend and Letitia Fell, dau of Thomas and Elizabeth of Londonberry.
Samuel Underwood, son of Alexander of Londongrove and Ann Trevilla 1738.3.10 at Londongrove.

William Underwood and Ruth Bails of Londongrove, dau of William dec'd.
William Underwood, son of Alexander of Londongrove and Ruth Bails 1742/3.1.2 at Londongrove.
Jehu Valentine, son of Jonathan and Lydia of E. Caln and Lydia Jones of Kennett, dau of Joseph and Rachel, dec'd, 1799.6.13 at West Grove.
Joseph Waler of Tredyffrin and Jane Rankin 1794.10.15 at Newgarden.
James Walter of Londongrove, son of Thomas and Rebecca, dec'd, and Ann Jackson, dau of Caleb and Hannah 1793.10.17 at Newgarden.
John Walter of Sadsbury, a carpenter and Martha Musgrove of Sadsbury, dau of John 1724.3.21 at Newgarden.
Isaac Walton of Newgarden, son of Joshua and Elizabeth and Isabel Starr, dau of Thomas and Sarah of Newgarden 1796.5.19.
Joshua Walton and Elizabeth Wilkinson of New London, dau of Thomas and Alice.
Philip Ward of Londongrove and Amy Allen, dau of John of Londongrove 1743.3.19 at Newgarden.
John Warner of Wilmington, son of William, dec'd, and Lydia Woodrow, dau of Isaac, dec'd, of Fallowfield 1766.5.14 at Londongrove.
Joshua Way and Sidney Hutton, dau of Hiett and Sarah of Newgarden.
George Webb, son of Daniel, dec'd, of Kennett and Ann Swayne, dau of William., dec'd, of E. Marlborough 1764.11.10 at Londongrove.
James Webb of Londongrove, son of Benjamin and Jane and Sarah Lamborn, dau of Robert and Ann of Londongrove 1783.11.12 at Londongrove.
Thomas Webb and Hester Paxson of Newgarden, dau of Henry and Matilda.
William Webb, son of William and Elizabeth of Kennett and Sarah Smith 1758.11.16 at Londongrove.
Isaac Webster of Bush River, MD, son of John and Margaret Lee 1722.9.2 at Bush River.
John Webster, son of William of E. Marlborough and Hannah Baily, dau of Joel of W. Marlborough 1750.3.22 at Londongrove.
John Webster of Bush River, Baltimore Co. and Sarah Giles of Patapsco River, Baltimore Co 1729.1.17 at Patapsco.
John Webster and Sarah Passmore, widow of Nathaniel of W. Marlborough.
John Webster of E. Marlborough, widower and Sarah Pennock 1783.6.11 at Londongrove.

Michael Webster of Baltimore Co., MD, son of John of Bush River and
Elizabeth Giles of Baltimore Co., dau of Nathaniel of Patapsco
1722.11.24 at Patapsco.

William Webster, son of William of E. Marlborough and Ann Smith,
dau of John of Marlborough 1748.3.25 at Londongrove.

Joshua West and Lydia Richards, dau of Isaac of Newgarden.

Samuel West, son of William and Hannah of Upper Derby and Mary
Pusey, dau of Joshua and Mary of Londongrove 1778.1.20 at
Londongrove.

John White of Nottingham, son of William, dec'd, of New Castle Co.
and Mary Jobe 1717.8.3 at Nottingham.

Samuel White of Cecil Co. and Hannah Piggott of Cecil Co 1726.2.21 at
Nottingham.

Henry Whitson of Newgarden, son of Thomas and Elizabeth and
Hannah Hutton, dau of Benjamin and Ann of Newgarden 1799.4.18
at Newgarden.

Thomas Whitson and Martha Hobson of Newgarden, dau of Francis
and Ann.

Abner Wickersham, son of James of E. Marlborough and Mary Taylor
1781.4.17 at Kennett.

Caleb Wickersham and Sarah Greenfield of Newgarden, dau of Daniel
Thompson.

Caleb Wickersham, son of William and Elizabeth of Newlin and Rachel
Swayne of E. Marlborough, dau of Samuel and Hannah 1789.11.5 at
Londongrove.

Enoch Wickersham and Elizabeth Hurford, dau of John and Hannah of
Newgarden and Martha Maris 1773.11.20 at Londongrove.

Enoch Wickersham, son of James and Ann of E. Marlborough and
Elizabeth Hurford 1764.8.15 at Londongrove.

Peter Wickersham, son of William and Rachel, dec'd, of Newlin and
Kezia Parker, dau of Abraham, dec'd, and Elinor of Kennett
1773.5.19 at Londongrove.

Robert Wickersham and Mary Taylor, dau of Joseph of W.
Marlborough.

Sampson Wickersham, son of James and Ann of E. Marlborough and
Elizabeth Jackson, dau of Jonathan and Mary of E. Marlborough
1775.11.22 at Londongrove.

Thomas Wickersham and Priscilla Jones, dau of Joseph and Elizabeth
of Newgarden.

William Wickersham, son of William of Newlin and Elizabeth Pusey,
dau of William of W. Marlborough 1764.5.23 at Londongrove.

William Wickersham of Newlin and Jane Hayes, widow of Joseph
Hayes of E. Marlborough 1750.9.22 at Londongrove.

Thomas Wiley, son of Allen of Newgarden and Rachel Rowland, dau of Thomas, dec'd, of Newgarden 1729.9.13 at Newgarden.
Francis Wilkinson, son of Joseph and Eliza of E. Caln and Hannah Mode, dau of Alexander and Rebecca of E. Fallowfield 1770.4.11 at Londongrove.
Joseph Wilkinson, of Kent Co. Md, son of Joseph, dec'd, of Paxton, Lancaster Co. and Mary Lamborn, dau of Robert and Ann of Londongrove 1775.10.3 at Londongrove.
Thomas Wilkinson of Londongrove, son of Joseph and Elizabeth and Alice Pyle of W. Marlborough, dau of Joseph and Alice 1778.11.11 at Londongrove.
Daniel Williams and Hannah Francina Cook, dau of Thomas and Hannah of Londongrove.
John Williams, son of Orion of Talbot Co. and Mary Grafton 1726.7.15 at Nottingham.
William Wills, son of Edward, dec'd, of Birmingham and Betty Harlan, dau of James of Londongrove 1753.11.30 at Londongrove.
Thomas Willy, son of Allen of Newgarden and Rachel Rowland 1729.9.13 at Newgarden.
Amos Wilson and Hannah Brown, dau of David and Hannah of Newgarden.
David Wilson and Sarah Hadley, dau of Samuel and Mabel of Mill Creek.
Ephraim Wilson and Elizabeth of Londongrove, dau of Joshua and Elizabeth, dec'd.
Isaac Wilson of Wilmington, son of John and Alisanna of Deer Creek, MD and Susanna Hoopes, dau of David and Esther of Newgarden 1789.4.14 at Newgarden.
James Wilson, son of James, dec'd, of Londongrove and Margaret Todd, dau of John of New London 1759.3.8 at Newgarden.
John Wilson and Hannah Oborn of W. Marlborough.
John Wilson of E. Marlborough and Elizabeth Jackson of E. Marlborough, dau of John, dec'd, 1741.10.24 at Londongrove.
John Wilson and Hannah Wilson of Birmingham 1738.9.8 at Londongrove.
John Wilson, son of Christopher of Christiana Hundred and Dinah Cook, dau of Isaac, dec'd, of Londongrove 1759.10.31 at Londongrove.
David Windle of E. Marlborough, son of Thomas and Mary and Abigail Kirk of Christiana Hundred, dau of Adam and Phebe 1780.5.10 Londongrove.
Francis Windle of Marlborough and Mary Jackson, dau of Isaac of Londongrove 1733.4.14 at Newgarden.
Thomas Windle, son of Francis and Mary of E. Marlborough and Abigail Wickersham, dau of William and Rachel of Newlin 1765.5.22

at Londongrove.

William Windle, son of Francis and Mary of E. Marlborough and Mary Jackson 1761.11.25 at Londongrove.

James Wollaston of Mill Creek, son of Jeremiah and Mary Chambers of White Clay Creek, dau of William 1752.11.11 at Newgarden.

Thomas Wollaston, son of Jeremiah of Mill Creek and Hannah Johnson, dau of Joshua of Londongrove 1758.5.17 at Londongrove.

James Wood and Lettice Chamberlain, dau of William and Martha of Westtown.

Thomas Wood, son of William and Margaret of Londongrove and Susanna Pusey, dau of John and Katharine of Londongrove 1773.11.24 at Londongrove.

Isaac Woodrow of Kennett, son of Isaac, dec'd, and Mary and Ruth Dixon, dau of Joseph and Sarah of Newgarden 1766.10.23 at Newgarden.

Simeon Woodrow, son of Isaac of W. Fallowfield and Lydia Pyle, dau of Moses of E. Marlborough 1757.6.16 at Londongrove.

James Woodward, son of John and Sarah of W. Bradford and Lettice Chamberlain 1789.9.15 at Londongrove.

Levi Woodward and Phebe Hutton, dau of Joseph and Sarah of Newgarden.

Samuel Woodward, son of Thomas and Elizabeth of E. Marlborough and Sarah Jackson, dau of John and Sarah, dec'd, of E. Marlborough 1773.5.12 at Londongrove.

Thomas Woodward, son of Thomas and Elizabeth of E. Marlborough and Mary Pusey, dau of Ellis and Susanna of W. Fallowfield 1777.10.15 at Londongrove.

Jacob Wright of E. Marlborough, son of Jacob, decd and Mary Jackson, dau of Thomas of W. Marlborough 1741.2.8 of Londongrove.

David Yarnall of Kennett, son of Phillip and Hannah Swayne, dau of Edward of Marlborough 1758.1.12 at Londongrove.

Nathan Yarnall of Edgmont and Hannah Mendenhall, dau of Benjamin, dec'd, of Concord 1750.3.10 at Middletown.

CERTIFICATES OF REMOVAL
1781-1800

Rumford Davis, and wife, Mary to Northern district of Philadelphia Monthly Meeting 1780.5.5.

Samuel Clark and his wife, Ruth to Kennett Monthly Meeting 1781.2.6.

Elizabeth Painter, wife of Joseph Painter to Concord Monthly Meeting 1781.2.6.

Mary Wickersham, wife of Abner to Kennett Monthly Meeting 1781.2.6.

NEW GARDEN MONTHLY MEETING

John Troth, an apprentice to Cecil Monthly Meeting, MD 1781.7.7.
Joel Morton to Newgarden Monthly Meeting 1781.4.8.
Samuel Jackson and his family to Hopewell, VA Monthly Meeting 1781.6.10.
Susanna, wife of John Bartlett to Newgarden Monthly Meeting 1781.6.10.
Samuel Hutton to Third Haven Monthly Meeting, MD 1781.6.10.
Hannah Butler to Bradford Monthly Meeting 1781.5.4.
Olive Thatcher, a young woman to Third Haven Monthly Meeting 1781.11.3.
William Common, to Cane Creek Monthly Meeting NC 1781.11.3.
Hannah, wife of Isaac Thomas, Jr. to Goshen Monthly Meeting 1782.2.2.
Hannah, wife of Caleb Harlan to Bradford Monthly Meeting 1782.2.2.
Elizabeth, wife of Joseph Gamble to Indian Spring Monthly Meeting 1782.2.2.
Thomas Cook to Hopewell Monthly Meeting, VA 1782.6.2.
Phebe, wife of William Downing, Jr. to Sadsbury Monthly Meeting 1782.3.2.
Joseph Morgan to Kennett Monthly Meeting 1782.3.2.
Moses Edward, Jr. to Sadsbury Monthly Meeting 1782.3.2.
Levi Woodward to Kennett Monthly Meeting 1782.4.6.
Lydia Hash to Bradford Monthly Meeting 1782.4.6.
Samuel Cleton to Bradford Monthly Meeting 1782.4.1.
Nathaniel Matter to Concord Monthly Meeting 1782.5.4.
Ann Taylor to Pipe Creek Monthly Meeting 1782.5.4.
Amos Ailes to Hopewell Monthly Meeting, VA 1782.5.4.
Hannah Hutten to Monallen Monthly Meeting 1782.6.1.
Catherine Kirk to Sadsbury Monthly Meeting 1782.6.1.
John Hutton and his wife, Rachel to Derby Monthly Meeting 1782.7.6.
Isaac Taylor, a young man to Haddonfield Monthly Meeting in W. Jersey 1782.7.6.
Elizabeth Webb, to Pipe Creek Monthly Meeting 1782.7.6.
Jacob Taylor, a young man to Abington Monthly Meeting 1782.8.3.
Phebe, wife of Garret Garretson to Bradford Monthly Meeting 1782.8.3.
Rachel Jordan to Kennett Monthly Meeting 1782.8.3.
Patience Jordan to Kennett Monthly Meeting 1782.8.3.
Mary Jordan to Kennett Monthly Meeting 1782.8.3.
Dinah Batten, a young woman to Hopewell Monthly Meeting, VA 1782.8.3.
Elizabeth Wobb to Pipe Creek Monthly Meeting 1782.7.6.
Elizabeth Pyle to Philadelphia Monthly Meeting southern district 1782.6.7.

Phebe Trimble to Concord Monthly Meeting 1782.10.5.
Lydia Windle to Wilmington Monthly Meeting 1782.10.5.
Gravener Baily, a young man to Kennett Monthly Meeting 1782.11.2.
Dinah Batten, a young woman to Kennett Monthly Meeting 1782.12.7.
Samuel Morton to Kennett Monthly Meeting 1782.12.7.
Isaac Jackson for his son, William placed as an apprentice at Bradford Monthly Meeting 1783.1.4.
John Davis who is placed as an apprentice to Kennett Monthly Meeting 1783.1.4.
Elisha Davis, a minor, to Kennett Monthly Meeting 1783.1.4.
Bennajah Brown and Jesse Davis, son and stepson of Amos Davis, dec'd to Uwchlan Monthly Meeting 1783.1.4.
Nathaniel Richards to Wilmington Monthly Meeting 1783.5.1.
Isaac Barger to Newgarden Monthly Meeting 1783.3.1.
Ebenezar Maule to Havarford Monthly Meeting 1783.3.1.
Robert Common and his wife, Ruth to Sadsbury Monthly Meeting 1783.5.7.
Sarah Hall to Philadelphia Northern District Monthly Meeting 1783.5.7.
Elizabeth Harvey to Wilmington Monthly Meeting 1783.5.7.
Ruth Milhous with her parents to Newgarden Monthly Meeting 1783.5.7.
Aaron Clayton and his wife Sarah to Bradford Monthly Meeting 1783.5.7.
John Milhous and his wife, Margaret with their apprentice, Daniel Smith to Nottingham Monthly Meeting 1783.5.7.
Samuel Pennock and his wife, Mary to Kennett Monthly Meeting 1783.5.7.
Philipp Price, Jr. to Darby Monthly Meeting 1783.6.7.
Margaret, wife of James Wilson and her eight children: Sarah, John, James, Margaret, Abner, Hannah, Jesse and Phebe to Nottingham Monthly Meeting 1783.6.7.
Mary Wilson to Nottingham Monthly Meeting 1783.6.7.
Ann, wife of David Hayse and her son, Nathan to Concord Monthly Meeting 1783.8.7.
Thomas Hutton, Jr. to Wilmington Monthly Meeting 1783.7.5.
Hannah Harlan, a young woman to Wilmington Monthly Meeting 1783.7.5.
David and Anna Hayes, children of David and Ann Hayes to Concord Monthly Meeting 1783.7.5.
Joseph, Mary and Joshua Baker, children of John Baker, dec'd with their mother, now the wife of John Edwards to Chester Monthly Meeting 1783.7.5.
Lydia, wife of Joshua Seal to Wilmington Monthly Meeting 1783.8.2.
Edward Stroud with his son, Edward to Wilmington Monthly Meeting

NEW GARDEN MONTHLY MEETING

1783.9.6.
Margaret Anderson with her mother to Hopewell Monthly Meeting, VA 1783.9.6.
Hannah Swayne with her husband, James Swayne and two of her children, Francis and Betty to Crooked Run Monthly Meeting 1783.11.1.
Sarah Jonston, a young woman to Wilmington Monthly Meeting 1783.11.1.
Hannah Bailey to Bradford Monthly Meeting 1783.12.30.
William, Isaac and Simon Warner who are placed as apprentices to Wilmington Monthly Meeting 1783.12.6.
Spencer Chandler to Kennett Monthly Meeting 1783.12.6.
Permanes Lamborn who is placed as an apprentice to Kennett Monthly Meeting 1784.2.7.
Lydia, wife of John Warner for herself and five children: Mary, Joseph, Rachel, Levi and Nanny Warner to Wilmington Monthly Meeting 1784.2.7.
Ruth Wood, a young woman to Pipe Creek Monthly Meeting 1784.1.3.
Sarah Leonard to Wilmington Monthly Meeting 1784.3.6.
Evan Baily, a young man to Kennett Monthly Meeting 1784.3.6.
Hannah Miller to Kennett Monthly Meeting 1784.4.3.
Thomas Moore to Sadsbury Monthly Meeting 1784.4.3.
Joanna Davis, wife of Isaac Davis to Wilmington Monthly Meeting 1784.5.1.
Thomas Cloud and his wife, Jane to Wilmington Monthly Meeting 1784.5.1.
Thomas Martin to Bradford Monthly Meeting 1784.6.5.
Moses Rowen and his wife, Hannah and their seven children: William, John, Elizabeth, Sarah, Amos, Mary and Phebe to Philadelphia Southern District Monthly Meeting 1784.6.5.
Rachel, wife of Joseph Johnson and their three children: Isaac, Joshua and Rachel to Uwchlan Monthly Meeting 1784.6.5.
Thomas Maule to Nottingham Monthly Meeting 1784.7.3.
Thomas Foulk, who is placed as an apprentice to Willimington Monthly Meeting 1784.7.3.
Joel Morton to Philadelphia Southern District Monthly Meeting 1784.7.3.
Hannah Hurford, a young woman to Wilmington Monthly Meeting 1784.9.1.
Isaac Cook to Pipe Creek Monthly Meeting 1784.9.1.
Jacob Taylor and his wife, Elizabeth and child, Ann to Bradford Monthly Meeting 1784.10.2.
Joseph Person to Kennett Monthly Meeting 1784.11.6.
Hannah and Ellis Baily, children of William Baily, dec'd to Kennett Monthly Meeting 1784.11.6.

Esther Townsend to Concord Monthly Meeting 1784.11.6.
Robert Wickersham to Philadelphia Northern District Monthly Meeting 1784.12.4.
Mordecai Churchman to Nottingham Monthly Meeting 1784.12.4.
Ann Hutton to Monallen Monthly Meeting 1784.12.4.
Rebecka Brinton, a young woman to Concord Monthly Meeting 1784.12.4.
Betty Baily to Kennett Monthly Meeting 1784.12.4.
Rachel Bernard, a young woman to Wilmington Monthly Meeting 1785.1.1.
Isaac Davis to Gunpowder Monthly Meeting 1785.2.5.
Isaac Chamberlain to Concord Monthly Meeting 1785.4.2.
Mary Atmore to Philadelphia Northern District Monthly Meeting 1785.4.7.
Margaret, wife of Garrett Garretson to Bradford Monthly Meeting 1785.5.7.
Hannah, wife of John Jackson, Jr. to Wilmington Monthly Meeting 1785.5.4.
James Moore and his wife, Lydia to Sadsbury Monthly Meeting 1785.6.2.
Andrew Moore to Chester Monthly Meeting 1785.6.4
Rachel Marsh to Willimington Monthly Meeting 1785.9.3.
Lydia Davis to Uwchlan Monthly Meeting 1785.7.2.
Jacob Wood and his wife, Isabell and their seven children: Joseph, John, Elizabeth, Jacob, Joshua, Enos and Lewis to Wilmington Monthly Meeting 1785.7.2.
Thomas Pusey, who is an apprentice to Bradford Monthly Meeting 1785.7.2.
Deborah, wife of Caleb Kimber to Uwchlan Monthly Meeting 1785.7.2.
Sarah, wife of Thomas Baker to Bradford Monthly Meeting 1785.7.2.
Margaret Flower, a young woman to Bradford Monthly Meeting 1785.7.2.
Joseph Lamborn who is placed as an apprentice to Kennett Monthly Meeting 1785.7.2.
Lewis Lamborn, a minor, who is placed as an apprentice to Willimington Monthly Meeting 1785.8.6.
Caleb Baily to Deer Creek Monthly Meeting 1785.8.6.
Isaac Trimble and his wife, Elizabeth with their five children: Joseph, John, Mary, Jane and James to Newgarden Monthly Meeting 1785.8.6.
Susanna Harlan a single woman, to Gun Powder Monthly Meeting 1785.9.3.
Abigail, wife of Paschall Milhous and her children: Amos, Thomas, Townsend, Lydia and Hannah to Kennett Monthly Meeting 1785.11.5.

NEW GARDEN MONTHLY MEETING 169

Susanna Milhous to Kennett Monthly Meeting 1785.12.3.
Joseph Baily, who is placed as an apprentice to Willimington Monthly Meeting 1785.12.3.
John Cook, who is placed as an apprentice to Kennett Monthly Meeting 1785.12.3.
Lewis Harlan to Nottingham Monthly Meeting 1786.2.4.
Thomas Welsh and his wife, Elizabeth to Kennett Monthly Meeting 1786.2.4.
Elisha Moore to live with his father to Sadsbury Monthly Meeting 1786.3.4.
Daniel Jonson to Goshen Monthly Meeting 1786.3.2.
Mary Webb to Sadsbury Monthly Meeting 1786.3.4.
Hannah Whiteside and her husband to Westland Monthly Meeting 1785.3.4.
Susanna Ailes to Kennett Monthly Meeting 1786.3.4.
Jane Taylor, wife of Joseph Taylor and their children: Jesse, James, Joseph, Israel and Sarah to Hopewell Monthly Meeting, Va 1786.4.1.
Joshua Wood to Crooked Run Monthly Meeting 1786.4.1.
Margaret Taylor, wife of John Taylor to Kennett Monthly Meeting 1786.5.6.
Rachel Pennock to Kennett Monthly Meeting 1786.5.6.
Jonathan Barnard, a young man to Hopewell Monthly Meeting, VA 1786.6.3.
Mary, wife of Solomon Harlan and their six children: Joseph, John, David, Ann, George and Lewis to Nottingham Monthly Meeting 1786.6.3.
Abigail Wickersham, a young woman to Hopewell Monthly Meeting, VA 1786.6.5.
Hannah Hurford to Crooked Run Monthly Meeting, Va 1786.6.3.
Deborah Bornard, a young woman to Hopewell Monthly Meeting, VA 1786.7.1.
Mary Common, dau of John Common, she being a child to Wilmington Monthly Meeting 1786.7.1.
Joshua Hallowell and his wife, Hannah and their six children: Margaret, Jesse, Joshua, Hannah, William and Joseph to Wilmington Monthly Meeting 1786.7.1.
David Lamborn to Kennett Monthly Meeting 1786.8.10.
Phebe Harry with her husband to Kennett Monthly Meeting 1786.8.10.
Joseph Hurford and his wife Naomi and their children: John, Ann, William, Nathan, Joseph, Benjamin, Thomas and Samuel to Crooked Run Monthly Meeting 1786.6.7.
Joseph Curle to Hopewell, VA Monthly Meeting 1786.9.2.
David Harlan and his wife Alice and their four minor children: Elisha, Hannah, Rebeckah and Alice to Nottingham Monthly Meeting

1786.9.2.
Jeremiah Harlan to Nottingham Monthly Meeting 1786.9.2.
Lydia Gatchel to Nottingham Monthly Meeting 1786.9.2.
James and Joseph Davis, both minors to Hopewell, VA Monthly Meeting. 1786.11.4.
Isaac Moore and his wife, Lydia to Sadsbury Monthly Meeting 1786.12.2.
Sarah Underwood, an ancient friend to Westland Monthly Meeting, Fegetta Co. 1786.12.2.
Samuel Hurford and his wife, Rachel and their children: Katharine, Rachel, Elizabeth, Samuel and Ruth to Crooked Run Monthly Meeting 1786.12.2.
Hannah Hurford to Crooked Run Monthly Meeting 1786.12.2.
Sarah Hurford with her parents to Crooked Run Monthly Meeting 1786.12.2.
Joseph Hurford, son of Samuel to Crooked Run Monthly Meeting 1786.12.2.
Silas Bennett to Kennett Monthly Meeting 1787.1.6.
Joseph Jackson to Indian Spring Monthly Meeting 1787.2.3.
Elizabeth Williams to Kennett Monthly Meeting 1787.3.3
Samuel Price to Duckcreek Monthly Meeting 1787.3.3.
William Bennett to Kennett Monthly Meeting 1787.4.7.
Isaac Barger to Nottingham Monthly Meeting 1786.3.3
James Curle to Kennett Monthly Meeting 1787.5.5.
Israel Harlan, a young man to Bradford Monthly Meeting 1787.5.5
Phebe Harlan to Wilmington Monthly Meeting 1787.5.5.
Amos Pyle to Nottingham Monthly Meeting 1787.7.7.
Caleb Kimber, and his wife Deborah to Philadelphia Monthly Meeting Southern District 1787.7.7.
John Fincher to Exeter Monthly Meeting 1787.7.7.
Ruth Wood, a young woman to Gunpowder Monthly Meeting 1787.8.4.
Margaret Davis with her husband and their five minor children: Elizabeth, George, Ellis, Benjamin and Hannah to Bradford Monthly Meeting 1787.8.4.
Thomas Barnard and his wife, Sarah to Nottingham Monthly Meeting 1787.9.1.
John Wilson, Jr. to Deer Creek Monthly Meeting to live with his father 1787.10.6.
Bernard Gilpin to Hopewell, VA Monthly Meeting 1787.10.6.
Joseph Taylor to Crooked Run Monthly Meeting 1787.10.6.
Hannah Taylor, a minor to Concord Monthly Meeting 1787.11.3.
John Jones and his wife, Hannah and their children, William and Joel to Nottingham Monthly Meeting 1787.11.3.
Arron Cox to Concord Monthly Meeting 1787.12.1.
Elizabeth Thompson to Kennett Monthly Meeting 1788.5.3.

NEW GARDEN MONTHLY MEETING 171

Thomas Marshall and Ann, his wife and their children: Martha, Hannah, Joseph, Esther and Ann to Kennett Monthly Meeting 1788.5.5.
Mary Baldwin to Sadsbury Monthly Meeting 1788.6.7.
Thomas Harlan to Kennett Monthly Meeting 1788.6.7.
Mary Taylor to Kennett Monthly Meeting 1788.3.1.
Sarah Stubbs to Nottingham Monthly Meeting 1788.7.5.
Olive Cookson to Nottingham Monthly Meeting 1788.7.5.
Joseph Newlin to Willimington Monthly Meeting 1788.8.2.
Hannah Wickersham to Bradford Monthly Meeting 1788.8.2.
Jacob Woods and his wife, Isabel and their children: Joseph, John, Elizabeth, Jacob, Joshua, Esau and Lewis to Westland Monthly Meeting 1788.9.6.
Elizabeth Hughs to Pipe Creek Monthly Meeting 1788.9.6.
Ann Betts with her husband to Westland Monthly Meeting 1788.9.6.
Joseph Hoopes, being placed as an apprentice to Willimington Monthly Meeting 1788.10.11.
Jonathan Miller to Nottingham Monthly Meeting 1788.10.4.
Reuben Bailey, a minor being placed as an apprentice to Kennett Monthly Meeting. 1788.10.4.
William Jackson to Westbury Monthly Meeting, Long Island 1788.10.11.
Isaac Johnson, and his wife, Lydia and their children: Kathrin, Reuben, Isaac, Hadly, Lydia, Ruel and Zilla refused a certificate to Westland Monthly Meeting 1788.10.4.
William Dixon, and his wife, Rebekah and their two sons, Joseph and William to Westland Monthly Meeting 1788.10.4.
Susanna Dixon with her parents to Westland Monthly Meeting 1788.10.4.
Mary Miller to Westland Monthly Meeting 1788.10.4.
David Michener to Abington Monthly Meeting 1788.11.1.
Lydia Edmundson with her husband to Motherkiln Monthly Meeting 1788.12.6.
Alice Woodward to Willimington Monthly Meeting 1788.12.6.
Isaac Wilson to Willimington Monthly Meeting 1788.12.6.
Thomas Lamborn for his son, Jonathan, a minor to live with his uncle to Bradford Monthly Meeting 1789.1.3.
Margaret Moody to Sadsbury Monthly Meeting 1789.1.3.
Isaac Chamberlain to Concord Monthly Meeting 1789.1.3.
Mary Taylor, wife of Joseph to Bradford Monthly Meeting 1789.1.3.
Betty Mendelhall to Hopewell, VA Monthly Meeting 1789.2.7.
William Chandler, Jr. to Westland Monthly Meeting 1789.3.7.
Ann, wife of John McIlvain to Chester Monthly Meeting 1789.3.7.
Elizabeth Milhous to Kennett Monthly Meeting 1789.3.7.
Margaret Milhous to Kennett Monthly Meeting 1789.3.7.

Jonathan Hartley and his wife, Elizabeth and their three children: Martha, David and Jesse to Sadsbury Monthly Meeting 1789.3.4.
Thomas Wilkson and his wife, Alice and their children: Joseph, Alice, Elizabeth and Thomas to Willimington Monthly Meeting 1789.4.4.
Margaret Moses to Philadelphia Monthly Meeting Southern District 1789.6.6.
Hiet Hutton to Nottingham Monthly Meeting 1789.7.4.
Jesse Huton and his wife, Lydia and their children: Enos, Katharine and Hannah to Nottingham Monthly Meeting 1789.7.4.
Joseph Ross to Kennett Monthly Meeting 1789.7.4
Samuel Smith, a minor to Kingwood Monthly Meeting, West Jersey 1789.7.4.
Susanna Wilson, wife of Isaac Wilson to Willimington Monthly Meeting 1789.7.4.
Simon Hadley to Willimington Monthly Meeting 1789.7.4.
Caleb Windle to Crooked Run 1789.7.4.
Thomas Stanfield to Newgarden Monthly Meeting, NC 1789.7.4.
John Pyle and his wife, Susannah and their two children, Jesse and Sarah to Westland Monthly Meeting 1789.7.4.
Esther Painter, a young woman to Kennett Monthly Meeting 1789.8.1.
Margaret Wilson to Kennett Monthly Meeting 1789.9.5.
Ruth Wood to Nottingham Monthly Meeting 1789.9.5.
Jesse Greave and his wife, Elizabeth and their two daughters, Tacy and Hannah to Westland Monthly Meeting 1789.10.3.
Thomas Parker, a minor placed as an apprentice to Philadelphia Monthly Meeting nd 1789.11.7.
Elizabeth Milhous, Jr. to Kennett Monthly Meeting 1789.11.7.
William Chambers, a young man to Sadsbury Monthly Meeting 1789.10.3.
James Woodward and his wife, Lettis to Nottingham Monthly Meeting 1789.11.7.
Joseph Pierce and his wife, Mary and their children, Ruth, Susanna to Burlington Monthly Meeting 1790.3.2.
Jacob Swayne and his wife, Elizabeth and their children: Deborah, David and Thomas to Bradford Monthly Meeting 1790.5.1.
Isaac Davis, a young man to Nottingham Monthly Meeting 1790.6.5.
Emer Harlan, a minor, to live with his parents to Nottingham Monthly Meeting 1790.6.5.
Ann Evans, a young woman to Gwynedd Monthly Meeting 1790.7.3.
Abraham Sharpless and his wife, Dinah to Concord Monthly Meeting 1790.8.7.
Ruth Hayse Wood to Uwchlan Monthly Meeting 1790.9.4.
George Churchman, Jr. to Nottingham Monthly Meeting 1790.10.9.
James Danisen to Third Haven Monthly Meeting 1790.11.6.
Joseph Pennock, a young man to Newgarden Monthly Meeting

NEW GARDEN MONTHLY MEETING

1790.12.4.
Mary Starr to Goshen Monthly Meeting 1790.12.4.
Rebeckah Hoopes, wife of William Hoopes to Cecil Monthly Meeting 1790.12.4.
Agnes Davies to Nottingham Monthly Meeting 1791.1.1.
Susanna Chambers to Sadsbury Monthly Meeting 1791.2.5.
Mary House to Kennett Monthly Meeting 1791.2.5.
Sarah Speakman to Concord Monthly Meeting 1791.3.5.
Betty Mercer to Concord Monthly Meeting 1791.3.5.
Ann Cloud to Willimington Monthly Meeting 1791.4.2.
Ann and Lydia Cloud to Willimington Monthly Meeting 1791.4.2.
Isaac Conrad and his wife, Mary to Sadsbury Monthly Meeting 1791.4.9.
Swithin Chandler to Kennett Monthly Meeting 1791.4.2.
Joshua Harvey to Kennett Monthly Meeting 1791.4.2.
George Hoopes to Goshen Monthly Meeting 1791.4.2.
Joshua Stroud and his wife, Martha and their three children: Samuel, Caleb and Mary to Willimington Monthly Meeting 1791.5.7.
Joseph Atkinson and his wife, Rachel and their two children: Sarah and Rachel to Indian Spring Monthly Meeting 1791.5.7.
Abigail Atkinson with her brother to Indian Spring Monthly Meeting 1791.5.7.
Isaac Lamborn to Bradford Monthly Meeting 1791.6.4.
Thomas Wayne and his wife, Mary and their children, Sarah and Jacob to Wilmington Monthly Meeting 1790.6.4.
Abigail Harlan, Jr. to Wilmington Monthly Meeting 1791.6.4.
Abigail Wickersham to Philadelphia nd Monthly Meeting 1791.7.2.
Sarah Woodrow to Sadsbury Monthly Meeting 1791.8.6.
Benejah Brown to Gunpowder Monthly Meeting 1791.8.6.
Hannah Hughes, widow to Gunpowder Monthly Meeting 1791.9.3.
Jesse Hoopes, being placed as an apprentice to Willimington Monthly Meeting 1791.9.3.
Mary Sidwell to Nottingham 1791.10.8.
Margaret Stephen to Robinson Monthly Meeting 1791.11.5.
Samuel Harlan to Concord Monthly Meeting 1791.11.5.
William Jackson to Fairfax, VA Monthly Meeting 1791.11.5.
Ruth McMillan with her husband to Warrington Monthly Meeting 1791.12.3.
Thomas Lamborn, Jr. to Kennett Monthly Meeting 1791.12.3.
Hannah Passmore to Nottingham Monthly Meeting 1791.9.3.
Katherine Evans, a young woman to Exeter Monthly Meeting 1792.1.7. Certificate returned to Newgarden Monthly Meeting 1792.10.6 and directed to Gwynedd Monthly Meeting.
Thomas Flower to Concord Monthly Meeting 1792.1.7.
Abraham Sinclair to Hopewell Monthly Meeting, VA 1792.2.4.

Tamzin Hoopes to Goshen Monthly Meeting 1792.2.4.
Caleb Pusey to Motherklin Monthly Meeting 1792.2.4.
Caleb Miller to Kennett Monthly Meeting 1792.3.3.
Esther Townsend to Westland Monthly Meeting 1792.2.4.
Nathan Pusey placed as an apprentice to Bradford Monthly Meeting 1792.3.3.
Sarah Lukins to Deer Creek Monthly Meeting 1792.3.3.
Mary Smith to Sadsbury Monthly Meeting 1792.5.5.
Martha Wilson, a minor to Middletown Monthly Meeting 1792.5.5.
Sarah Disses to Philadelphia Northern District Monthly Meeting 1792.5.5.
Stephen Cook, Jr. to Bradford Monthly Meeting 1792.5.5.
William Hoopes to Warrington Monthly Meeting 1792.5.5.
Reuben Starr placed as an apprentice to Goshen Monthly Meeting 1792.5.5.
Joseph Moore, Jr. and his wife, Merry to Nottingham Monthly Meeting 1792.6.2.
William Preston and his wife, Mary to Nottingham Monthly Meeting 1792.6.2.
Hannah Starr, a young woman to Goshen Monthly Meeting 1792.7.7.
Massey Jordon to Hopewell, Va Monthly Meeting 1792.7.7.
Elizabeth Wilson, wife of Benjamin and their children: Joseph, Agness and George to Middletown Monthly Meeting 1792.8.4.
Mark Evans to Sadsbury Monthly Meeting 1792.8.4.
Peter Cook to Bradford Monthly Meeting 1792.8.4.
Susanna Jackson to Gunpowder Monthly Meeting, MD 1792.8.4
Margaret Garretson to Bradford Monthly Meeting 1792.8.4.
Betty Story to Wilmington Monthly Meeting 1792.8.4.
Jacob Miller placed as an apprentice by his father to Willimington Monthly Meeting 1792.9.1.
Rebecca Sharpless to York Monthly Meeting 1792.9.1.
Martha Mendenhall to Fairfax, VA Monthly Meeting 1792.11.3.
Rebecca McMillan to Warrington Monthly Meeting 1793.11.6.
Isaac Shortridge placed as an apprentice to Willimington Monthly Meeting 1793.1.5.
Isaac Wickersham being placed with a friend to Bradford Monthly Meeting 1793.1.5.
William Pennock, who was disowned by this meeting many years ago for going out in marriage, having made an acknowledgement requests a certificate to South River Monthly Meeting, Campbell Co., VA 1793.2.2.
Jesse Pennock to Londongrove Monthly Meeting 1793.3.2.
Joel Richardson to Philadelphia Monthly Meeting 1793.3.2.
Sarah Pennock a young woman to Londongrove Monthly Meeting 1793.3.2.

NEW GARDEN MONTHLY MEETING 175

William Jackson to Cedar Creek, VA 1793.3.2.
Permela Marshall to Philadelphia nd Monthly Meeting 1793.3.2.
Jacob Lindley to visit among the Indians 1793.4.11.
John Richardson to Sadsbury Monthly Meeting 1793.5.16.
Hannah Jackson to Philadelphia Northern District Monthly Meeting 1793.5.16.
Isaac Jackson, Jr. to Philadelphia Northern District Monthly Meeting 1793.5.16.
Rachel Gray with her husband to Bradford Monthly Meeting 1793.7.6.
Sarah Batten to Londongrove Monthly Meeting 1793.9.7.
Susanna Walton to Buckingham Monthly Meeting 1793.10.5.
Joshua Walton placed as an apprentice to Kennett Monthly Meeting 1793.11.2.
James Walter and his wife Ann to Philadelphia Southern District Monthly Meeting 1793.8.4.
Samuel Richardson to Nottingham Monthly Meeting 1794.1.4.
Jesse Pugh and his wife, Catharine to Nottingham Monthly Meeting 1794.1.4.
Jonathan Lamborn placed as an apprentice to Kennett Monthly Meeting 1794.2.1.
George Churchman, Jr. to Nottingham Monthly Meeting 1794.4.5.
William Jones to Wilmington Monthly Meeting 1794.5.3.
Margaret Conrad, a young woman to Willimington Monthly Meeting 1794.5.3.
Benjamin Cutler and his wife Susanna and their eight children: Jonathan, Susannah, Jesse, Anna, Benjamin, Jacob, Hannah and Ruth to Nottingham Monthly Meeting 1794.5.3.
Hannah Cook with her husband to Londongrove Monthly Meeting 1794.7.5.
Jesse Way, a minor placed with a friend to Kennett Monthly Meeting 1794.9.6.
John Jackson, a minor to Philadelphia Southern District Monthly Meeting 1794.10.11.
Eli Swayne, a minor to Kennett Monthly Meeting 1794.10.11.
Permenas Lamborn to Fairfax, VA Monthly Meeting 1794.11.1.
Caleb Pusey to Nottingham Monthly Meeting 1794.12.4.
Jane Malher with her husband, from Canada to Haverford Monthly Meeting 1794.12.6.
Alice Murry to Philadelphia Southern District Monthly Meeting 1795.1.3.
Enos Painter to Concord Monthly Meeting 1795.2.7.
Samuel Fisher to Menallen Monthly Meeting 1795.3.7.
Susannah Jackson to Philadelphia Southern District Monthly Meeting 1795.3.7.
Benjamin Mason and his wife, Sarah and their five children: George,

Benjamin, Jane, Mary and Sarah to Nottingham Monthly Meeting 1795.4.4.
James Harlan and his wife, Elizabeth and their six children: Elwood, Hannah, Mary, Benjamin, Milton and Jonathan all in their minority, to Nottingham Monthly Meeting 1795.4.4.
Mary Swayne and her children to Nottingham Monthly Meeting 1795.4.4.
Joel Jackson to Philadelphia nd Monthly Meeting 1795.5.2.
Jonathan Dickenson, a minor with his parents to Haverford Monthly Meeting 1795.5.2.
Amos Davis to Willimington Monthly Meeting 1795.5.2.
Hezekiah Linton and his wife, Esther and their children: Joshua, Sarah, Hezekiah, William and Jane to Buckingham Monthly Meeting 1794.6.2.
Hezekiah Linton to Sadsbury Monthly Meeting 1795.5.2.
Mark Fell placed as an apprentice to Buckingham Monthly Meeting 1795.5.2.
Ann Dickenson, wife of John Dickenson for herself and her two children: Nathan and Solomon to Haverford Monthly Meeting 1795.5.2.
Esther Jackson with her parents to Philadelphia Southern District Monthly Meeting 1795.6.6.
Caleb Jackson and his wife, Hannah and their three minor children: Joshua, William and Hannah to Philadelphia Southern District Monthly Meeting 1795.6.6.
Jacob Jackson to Philadelphia Southern District Monthly Meeting 1795.6.6.
George Mason and his wife, Susanna with their four children: William, George,, Rachel and Susanna to Baltimore Monthly Meeting 1795.6.6.
Hannah Brown, wife of Jacob with her husband and children: Elizabeth, Robert, Caleb, Rebeckah and Hannah to Nottingham Monthly Meeting 1795.6.6.
John Common and his three children: Isaac, William and Thomas to Londongrove Monthly Meeting 1795.6.6.
William Walton and his wife, Hannah and their children, Rebekah and Joseph to Londongrove Monthly Meeting 1795.6.6.
Hannah Common to Wilmington Monthly Meeting 1795.6.6.
Joshua Seal to Wilmington Monthly Meeting 1795.7.4.
Abraham Seal to Willimington Monthly Meeting 1795.4.4.
David Dickenson to Bradford Monthly Meeting 1795.10.10.
Elizabeth Johnson with her husband and children: Hadley, Isaac, Lewis, Joshua and Robert to Westland Monthly Meeting 1795.11.7.
Hannah Johnson with parents to Westland Monthly Meeting 1795.11.7.
Jonathan Johnson, Jr. with his parents to Westland Monthly Meeting

NEW GARDEN MONTHLY MEETING 177

1795.11.7.
William Johnson to Westland Monthly Meeting 1795.11.7.
Stephen Webb to Kennett Monthly Meeting 1795.11.7.
Robert Pyle to Londongrove Monthly Meeting 1796.2.6.
Hannah Wilson to Londongrove Monthly Meeting 1795.10.10.
Jacob Taylor to Warrington Monthly Meeting 1796.2.6.
Levi Lambourn to Warrington Monthly Meeting 1796.3.5.
Elizabeth Harry, a young woman to York Monthly Meeting 1796.4.2.
Ellis Baily from Westland Monthly Meeting 1796.4.2.
William Keeran and his wife, Rebecca and their children: Levi, John, Thomas, William, Eli, Simon, and Sarah to Haverford Monthly Meeting 1796.4.2.
Elizabeth Keerans with her parents to Haverford Monthly Meeting 1796.11.4.
Ann Gray and her husband and children: Jacob, Ann, Margaret and Joseph to Nottingham Monthly Meeting 1796.4.2.
Elizabeth Gray to Nottingham Monthly Meeting 1796.4.2.
Elisha Davis and his wife, Alice who removed earlier to Huntington Co. request a certificate to Warrington Monthly Meeting 1796.5.7.
Joseph Johnson and his wife, Sarah and their apprentice William Cole to Willimington Monthly Meeting 1796.5.7.
Jesse Garrett and his wife, Elizabeth to Gwynedd 1796.5.7.
Aaron Smith to Philadelphia Monthly Meeting 1796.5.7.
Aaron Smith by his father to Newgarden Monthly Meeting 1795.5.20.
Abraham Conrad to Sadsbury Monthly Meeting 1796.11.5.
Lydia Smith to Newgarden Monthly Meeting 1796.6.4.
Thomas Lindley and his wife, Jane to Spring Monthly Meeting in Orange Co., NC 1796.11.6.
Margaret Bunting to Nottingham Monthly Meeting 1796.6.4.
William Richards and his wife, Catharine to Willimington Monthly Meeting 1796.11.6.
Hannah Embra and her husband to Bradford Monthly Meeting 1796.7.2.
Sarah Wilson, a minor who resides with her uncle, Oliver Wilson to Abington Monthly Meeting 1796.11.2.
Abraham Hoops, a minor placed as an apprentice to Londongrove Monthly Meeting 1796.10.6.
Mary Neal with her husband and children to Newhope Monthly Meeting, Green Co., TN 1796.10.20.
Thomas Maul and his wife, Margaret and two children, Elizabeth and Caleb to Gunpowder Monthly Meeting 1796.11.30.
Thomas Mall to Cedar Creek Monthly Meeting in VA 1796.12.5.
John Miller, son of Jesse to Motherkiln Monthly Meeting 1796.11.10.
Caleb Davis, Jr. to Warrington Monthly Meeting 1796.12.3.
Isaac Clayton to Bradford Monthly Meeting 1797.3.4.

Joseph Richardson and his wife, Dinah and their five minor children: Joseph, Mary, Lydia, Isaac and Caleb to Nottingham Monthly Meeting 1797.11.4.
Elijah Gray and his wife, Mary to Bradford Monthly Meeting 1797.4.1.
David Garrett and his wife, Rebeckah to Horsham Monthly Meeting 1797.5.6.
Mary Sharpless and her children: Lydia, Phebe, Esther, Rebekah and Joseph to Chester Monthly Meeting 1797..11.6.
Joshua Foullk to Gwynedd Monthly Meeting 1797.5.6.
Richard Lamborn to Salem Monthly Meeting 1797.6.3.
Hannah Pusey to Rahway Monthly Meeting 1797.6.3.
Thomas Wickersham and his wife Sarah and their children: John, Mary, Isaac, Thomas and James to Willimington Monthly Meeting 1797.5.3.
Mary Haines and her husband to Concord Monthly Meeting 1797.11.7.
William McConnel to Derby Monthly Meeting 1797.11.7.
William Studdy to Londongrove Monthly Meeting 1797.11.7.
Rachel Thomas to Londongrove Monthly Meeting 1797.11.5.
Cornelius Conrad and his wife, Susanna and their children: Lydia, William and Margaret to Radner Monthly Meeting 1797.11.8.
Hannah Williams to Fairfax Monthly Meeting, VA 1797.11.2.
John Taylor to Kennett Monthly Meeting 1797.11.10.
Ann Lee to Wilmington Monthly Meeting 1797.11.11.
William Seal, being free from his apprenticeship to Wilmington Monthly Meeting 1797.11.7.
Mary Sharpless, a young woman to Chester Monthly Meeting 1797.11.4.
Elizabeth Johnson with her husband and children: Hadley, Isaac, Lewis, Robert and Richard to Westland Monthly Meeting 1797.11.4.
Hannah Johnson with her parents to Westland Monthly Meeting 1797.11.4.
Hannah Brown to Philadelphia Monthly Meeting 1797.12.2.
John Hoopes, a minor to Concord Monthly Meeting 1798.2.3.
Mary Sharp to Willimington Monthly Meeting 1798.2.3.
Robert Johnson to Philadelphia Monthly Meeting 1798.2.3.
Elizabeth Johnson to Philadelphia Monthly Meeting 1798.2.3.
Amos Davis to Cattawafive Monthly Meeting 1798.2.3.
Samuel Dobson and his wife, Sarah and her son William Black to Radnor Monthly Meeting 1798.3.3. The certificate stated that William Black led an offensive life and conversation.
Elizabeth Black and Sarah Dobson with their parents to Radnor Monthly Meeting 1798.3.3.
Rebecca Maul to Radner Monthly Meeting 1798.3.3.
Hannah Gray to Nottingham Monthly Meeting 1798.4.7.

NEW GARDEN MONTHLY MEETING

Daniel Pennigton to Radnor Monthly Meeting 1798.4.7.
Jane Pyle to Nottingham Monthly Meeting 1798.5.5.
Thomas Wood and his wife, Susanna to Pipe Creek Monthly Meeting, MD, he as a minister 1798.5.5.
William Wood with his parents to Pipe Creek Monthly Meeting, MD 1798.5.5
Lydia Wood with her parents to Pipe Creek Monthly Meeting, MD 1798.5.5
Daniel Temple to Goshen Monthly Meeting 1798.5.2.
Sarah Griffin to Concord Monthly Meeting 1798.6.2.
Caleb Hurford to Londongrove Monthly Meeting 1798.6.2
Margaret Stephen to Kennett 1798.11.7.
Permanes Lamborn to Fairfax Monthly Meeting, VA 1798.7.7.
Miriam Atkinson to Third Haven Monthly Meeting, MD, Talbot Co. 1798.7.7.
Caleb Jackson to Londongrove Monthly Meeting 1798.9.1.
Hannah Sharpless to Chester Monthly Meeting 1798.8.4.
James Taylor, a young man to Bradford Monthly Meeting 1798.10.6.
Joseph Taylor to Southland Monthly Meeting, VA 1798.10.6.
Joseph Taylor, JR. to Bradford Monthly Meeting 1799.1.3.
Samuel Jackson, placed as an apprentice to Baltimore Monthly Meeting 1799.2.2.
Edith Gray to Bradford Monthly Meeting 1799.4.6.
Elizabeth Smith to Sadsbury Monthly Meeting 1799.4.6.
Benjamin Hillard and his wife and their two children, 1799.5.4.
William Moore and his wife, Sarah to Nottingham Monthly Meeting 1799.5.4.
John Pennock to Londongrove Monthly Meeting 1799.5.4.
Thomas Richards and his wife, Hannah and their children: Isaac, Hannah, Thomas, Mary, Jacob and Rachel to Nottingham Monthly Meeting 1799.6.1.
Samuel Temple and his wife, Elizabeth and their five children: William, Samuel, Clemens, Sarah and Mary to Concord Monthly Meeting 1799.6.1.
Henry Whitson and his wife, Hannah to Sadsbury Monthly Meeting 1799.7.6.
Alice Lewis to Radner Monthly Meeting 1799.8.5.
Caleb Hurford, Jr. to Londongrove Monthly Meeting 1799.8.3.
Lydia Valentine to Bradford Monthly Meeting 1799.8.3.
Dorothy Kinsey to Wrightstown Monthly Meeting 1799.9.7.
George Sharp placed as an apprentice to Sadsbury Monthly Meeting 1799.11.5.
Sarah Kinsey to Wrightstown Monthly Meeting 1799.11.2.
Rebeccah Taylor to Concord Monthly Meeting 1799.12.7.
Eli Plumbers and his wife, Alice to Baltimore Monthly Meeting

1799.12.7.
John Wells and his wife Catharine and six minor children: Mary, Isaiah, Elizabeth, Susanna, Thomas and Sarah to Hopewell Monthly Meeting, VA 1800.1.4.
Ann Cain to Sadsbury 1800.1.4.
Elizabeth Lees to Hopewell Monthly Meeting, VA 1800.1.4.
James Kinsey placed as an apprentice to Wrightstown Monthly Meeting 1800.3.1.
Robert Plumbly to Bradford Monthly Meeting 1800.6.7.
Isaac Wilson and his wife, Rebeccah to Nottingham Monthly Meeting 1800.6.1.
Reuben Miller to Nottingham Monthly Meeting 1800.6.7.
Sarah Wilson to Nottingham Monthly Meeting 1800.7.5.
William Hambleton and his wife, Mary to Baltimore Monthly Meeting 1800.7.5.
Elizabeth Mendinghall to Kennett Monthly Meeting 1800.7.5.
Thomas Gilpin and his wife, Mary and two minor children, to Warrington Monthly Meeting 1800.10.4
Jonathan Lamborn to Concord Monthly Meeting 1800.11.1.

INDEX

-A-

ABRELL, Mary, 151; Richard, 151
ACHE, Catharina, 72; Jacob, 72; Margareth, 72
ACHEN, Abraham, 49; Jacob, 45, 49; Maria, 49; Sophia, 45
ACHY, Herman, 57; Johannes, 57; Magdalena, 57
ACKER, Anna Maria, 42, 46; Anthonay, 42; Anthony, 42; Anton, 46, 72; Antony, 71; Barbara, 42; Catharina, 42, 72; Elisabeth, 46; Jacob, 42; Magdalena, 42; Maria, 42, 48, 71
ADES, Ann, 136; Elizabeth, 136; Stephen, 136; William, 136
AILES, Amos, 165; Ann, 144; Hannah, 112; Mary, 112; Stephen, 112, 144; Susanna, 169; William, 112
AITKESON, Agnes, 76
AKER, Barbara, 52, 57; Conrad, 52, 57; Henna, 57
ALBIN, Jane, 83; Thomas, 83
ALEXANDER, Elianor, 74
ALFORD, Ann, 119
ALLEN, Alice, 109; Amy, 112, 161; Ann, 112; Benjamin, 136; Deborah, 136; Elizabeth, 142, 153; Emey, 112; Hannah, 112, 136; Jane, 140; John, 112, 136, 142, 143, 161; Joseph, 136; Mary, 143; Phebe, 136; Rebecca, 153; Samuel, 112; Sarah, 78, 140; Thomas, 112; William, 78, 140
ALSDDORFF, Anna Maria, 55; Christian, 55
ANDER, Anna Margareth, 70; Magdalena, 71; Phillip, 71
ANDERSON, Margaret, 167
ANDRA, Philip, 39; Susanna, 39
ANDRE, Adam, 51; Anna Maria, 67; Catharina, 51; Elisabeth, 51; Philip, 67
ANDREE, Adam, 53, 55, 56; Catharina, 53, 55, 56; Magdalena, 53; Philip, 55
ANDREN, Barbara, 68; Oatharina, 68; Phillip, 68
ANDREWS, Alexander, 74
ARENDORFF, Ludwig, 69; Phillip, 69

ARENDORFT, Eva Barbara, 43; Johann Phillip, 43; Johannes, 43
ARMSTRONG, Francis, 75
ASBRIDGE, Joseph, 82; Priscilla, 82
ASHBRIDGE, Aaron, 78; Amos, 78; David, 78; Elizabeth, 78, 103, 105; George, 78; Hannah, 78, 90; Jane, 6, 78, 83, 104; John, 78; Jonathan, 78, 92; Joseph, 78, 79; Joshua, 78; Lydia, 35, 78, 82, 97; Margaret, 78; Mary, 35, 78, 79, 102, 111; Phebe, 78, 105; Priscilla, 78; Rebecca, 78, 79; Sarah, 78, 79, 92; Susan, 78; William, 35, 78
ASHTON, Isaac, 79; Lydia, 79, 111; Susanna, 79, 94
ATHERON, Thomas, 24
ATHERTON, Abigail, 19, 79; Caleb, 79; Charles, 32; Elizabeth, 19; George, 32; Hannah, 31, 32; Henry, 19, 20, 32, 79; Humphrey, 32; Isaac, 32; Richard, 19; Ruth, 32; Susannah, 79; Thomas, 19, 79; William, 79
ATKINSON, Aaron, 136; Abigail, 173; Joseph, 173; Miriam, 136, 179; Rachel, 173; Sarah, 173; William, 136
ATMORE, Mary, 136, 168; Thomas, 136; William, 136

-B-

BAART, Catharina, 44; Johannes, 44; Vallentin, 44
BACH, Anna Maria, 54; Elisabeth, 54, 57; Heinrich, 54, 57; Sara, 57
BACON, Thomas, 76
BAEDENBACH, Jost, 48; Magdalena, 48; Philip, 48
BAELS, Jacob, 136; John, 136, 137, 149; Mary, 136; Patience, 149; Rebecca, 137; Sarah, 136; William, 137
BAILEY, Abigail, 136; Alice, 112; Ann, 112, 136; Betty, 112, 132; Edward, 136; Elisha, 112; Elizabeth, 153; Hannah, 112, 136,

167; Isaac, 112, 136; Isarel, 112; Jemima, 112; Joel, 112, 132, 136; John, 74, 76, 112, 130, 136, 140; Joseph, 112; Joshua, 112, 136; Josiah, 112; Judith, 112; Lewis, 112; Lydia, 112, 136, 145; Margaret, 137; Mary, 112, 130, 140; Phebe, 112; Reuben, 112, 171; Sarah, 112, 140; Susanna, 112; Tacy, 153; Thomas, 112, 136; William, 112, 136, 153
BAILS, Ruth, 161; William, 161
BAILY, Ann, 137, 146; Betty, 137, 143, 152, 168; Bety, 159; Caleb, 168; Daniel, 137; Elizabeth, 79, 137; Ellis, 167, 177; Emmor, 137; Evan, 167; Gravener, 166; Hannah, 79, 137, 144, 149, 156, 161, 167; Hoopes, 79; Isaac, 137, 152; Jane, 76; Jesse, 79; Joel, 137, 146, 149, 159, 161; John, 79, 137, 143, 156; Joseph, 79, 169; Joshua, 137; Josiah, 137, 146; Lydia, 137, 146, 149, 152; Mary, 137, 143, 146, 156; Pennock, 79; Sarah, 137, 146; Susanna, 156; William, 137, 144, 167; Yarnall, 79
BAILYU, Lydia, 166
BAKER, Aaron, 137, 139, 140; Adam, 79; Ann, 79, 137; Caleb, 79; Elizabeth, 92; Hannah, 79, 137; John, 79, 137; Joseph, 166; Joshua, 79, 137, 166; Levi, 137; Margaret, 79; Martha, 140; Mary, 79, 137, 139, 140, 166; Mercy, 79; Rachel, 79, 137; Rebecca, 79; Richard, 137; Robert, 79; Samuel, 79; Sarah, 79, 168; Sidney, 79; Thomas, 137, 168; William, 79
BALDERSON, Deborah, 113; Hannah, 112, 113; Isaiah, 113; Jacob, 113; John, 112; Jonathan, 113; Joseph, 113; Katherine, 113; Mary, 113; Mordecai, 112, 113; Sarah, 113
BALDWIN, Ann, 5; Caleb, 5, 17; Catharine, 15; Charity, 17; Deborah, 17; Elizabeth, 137; George, 34; George S., 18; Grace, 15; Hannah, 1, 5, 9, 113, 128, 155; Isaac, 18, 34; Israel, 18, 34; Jane, 1, 18, 34; John, 1, 5, 15, 17, 19, 36, 137; Jonathan, 17; Joseph, 15; Joshua, 1, 9, 18, 19, 34, 83; Lydia, 15, 18, 34; Marcy, 1; Mary, 5, 15, 18, 19, 34, 87, 171; Mercy, 1, 9, 18, 34; Rachel, 1, 18; Richard T., 15; Samuel, 1, 17, 18, 34, 36; Samuel S., 18; Sarah, 83, 113, 128, 155; Thomas, 15, 113, 128, 155; William, 15, 137
BALDWINI, Hannah, 9
BALING, Margrith, 55
BALLINGER, Hannah, 137; Henry, 137; Josiah, 137; Mary, 137
BANE, Abner, 79; Alexander, 79, 80; Amy, 79; Catharine, 79; Daniel, 79; Deborah, 16, 101; Elizabeth, 79; James, 79; Jane, 79, 153; Jesse, 79; Jonathan, 80; Margaret, 79, 119, 153; Mary, 16, 79; Mordecai, 79; Nathan, 16, 79, 153; Ruth, 79; Thomas, 79, 80; William, 79, 80, 119
BARGER, Elizabeth, 140; Isaac, 166, 170; John, 140; Joseph, 32
BARKER, Edward, 67; Esther, 67; Henrich, 67; William, 67
BARNARD, Ann, 138, 139; Elizabeth, 138; Jeremiah, 138; Jonathan, 169; Mary, 138; Richard, 138; Sarah, 138, 139, 170; Susanna, 138; Thomas, 138, 139, 170
BARR, Robert, 75
BARTLETT, John, 138, 165; Joseph, 138; Martha, 138; Susanna, 138, 165
BASSETT, Arthur, 113; John, 113; Lydia, 113; Richard, 113; Thomas, 113; William, 113
BATEMAN, Elizabeth, 27; William, 27
BATTEN, Dinah, 165, 166; Elizabeth, 80; John, 80; Mary, 80; Richard, 80; Sarah, 175

INDEX

BAUER, Anna, 62, 63, 64; Catharina Margretha, 68; Christian, 68; Elisabeth, 62; Friedrich, 70; Jacob, 62, 63; Jaocb, 64; Maria, 64; Niclas, 63; Rosina, 63; Uhlrich, 68, 70
BAYRS, Benedict, 42; Johannes, 42; Margaretha Elisabeth, 42
BEAL, Mary, 19
BEALE, Joshua, 20; Mary, 1; William, 1
BEALS, Jacob, 113; John, 113; Lydia, 113; Mary, 113; Patience, 113; Rebecca, 113; Sarah, 113; Thomas, 113; William, 113
BEARD, William, 75
BEAUMONT, Elizabeth, 80; William, 80
BECHTEL, Abraham, 60; Borg, 55, 58, 59, 60, 63; Elisabeth, 55, 58, 60; Elizabeth, 59; Joh. Heinrich, 58; Margrith, 63; Maria, 63; Maria Philippina, 55
BEESON, Charity, 152; John, 138, 152; Martha, 152; Mary, 138, 152; Richard, 138
BELL, Ann, 21; Deborah, 21; Elizabeth, 21; Jacob, 21
BEMBROW, Gershon, 80; Sarah, 80
BENDER, Anna, 59; Catharina, 59, 73; Catharine, 67; Friderich, 67; Jacob, 59, 73
BENER, John Heinrich, 73
BENNER, Anna Maria, 55, 57; Barbara, 39; Catharina, 63; Christian, 55, 57, 61, 64; Daniel, 40; Elisabeth, 43, 59, 61, 64; Heinrich, 55, 59, 61, 63; Henna(Hanna), 61; Jacob, 40; Joh. Daniel, 40; Johannes, 40; Joshua, 61; Maria, 61, 64; Maria Catharina, 43; Paul, 39, 43; Sophia, 59; Zusanna(Susanna), 59
BENNETT, Alice, 80, 91; Amos, 113; Deborah, 122; Elizabeth, 113; Grace, 113; Hannah, 80, 91, 113; Harriet, 80; Imlah, 80; Isaac, 113; James, 80, 91, 113; Jane, 113; Joseph, 122; Juliet, 80; Lewis, 80; Malinda, 80; Martha, 80; Matilda, 80; Minerva, 80; Rachel, 113; Silas, 170; Titus, 80; Warner, 80; William, 30, 80, 91, 113, 170
BENSON, Abraham, 27; Alice, 25; Ann, 27, 80; Benjamin, 27; Catharine, 80; Elisabeth, 27; Hannah, 27, 80; James, 27, 80; Jane, 25, 80; John, 80; Margaret, 80; Reuben, 27; Robert, 20, 24, 80; William, 25, 80
BERGER, Joh. Jost, 40
BERNARD, Abner, 113; Ann, 113; Deborah, 113; Hannah, 113; John, 113; Jonathan, 113; Joseph, 32; Joshua, 113; Lydia, 113; Mary, 32; Rachel, 113, 168; Sarah, 113; Thomas, 113
BERTHWAITE, Margaret, 122
BETTS, Ann, 171; Margaret, 83
BEVAN, Elizabeth, 105
BEVERLY, Mary, 152; Ruth, 138; Samuel, 138, 152
BIBBS, Charles, 153; Rachel, 153
BIBER, Georg, 57; Susanna, 57
BICKET, Mary, 142; Phebe, 142; Samuel, 142
BIERBAUER, Abraham, 55; Caspar, 40, 41; Christina, 42, 52, 55, 56; Henna/Hanna, 52; Henrich, 68; Herman, 52, 55, 56; Hermann, 42; Magdalena, 42; Margaretha, 41; Phillip, 68; Sara, 41; Vincent, 68
BIERBAURER, Christina, 48, 51; Elisabeth, 48; Herman, 48, 51; Maria, 51
BIERBRAUER, Christina, 49; Herman, 49; Johannes, 49
BIERY, Barbara, 57; Georg, 57
BIGGER, Mary, 76
BIKERT, Johannes, 61
BIKERTH, Maria, 58
BIRD, John, 74
BLACK, David, 138; Elizabeth, 178; Jane, 77; Newton, 138, 142; Rachel, 138; Sarah, 138, 142; William, 178
BLACKBURN, John, 126; Mary, 76, 126
BLAIR, Susanna, 74

EARLY CHURCH RECORDS OF CHESTER CO.

BLUMSTON, Samuel, 151
BOAKE, Sarah, 89
BOLDIN, Henna(Hanna/Anna), 59; John, 59
BOLEN, Rachel, 76
BOLTON, Rhoda, 26
BOND, Hannah, 80; Joseph, 32, 80; Paul, 80; Samuel, 32, 80, 83; Sarah, 32; Thamzin, 80, 83
BONLONG, John, 75
BONSALL, Anna, 17; Charles, 17; Edward, 17; Hannah, 16; Isaac, 16; Joseph, 17; Mary, 30; Mercy, 16; Sidney, 17; Thomas, 17; William, 17
BONSELL, Jesse, 36
BOOTH, Lydia, 96
BORNARD, Deborah, 169
BOSSART, Johannes, 57
BOURNE, Ann, 150; Jesse, 150
BOWATER, Sarah, 136; Thomas, 136
BOWEN, Gaynor, 102; Henry, 150; Jane, 150
BOYCE, Mary, 138; Robert, 138
BOYD, Jane, 76; John, 75
BRAMBACH, Ann, 53; Edward, 66; Elisabeth, 61; Heinrich, 53, 60; Johannes, 60, 61; Margrith, 60, 61; Susanna, 66
BRANSON, Mary, 101
BRAUN, Jacob, 39; Maria Catharina, 38
BRENHOLTZ, Catharina, 42; Friedrich, 42
BRENNHOLTZ, Elisabeth, 43; Eva, 44; Friedrich, 44
BRINTON, Rebecka, 168
BROOKS, David, 113, 138; Eleanor, 113; Elinor, 138; Isaac, 113
BROOKSLEY, John, 136; Mary, 136
BROWN, Agnes, 21; Ann, 1, 113; Benejah, 31, 173; Benjamin, 114; Bennajah, 166; Caleb, 176; Catharine, 113; Catherine, 114; Daniel, 20, 23, 114; David, 138, 163; Deborah, 114, 152; Dinah, 138; Dorothy, 113; Elgar, 4; Elinor, 114; Elisha, 4; Elizabeth, 4, 19, 114, 138, 145, 151, 152, 176; Esther, 4, 114; Hannah, 114, 145, 163, 176, 178; Henry, 114; Isaac, 114, 138; Israel, 4; Jacob, 114, 138, 176; James, 4, 19; Jane, 113, 114; Jeremiah, 114; Joel, 23; John, 23, 113, 114; Jonathan, 20; Joseph, 4, 23, 113, 114, 138, 145, 151, 152, 155; Joshua, 114; Lydia, 138; Marcy, 1; Margaret, 23, 113, 114, 138, 140, 150, 155; Margaretta, 138; Mary, 23, 113, 114, 138, 156; Messer, 113, 114, 138; Miriam, 4; Nathan, 114; Phebe, 138; Rachel, 114; Rebecca, 114, 151; Rebeckah, 176; Richard, 113, 114; Robert, 176; Samuel, 1, 113; Sarah, 22, 114; Susanna, 19, 138; susanna, 23; Tabitha, 114; Thomas, 20, 113, 114, 138; William, 4, 21, 113, 114, 138, 140, 150, 156
BRUNNER, Peter, 39
BRYAN, Ann, 157
BRYNES, Mary, 75
BUCHANAN, Elizabeth, 75; George, 18; Mary, 18, 25; Thomas, 18
BUCHANNAN, Thomas, 34
BUCHER, Elisabeth, 64
BUCKINGHAM, Caleb, 8; Hannah, 8; James, 138; John, 8, 138; Lydia, 8; Mary, 8, 138; Rachel, 8; Rebecca, 8; Ruth, 8; Sarah, 8; Tamor, 8
BUFFINGTON, Ruth, 2; Susannah, 2; Thomas, 2
BULLER, Elizabeth, 114; Hannah, 114; Jane, 114; John, 114; Mary, 114; Richard, 114; sarah, 114; Susanna, 114
BULLET, Ames, 35
BUNTING, Jane, 74; Margaret, 177
BUNTON, --, 74
BUNTY, Walter, 76
BURK, James, 79, 80; Mary, 79, 80
BUTLER, Amos, 13, 32; Ann, 32; Elijah, 33; Hannah, 165; James, 13; Jane, 13, 32; John, 26, 36; Noble, 13, 80; Rachel, 13, 32, 80; Samuel, 13, 21, 33; Sarah, 32; Susanna, 25; William, 13, 32

INDEX

BUTTERFIELD, Mary, 76
BUZBY, Joseph, 80; Mary, 80; Sarah, 80

-C-

CABUCH, Christina, 71; Johannes, 71
CADWALADER, Abigail, 80; David, 80, 81; Dinah, 80; Elizabeth, 80, 81; Hannah, 80; James, 80; John, 80, 81; Lydia, 80; Mary, 80, 81; Moses, 80; Nathan, 80; Sarah, 81; Vincent, 80
CADWALDER, Charles, 7; David, 7; Elizabeth, 7, 27; Hannah, 7, 29; Isaac, 7; Jesse, 7; Judah, 7, 25; Mary, 7, 22; Nathan, 7, 19; Phebe, 7, 29
CADWALLADER, Elizabeth, 96; Nathan, 36
CAER, John, 81; Mary, 81
CAIN, Ann, 114, 180; Hannah, 114, 125, 152; John, 114, 125, 138, 152; Margaret, 160; Robert, 114, 138; Ruth, 114, 138; Sara, 114; Sarah, 114, 125, 138, 152, 155
CALVON, Eleanor, 75
CAMBLE, Sarah, 76
CAMERON, Douglald, 35
CAMM, Esther, 81, 105; Henry, 81; Sarah, 81, 105
CANBY, Hannah, 114, 130; Joseph, 114, 130; Rebecca, 135
CANNON, William, 76
CARAS, Ann, 125; John, 125
CARL, Abraham, 47, 49; Anna Maria, 55, 61; Catharina, 46, 47, 52, 54, 55, 56, 57, 59, 61, 64, 66, 69, 73; Christina, 52, 57, 59, 60, 62; Clara Elisabeth, 69; Conrad, 46, 47, 53, 55, 61, 72; Daniel, 55; David, 61; Elisabeth, 41, 47, 49, 56, 60, 70; Hanna, 62; Heinrich, 55, 56, 59; Henrich, 41, 47, 49, 70; Iesajas(Isaiah), 73; Ieseias(Isaias), 69; Isaias, 69, 70; Jacob, 46, 52, 57, 60, 62, 70; Jesajas(Isaiah), 59; Johanes, 54; Johann Peter, 41; Johannes, 37, 46, 51, 54, 56, 59, 66, 69, 70; John, 47, 61, 64; Joseph, 61; Magdalena, 53, 59, 72; Maria, 46, 47, 53, 72; Maria Magdalena, 56; Peter, 51, 52; Philippina, 59; Philippine, 55, 56; Rachel, 54; Rebecca, 64; Rebecka, 47
CARLETON, Sarah, 81; Thomas, 81
CARLIN, Catharina, 38; Catharina Elisabetha, 37; Elisabeth, 37
CARLISLE, Nancy, 75; William, 76
CARPENTER, Francis, 112; Hannah, 81, 93; Margaret, 144; Sarah, 112, 144; William, 144
CARRINGTON, Mary, 139; Phebe, 146; Thomas, 139, 146
CARSON, Dinah, 114, 124; Elinor, 139; George, 114, 139; Hannah, 114, 139; Lydia, 114; Martha, 124; Richard, 124; Sarah, 114
CARTER, Hannah, 146; Robert, 146
CATORARA, John Duglas, 76
CHALFANT, Abner, 115; Ann, 114, 139, 150; Caleb, 115; Elizabeth, 114, 139; Henry, 114, 115, 139; Jacob, 114; John, 114, 139, 150; Jonathan, 114, 139; Mary, 115; Phebe, 115, 139; Susanna, 139; Thomas, 114, 139
CHALFONT, Elizabeth, 139, 141; Hannah, 139; Henry, 139; James, 139; John, 139; Phebe, 139; Thomas, 139
CHALFTON, Henry, 141
CHAMBERLAIN, Hannah, 155; Isaac, 168, 171; Jane, 81; John, 81; Lettice, 164; Martha, 164; William, 164
CHAMBERS, allen, 139; Caleb, 115; Caroline, 143; David, 115; Deborah, 115, 139, 154; Elener, 139; Elisabeth, 115; Elizabeth, 115, 139, 156, 160; Emey, 139; Hannah, 115, 139; Isaac, 115; Jesse, 115; John, 115, 137, 139, 156; Joseph, 115, 139, 154; Joshua, 115; Leah, 115; Martha, 160; Mary, 115, 138, 148, 164; Patience, 115, 139; Phebe, 115; Rebecca, 115, 137, 139,

156; Reuben, 115; Richard, 138, 139, 143, 144, 160; Samuel, 139; Sarah, 115, 139, 144, 154; Susanna, 139, 143, 173; William, 115, 139, 164, 172
CHANDLER, Ann, 115; Benjamin, 22; Jacob, 10; Jane, 115; John, 115; Lydia, 10, 115; Martha, 10; Samuel, 115; Spencer, 167; Swithin, 173; Thomas, 115; William, 115, 171
CHILDS, Elizabeth, 81; Francis, 81; John, 81
CHRIST, Herman, 70; Wilhelm, 70
CHRISTMAN, Georg, 52; Sophia, 52
CHRISTMANN, Elisabeth, 43; Georg, 43; Heinrich, 55; Sophia, 43; Susanna, 55
CHURCHMAN, Dinah, 115, 138; Edward, 115; George, 115, 172, 175; Hannah, 115; John, 115, 140; Margaret, 140; Miriam, 115; Mordecai, 168; Sarah, 115; Susanna, 115, 138; Thomas, 115; William, 115
CLAP, Benjamin, 74
CLARK, John, 140; Mary, 140; Ruth, 140, 164; Samuel, 23, 140, 164; Walter, 140
CLAUS, Catharina, 44, 70; Christina, 43; Conrad, 70; Cunigunda, 43; Maria Elisabeth, 41; Wilhelm, 41, 43, 44
CLAYTON, Aaron, 112, 140, 166; Ann, 140; Edward, 140; Isaac, 177; Joshua, 140, 158; Martha, 140, 158; Mary, 158; Sarah, 112, 140, 166
CLEER, Johannes, 60; Maria, 59, 60; Philip, 59, 60
CLEER(KLEER), Benjamin, 63; Elisabeth, 62; Maria, 62, 63; Philip, 62, 63
CLENDENAN, Elisabeth, 13
CLENDENON, Elizabeth, 140; Isaac, 115, 140; Phebe, 115; Rebeka, 159; Robert, 115, 140, 159
CLETON, Samuel, 165
CLINGAN, William, 77
CLINGER, Barbara, 60; Johannes, 68; Maria, 68; Philip, 60
CLOUD, Ann, 140, 173; Jane, 140, 167; Joshua, 140; Lydia, 173; Mary, 140; Mordecai, 140; Ruth, 140; Thomas, 140, 167; William, 140
COATE, Tacey, 33
COATES, Abner, 29; Ann, 3, 26, 28, 81; Aquila, 14; Aron, 20; Benjamin, 3, 20, 26, 28, 35, 81; Beulah, 20; Charles, 14; Cyrus, 14; Deborah, 140; Elizabeth, 3, 28; Grace, 20, 28; Hannah, 3, 14, 28; Isaac, 28; James, 3, 28; Jane, 3, 14, 19, 26, 28; John Hutchison, 14; Jonathan, 3, 19, 27, 28; Kezia, 3; Keziah, 28; Moses, 3, 81; Phebe, 3, 28; Rachel, 20, 34; Sarah, 14, 27; Seymour, 140; Susanna, 3, 10, 28; Tacy, 28
COATS, Phebe, 32
COCHRAN, David, 76; Jane, 75; Robert, 76
COCK, Elizabeth, 140; Thomas, 140
COCKS, John, 140; Mary, 140
CODDEN, Ann M., 77
COELEBS, Peter Schumann, 39
COLB, Elisabeth, 64; Michel, 64
COLE, Lydia, 115; Samuel, 115
COLES, Mary, 115, 145; Prudence, 140; William, 115, 140
COLGAN, Grace, 144; Hannah, 144; William, 144
COLINS, Joseph, 140; Mary, 140; Thomas, 140
COLLINS, Amey, 81; Ann, 81, 84; Elizabeth, 81, 84; Jacob, 24; John, 81, 84; Joseph, 81, 84; Mary, 79; Rebecca, 81; Sarah, 96, 140; Thomas, 96; Timothy, 76; William, 81
COLLMAN, Jacob, 37
COLMERRY, William, 75
COMFORT, Mary, 115; Robert, 115
COMISTON, --, 76
COMMON, Hannah, 140, 176; Isaac, 140, 176; John, 176; Mary, 169; Robert, 141, 166; Ruth, 141, 166; Sarah, 141; Thomas, 176; William, 141, 165, 176
COMMONS, Isaac, 115; John, 115; Mary, 115; Sarah, 115

CONARD, Ann, 141; Evard, 145; Jesse, 141; Margaret, 145; Sarah, 145
CONELY, Eunice, 157
CONN, Barbara, 58; Henna, 58; Jeremias, 58
CONNER, David, 74
CONRAD, Abraham, 177; Anna Margaretha, 41; Cornelius, 178; Evard, 141; Isaac, 141, 173; Jacob, 41; Margaret, 141, 175, 178; Mary, 141, 173; Samuel, 41; Susanna, 178; William, 178
CONRAT, Jacob, 40; Sara, 40
COOK, Dinah, 163; Elinor, 158; Elizabeth, 138, 141, 149; Ennion, 115; Hannah, 115, 149, 152, 163, 175; Hannah Francina, 163; Isaac, 115, 167; Job, 115; John, 115, 138, 141, 155, 158, 169; Lydia R., 152; Margaret, 76, 115, 141; Peter, 115, 141, 174; Phebe, 155; Rebecca, 138, 141, 158; Ruth, 141; Samuel, 141; Sarah, 141; Stephen, 115, 141, 174; Thomas, 149, 152, 163, 165
COOKE, John, 156; Mary, 156
COOKSON, Jane, 141; Olive, 141, 171; Samuel, 141
COOPE, Amy, 79; Jane, 81; John, 81; Jonathan, 29; Nathan, 79, 81
COOPER, Isaac, 10, 33; Jeremiah, 81, 99; John, 77; Joshua, 10, 33; Leah, 81, 99; Lettice, 74; Margaret, 74; Mary, 10, 33, 141; Rachel, 10, 33; Samuel, 10, 33; Sibilla, 10, 33; William, 10, 33, 141
COPPOCK, Aaron, 141, 149, 158; Aston, 141; Mary, 158; Miriam, 141, 149
CORSBY, David, 75; John, 75
COTES, William, 26
COWEN, Mary, 75
COWGILL, Sarah, 24
COWPERTHWAITE, Asenath, 141; Job, 141
COX, Abner, 82; Amy, 81; Arron, 170; Benjamin, 0, 25, 81, 82; Catharine, 8, 23, 81; Elizabeth, 9, 82; Ellen, 81; George, 81; Hannah, 8, 24, 81, 82; 154; Jane, 81; Jeffery, 82; John, 81, 82, 84, 141; Jonathan, 82; Joseph, 8, 23, 81; Joshua, 81; Lawrence, 81; Levi, 82; Lydia, 82; Margaret, 8, 23, 81; Mary, 8, 81, 84, 87, 141; Richard, 8; Sarah, 81, 102; Thomas, 82, 154; William, 8, 81, 82, 141
CRAWFORD, --, 76
CRESCHER, Elias, 39; Johannes, 39
CRISPIN, Susannah, 30
CRISURI, Charles, 75
CRISWEL, Hannah, 76
CRISWELL, William, 77
CROPFROCK, Ann, 110
CROSBY, David, 75
CUNIGUNDA, Anna, 41, 44
CURLE, Benjamin, 115; Deborah, 115, 141; Elizabeth, 141; James, 170; John, 115, 141; Joseph, 169; Mary, 115; Richard, 141, 144; Susanna, 144
CURREY, Ann, 106
CURROTHERS, Isabel, 75; Robert, 74
CUTLER, Anna, 175; Benjamin, 151, 153, 175; Hannah, 175; Jacob, 175; Jesse, 175; Jonathan, 175; Mercy, 153; Rebecca, 151; Ruth, 175; Susanna, 151, 153, 175
CUTTER, Mercy, 153

-D-

DALBY, Hannah, 25
DALLICHER, Friedrich, 72
DALLICKER, Friederich, 51
DALLIKER, Freiderich, 67
DANISEN, James, 172
DARLINGTON, Abraham, 116, 130; Elizabeth, 116, 130; John, 20; Mary, 20
DAUBEL, Apollonia, 47; Leonhardt, 47; Margaretha, 47
DAUBIL, Apellano, 46; Apollonia, 42; Appellona, 44; Catharina, 42; Elisabeth, 46; Joh. Georg, 44; Lenhard, 42; Leonhart, 46; Leonharth, 44
DAUGHERTY, Elizabeth, 74; Sarah, 27
DAVID, Ellis, 82; Thomas, 82
DAVIES, Agnes, 23, 173; Amos,

3, 14, 23, 82; Ann, 82;
Benjamin, 14; David, 82;
Elisabeth, 14; Elisha, 3,
23; Eliza, 3; Elizabeth,
1, 3, 83; Ellis, 78, 82;
Esther, 82, 108; George,
82; Grace, 3; Hannah, 14,
82; Isaac, 3, 23, 82;
Israel, 82; Jane, 82, 104;
Jesse, 82; Joel, 3, 23;
John, 1, 3, 14, 23;
Jonathan, 82; Lydia, 78,
82; Mary, 14, 82; Phebe,
82; Priscilla, 82; Rachel,
82, 85; Richard, 82; Ruth,
1, 3, 14, 23, 108;
Sabilla, 14; Samuel, 14;
Sarah, 14, 82; Susanna,
82, 90; Tace, 14; William,
82
DAVIS, Abiather, 25; Abigail,
33; Alice, 116, 177; Amos,
82, 87, 99, 166, 176, 178;
Ann, 82; Benjamin, 170;
Caleb, 141, 177; David,
82; Elisha, 32, 116, 166,
177; Elizabeth, 4, 8, 82,
86, 141, 157, 170; Ellis,
170; George, 170; Grace,
27; Hannah, 24, 78, 80,
141, 170; Hugh, 82; Isaac,
167, 168, 172; James, 170;
Jane, 82, 160; Jesse, 30,
82, 166; Joanna, 167;
Joel, 27; John, 4, 8, 24,
82, 116, 166; Joseph, 82,
116, 141, 170; Lydia, 30,
168; Margaret, 116, 138,
141, 170; Martha Emily,
82; Mary, 23, 35, 116,
164; Nathan, 116; Phebe,
91; Priscilla, 78; Rachel,
4; Rumford, 164; Samuel,
82; Sarah, 78, 82, 83;
Sibella, 8; Susanna, 82,
87; William, 36, 82
DAVISON, Dorothy, 36
DAWSON, Ann, 141; Benjamin,
141; Deborah, 20;
Elizabeth, 141; James,
141; Joseph, 141
DAY, Ann, 151; John, 151;
Rebecca, 151
DE FRIDERICH, Elisabeth, 53;
Johannes, 53; Philip, 53
DEARMIN, Margaret, 76
DEAVES, Abraham, 82; Mary, 82;
Priscilla, 82; Samuel, 82
DECK, Catherina, 51; Johannes,
51; Susanna, 51
DECK(DICK), Catharina, 51;
Christina, 51; Johannes,
51
DEFRAIN, Adam, 40, 41;
Bernhart, 41; Phillipps
Henrich, 40
DEFREHN/DUVRAIN/DEFRAIN, Anna
Maria, 45; Catharina, 45;
Elizabeth, 45; Johannes,
45; Magdalena, 45;
Margaretha, 45; Peter, 45;
Susanna, 45
DENNIS, Elizabeth, 141;
Thomas, 141
DENY, Abraham, 56; Anna Maria,
51, 56; Catharina, 37;
Christoph, 56;
Christophel, 49, 51, 52;
Christopher, 60;
Christophorus, 37;
Elisabeth, 51; Jacob, 49,
70; Johannes, 60, 70;
Margareth, 69; Margaretha,
38; Maria, 49, 60; Maria
Barbara, 52; Maria
Elisabeth, 38; Michael,
37, 38, 69
DICKENSON, Ann, 176; David,
176; John, 176; Jonathan,
176; Nathan, 176; Solomon,
176
DICKES, Peter, 82; Rebecca,
82; Roger, 82; Sarah, 82
DICKINSON, Elizabeth, 141;
Joseph, 99, 141; Phebe, 99
DICKS, Rebecca, 97; Roger, 97
DICKSON, Hannah, 141; Joseph,
141; Mary, 141; Thomas,
141
DIEFFENDORFER, Barbara, 65;
Elisabeth, 65; Philip, 65
DIERY, Johan, 67
DIFFENDORFER, Heinrich, 64;
Henrick, 67; Jacob, 67;
Juliana, 64, 67; Philip,
64
DIFFENDORFFER, Heinrich, 62;
Johannes, 62; Juliana, 62
DILLIN, Elisabeth, 17; Hannah,
17; Isaiah, 17; Mary, 17;
Mercy, 17; Owen, 17;
Rebecca, 17; Sarah, 17;
William, 17
DILWORTH, Ann, 83; Caleb, 83;
James, 83
DISSES, Sarah, 174
DIXON, Elizabeth, 142; Emey,
142; Henry, 142; Isaac,
142; John, 130, 142;
Joseph, 116, 142, 147,
157, 164, 171; Mary, 142,
157; Rachel, 147; Rebecca,

INDEX 189

116, 142; Rebekah, 171;
Ruth, 164; Sarah, 116,
130, 142, 147, 157, 164;
Simon, 142; Susanna,
171; Thomas, 116; William,
116, 142, 171
DOBSON, John, 142; Samuel,
142, 178; Sarah, 142, 178
DOLBY, Hannah, 15, 31; John,
15, 31; Rebecca, 15
DONALDSON, Violet, 77
DONNING, Elizabeth, 24;
Richard, 24
DONY, Christopher, 47;
Henrich, 47; Maria, 47
DORSEY, Benedict, 5
DOUGLAS, Elizabeth, 116;
Joseph, 116; Mary, 116
DOWNING, Ann, 11, 17; Charles,
17; David, 17; Deborah,
17; Elen, 83, 93;
Elizabeth, 17, 83, 102;
Ellen, 142; George, 6, 17;
Hannah, 6, 83; Harriet,
17; Hester, 17; Jacob, 6,
26; James, 11; Jane, 6,
19, 83, 102; John, 6, 83;
Joseph, 6, 10, 11, 17;
Joshua, 1; Marcy, 1; Mary,
10, 16, 17, 83; Miller,
17; Phebe, 17, 142, 165;
Richard, 6, 11, 16, 17,
19, 83, 102; Robert, 19;
Samuel, 6, 17, 83; Sarah,
1, 11, 79, 83; Thamzin,
80, 83; Thomas, 1, 6, 10,
17, 19, 83; Thomasin, 1;
Thomzin, 6, 10; Thornzin,
16, 17; William, 6, 17,
83, 93, 142, 165
DRIT, Elizabeth, 45; Henrich,
45; Jacob, 45
DRITT, Christian, 44;
Elisabeth, 44; Henrich, 44
DUCKILL, Thomas, 23
DUFF, Mary, 75
DUFRAINE, Catharine, 72;
Jacob, 72
DUNKIN, Aaron, 11, 28; Ann,
28; Aron, 25; Elisabeth,
11; Gulielma, 11; Martha,
11; Sarah, 28; Susanna,
11, 25; Susannah, 28
DUNN, Alice, 152; Anne, 125,
152; Elizabeth, 83;
George, 83; Philip, 83;
Ralph, 125, 151; Sarah,
83; Susanna, 83
DURBOROW, Ann, 83; Daniel, 83,
87; Hugh, 83; Margaret,
83; Phebe, 83, 87

DUTTON, Ann, 116; Elizabeth,
116; James, 154; Mary,
116; Robert, 116; Sarah,
154
DUVIN, Katharine, 77
DUVRAIN, Adam, 40, 41;
Bernhart, 41; Peter, 39;
Phillipps Henrich, 40
DYSERT, Eliz., 76; May, 76

-E-
EACHUS, Elizabeth, 86; Hannah,
83; John, 83; Mary, 20;
Phinehas, 83; Robert, 20,
83; Sarah, 83; William,
20, 83
EAVENSON, Alice, 83; Enoch,
83; Esther, 83; Hannah,
83; Isaac, 83; Richard,
83; Thomas, 83
EDGE, Ann, 34; Fanny, 35;
George, 35; Jane, 34;
John, 3, 6, 22, 34, 35;
Mary, 3, 6, 35; Rachel, 3,
4, 107; Thomas, 32, 35
EDMUNDSON, Elinor, 138; John,
142, 151; Lydia, 142, 151,
159, 171; Sophia, 142;
Thomas, 142
EDWARD, Moses, 165
EDWARDS, Ahab, 17; Alexander,
83; Ann, 83; Caleb, 116;
Dinah, 83; Elinor, 116;
Ellin, 83; Esther, 116,
142; Hannah, 29, 83, 116,
145; Isabel, 116;
Isabella, 142; James, 1,
83; Jane, 116; John, 1,
83, 116, 142, 166;
Jonathan, 116, 142;
Joseph, 83; Joshua, 116;
Lydia, 116; Martha, 145;
Mary, 1, 116; Moses, 116,
142; Nathan, 116; Phebe,
116; Priscilla, 83;
Robert, 116; Rowland, 1;
Sarah, 83, 116; Sibbilla,
83; Thomas, 83, 116;
William, 83, 145
EHMICH, Catarina, 51;
Catharina, 54; Christian,
51, 54; Elisabeth, 54;
Sophia, 51
EHMIG, Christian, 48;
Elissabeta, 48; Maria
Catarina, 48
ELDRIDGE, Jonathan, 83; Sarah,
78, 83; Thomas, 83
ELEMAN, Dorcas, 84; Enos, 84;
Esther, 84; John, 84;
Margaret, 84; Mary, 84;

Sarah, 84; Thomas, 84
ELER, Henna (Hanna), 57;
  Maria, 57; Philip, 57
ELGAR, Elizabeth, 4; Joseph,
  4; Mary, 4
ELIOT, Nancy, 77
ELLICOTT, Hannah, 142; Mary,
  142; Thomas, 142
ELLIOT, Mary, 75
ELLIOTT, Eli, 116; Hannah,
  116; John, 116, 142; Mary,
  142; Sarah, 116, 142;
  William, 142
ELLIS, Elisha, 24; Elizabeth,
  28; Rebecca, 102; Sarah,
  27, 110
ELSASS, Anna Christina, 47;
  Anna Magdalena, 47; Jacob,
  47
ELSAZ, Christina, 44;
  Christina Margaretha, 44;
  Georg Jacob, 44; Jacob,
  46; Magdalena, 46;
  Rebecka, 46
ELTON, Susanna, 76
EMBRA, Hannah, 177
EMBREE, Hannah, 142; James,
  28, 142; Phebe, 142;
  Rebecca, 28; Samuel, 142
EMELEN, Ann, 125; George, 125;
  Hannah, 125
EMIG, Christian, 71, 72;
  Christina, 72; Wilhelmina,
  71
EMLEN, Ann, 116; George, 116;
  Hannah, 116
EMMERIC, Catharina, 53
EMPSON, Phebe, 150
ENGLAND, David, 116, 142;
  Elizabeth, 116, 123, 145;
  Isaac, 116; Israel, 116;
  John, 116, 123, 142, 145;
  Mary, 116, 142, 145;
  Sarah, 116, 142; Susanna,
  83; William, 83
ERISTMAN, Daniel, 41; George,
  41; Sophia, 41
ERNSTIN, Catharina, 37
ESCH, Elizabeth, 40
ESCHENFELDER, Anna Barbara,
  53; Ludwig, 53; Maria, 53;
  Thomas, 43
ESCHENTZELLERIN, Margaretha,
  38
ESPIN, Israel, 31; Jane, 31;
  Lillah, 31; Mary, 31
ESSIG, Anna, 53; Heinrich, 53
EVAN, Elizabeth, 93; Gainer,
  93; Hannah, 84, 93;
  Jefferis, 93; John, 93;
  Mary, 84, 93; Samuel, 93;

Thomas, 84
EVANS, alice, 143; Amos, 95;
  Ann, 121, 141, 172;
  Catharina, 67; Catharine,
  84; Catherine, 26; David,
  84; Elihu, 17, 19, 20;
  Elim, 17; Elizabeth, 84,
  95; Evan, 84; Hannah, 84;
  Isaac, 141, 143; James,
  75; John, 67, 77, 84, 93;
  Jonathan, 17, 20; Josiah,
  84; Katherine, 173;
  Margaret, 26, 84, 93;
  Margery, 75; Mark, 174;
  Mary, 19, 26, 84, 141;
  Phebe, 26, 84; Rachel, 17,
  107, 159; Richard, 26;
  Robert, 75; Roland, 121;
  Ruth, 84; Samuel, 67;
  Sarah, 20, 26, 103;
  Thomas, 26, 84; William,
  143
EWEN, James, 76
EWING, Mary, 75; Robert, 75

-F-

FAEGER, Catharina, 67; Jacob,
  67
FAIRLAMB, Hannah, 116, 119;
  Katharine, 116; Katherine,
  119; Nicholas, 116, 119
FAIRLAND, John, 78; Susanna,
  78
FALKNER, Jesse, 9; Martha, 9;
  Mary, 9
FALLS, Jane, 77
FARLOW, Ann, 116; Elizabeth,
  116; Isaac, 116; James,
  116; Jemima, 116;
  Margaret, 116; Rebecca,
  116; William, 116
FARQUAR, Allen, 143; Ann, 143;
  Mary, 143; William, 143
FARQUHAR, Allen, 88; Ann, 84;
  Mary, 112; Phebe, 84, 88;
  Samuel, 84; William, 84,
  112
FARR, Abraham, 84; Edward, 84;
  Isaac, 84; James, 84;
  Jane, 84; John, 84; Mary,
  81, 84; Phebe, 84, 107;
  Richard, 84; William, 84
FARRIN, Eliz., 75
FAWKES, Ann, 84; John, 84;
  Mary, 84, 89; Rachel, 84,
  99; Richard, 84; Samuel,
  84, 99; Sarah, 84
FELL, Alice, 116; Cynthia,
  117; David, 117;
  Elizabeth, 116, 117, 125,
  160; Esther, 117; Hannah,

117, 143; John, 117;
Joseph, 117; Letitia, 116,
160; Lewis, 117; Mark,
143, 176; Mary, 143;
Rebecca, 117, 125; Robert,
143; Sarah, 116, 117;
Thomas, 116, 117, 125, 160
FELLOWFIELD, Alexander, 126;
Rebecca E., 126
FERGUSON, Agnes, 75; Jessica
C., 74
FERREE, Betty, 112, 143; John,
112, 143; Susanna, 21
FERRIS, David, 7; Mary, 7
FERRISS, Hannah, 21
FERTIG, Elisabeth, 57;
Johannes, 57
FETTER(VETTER), Peter, 70;
Phillip, 70
FILLEMAN, Conrad, 51;
Elisabeth, 51; Phillip, 51
FINCHER, Elizabeth, 140;
Francis, 143; Hannah, 143,
157; Jane, 157; John, 140,
143, 157, 170; Jonathan,
143; Rachel, 143; Sarah,
159; Thomas, 143
FINLEY, Ebenezer, 74;
Elizabeth, 74; Hannah
Evans, 73; James, 73; John
E., 73, 77
FISHER, Ann, 143; Elizabeth,
117, 125, 143; Hannah, 20,
27; John, 117, 125; Mary,
93; Ruth, 21; Samuel, 21,
143, 175; Sarah, 117, 125;
Thomas, 143; William, 27
FITZWATER, Caroline, 143;
George, 143
FLEMING, George, 75
FLOWER, Abigail, 117; Alice,
143, 157; Dinah, 157;
Margaret, 168; Mary, 117;
Richard, 117, 143, 157;
Thomas, 117, 173
FOREMAN, Alexander, 147;
Esther, 147; Rachel, 147
FORSYTHE, John, 25
FOTTER, Elizabeth, 141;
Francis, 141
FOULK, Johsua, 178; Thomas,
167
FRAUNFELTZ, Eva, 41;
Friedrich, 41; Ludwich, 41
FRAZIER, Alexander, 143; Mary,
143; Moses, 143
FRED, Ann, 117; Benjamin, 117,
143, 147; Deborah, 143,
147; John, 143, 152;
Joseph, 117, 143; Joshua,
117; Nicholas, 117, 143;
Rachel, 152; Sarah, 117,
143; Thomas, 117
FREEBEE, Joseph, 25
FREHM, Anna Maria, 70; Peter,
70
FREHN, Catharina, 70; Peter,
70
FRIDERICH, Elisabeth, 57;
Maria, 56; Philip, 56
FRIEDERICH, Elisabeth, 61;
Philip, 60
FRIES, Elianor, 77
FUCH(FUES), Rosina, 63;
Valentine, 63
FULKER, Henrich, 56
FULKERT, Anna, 63; Christoph,
67; Heinrich, 63, 67;
Margrith, 63, 67
FUSSELL, Bartholomew, 9, 25,
36; Esther, 9; Jacob, 9;
Joseph, 9; Rebecca, 9;
Rebekah, 9; Sarah, 9, 10;
Solomon, 9, 10; William, 9
FUSSILL, Solomon, 24

-G-
GALBRAITH, Ann, 112; Thomas,
112
GALLOWAY, James, 76; Joseph,
143; Mary, 143; Richard,
143; Susana, 143
GAMBLE, Catharine, 143;
Elizabeth, 143, 165;
Joseph, 143, 165; Leah,
77; Samuel, 143
GARDINER, John, 74; Lettice,
74
GARNETT, Mary, 148
GARRATT, Amy, 87
GARRETSON, Cornelius, 32;
Eliakim, 144; Garret, 165;
Garrett, 143, 144, 168;
Hannah, 32; Lydia, 144;
Margaret, 143, 168, 174;
Phebe, 144, 165
GARRETT, Aaron, 35, 85;
Abigail, 85, 111; Abner,
85, 86; Abraham, 85;
Agnes, 85; Alice, 84, 103;
Amey, 85; Amos, 84, 85;
Ann, 81, 84, 85, 86;
Benjamin, 86; David, 85,
86, 178; Davis, 84; Debby,
85, 86; Debby L., 86;
Debbye, 86; Deby, 95;
Edith, 85, 91; Eli, 86;
Elizabeth, 84, 85, 86,
109, 177; Ellen, 84; Enos,
86; Esther, 86, 109; Ezra,
85; George, 84, 85, 86,
102; Gideon, 86; Hannah,

85, 86, 89, 94, 102, 111;
Isaac, 85; James, 84, 86;
Jane, 85, 86, 105, 109;
Jehu, 86; Jeru, 86; Jesse,
85, 86, 111, 177; Joel,
85, 86; John, 84; Jonah,
86, 109; Joseph, 86;
Josiah, 84, 85, 89, 111;
Levi, 85; Lydia, 82, 84,
85, 86, 89, 94; Margaret,
85; Martha, 86; Mary, 84,
85, 89, 90, 97, 111;
Nathan, 86; Peter, 85, 86;
Rachel, 22, 84, 85, 86;
Rebecca, 78, 84, 85, 86,
110; Rebeckah, 178; Reece,
86; Reese, 85; Robert, 85;
Samuel, 84, 85, 86, 109;
Sarah, 85, 106, 108, 111;
Susanna, 85, 86, 90;
Susannah, 79; Thomas, 84,
85, 86, 108, 111; Unity,
86; William, 84, 85, 94,
95
GASTMAN, Joh. Daniel, 50;
Johannes, 50; Maria
Elisabeth, 51
GATCHEL, Elisha, 147;
Elizabeth, 147; Lydia, 170
GATCHELL, Elisha, 149; Sarah,
149
GATLEIF, Charles, 5; Mary, 5
GATLIFF, Charles, 86;
Elizabeth, 80, 86; Mary,
86
GATLIVE, Charles, 7;
Elizabeth, 7; Mary, 7
GAVIN, Edward, 74
GAWTHORP, Elizabeth, 144;
George, 158; Hannah, 158;
Jane, 158; Thomas, 144
GAWTHROPE, Elizabeth, 157,
160; George, 160; Jane,
160; Sarah, 157; Thomas,
157
GEBEL, Elisabeth, 53, 55, 56,
61; Georg, 61; Heinrich,
53, 55, 56, 59, 61;
Johannes, 55; Magdalena,
59; Sophia, 59
GEHRICH, Anna Catharina, 46;
Peter, 46; Phillipina, 46
GEIDLING, Anna Maria, 56;
Friderich, 56; Johannes,
56
GEITLING, Eliesabetha, 46;
Elisabeth, 44, 46;
Johannes, 44, 46;
Margareda, 44
GELER, Johannes, 44;
Margaretha, 44; Michel, 44

GEOTZ, Anna Maria, 44;
Elisabeth, 44; Johannes,
44
GERBER, Carl, 60; Elisabeth,
60
GIBBONS, Joseph, 14, 31, 36;
Sarah, 14, 31
GIBSON, Hannah, 34; James, 76;
Nancy, 77; Nathaniel, 34
GILBERT, Joseph, 86; Sarah, 86
GILES, Elizabeth, 162; Hannah,
144; Jacob, 144;
Nathaniel, 162; Sarah, 161
GILL, Ann, 34; Charles, 34;
David, 34; Francis, 34;
Margaret, 34; Susannah, 34
GILPIN, Bernard, 170; Mary,
117, 180; Sarah, 117;
Thomas, 117, 180
GINTER, Catharina, 58, 61;
Johannes, 58, 61; Maria,
58
GISSONS, Abraham, 85; Lydia,
85
GLEAVE, Elizabeth, 86; John,
86
GLEEN, William, 75
GONDEL, Adam, 40; Joh. Adam,
40; Philip, 40
GONDELT, Adam, 39; Maria
Chattharina, 39; Maria
Magdalena, 39
GONN, Barbara, 53; Jeremiah,
53; Maria, 53
GOOD, Charles, 117; Esther,
136, 152; Evan, 117; Jane,
117; Miriam, 136; Rebecca,
152; Thomas, 117, 136, 152
GOODSON, Ann, 144; William,
144
GOODWIN, Ann, 86; Elizabeth,
87; Enoch, 86; Ezra, 87;
George, 87; Gideon, 87;
Hannah, 86; Isaac, 86;
Jane, 87, 97; Jesse, 86;
John, 86, 87; Lydia, 86;
Mary, 86, 87, 88; Naomi,
98; Naomy, 86; Richard,
21, 86, 87; Sarah, 87,
108; Susanna, 82, 87;
Thomas, 86, 87, 88
GORDON, John, 36
GRAFTON, Mary, 163
GRAHAM, --, 76
GRAST, Johannes, 43; Julianna,
43
GRAY, Ann, 117, 177; Anthony,
34; Edith, 179; Elijah,
144, 178; Elizabeth, 34,
117, 177; Enoch, 144;
Hannah, 117, 144, 178;

INDEX

Jacob, 117, 177; John, 34;
Joseph, 117, 177;
Margaret, 117, 177;
Margery, 144; Marta, 75;
Mary, 32, 34, 144, 178;
Rachel, 144, 175; Samuel,
144; Sarah, 117; William,
117
GREACY, Dorothy, 144; Emey,
144; John, 144; Katherine,
144; Ruth, 144; William,
144
GREAVE, Elizabeth, 172;
Hannah, 172; Jesse, 172;
Tacy, 172
GREEN, Hannah, 87; Mary, 79,
87; Robert, 87; Silas, 79,
87
GREENFIELD, Amos, 117, 119;
Ann, 119, 144; Benjamin,
117; Betsy, 117;
Elizabeth, 117; Hannah,
136; James, 136, 144;
Margaret, 117, 119; Mary
Ann, 117; Phebe, 119;
Reuben, 119; Sarah, 162
GREGG, Anne, 144; Benjamin,
144; Dinah, 144; George,
144; Hannah, 144; John,
144; Joseph, 144; Mary,
87; Michael, 87, 144;
Richard, 144; Ruth, 144;
Sarah, 87, 144; Susanna,
144; Thomas, 144; William,
87
GREGORY, Walpole, 22
GREY, Edwin, 117; Enoch, 117;
Ezra, 117; Hannah, 117;
Margaret, 117; Matilda,
117; Michajah, 117;
Samuel, 117; Sarah, 117
GRIER, Susanna, 74
GRIFFIN, Sarah, 179
GRIFFITH, Abigail, 143; Abner,
87; Amy, 87; Benoni, 6,
87; Catharine, 87;
Catherine, 6; Elizabeth,
87, 108; Esther, 144;
Ezekiel, 21; Hannah, 87,
111, 145; Isaac, 77;
Jesse, 9; John, 9, 25, 87,
93, 144; John G., 143;
Joseph, 145; Martha, 9;
Mary, 9, 25, 93; Nathan,
87; Phebe, 87; Rachel, 6,
87, 101; Sarah, 99, 145;
Sibella, 9; Susanna, 89,
103; William, 87, 111, 145
GRISSEL, Agnes, 30; Joseph,
30; Precilla, 30; Thomas,
30

GRISTO, Christoph, 68;
Matheiss, 68
GROB, Barbara, 51; Elisabeth,
52, 53; Heinrich, 51, 52;
Jacob, 52, 53; Verena, 52
GROLL, Michel, 68; Sara, 68
GRUB, Nathaniel, 102; Sarah,
102
GRUBB, Ann, 87, 104; Jane, 77;
Nathaniel, 87; Phebe, 87,
110; Sarah, 87
GRUENSTEIN, Catharina, 47;
Jacob, 47
GRUND, Abraham, 41; Catarina,
47; Elisabeth, 43, 67;
Eva, 41, 43, 47, 49;
Hannickel, 47; Hans
Nicholaus, 47; Joh.
Nickel, 43; Johann Michel,
41; Johannes, 49; Peter,
67
GRUNDT, Elisabeth, 66; Eliza,
45; Eva, 51; Henrich, 66;
Joh. Nickel, 51;
Magdalena, 45; Nickel, 45;
Nicolaus, 51; Peter, 66
GUNTER, Catharina, 41;
Dorrothea, 41; Jacob, 41
GUNTHER, Anna Dorothea, 42;
Dorothea, 44; Jacob, 42,
44; Johann Phillip, 42
GUTHRIE, Abigial, 74; John, 76

-H-
HAAS, Heinrich, 65; Johannes,
54; Maria, 54
HADLEY, Anne, 144; Deborah,
141, 143; Elizabeth, 142,
160; Emey, 142; Hannah,
141, 160; John, 128, 142,
145, 155, 160; Joseph,
141, 145; Joshua, 143,
145, 146, 151; Katherine,
149; Mabel, 119, 163;
Mable, 145, 146; Margaret,
128, 142, 145, 155, 160;
Mary, 128, 145, 146, 154,
155; Ruth, 150, 151;
Samuel, 145, 163; Sarah,
143, 163; Simon, 141, 143,
144, 149, 150, 172;
Thomas, 145
HAGERIN, Eva Elisabeth, 38
HAHLMAN, Esther, 49, 51;
Johannes, 51; John, 49;
Susanna, 49
HAHLMANN, Maria, 53
HAHNVOIN(HAUGEN), Christina,
69; John, 69
HAINES, Catharine, 87; David,
87; Dorothy, 118;

Elizabeth, 80, 145; Ellis,
87; Esther, 82, 87; Ezra,
87; George, 87; Hannah,
83, 87; Isaac, 87, 145;
Jacob, 145; Jane, 87, 110;
Joseph, 118, 145; Josiah,
87; Lydia, 87, 108, 145;
Mary, 87, 108, 145, 178;
Meriam, 118; Miriam, 145;
Patience, 118; Phebe, 83,
87; Ruth, 118; Sarah, 118;
Solomon, 118; William,
118, 145; William D., 87
HAINGE, Georg, 52; Johannes,
52; Maria Catharina, 52
HAINS, Jacob, 17; Phebe, 17;
Samuel, 17
HALL, Caleb, 87; Eliz., 75;
John, 87, 97; Maris, 87;
Mary, 87, 88; Mary Ann,
87; Phebe, 87; Samuel, 87;
Sarah, 87, 88, 107, 166;
Seth, 87; Susanna, 83, 87,
97; Thomas, 87, 88
HALLIDAY, Deborah, 118, 150;
Hannah, 147; Jacob, 118,
145; Mable, 148; Margaret,
152; Marget, 118; Miriam,
145; Phebe, 145, 148;
Rachel, 118; Robert, 118,
145, 147, 148; Sarah, 118;
William, 118, 145, 150,
152
HALLMANN, Elisabeth, 51;
Esther, 51; John, 51
HALLOWELL, Alice, 12; Ann, 13;
Daniel, 12; Elizabeth,
118; Grace, 118; Hannah,
169; Jesse, 118, 169;
John, 12, 118; Joseph,
118, 169; Joshua, 169;
Lebulon, 12; Lydia, 118;
Margaret, 118, 169;
Martha, 12; Mary, 12;
Nathaniel, 12; Susanna,
12; Thomas, 118; William,
12, 169
HALMANN, Esther, 54; Jean, 54;
Jones(Jonas), 54
HAMBLETON, Charles, 118; Eli,
118; Hannah, 118, 145;
John, 118; Mary, 180;
Rachel, 118; Samuel, 145;
Sarah, 118; Thomas, 118;
William, 118, 180
HAMMANS, Lowry, 88; Sarah, 88;
William, 88
HAMPTON, David, 77; Eli, 145;
Rachel, 145
HANBE, Elizabeth, 118; Mary,
118; William, 118

HANCOCK, Benjamin, 6, 22;
Elizabeth, 6, 22; James,
5, 6, 22; Jane, 21; Joel,
6, 22; John, 6, 22;
Joseph, 5, 22; Rebekah, 5;
Sarah, 5, 6, 21, 22;
William, 5, 21
HANGAN, Christiana, 40; Joh.,
40
HANGIN, Christina, 39
HARDLEY, Hannah, 133; John,
133; Margaret, 133
HARLAN, Abigail, 117, 118,
145, 173; Alice, 143, 145,
169; Ann, 145, 169;
Benjamin, 176; Betty, 163;
Caleb, 118, 145, 165;
David, 145, 169; Dinah,
117, 118, 144; Elisha,
169; Elizabeth, 176;
Elwood, 145, 176; Emer,
172; Ezekiel, 145, 146;
George, 118, 145, 169;
Hannah, 88, 118, 137, 145,
146, 165, 166, 169, 176;
Israel, 170; James, 145,
163, 176; Jeremiah, 170;
Jesse, 112, 145, 146;
Joel, 88, 118, 145; John,
169; Jonathan, 176;
Joseph, 169; Joshua, 118;
Lewis, 169; Lydia, 88,
112, 145, 146; Mary, 118,
140, 145, 146, 154, 169,
176; Michael, 117, 137,
144, 145, 146, 159;
Milton, 176; Moses, 140;
Phebe, 170; Rachel, 145;
Rebeckah, 169; Ruth, 118;
Samuel, 173; Sarah, 159;
Solomon, 145, 169;
Stephen, 146; Susanna,
137, 145, 168; Thomas,
146, 171; William, 143,
154
HARLEY, Levi, 118; Levinia,
118; Ruth, 118; Samuel,
118; Sidney, 118; Susanna,
118; Thomas, 118; William,
118
HAROLD, Elizabeth, 153
HARPER, Samuel, 76
HARRIS, Elizabeth, 118, 120,
154; Evan, 118; Hannah,
139; Rebecca, 31; Roger,
154; Sarah, 154
HARRISON, Caleb, 88; Hannah,
88; John, 88; Mary, 88
HARROLD, Elizabeth, 118; John,
118; Jonathan, 118;
Levinia, 118; Mary, 118;

INDEX

Rachel, 118; Richard, 118;
Samuel, 118
HARRY, Amos, 146; Ann, 147;
Catharine, 35; Elisabeth,
47; Elizabeth, 148, 158,
177; George, 146; Hannah,
35; James, 47; Jesse, 35,
158; Martha, 47; Mary,
158; Phebe, 146, 169;
Sarah, 35; William, 35
HARTENSTEIN, Catharina, 56
HARTLEY, David, 172;
Elizabeth, 153, 172;
Jesse, 172; Jonathan, 172;
Martha, 172
HARTMAN, Elisabeth, 61; Jacob,
62; Michal, 61; Sara, 62
HARTMANN, Jacob, 60; Sara, 60
HARTS, Catharina, 40; Georg,
40; Joh. Henrich, 40
HARTSHORN, Rebecca, 75
HARVARD, David, 88; John, 88;
Susanna, 88
HARVEY, Ann, 146; Elizabeth,
166; Esther, 147; Joshua,
173; Mary Ann, 147;
Samuel, 147; Susanna, 146;
William, 146
HASH, Lydia, 165
HATTEN, Ann, 34; Edward, 34;
Eliza, 34; Grace, 34;
Jarves, 34; Rachel, 34;
Robert, 34; Susanna, 34
HATTON, Ann, 36; Edward, 15,
29; Jesse, 29; John, 36;
Joseph, 15, 25; Mary, 15,
29; Robert, 20; Sarah, 15,
29; Susanna, 15, 28, 29,
31; Thomas, 15, 29
HAUBEY, Rebecca, 35
HAUENSTEIN, Catharina, 46;
Jacob, 46
HAUGE, Johan Georg, 70; Johan
Peter, 70; Johannes, 70
HAUGEN, Elisabeth, 71;
Johannes, 71; Maria
Elisabeth, 71
HAUS, Elisabeth, 63; Jacob,
63; Samuel, 63
HAUSM, Elisabeth, 54;
Friderich, 54
HAUTERSTEIN, Catharina, 46;
Jacob, 46; Magdalena, 46
HAVARD, Susanna, 97
HAVARD(HARVARD), David, 97
HAWLEY, Benjamin, 11, 88;
Dinah, 11, Joana, 11;
Joel, 11; Joseph, 11;
Mary, 11; Phebe, 88;
Rebecca, 11; Robert, 33;
Simon, 11; William, 88

HAWORTH, Mahlon, 26
HAYCOCK, Ann, 88; Hannah, 88,
97; Jonathan, 88; Joseph,
88, 97
HAYDON, Catherine, 159
HAYES, Ann, 139, 146; Anna,
166; Caleb, 112; David,
139, 146, 166; Elizabeth,
118, 137; Hannah, 118,
133, 141, 146, 159; Henry,
118, 137, 146, 154; Isaac,
141, 146; Israel, 150;
Jane, 118, 133, 146, 150,
162; John, 146; Joseph,
146, 153, 162; Jospeh,
162; Lydia, 154; Lysia,
150; Margaret, 158; Mary,
112, 158; Phebe, 139;
Rachel, 153; Rebecca L.,
150; Richard, 146, 158;
Ruth, 141; Sarah, 150;
William, 118, 133, 146,
150, 159
HAYS, Ruth, 33
HAYSE, Ann, 166; David, 166;
Nathan, 166
HEAD, Mary, 150
HEADLEY, Anna, 117; Deborah,
117; Elizabeth, 118; Emey,
118; Hannah, 117, 118;
John, 118; Joseph, 117;
Joshua, 117; Katharine,
117; Margaret, 118; Mary,
117, 118; Ruth, 117;
Samuel, 118; Sarah, 117;
Simon, 117, 118
HEAYES, Sarah, 107
HECK, Andreas, 43; Anna Maria,
42; Barbara, 43;
Christian, 70; Elisabeth,
46; Esther, 71; Jacob, 43;
Jonah, 42; Jonas, 46, 70,
71; Peter, 70; Susanna,
46; Sussanna, 42
HECKE, Johne, 72; Jonas, 72
HEID, Christina, 58; Johannes,
58
HEILMAN, Johannes, 72
HEINRICH, Christel, 61; Georg,
61; Johannes, 59;
Magdalena, 59
HEINY, Georg, 73; Hanna, 73
HEITZEL, Catharina, 60; Georg,
60
HELL, Conrath, 45; Elisabeth,
43; Hans Jacob, 43, 47;
Jacob, 45; Margareth, 47;
Maria, 45; Maria Susanna,
43, 45; Susanna, 47
HELLWEIS(HELLWICH), Catharina,
69

HELLWICH, Dorrothea, 43;
    Jacob, 43, 69; Maria, 43
HELSBY, Jane, 88; Joseph, 88;
    Mary, 88, 100; Sarah, 26
HELWICH, Margrith, 51
HELWIG, Catharina, 38; Eva
    Elisabeth, 38; Jacob, 38
HENCH, Elisabeth, 52
HENCHY, Catharina, 55; Georg,
    55; Johannes, 55;
    Margrith, 55; Maria, 55
HENCKE, Peter, 41
HENCKEN, Anna Margaretha, 42;
    Anna Margreth, 44; Georg,
    45; Henrich, 44, 45;
    Johann Henrich, 42; Johann
    Peter, 42; Margaretha, 45;
    Philip, 44
HENDERSON, Eliz., 75
HENGE, Christina, 40; Jacob,
    40; Jah. Jacob, 40; Joh.,
    40
HENNER, Johannes, 40
HENNING, Andrew, 75
HENRY, Jane, 74
HERLIN, Joel, 122; Mary, 122
HERMAN, Frederick, 66
HERTZ, Christina, 69; Georg,
    69
HIBBARD, Aaron, 89; Abraham,
    88, 89; Alice, 89; Allen,
    89; Amos, 88, 89; Ann, 88;
    Anna, 89; Benjamin, 88,
    89; Caleb, 88; Deborah,
    88, 89; Edith, 89;
    Elizabeth, 88, 89; Enos,
    89; Esther, 89; George,
    89; Hannah, 88; Isaac, 88,
    89; Jacob, 88; James, 89;
    Jane, 88, 89, 109; John,
    88, 89, 98; Joseph, 88,
    89; Joshia, 89; Joshua,
    88; Josiah, 88, 89; Lydia,
    88, 89; Martha, 88, 89;
    Mary, 88, 89, 98; Naomi,
    89; Owen, 89; Phebe, 89;
    Philena, 89; Phinehas, 88;
    Preston, 89; Rachel, 89;
    Rebecca, 89; Rhoda, 88;
    Samuel, 88, 89; Sarah, 88,
    89; Sidney, 89; Silas, 89;
    Susanna, 89; Thomas, 89;
    Walter, 89; William, 88,
    89, 109
HIBBERD, Ann, 103; Benjamin,
    85; Deborah, 94; Hannah,
    103; Jane, 111; Joshua,
    94; Mary, 85, 103
HIBBERT, James, 35
HIETT, Ann, 119, 148;
    Elizabeth, 118, 120;
    Katharine, 119, 148;
    Thomas, 118
HILL, Deborah, 136; Elizabeth,
    152; Mary, 137; Robert,
    146; Samuel, 136, 152;
    Shem, 76; Violeta, 146
HILLARD, Benjamin, 179
HILLES, Ann, 14, 34; David,
    14, 34; Dinah, 14; Eli,
    14, 34; Hannah, 14; Hugh,
    14, 34; Jesse, 14;
    Jonathan, 14; Lydia, 14;
    Mary, 14, 34; Nathan, 14;
    Phebe, 14; Rachel, 14;
    Rebecca, 34; Rebeckkeh,
    14; Robert, 14; Samuel,
    14, 34; William, 14, 34
HILLIS, --, 77
HIMELREICH, Catharina, 73;
    Elisabeth, 59; Philip, 59,
    73; Simon, 72; Sophia, 59,
    73
HIMMELREICH, Anna Maria, 55;
    Catharina, 56; Philip, 55,
    56; Samuel, 55; Sarah, 55;
    Sophia, 56
HIMMELSREICH, Phillip, 72;
    Simon, 72
HIPP, Elisbeth, 62
HIPPEL, Abraham, 59; Anna, 55,
    68; Anna Catharina, 39;
    Anna Christina, 40; Anna
    Elisabeth, 40; Anna Maria,
    37, 40, 43, 44, 45, 47,
    48, 54; Anna Maria
    Margaretha, 40; Annamaria,
    48; Borentz, 48; Caspar,
    55; Catarina, 40;
    Catharina, 46, 49, 54, 60,
    64, 71; Catharine, 66;
    Elisabeth, 44, 45, 47, 51,
    54, 58, 60, 63, 65, 68;
    Friedrich, 48, 71;
    Friedrick, 43; Frierich,
    44; Frietrich, 40; Hanna,
    51, 52, 58, 64, 66;
    Hannah, 66; Hannes, 48,
    51, 64, 68; Heinrich, 52,
    54, 55, 58, 60, 61, 64;
    Henna(Hanna/Anna), 61;
    Henrich, 38, 39, 40, 48,
    49, 51, 69, 70, 71, 72;
    Herich, 66; Jacob, 39, 51,
    54, 55, 56, 60, 63, 70;
    Jacobz, 58; Jesse, 66;
    Joh. Georg, 53, 58; Johan,
    66; Johann Jost, 40;
    Johannes, 37, 38, 39, 43,
    47, 52, 60, 69, 70; Jost,
    71; Laurens, 59; Laurentz,
    73; Lorentz, 38, 39, 40,

INDEX

43, 45, 46, 47, 51, 52, 53, 54, 55, 68, 69, 70, 71; Lorenz, 56, 57, 58, 60, 62; Magdalena, 39, 47, 51; Margaretha, 47; Margrith, 51, 52, 55, 57, 58, 60; Maria, 60, 62, 63, 71, 72; Maria Elizabeth, 49; Peter, 43; Rosina, 53, 54, 56, 59, 62; Wilhelm, 48; Zacharias, 54
HIRSCH, Anna Maria, 67; Elisabeth, 62; Georg, 54, 59, 62, 65, 67, 72; Johannes, 53; Magdalena, 54, 55, 59, 62, 65, 72; Philip, 67, 73; Rebecca, 72; Samuel, 53, 55, 59, 62, 65, 73; Susanna, 54, 55, 62, 65, 73; susanna, 53; Zusanna, 60
HOBSON, Ann, 119, 146; ann, 162; Elizabeth, 119, 146, 150; Francis, 138, 146, 152, 162; Joseph, 119, 146, 150; Martha, 119, 146, 152, 162; Mary, 138; Phebe, 150
HOFF, Catharina, 44; Christjan, 44; Elisabeth, 44
HOFFMAN, Anna Maria, 55; Catharina, 72; Elisabeth, 59, 72; Henrich, 67; Johannes, 59, 72
HOFFMANN, Catharina, 53; Elisabeth, 53; Johannes, 53
HOFMAN, Elisabeth, 62; Johannes, 61
HOFMANN, Elisabeth, 55; Johannes, 55
HOLLAND, Deborah, 96; Hannah, 89; John, 89; Margaret, 119, 135; Mary, 89; Samuel, 89; Sarah, 88, 89; Thomas, 119, 135
HOLLEY, Joshua, 117; Mary, 117; Sarah, 117
HOLLIDAY, Rachel, 153; William, 153
HOLMES, --, 76
HOOD, James, 89; Jonathan, 30, 89; Joseph, 84, 89; Margaret, 76; Mary, 84, 89; Rachel, 89; Rebecca, 89; Richard, 89; Thomas, 89; William, 89
HOOPER, Elizabeth, 26; Israel, 26; Jane, 26; Jonathan, 26; Margaret, 26; Thamzen, 26; William, 26
HOOPES, Aaron, 91; Abner, 90, 91; Abraham, 90, 109; Albinah, 90; Alice, 80, 90, 91; Amos, 90, 91; Amy, 90, 104; Amy C., 90; Amyu, 90; Ann, 90, 91, 119; Benjamin, 90, 119, 146; Caleb, 90; Christian, 91, 98; Curtis, 90; Daniel, 79, 90, 91; David, 90, 91, 146, 163; Edith, 91; Eli, 90; Elijah, 91; Elisha, 91; Elizabeth, 79, 90, 91, 92, 93, 98, 119, 146; Enos, 91; Esther, 91, 146, 163; Ezra, 90; Francis, 91, 100; Garrett, 90; George, 90, 92, 173; George M., 91; Gimlah, 91; Grace, 107; Hannah, 78, 80, 90, 91; Henry, 91; Israel, 90, 119, 146; James, 90, 91, 119; Jane, 90, 97, 100, 105, 119, 150; Jesse, 90, 91, 173; Joel, 91, 119; John, 91, 100, 178; Jonathan, 91, 119; Joseph, 90, 171; Joshua, 78, 85, 90, 91, 146; Kesse, 90; Lavinah, 90; Lewis, 91; Lydia, 90, 91, 100, 104, 106; Mabel, 119; Mable, 146; Margaret, 90, 91, 119, 147; Marshall, 90; Martin, 91; Mary, 85, 90, 91, 108, 109, 145, 146; Moses, 90, 91; Nathan, 90, 91, 147; Phebe, 88, 90, 91, 119, 147; Rachel, 90; Rebecca, 91, 146; rebecca, 119; Rebeckah, 173; Samuel, 91; Samuel G., 90; Sarah, 81, 90; Susanna, 90, 91, 119, 163; Tamzin, 174; Thomas, 90, 91, 119, 146; Tomzin, 119; William, 90, 91, 119, 146, 147, 174; William Lewis, 91
HOOPS, Abraham, 177
HOPE, Frances, 32; William, 24
HOPF, Heinrich, 64
HOUCK, Henrich, 41; Margaretha, 41; Susanna, 41
HOULTON, Martha, 147; Nathaniel, 147
HOUSE, Amos, 147; James, 147; Mary, 147, 173
HOWELL, David, 92; Deborah,

147; Elizabeth, 92, 147;
Jacob, 147; Jonathan, 92,
105; Magdalen, 103; Rees,
92; Sarah, 147; Stephen,
147
HOYT, Catharina, 71;
Christian, 71
HUBENER, Abraham, 65;
Catharina, 60, 61, 63, 65;
Georg, 60, 61, 63, 65, 67;
Katharina, 67; Wilhelm, 63
HUBNER, Catharina, 64; Daniel,
64; Georg, 64
HUDSON, Joseph, 24
HUGHES, Beulah C., 160;
Elizabeth, 147; Hannah,
173; Jesse, 147, 156; Mary
Ann, 147; Samuel, 147;
Sarah, 156; Thomas, 147
HUGHS, Elizabeth, 171
HUMPHREY, Margaret, 92; Mary,
12; Owen, 12; Richard, 92;
Sarah, 12; Solomon, 92
HUMPHRIES, Edward, 31; Hannah,
31; Jacob, 31; Rebeckah,
31; Samuel, 31; Sarah, 31
HUNT, Mary, 23; Samuel, 23
HUNTER, Alice, 89
HURFORD, Ann, 169; ann, 120;
Benjamin, 120, 169; Caleb,
119, 147, 179; Catharine,
119; Eli, 119; Elizabeth,
119, 162, 170; Hannah,
119, 120, 147, 162, 167,
169, 170; Isaac, 119;
John, 116, 119, 120, 147,
162, 169; Joseph, 119,
120, 169, 170; Katharine,
116, 170; Katherine, 119;
Martha, 119, 147; Mary,
147; Naomi, 120, 169;
Nathan, 120, 169;
Nicholas, 147; Rachel,
119, 147, 170; Ruth, 119,
170; Samuel, 119, 120,
147, 169, 170; Sarah, 119,
170; Thomas, 120, 169;
William, 119, 120, 169
HUSBAND, Joseph, 147; Mary,
147; William, 147
HUSEY, Catharina, 69;
Johannes, 69
HUTCHINSON, Hannah, 32; John,
32
HUTTEN, Hannah, 165
HUTTON, Ann, 114, 120, 127,
138, 147, 148, 156, 162,
168; Benjamin, 120, 127,
133, 138, 147, 156, 162;
Betty, 147; Caleb, 120;
Catharine, 147; Deborah,
148; Ebenezer, 120;
Elizabeth, 120, 133, 148;
Emmer, 120; Enos, 172;
Ephraim, 120; Evan, 120;
Hannah, 120, 147, 148,
160, 162, 172; Hiatt, 156;
Hiet, 172; Hiett, 120,
161; Hutton, 120; Isaac,
120; Jesse, 120, 172;
John, 120, 147, 165;
Joseph, 10, 120, 147, 148,
164; Joshua, 120;
Katharine, 120, 148, 160,
172; Lydia, 120, 138, 172;
Martha, 120; Mary, 120,
147, 156; Nehemiah, 114,
120, 138, 147; Phebe, 164;
Rachel, 120, 147, 165;
Samuel, 120, 165; Sarah,
114, 120, 138, 147, 156,
161, 164; Seph, 148;
Sidnee, 120; Sidney, 161;
Susanna, 10, 120; Thomas,
120, 147, 148, 160, 166;
William, 120, 148
HYLMAN, Georg Adam, 39

-I-

IMHOFTT, Johannes, 39;
Magdalena, 39
INGRAM, Mary, 35
INNER, John, 74
IVES, Elizabeth, 24

-J-

JACKSON, Alice, 121, 122, 124,
148, 150; Ann, 112, 121,
122, 136, 137, 140, 145,
149, 161; Caleb, 121, 122,
148, 161, 176, 179;
Catharine, 121, 122, 155;
Deborah, 33, 121, 122,
156; Dinah, 156;
Elizabeth, 33, 121, 139,
162, 163; Ephraim, 121,
148, 149; Esther, 122,
176; Hannah, 121, 122,
124, 148, 155, 157, 160,
161, 168, 175, 176; Isaac,
30, 33, 121, 122, 124,
136, 148, 149, 155, 163,
166, 175; Isaiah, 122;
Israel, 122; Jacob, 122,
176; James, 121, 122, 148;
Jane, 148, 149; Jarries,
121; Jesse, 121; Joel,
148, 176; John, 75, 112,
121, 122, 135, 136, 148,
156, 157, 164, 168, 175;
Jonathan, 140, 148, 149,
162; Joseh, 149; Joseph,

INDEX

29, 121, 150, 170; Joshua, 121, 122, 176; Josiah, 121; Katharine, 121, 126, 149, 160; Katherine, 122; Lydia, 121, 122, 148, 149; Mabel, 119; Mable, 145; Margaret, 148; Mary, 32, 121, 122, 134, 136, 140, 148, 149, 158, 159, 162, 163, 164; Mercy, 33; Mray, 148; Nathaniel, 121; Phebe, 122, 148; Rachel, 121, 122, 149, 156; Rachell, 121; Rebecca, 122, 133, 151; Rebekah, 121; Ruth, 121, 138, 140; Samuel, 121, 122, 134, 137, 138, 149, 156, 159, 165, 179; Sarah, 33, 112, 121, 122, 135, 136, 137, 148, 149, 150, 157, 164; Sidney, 33; Susanna, 121, 148, 150, 174; Susannah, 122, 175; Tacy, 148; Thomas, 114, 121, 122, 136, 139, 140, 148, 149, 164; William, 121, 122, 126, 133, 148, 149, 160, 166, 171, 173, 175, 176
JACOB, Isaac, 36
JACOBS, Ann, 11; Benjamin, 92; Elizabeth, 11, 19, 92; elizabeth, 31; Hannah, 11, 31; Isaac, 11, 31, 92; Israel, 92, 97; John, 11, 19, 92; Joseph, 11, 31, 92; Lydia, 33; Mary, 11, 31, 92; Phebe, 11, 31, 33; Rachel, 11, 31; Richard, 33; Sarah, 11, 31, 92, 97; Susannah, 33; Thomas, 92; William, 11, 31
JACSON, --, 76
JAGER, Anna Catharina, 40; Anna Maria, 39, 41, 45, 47, 70; Georg, 40, 41, 44, 47, 70, 72; Gorg, 39; Jacob, 44; Johan Gorg, 39, 40; Johannes, 39; Peter, 40, 72
JAGERIN, Anna Maria, 38
JAMES, Aaron, 92; Ann, 92, 110; Caleb, 92; Elizabeth, 80, 90, 92; Esther, 92, 109; Ezekiel, 92; Gainor, 92; Hannah, 27, 29, 33, 80, 92, 97; Jacob, 92; Jane, 88; Jesse, 92; Joanna, 92; John, 92; Joseph, 21, 92; Keziah, 92; Lydia, 92, 104, 114; Mary, 92; Mordecai, 92; Moses, 92; Phebe, 92; Rebeckah, 92; Ruth, 92; Samuel, 92; Sarah, 79, 86, 92; Susanna, 92
JAYS, John, 75
JEFFERIS, Carpenter, 93; Hannah, 81; John, 81; Malinda, 93; Minerva, 93; Phebe Baily, 93; Townsend, 93; William Walter, 93
JEGER, Anna Maria, 56; Catharina, 68; Elisabeth, 55, 56, 61; Elisbeth, 64; Georg, 56, 61, 68; Hanna, 59; Heinrich, 55; Johannes, 52, 54, 56, 59, 63; Magdalena, 54, 59, 63; Magdalnea, 56; Maria, 56; Maria Magdalena, 52; Peter, 55, 56, 61, 64
JEGER(YEAGER), Georg, 73
JENKIN, Ann, 7; Evan, 7; Sarah, 7
JENKINS, Anne, 93; Evan, 93; Mary, 93, 101; Sarah, 93
JERIAR, Eleanor, 77
JIPY, Isbel, 75
JOB, Abraham, 122, 149; Andrew, 122, 149; Caleb, 122; Elizabeth, 122, 149; Enoch, 122; Hannah, 122; Jacob, 122; Joshua, 122; Mary, 122, 162; Patience, 122; Sarah, 149; Thomas, 122, 149
JOHN, Abel, 20, 93; Abner, 4, 33, 93; Adam, 51; Ann, 4, 5, 7, 18, 19, 22, 33, 34, 93; Anne, 93; Asa, 93; Barbara, 51; Daniel, 93; David, 93; Ebenezer, 7, 22; Elen, 83, 93; Elizabeth, 4, 93; Ellen, 93; Emy, 33; Esaiak, 4; Esther, 93; Gedeon, 33; Griffith, 4, 5, 19, 33, 93, 96; Gwen, 93; Hannah, 4, 93; Isaac, 7; Isaiah, 33; Israel, 18, 34; Jane, 5, 93; Jehurr, 51; Joanna, 18; Joannah, 34; John, 7; Joseph, 93; Joshua, 4, 10, 33, 93; Lisa, 4; Lydia, 7, 18, 34; Lydiah, 34; Margaret, 7, 93; Martha, 18; Mary, 7, 22, 93; Owen, 93; Pamela, 18; Pameliah, 34; Phebe, 18, 34; Rachel, 10, 33, 93; Rebecca, 153; Reuben, 18, 36; Robert,

18, 93; Ruben, 34, 36;
Ruth, 7, 22; Samuel, 7,
22, 93; Sarah, 4, 7, 17,
18, 22, 33, 34, 93, 96,
97; Sibilla, 4, 10, 93;
Thomas, 19, 93; Townsend,
18, 34; William, 93
JOHNSON, Abigail, 122; Ann,
144, 146, 149; Benjamin,
123; Caleb, 122, 142, 144;
David, 123; Davies, 123;
Dinah, 123; Elizabeth,
116, 123, 176, 178;
Hadley, 123, 149, 176,
178; Hadly, 171; Hannah,
122, 123, 160, 164, 176,
178; Isaac, 30, 122, 123,
167, 171, 176, 178; James,
122, 123, 149; Jane, 123;
Joanna, 123, 149;
Jonathan, 122, 123, 176;
Joseph, 167, 177; Joshua,
30, 116, 122, 123, 139,
140, 145, 149, 164, 167,
176; Katharine, 122, 123;
Katherine, 149; Kathrin,
171; Lewis, 123, 176, 178;
Lydia, 122, 123, 145, 171;
Margaret, 122, 123, 149;
Martha, 142, 144; Mary,
122, 123; Rachel, 30, 167;
Rebecca, 115, 123, 139,
142; Reuben, 123, 171;
Richard, 178; Robert, 122,
123, 149, 160, 176, 178;
Ruel, 123, 171; Ruth, 123,
149; Sarah, 122, 123, 140,
177; Simon, 122; Stephen,
122; William, 123, 177;
Zilla, 171
JOHNSTON, Catherine, 23;
Robert, 23
JOLLY, David, 76
JONATHAN, Rebecca, 13; Reuben,
13; Thomas, 13
JONES, Abner, 2; Acquila, 29;
Agnes, 2; Amey, 81; Amy,
94; Ann, 14, 16, 86, 94,
112; Aquila, 2; Benjamin,
94; Cadwalader, 5;
Cadwalader, 2, 86, 93;
Cadwalder, 6, 8, 19;
Cadwaller, 94; Catharine,
19; Charity, 123; Deborah,
94, 107; Edward, 23, 30;
Eleanor, 8, 123, 149;
Elenor, 5, 93; Elinor, 2,
93, 94; Elisabeth, 16;
Elisha, 93; Elizabeth, 27,
86, 97, 162; Ellinor, 6;
Evan, 2, 11, 19, 36, 93,
94; Gwen, 93; Hannah, 2,
94, 123, 149, 170; Henry,
94, 123, 149; Isaac, 112;
James, 16; Jane, 76, 80,
94, 146; Jesse, 5, 30, 36,
78; Joel, 123, 170; John,
26, 93, 123, 149, 170;
Jonathan, 5, 79, 94;
Joseph, 94, 123, 143, 149,
155, 161, 162; Judith,
123; Levi, 23; Lydia, 123,
149, 161; Margaret, 26;
Mary, 2, 5, 11, 19, 30,
78, 86, 93, 94, 101, 112,
123, 143, 157; Miriam,
149; Nathan, 86; Nehemiah,
94; Patience, 123, 149;
Priscilla, 162; Rachel,
80, 123, 143, 155, 157,
159; Rebecca, 2, 29, 35,
93, 94; Rebecka, 22;
Rebeckah, 14; Rebekah, 6;
Rees, 94; Reese, 94;
Richard, 94, 112, 149,
161; Robert, 93; Ruth, 2,
22, 102; Samuel, 159;
Sarah, 8, 30, 34, 93, 123;
Susanna, 2, 11, 19, 79,
94; Susannah, 2; William,
14, 35, 94, 123, 170, 175;
Yearsley, 2
JONSON, Daniel, 169
JONSTON, Sarah, 167
JORDAN, Elizabeth, 154; John,
147, 149, 154; Margaret,
77; Martha, 147; Mary,
165; Patience, 165;
Rachel, 149, 165
JORDON, Massey, 174
JOYCE, Deborah, 35
JUDGE, Hugh, 10, 27; Margaret,
10; Susanna, 10, 27, 28;
Thomas, 10
JUNG, Barbara, 62; Catharina,
62, 63; Elisabeth, 46;
Jacob, 46; Peter, 62, 63
JUNG (YOUNG), Catharina, 56;
Peter, 56
JUNGBLUT, Anna, 62; Elisabeth,
57; Johannes, 62; John,
57, 62; Magdalena, 57, 62;
Willy, 62
JUST, Heinrich, 64

-K-

KARL, Catharina, 43;
Elisabeth, 43, 44, 46;
Henrich, 43, 44, 46;
Johannes, 46
KEELAR, Mary, 142; Owen, 142
KEERAN, Eli, 177; John, 177;

INDEX 201

Levi, 177; Rebecca, 177; Sarah, 177; Simon, 177; Thomas, 177; William, 177
KEERANS, Elizabeth, 177
KEHR, Anna Margaret, 68; Jacob, 68
KELLER, Andreas, 40; Elisabeth, 40; Maria Catharina, 40
KELLY, Dennis, 74
KENNEY, Betty, 94; Daniel, 36, 94; Edith, 94; Hannah, 94; James, 5; Samuel, 94; Thomas, 94
KENNY, Mary, 35, 36; Richard, 35, 36
KERCHER, Maria, 55; Niclas, 55
KERSEY, Ann, 18; Elizabeth, 18; Esther, 18; Hannah, 18; Jesse, 18, 36; Joseph, 18; Lydia, 18; Mary, 18; Rachel, 18; Sarah, 18; William, 18
KEYS, William, 77
KIEHLY, Eva, 52; Maria Margaretha, 52; Matthias, 52
KIHLY, Conrad, 51, 55, 57, 60; Eva, 57; Jacob, 56, 57, 60; Johannes, 55; Magdalena, 60; Margreth, 51; Margrith, 55, 57, 60; Maria, 56, 60; Mattheis, 57; Rebecca, 51
KIHTY, Andreas, 52; Maria, 52; Sophia, 52
KIMBER, Caleb, 30, 149, 168, 170; Deborah, 30, 149, 168, 170; Gertrude, 149; Predy, 149
KIND, Isabella, 77; Jacob, 77; Mary, 76
KING, Anna, 61; Anna Maria, 56; Hannah, 123; Isabel, 123; Jacob, 61; James, 123; Johannes, 56; John, 61; Margaret, 123; Mary, 123; Michael, 123; Thomas, 123; Vincent, 123
KINKAID, Jane, 74
KINSEY, Abigail, 143; Dorothy, 179; Elizabeth, 149; James, 180; John, 143; Margaret, 143; Margaretta, 138; Rachel, 138; Samuel, 138; Sarah, 179; Thomas, 149
KIRK, Abigail, 8, 163; Adam, 94, 163; Alfansus, 8; Alphonsus, 94, 146, 150; Caleb, 94; Catherine, 165;

Elisabeth, 16; Elizabeth, 8, 11, 32, 135; Ezekiel, 22, 94; Hannah, 16, 22, 94, 146; Isaac, 22; Isaiah, 8, 16, 32; Jacob, 22, 94, 157; Jane, 150; Jonathan, 22; Joseph, 19, 94; Lydia, 94; Margaret, 150; Mary, 19, 94, 150; Phebe, 163; Rachel, 8, 16, 22, 32, 94; Rebecca, 8, 94, 157; Roger, 135, 150; Ruth, 8, 94; Samuel, 16, 32, 150; Sarah, 12, 22, 94; Sibbilla, 32; Sibella, 8; Sibilla, 8; Sibille, 16; Sybilla, 11; Tamar, 94; Thomas, 19, 94; Timothy, 19, 22, 94, 150; William, 8, 11, 16, 19, 30, 94, 150
KLAUS, Anna Catharina, 48; Catharina, 47; Christoff, 47; Christoph, 48; Johannes, 47
KLEIN, David, 45; Johan Jacob, 40; Johannes, 40, 45, 70; Margaretha, 45; Wilhelm, 70
KLIEN, Daniel, 42; Henrietta, 42; Johannes, 42
KLINGER, Johannes, 72; Margaret, 72
KNAUER, Christoph, 63; Elisabeth, 63
KNEEL, Ann, 127; Henry, 127; Sarah, 127
KNERR, Elisabeth, 52; Henrich, 52
KNUT, Maary, 76
KOENIG, Anna Maria, 70; Hannes, 68; Jacob, 70; Maria Elisabeth, 68; Susanna, 72
KOLB, Anna, 66; Elisabeth, 66; George Michael, 66; Hanna, 67; Maria, 67; Peter, 67
KONIG, Eva, 51; Jacob, 69; Margareth, 69; Michel, 51
KREBS, Heinrich, 65; Thomas, 65; Violetta, 65
KYLE, Henrich, 38
KYLER, Martin, 37

-L-
LAAR, Magdalena, 55; Niclas, 55
LABACH, Anna Maria, 60, 70, 73; Catharina, 55, 58, 60, 68; Elisabeth, 72; Heinrich, 58, 60, 73;

Johannes, 55, 58, 60, 64, 68, 70, 72; Ludwig, 68; Magdalena, 60; Margrith, 73; Maria, 58, 68
LABUCH, Christina, 71; Johannes, 71
LAMBERT, Mary, 94; Matthew, 94
LAMBORN, Alice, 124, 150; Ann, 123, 141, 143, 150, 161, 163; David, 169; Dinah, 124; Elizabeth, 123, 143; Ephraim, 124; Ezra, 124; Francis, 123; Hannah, 12, 124; Hobson, 150; Isaac, 124, 173; Jacob, 124; John, 123, 124; Jonathan, 124, 171, 175, 180; Joseph, 124, 168; Josiah, 123, 124, 150; Levi, 124; Lewis, 119, 168; Mary, 163; Miriam, 124; Parmena, 124; Permanes, 167, 179; Permenas, 175; Phebe, 119, 150; Rebecca L., 150; Richard, 124, 150, 178; Robert, 123, 124, 143, 150, 161, 163; Samuel, 124, 150; Sarah, 12, 123, 124, 150, 152, 161; Susanna, 124; Thomas, 123, 124, 150, 171, 173; William, 12, 123, 150
LAMBOURN, Levi, 177
LANDES, Carl, 68; Catharina, 68
LARKIN, Ann, 94; John, 94; Joseph, 94; Martha, 94
LAUBACH, Anna Catarina, 47; Anna Margaretha, 39; Anna Maria, 39, 47, 48, 51, 55, 56, 72; Catharina, 46, 51, 52; Christina, 40; Elisabeth, 49; Heinrich, 52, 55, 56; Hennerch, 47; Henrich, 38, 48, 49, 51, 68; Henry, 72; Johannes, 38, 39, 40, 46, 48; John, 68; Margrith, 56; Maria, 50, 52; Peter, 51, 72; Rebecca, 46
LAUDERBACH, Christina, 40; Phillipp, 40
LEE, Ann, 178; Margaret, 161
LEES, Elizabeth, 180
LEHR, Jacob, 69
LEONARD, Jemima, 112; Sarah, 167; William, 112
LEWES, Elija, 35
LEWIS, Abel, 33; Abner, 36; Agnes, 85; Alice, 124, 150, 179; Ambrose, 95, 96;
Amos, 4; Ann, 16, 84, 96, 102; Azariah, 95; Benjamin, 96; Catharine, 16; David, 94, 95, 96; Debbe, 96; Debby, 85; Debbye, 86; Debe, 95; Deborah, 88, 94; Deby, 95; Didymus, 95, 96; Dinah, 3, 31, 104; Eli, 96, 150; Elija, 35; Elizabeth, 4, 94, 95, 105, 124, 129; Ellis, 124, 129, 150; Elziabeth, 95; Enoch, 150; Enos, 95, 96; Esther, 95, 97; Evan, 24, 95, 97, 150; Gabriel, 94; Gideon, 95, 96; Grace, 16, 25; Griffith, 3, 4, 16, 95, 109; Gwen, 94; Hannah, 3, 4, 16, 21, 94, 95, 109, 150; Henry, 21, 95; Isabella, 142; Jabez, 84, 94, 95; Jacob, 28; James, 94, 95; Jane, 24, 76, 96, 150; Jephthah, 96; John, 16, 27, 36, 95; Jonathan, 94, 95; Joseph, 95, 96; Katharine, 95; Lamar, 96; Leah, 95; Levi, 95; Lewis, 94, 95; Lowry, 88, 96; Lydia, 16, 84, 94, 109, 110; Margaret, 3, 16, 92, 95, 96; Mary, 3, 4, 16, 84, 94, 95, 102, 108, 124, 150; Miles, 95; Nathan, 16, 95, 96; Pamela, 150; Peter, 95; Phebe, 84, 96; Phinehas, 94; Rachel, 82; Rebecca, 3, 4, 94, 104; Robert, 95, 150; Rose, 95; Ruth, 95, 96; Samuel, 3, 16, 95; Sarah, 4, 95, 109; Susanna, 76, 85, 95; Tacy, 96; Tamar, 95; Thomas, 94, 96; Unity, 86, 95; William, 4, 95, 96, 105
LIGET, Mary, 76
LIGHTFOOT, Benjamin, 11, 35; David, 7, 36; Deborah, 7; Elinor, 124; Katharine, 124; Margaret, 158; Mary, 6, 7, 124, 140; Michael, 124, 140, 154; Rachel, 11; Samuel, 5, 6, 7; Sarah, 7, 124, 147; Susanna, 7, 11, 28; Susannah, 35; Thomas, 11, 19, 124; William, 6, 7, 11, 19, 124
LIGHTFOTT, Mary, 150; Samuel, 150; Thomas, 150
LINDLEY, Alice, 124; Deborah,

INDEX 203

124, 150; Eleanor, 123, 124, 149; Elinor, 124; Elizabeth, 124; Hannah, 124, 151; Jacob, 124, 151, 175; James, 123, 124, 150; Jane, 150, 177; Jonathan, 124, 150; Katharine, 124; Marget, 124; Mary, 124; Rachel, 124; Robert, 124; Ruth, 124, 150; Simon, 124; Thomas, 124, 150, 177; William, 124, 150
LINERD, Christian, 151
LINNARD, Mary, 153
LINTON, Esther, 176; Hezekiah, 176; Jane, 176; Joshua, 176; Sarah, 176; William, 176
LINUS, Thomas, 146; Violeta, 146
LITTLER, John, 124, 151; Joshua, 124; Mary, 151; Minshall, 124; Rachel, 124; Samuel, 124, 151; Sarah, 124
LLOYD, David, 96; Grace, 96; Hannah, 96; Humphrey, 33, 96; John, 32, 96; Jones, 96; Joshua, 32; Margaret, 96, 108; Mercy, 32; Rebecca, 96, 100; Sarah, 93, 96; Thomas, 31
LOBB, Abraham, 96; Benjamin, 96; Dinah, 96; Jacob, 96; Sarah, 96
LOGAN, Ann, 75; Eliz., 74
LONGSTREET, Hannah, 14
LONGSTRETCH, Ann, 3, 10, 81; Bartholomew, 3, 10; Benjamin, 19; Elisabeth, 10; Hannah, 36; Jammaj, 3; Jane, 3; Joseph, 35; Kame, 3; Kpjm, 3; Moses, 3; Samuel, 36; Sarah, 3, 36
LONGSTRETH, John, 19
LOUDEN, Elizabeth, 24, 27
LOVE, Sarah, 76
LOW, Ann, 76
LOWDEN, Richard, 151
LOWNES, Alice, 96, 109; Benanuel, 96; Bennuel, 109; George, 96
LOWRY, Andrew, 76
LUBACH, Catharina, 44; Johann, 44; Johann Ludwig, 44
LUCKIE, George, 75
LUDWIG, Anna Maria, 55; Jacob, 55; Peter, 61; Susann, 67
LUKINS, Sarah, 174
LYET, James, 75

-M-
MCAFEE, Daniel, 75
MCBRIDE, Archibald, 76; John, 76
MCCONNEL, William, 178
MCCONNELL, Mary, 151; Matthew, 151; Rebecca, 151; Thomas, 151
MCCORCKLE, Isbella, 75
MCCORD, Hannah, 98; John, 98; Mary, 98
MCCOWEN, Bathshebba, 20; John, 20
MCCOY, --, 76
MCCULLOCH, James, 75
MCCURDIE, Alexander, 74
MACDANIL, Henrich, 71; Susanna, 71
MCFADGEN, James, 151; Rebecca, 151
MCGAHEN, Joseph, 75
MCGIFFEN, Thomas, 76
MCILHENNY, Thomas, 77
MCILVAIN, Ann, 151, 171; John, 151, 171; Lydia, 151
MACK, Conrad, 51; Jacob, 49; Magdalena, 49, 51; Margrith, 51; Nicklas, 51; Nicolaus, 49, 70; Niklas, 51
MACKAY, Mary, 157
MCKEE, William, 74
MACKEY, James, 75, 76; Kathrine, 75; Rachel, 75
MCMASTER, --, 76
MCMILLAN, Ann, 151; George, 151; Jane, 151; John, 151; Rebecca, 151, 174; Ruth, 151, 173; Thomas, 151
MCMILLIAN, Deborah, 96; Thomas, 96; William, 96
MCNEIL, Sarah, 112; William, 112
M'VEAGH, Alice, 13; Ellen, 13; Mary, 13; Rachel, 13
MAGEVER, Bastian, 69; Catharina, 69
MAHONY, John, 76; Kat., 76
MALHER, Jane, 175
MALIN, Alice, 96, 97, 101; Elisha, 97; Elizabeth, 102; elizabeth, 96; Ezra, 96; George, 96; Isaac, 96; James, 96; Jane, 96, 97; John, 96, 97; Joseph, 78, 97; Lucy, 97; Lydia, 78, 96, 97; Mary, 96, 97; Randal, 96, 97; Randall, 96, 97; Rebecca, 16, 96, 106; Sarah, 96, 97; Sophia, 96; Susanna, 88,

96, 97; Thomas, 96
MALL, Thomas, 177
MANSFIELD, William, 26
MARCHBANCH, David, 76
MARIS, Ann, 84, 97; Caleb, 84, 97; Catherine, 147, 159; Elizabeth, 97; George, 97; Hannah, 97; Jane, 78; Jesse, 78; John, 97, 124, 129, 132, 139, 147, 159; Jonathan, 97; Katharine, 124, 129, 132; Katherine, 139; Martha, 124, 147, 162; Mary, 97; Phebe, 97; Rebecca, 82, 86, 97; Richard, 97; Susanna, 97, 124, 129, 139, 159
MARISON, Barbara, 64
MARQUIS, Samuel, 76
MARSH, Abigail, 79; John, 151; Rachel, 168; Ruth, 151; Sarah, 137; William, 151
MARSHALL, Abraham, 151; Ann, 171; Elizabeth, 119, 124, 146; Esther, 171; Hannah, 92, 97, 134, 145, 151, 171; Humphrey, 151; Jacob, 151; James, 124, 146; John, 92, 97, 134, 145, 151; Joseph, 171; Margaret, 124, 146; Martha, 171; Mary, 145, 151; Permela, 175; Ruth, 151; Sarah, 151; Thomas, 26, 97, 171
MARTIN, Aaron, 5, 8, 29, 97; Ann, 29; Eleanor, 8, 97; Elizabeth, 8; Hannah, 8, 97; John, 8, 30, 97; Mary, 8, 20, 22, 77; Samuel, 77; Sarah, 8, 97; Susanna, 8, 97; Thomas, 8, 19, 29, 97, 167
MASH, Mary, 137
MASON, Benjamin, 124, 175, 176; George, 124, 154, 175, 176; Hannah, 151; Jane, 124, 154, 176; Joshua, 151; Mary, 124, 176; Rachel, 124, 176; Rebecca, 151; Samuel, 151; Sarah, 124, 175, 176; Susanna, 124, 176; William, 176
MASSEY, Aaron, 97; Ann, 97, 98; Catharine, 98; Elizabeth, 97; Esther, 95, 97, 98; George, 9, 36, 98; Hannah, 88, 97, 100; Isaac, 9, 78, 97, 98; Israel, 98; James, 97;
Jane, 87, 96, 97, 98; John, 98; Joseph, 97, 98; Levi, 98; Lewis, 97; Lydia, 97; Mary, 97, 98; Mordecai, 97; Phebe, 78, 97, 98, 99, 105; Phinehas, 97; Rachel, 9; Rebecca, 97; Robert, 9; Sarah, 92, 97, 98; Sidney, 79; Susannah, 9, 98; Thomas, 87, 97, 98; William, 9, 97, 98
MATHEWS, Esther, 31; Sarah, 127; Thomas, 127
MATLACK, Ruth, 103
MATLOCK, Jemima, 100
MATLOCK(MATLACK), Amos, 98; Esther, 98; Hannah, 98; Isaiah, 98; Jemima, 98; Jesse, 98; Jonathan, 98; Joseph, 98; Mary, 98; Nathan, 98; Rebecca, 98; Ruth, 98; Simeon, 98; William, 98
MATSON, Alice, 98; John, 98; Rebecca, 98
MATTER, Nathaniel, 165
MATTHEWS, Esther, 74; Katherine, 144
MATTISON, Hannah, 104
MATTSON, Hannah, 24; Jacob, 24; Mary, 24; Sarah, 24
MAUL, Caleb, 177; Elizabeth, 177; Rebecca, 178; Thomas, 177
MAULE, Ann, 28; Benjamin, 28; Ebenezar, 166; Jane, 33; Joshua E., 142; Lewis, 29; Rebecca, 142; Thomas, 167
MAULSBY, John, 21; Lydia, 21
MAURER, Elisabeth, 65; Peter, 65
MAUSER, Elisabeth, 54; Hannes, 54
MAXWELL, Eleanor, 15; Elizabeth, 149
MAXWIL, --, 76
MAYER, Catharina, 72; Daniel, 51; Margareth, 51; Peter, 72; Sebastian, 51
MEAD, John, 151; Mary, 151; William, 151
MECHAM, John, 36
MECHEM, Francis, 98; John, 98; Naomi, 98
MEDCALF, Abraham, 151; Esther, 154; James, 151; Margaret, 151; Mary, 151
MEDLEY, Ann, 17; Betty, 17; George, 17; Hannah, 17; Jane, 17; Mary, 17;

Rachel, 17
MEEK, Mat., 76
MEHAFFY, Hugh, 75
MELONY, Ann, 74; Jane, 75
MENDELHALL, Betty, 171
MENDENHAL, Aaron, 98; Hannah, 98; James, 98
MENDENHALL, Aaron, 1, 152; aaron, 152; Alice, 98; Benjamin, 98, 164; Betty, 94; Beulah, 152; Charity, 152; Daniel, 98; Deborah, 152; Elizabeth, 98; Esther, 98, 109; Griffith, 152; Hannah, 105, 164; Jacob, 152; James, 105, 152; Jane Newlin, 98; John, 98, 152; Martha, 98, 152, 174; Mary, 88, 98, 152; Mordecai, 152; Moses, 98; Robert, 98; Rose, 1; Samuel, 98, 109; Sarah, 152; William, 152
MENDINGHALL, Elizabeth, 180
MERCER, Alice, 112; Betty, 152, 173; Caleb, 98, 112; Daniel, 112; Hannah, 112; Jane, 152; Jesse, 152; Mary, 98; Robert, 98; Thomas, 152
MEREDETH, Grace, 34; James, 30
MEREDITH, Abel, 5; Abraham, 15; Ann, 7, 99; Bulah, 11; David, 84; Dinah, 9, 98; Elizabeth, 3, 5, 7, 9, 11, 12, 82, 98, 99; Ellen, 84; Enoch, 5, 7, 12, 15, 98, 99; Ezra, 5, 99; Grace, 3, 5, 7, 9, 11, 16, 23, 98, 99; Hannah, 5, 7, 99; Hugh, 33, 35; Isaac, 15; Isaiah, 12; James, 5, 7, 9, 15, 29, 30, 98, 99; Jane, 5, 7, 15, 98, 99; Jese, 9; Jesse, 31, 35; Joel, 9; John, 3, 5, 7, 9, 11, 12, 15, 16, 19, 34, 35, 36, 98, 99; Mary, 9, 11, 32; Rebecca, 9, 11, 12, 15, 29, 30; Ruth, 7, 99; Simon, 7, 9, 11, 19, 98; Thomas, 5; William, 12
MERRDITH, Ann, 2; Grace, 2; John, 2
MERTZ, Anna Maria, 52; Barbara, 47; Catarina, 47; Catharina, 44, 46, 52; Cathrina, 51; Elisabeth, 46; Hannes, 47; Joh., 40; Joh. Conrad, 51; Johan, 52; Johannes, 42, 44, 46, 51; Maria Magdalena, 51; Michel, 64; Susanna, 72
MERZ, Catrina, 49; Johan Georg, 49; Johannes, 49; Peter, 49
METEER, Sarah, 24; Thomas, 24
METZ, Heinrich, 59, 64; Jacob, 59; Johannes, 72; Magdalena, 59, 64; Susanna, 72
MICHEM, Ann, 7; Ellen, 7; Francis, 7; George, 7; Jane, 7; John, 7; Mary, 7; Naomi, 7
MICHENEER, Joseph, 152; Rebecca, 152
MICHENER, Barak, 152; David, 171; Hannah, 152; John, 1; Lydia R., 152; Mary, 1; Sarah, 1; William, 152
MICHNER, Mordecai, 117; Sarah, 1, 117
MICKLE, Ann, 125; Jane, 125; John, 125; Mary, 125, 152; Robert, 125, 152; Ruth, 149; Sarah, 125
MILHAUS, John, 22; Lydia, 22; Margaret, 22; Mary, 22; Ruth, 22; Sarah, 22; Thomas, 22
MILHENER, Abie, 125; Alice, 125; Ann, 125; Anna, 125; Barak, 125; Deborah, 125; Ezra, 125; Hannah, 125; Jane, 125; Jesse, 125; Joseph, 125; Lydia, 125; Martha, 125; Mary, 125; Mordecai, 125; Phebe, 125; Rebecca, 125; Robert, 125; Sarah, 125; William, 125
MILHOUS, Abigail, 168; Amos, 168; Ann, 2; Anna, 15; Deborah, 2, 23, 149; Dinah, 2; Elizabeth, 2, 19, 23, 133, 149, 159, 171, 172; Enos, 2; Hannah, 2, 15, 23, 168; Isaac, 2; Jesse, 2, 28; Joanna, 2; John, 2, 15, 19, 142, 166; Joseph, 15; Lydia, 2, 168; Margaret, 2, 19, 142, 166, 171; Martha, 15; Mary, 2; Mercy, 15, 16; Paschall, 2, 23, 168; Phebe, 2, 23, 133, 159; Robert, 2; Ruth, 166; Samuel, 2, 23; Sarah, 1, 2, 9, 14, 23, 142; Seth, 2; Susanna, 169; susanna, 23; Susannah, 2; Thomas, 1, 2, 9, 24, 133, 149, 159, 168; Townsend,

168; William, 2, 9, 15, 36
MILHOUSE, Elizabeth, 99; John, 99; Margaret, 99; Sarah, 99, 100; Thomas, 99
MILLER, Ann, 113, 125, 126, 129, 143, 152, 156; Benjamin, 125; Caleb, 126, 174; Caspar, 40; Deborah, 125; Elener, 139; Elisabeth, 66; Elizabeth, 115, 126, 139, 152; Gayen, 123, 153; George, 97, 99; Grifen, 126; Hannah, 126, 150, 151, 152, 167; Henrich, 66; Henry, 99; Isaac, 125, 126; Jacob, 40, 174; James, 113, 122, 125, 126, 138, 143, 148, 149, 151, 152, 154, 157; Jane, 157; Jesse, 125, 151, 177; John, 75, 115, 125, 126, 139, 147, 152, 177; Jonathan, 171; Joseph, 125, 126, 152, 157; Joshua, 125; Katharine, 125, 126, 149; Lydia, 126, 142, 151; Margaret, 123, 126, 141, 142, 152; Martha, 147, 152; Mary, 115, 125, 126, 129, 141, 142, 148, 151, 156, 171; Phebe, 97, 99; Rachel, 122, 123, 125, 152; Rebecca, 126, 151, 152, 157; Reuben, 152, 180; Robert, 123; Rosina, 40; Ruth, 34, 123, 144, 152, 153; Samuel, 125, 141, 142, 152; Sarah, 99, 113, 122, 123, 125, 126, 138, 147, 148, 151, 154; Sibilla, 40; Susanna, 148; Susannah, 125; Thomas, 125, 126; William, 126, 129, 142, 151, 153, 156
MILLHOUSE, Elizabeth, 126; James, 126; John, 126; Phebe, 126; Robert, 126; Sarah, 126; Thomas, 126; William, 126
MILLIR, --, 76
MILLS, Elizabeth, 153; John, 153; Thomas, 153
MILLSON, Elizabeth, 153; Grace, 153; James, 153; William, 153
MILTON, Elizabeth, 143
MINCHENER, Alice, 152; Mordecai, 152; Sarah, 152
MININCH, --, 76
MINSHALL, John, 13, 104;
Sarah, 13, 104
MITCHEL, Alexander, 75
MITCHELL, Hannah, 139; Lucy, 139; Thomas, 139
MODE, Alexander, 153, 163; Elizabeth, 153; Emey, 144; Hannah, 163; James, 153; John, 153; Phebe, 153; Rebecca, 153, 163; William, 153
MONEY, James, 153; Mary, 153; Neal, 153
MOODE, Alexander, 126, 134, 141; Hannah, 126, 134; Rebecca, 126, 134; Ruth, 141
MOODY, Margaret, 171
MOOR, Elizabeth, 27; Thomas, 27
MOORE, Abner, 99, 108; Andrew, 153, 168; Ann, 99, 126, 153; Benjamin, 99; Caleb, 126; David, 126, 144, 153; Dinah, 126; Elisha, 169; Elizabeth, 153; Esther, 126; Hannah, 99, 126; Hibberd, 126; Isaac, 99, 126, 153, 170; Jacob, 126; James, 26, 153, 168; Jane, 126, 151, 153, 158; Jesse, 126; John, 99, 153; Joseph, 20, 126, 151, 153, 158, 174; Joshua, 126, 153; Leah, 99; Lewis, 99; Lydia, 126, 153, 168, 170; Martha, 126, 144, 153; Mary, 100, 119, 126, 144, 153, 155; Mercy, 153; Merry, 174; Mordecai, 99; Phebe, 99, 126, 153, 158; Rachel, 17, 99, 126, 153, 158; Rebecca, 99, 153; Robert, 17, 153; Ruth, 99, 126, 151; Sarah, 99, 111, 126, 153, 179; Sharpless, 126; Sidney, 126; Susanna, 99; Thomas, 99, 167; Walker, 99; William, 99, 126, 153, 179; Zeba, 126
MORGAN, Ann, 23; David, 21; Elizabeth, 24, 99; Hannah, 23, 99; Hugh, 23; Jacob, 99; Jesse, 23; John, 99; Joseph, 165; Rebecca, 23; Rebuen, 99; Rees, 99; Ruth, 99; Sarah, 99; Thomas, 99; William, 23, 24
MORITZ, Barbara, 65; Jacob, 65
MORRIS, Alice, 148; Ann, 99; David, 12, 29; Edward, 12,

29; Elizabeth, 29, 100;
Hannah, 12, 29, 99, 103;
Isaac, 23, 99; Jane, 30;
John, 99, 103; Jonathan,
12, 15, 29; Joseph, 99;
Leah, 81, 99; Lewis, 81,
99, 107; Mary, 15, 99;
Nicholas, 30, 32; Phebe,
99; Priscilla, 99; Rachel,
81, 84, 99, 107; Sarah,
15, 99
MORTON, Benjamin, 126; Elinor,
126; Eliza, 126, 150;
Elizabeth, 118, 126;
Hannah, 126; Joel, 165,
167; John, 126, 154;
Margaret, 126, 145; Mary,
126, 150, 154; Samuel,
118, 126, 145, 150, 166;
Sarah, 127; thomas, 126;
William, 126
MOSER, Henrich, 40;
Phillippina, 40
MOSES, Hannes, 54; Heinrich,
58; Magdalena, 54;
Margaret, 172
MULHOUS, Hannah, 9; Jane, 9;
Joshua, 9; Mercy, 9;
Phebe, 9; Rachel, 9;
Samuel, 9; Sarah, 9;
William, 9
MULLER, Adam, 62; Christoph,
52, 60, 73; Christopher,
52; Clar Elis(abeth), 60;
Clara Elisabeth, 52, 54;
Clorliss(Ehefrau), 73;
Danjel(Daniel), 60;
Elisabeth, 56, 57; Jacob,
39, 54;
Jesajas/Isaias/Isaiah, 52;
Johannes, 39; Margrith,
56; Maria, 63; Philip, 63;
Stoffel, 54, 56
MULOUS, Ann, 14; Dinah, 14;
Robert, 14
MUNDSCHAUEER, Catharina, 67;
Michal, 67; Susanna, 67
MUNDSCHAUER, Jacob, 67
MUNSCHAUER, Catharina, 65;
Esther, 65; Michel, 65;
Philip, 65
MURRY, Alice, 175
MUSGROVE, Aaron, 158;
Christian, 151; Esther,
144; Hannah, 154; James,
154; John, 144, 151, 154,
161; Martha, 161; Mary,
112, 137; Rachel, 158

-N-
NAGEL, Carl, 68, 69; Jacob,
68; Johannes, 69
NAILOR, Cathrina, 49; Jacob,
49
NAYLE, Henry, 120; Sarah, 120
NEAL, Mary, 177
NEAL/NOYLE, Ann, 147; Hannah,
156; Henry, 147, 156;
Sarah, 147, 156
NEIL, James, 76
NEILER, Cathrina, 51; Jacob,
51; Mary, 51
NEWLIN, Ellis, 154; Esther,
154; Hannah, 130; Jane,
154; Joseph, 154, 171;
Mary, 130; Moses, 130;
Nathaniel, 154; Phebe, 154
NICHOLS, Ann, 154; Elizabeth,
154; James, 154; John,
154; Lydia, 154; Samuel,
154; Thomas, 154
NORBURY, Mary, 94

-O-
OBORN, Hannah, 163
OHLWEYN, Abraham, 58;
Johannes, 73; Rebecca, 58;
Samuel, 58
OHYWEYN, Heinrich, 58
OLDHAM, Mary, 157; Thomas, 157
ORROK, Ann, 27
ORVEN, Rebecca, 96; William,
96
OSBORNE, Hannah, 100; Peter,
100
OWEN, David, 19, 28; Elisha,
13, 28; Elizabeth, 28;
Evan, 28; Jane, 19, 28;
Mordecai, 28; Rebecca,
100; William, 100
OWENS, Alice, 150; George,
150; Mary, 150

-P-
PACA, Mary, 143; Susana, 143
PACKER, Aaron, 1, 31, 36;
Amos, 1, 36; Amy, 36; Ann,
1, 31; Eli, 1, 31, 36;
Elizabeth, 31, 36; Hannah,
1, 12, 29; James, 1, 12,
19, 36; Job, 1, 12, 29;
John, 36; Lillah, 36;
Lydia, 1; Moses, 1, 31;
Phillip, 1; Rachel, 31;
Ropse, 1; Rose, 12, 36;
Sarah, 12, 29; William,
12, 29
PACKSON, John, 154; Sarah, 154
PAIN, Alice, 127; Elizabeth,
127; George, 127; Josiah,
127; Marary, 127; Martha,
127; Mathew, 127; Ruth,

127
PAINTER, Elizabeth, 129, 164;
  Enos, 175; Esther, 172;
  Grace, 129; Joseph, 164;
  Phebe, 139, 145; Thomas,
  129
PARK, Ann, 22
PARKE, Abiah, 31, 36;
  Jonathan, 27; Thomas, 34
PARKER, Abraham, 162;
  Alexander, 100, 127; Ann,
  83; Elinor, 162;
  Elizabeth, 105, 112;
  George, 127; James, 19;
  Kezia, 162; Rose, 21;
  Sarah, 99, 100, 127;
  Thomas, 127, 172;
  Thompson, 99, 100, 127
PARKS, Susanna, 139
PARSON, Charles, 154; Joseph,
  154; Sarah, 154
PARSONS, Henry, 127; Margaret,
  127
PARVIN, Benjamin, 23; Eleanor,
  154; Francis, 154
PASCHALL, Elizabeth, 2, 99;
  Grace, 100; Hannah, 2,
  100; Joanna, 92; Margaret,
  2, 78, 99; William, 2, 100
PASEMORE, Elinor, 139
PASSMORE, Abigail, 100;
  Abijah, 100; Abram, 127;
  Alice, 154; Ann, 127, 154,
  156; Beulah, 100; Caleb,
  154; Deborah, 100;
  Elizabeth, 127, 138, 154;
  Ellis, 127; Everatt, 100;
  George, 127, 138, 141,
  154, 156; George S., 127;
  Hannah, 100, 127, 154,
  156, 173; Imlah, 127;
  Jesse, 127, 156; John,
  127, 130, 154; Joseph,
  127, 154; Lydia, 127;
  Margaret, 127, 137, 138,
  141, 154, 156; Margery,
  127; Mary, 100, 127, 130,
  138, 154, 156; Mary Ann,
  156; Nathaniel, 161;
  Pennock, 127; Phebe, 127,
  154; Rachel, 100, 127,
  154; Richard, 100; Samuel,
  154; Sarah, 161; Susanna,
  127; Thomas, 127; William,
  154; William Pennock, 127
PATTEN, William, 76
PATTERSON, John, 74
PATTON, Mary, 35
PAXSON, Henry, 145, 161;
  Hester, 161; Matilda, 145,
  161; Rachel, 145

PAYNTER, Ann, 100; Richard,
  100
PEARSON, Benjamin, 100;
  Charity, 100; Elijah, 34;
  Elizabeth, 100; Esther,
  100; Hannah, 100; Jane,
  34; Lawrence, 100; Lydia,
  100; Margerty, 100; Phebe,
  100; Sibilla, 100; Thomas,
  100; William, 19, 26, 100
PEIRCE, Ann, 100; Elizabeth,
  100; Gainer, 100; George,
  100; Hannah, 100; James,
  100; Mary, 98, 100; Sarah,
  83, 100, 105; Susanna, 100
PENNEL, James, 98; Jemima, 98
PENNELL, James, 100; Jemima,
  100; John, 100; Joshua,
  100; Mary, 100; William,
  100
PENNINGTON, Ann, 141; Daniel,
  179; Katharine, 155;
  Rachel, 155; Sarah, 155;
  Susanna, 141; Thomas, 141,
  155; william, 155
PENNOCK, Abraham, 127; Alice,
  128, 143; Ann, 127, 128,
  149, 151, 155; Caleb, 128,
  155; Elizabeth, 127, 128,
  159; George, 127; Grace,
  128, 155; Hannah, 112,
  113, 127, 128, 137, 151,
  155; Isaac, 127; Jacob,
  127; Jane, 155; Jesse, 21,
  113, 127, 128, 155, 174;
  John, 127, 155, 179;
  Joseph, 127, 128, 133,
  137, 143, 151, 155, 159,
  172; Levis, 127, 154;
  Margaret, 128; Mary, 127,
  128, 143, 154, 155, 166;
  Moses, 155; Nathaniel,
  151, 155; Phebe, 119, 128;
  Rachel, 155, 169; Ruth,
  127, 154; Samuel, 128,
  155, 166; Sarah, 127, 128,
  133, 137, 151, 155, 161,
  174; Simon, 128; Thomas,
  128; William, 127, 128,
  155, 174
PERRY, John, 155; Margaret,
  155
PERSON, Joseph, 167
PERSONS, Henry, 155; John,
  155; Margaret, 155
PETERS, Robert, 95
PHILIPS, Hannah, 33
PHILLIPPINA, Maria, 41
PHILLIPS, David, 26; Deborah,
  128, 139; Hannah, 26;
  Isaac, 128; Jediah, 128;

INDEX

John, 128, 139; John J., 128; Lydia, 128, 139; Mahlon, 128; Sarah, 128; William, 128
PHIPPS, Joseph, 100; Mary, 100
PIERCE, Ann, 5; Caleb, 5; Joseph, 172; Mary, 5, 172; Ruth, 172; Susanna, 172
PIERSON, Phebe, 35; Sarah, 35
PIGGOTT, Elizabeth, 128; Hannah, 128, 155, 162; Henry, 128, 155; John, 128, 155; Margery, 128; Mary, 128; Moses, 128; Rachel, 128; Rebecca, 128; Samuel, 128
PIKE, Sarah, 88
PILE, Esther, 33
PIMM, Moses, 30
PLUMBERS, Alice, 179; Eli, 179
PLUMBLY, Robert, 180
PLUMMER, Alice, 155; Eli, 155; Elinor, 116, 128; Esther, 128, 142; Phebe, 155; Robert, 128, 142, 155; Thomas, 155
POGUE, Sarah, 75
PORTER, Katarine, 75; Samuel, 75
POSY, Susanna, 73; William, 73
POTTS, Alice, 12; Lebelon, 12; Martha, 12
POWELL, Ann, 112, 155; Evan, 128, 142, 155; Hannah, 112; Isaac, 112; James, 112; John, 155; Mary, 128, 155; Sarah, 80, 128, 142; Thomas, 155
PRATT, Abraham, 100, 101; Alice, 96; Ann, 82, 101; Christian, 101; David, 100, 101; Davis, 91; Elizabeth, 100, 103; Hannah, 100, 101; Henry, 101; Jane, 100, 101; Jeromia, 101; John, 101; Joseph, 100, 101; Lydia, 91, 100, 101; Mary, 91, 100; Massey, 101; Orpah, 101; Phinehas, 101; Priscilla, 100, 101; Randal, 96, 101; Rose, 95; Sarah, 99, 100; Susanna, 101; Thomas, 100, 101
PREISER, Danjel, 58; Sophia, 58
PRESTON, Anna, 128; David, 128; Deborah, 128, 140; Eliza, 128; Hannah, 128; Isaac, 158; Isaac Hollingsworth, 128; Jonas, 128; Joseph, 128, 131, 140, 155, 158; Judith, 128; Mahlon, 128; Mary, 155, 158, 174; Rachel, 128, 131, 158; Rachel G., 158; Rebecca, 128, 131, 140, 155, 158; Sarah, 128; Sylvester Bills, 128; William, 128, 155, 174
PREUSSER, Daniel, 59; Sophia, 59; Susanna, 59
PRICE, Hannah, 32; Martha, 32; Philip, 29, 32; Philipp, 166; Rachel, 29, 32; Ruth, 31; Samuel, 170; Sibbilla, 32; William, 32
PRICHARD, Joseph, 19
PRINZIN, Catharina, 64
PRITCHARD, Joseph, 20
PRYOR, Elizabeth, 150; James, 150; Mary, 150
PUGH, Alice, 101; Ann, 129; Cabel, 129; Catharine, 102, 128, 175; David, 128; Dinah, 9, 98, 101; Hannah, 101, 128, 155; Hugh, 9, 14, 22, 93, 101; Isaac, 128; James, 101; Jesse, 96, 101, 128, 155, 175; Joan, 108; John, 93, 101; Jonathan, 101; Joseph, 101; Joshua, 101, 155; Lewis, 156; Margaret, 101; Mary, 9, 14, 17, 93, 101, 102, 128, 156; Rebecca, 101; Rebeckkeh, 14; Sarah, 101, 128; Thomas, 101
PURTLE, Eliza, 156; Nicholas, 156; Samuel, 156
PUSEY, Abigail, 130; Abner, 129; Ann, 129, 130, 132, 156, 159; Benjamin, 130; Betty, 130; Cabel, 129; Caleb, 112, 132, 155, 156, 159, 174, 175; David, 116, 129, 130, 147; Edith, 130; Elenor, 130; Elinor, 130; Eliza, 156; Elizabeth, 124, 129, 130, 133, 137, 139, 156, 158, 162; Ellis, 112, 130, 156, 164; Enoch, 130; George, 129; Hannah, 112, 114, 129, 130, 139, 178; Isaac, 129, 130; Jacob, 130; James, 129, 156; Jane, 129, 130, 155; Jesse, 129, 156; John, 124, 129, 130, 135, 136, 139, 156, 164; Jonas, 130; Jonathan, 130, 156; Joseph, 115, 130; Joshua,

114, 118, 124, 129, 130, 146, 147, 154, 156, 158, 162; Katharine, 124, 129, 136, 156, 164; Katherine, 129, 135; Lea, 130; Lewis, 129, 130, 133; Lydia, 115, 129, 130, 136, 137; Margaret, 129, 155; Mary, 129, 130, 141, 142, 146, 147, 154, 156, 162, 164; Mary Ann, 130; Miller, 129; Nathan, 129, 174; Phebe, 129, 130, 154; Philema, 130; Prudence, 129, 132, 159; Rachel, 129; Rebecca, 130; Robert, 129; Ruth, 129; Samuel, 129; Sarah, 116, 130, 147, 156; Solomon, 130; Susanna, 112, 118, 135, 139, 146, 156, 164; susanna, 130; Thomas, 129, 156, 168; William, 129, 130, 133, 137, 139, 141, 155, 162
PYLE, Alice, 137, 139, 163; Amos, 170; Ann, 137, 156; Deborah, 156; Elizabeth, 116, 130, 141, 158, 165; Hannah, 130, 155, 156; Isaac, 116, 130, 141; James, 156, 158; Jane, 179; Jesse, 172; Job, 130; John, 130, 156, 172; Joseph, 137, 139, 156, 163; Lydia, 164; Mary, 130, 151, 156, 158; Moses, 151, 155, 156, 164; Olive, 130, 141; Rachel, 156; Rahgel, 156; Robert, 156, 177; Sarah, 139, 172; Susannah, 172; Thomas, 130; William, 156

-R-
RAKESTRAW, John, 156; Mary Ann, 156
RAMSEY, Isbel, 75
RANDAL, Abraham, 22; Charles, 28; Elizabeth, 5, 28; Hannah, 28; Jane, 28; John, 28; Joseph, 5, 28; Mary, 28; Rachel, 28; Rebecca, 5; Rebekah, 28; Ruth, 28
RANDALL, Abraham, 20; Elizabeth, 6, 23; Hannah, 6, 23; John, 6, 23; Joseph, 6, 23, 101; Jospeh, 23; Levi, 21; Rachel, 6, 23, 101;
Rebecca, 6, 23; Ruth, 6, 23; Sarah, 6, 23, 96
RANKIN, Ann, 83; James, 77; Jane, 161
RAP, Benjamin, 66; Bernhard, 65, 67; Elisabeth, 66; Esther, 65, 67; Isabel, 75; Johann, 65; Johannes, 65; Magdalena, 63; Maria, 66; Peter, 63, 66; Philip, 63
RAPP, Benjamin, 64, 65; Bernhard, 58, 61, 63; Catharina, 64, 68; Elisabeth, 58, 61, 63, 65; Esther, 58, 61, 63; Hanna, 63; Johannes, 64; Maria, 61, 64, 68; Peter, 68; Philip, 61, 68, 73; Philipp, 64; Regina, 64
RAPPIN, Elisabeth, 65
RASETER, Benjamin, 64; Elisabeth, 64; John, 64
RATTARIN(RADER), Catharina, 69; Melcher(Melchior), 69
RATTEW, Abigail, 101; Edith, 101; Hannah, 101; Jesse, 101; John, 101; Mary, 101, 107; Rebecca, 101; William, 101
RAUBEY, Rebecca, 35
RAWLINGS, Greenbury, 76
REA, Deborah, 16, 101; Elizabeth, 29; Evan, 16; John, 16, 101; Mary, 16; Moses, 30; Samuel, 16, 101; Sarah, 30; Sidney, 16
REECE, Lewis, 102; Mary, 102; Mordecai, 102; Orpha, 102; Rebecca, 99; Sarah, 87; Sidney, 102; William, 102
REED, James, 101; Mary, 101; Ruth, 101; William, 101
REES, Ann, 101; Caleb, 101, 102; David, 101, 102; Elizabeth, 93, 101, 102; George, 84; Hannah, 84, 102; John, 130; Joshua, 101; Judith, 76; Lewis, 101, 102; Margaret, 101; Mary, 100, 102; Morris, 130; Rachel, 101; Sarah, 102, 130; Thomas, 101; William, 102
REESE, David, 102, 110; Elizabeth, 83; Ellin, 83; Grace, 102; Jane, 102, 110; Lewis, 102; Samuel, 25
REFFERT, Johannes, 54; Philip, 54; Ursula, 54

INDEX 211

REGESTER, Abigail, 102;
Catherine, 102; Daniel,
102; David, 102;
Elizabeth, 102; Jane, 102,
109; Lydia, 102; Mary,
102; Robert, 102, 109;
William, 102
REIMS, Thomas, 64
REIS, Joh. Georg, 58; Maria,
63; Peter, 63
REISS, Catharina, 44; Johann
Georg, 44; Johannes, 44
REMY, Adam, 69; Jacob, 69, 72;
Susanna, 72
RENER, Maria, 68
RENNER, Adam, 64; Regina, 64
RENNY, David, 15; Eleanor, 15;
Maxwell, 15
RESE (ROSE), Moses, 29
REUSSER, Daniel, 58; Sophia,
59
REYNOLDS, David, 130; Dinah,
156; Hannah, 130; Henry,
102, 130; Jacob, 130;
Jeremiah, 130; John, 74;
Mary, 130, 156; Rachel,
130; Rebecca, 102;
Richard, 102; Samuel, 130;
William, 130, 156
RHEA, --, 76
RHOADS, Adam, 102; Ann, 102;
Benjamin, 102; Catharine,
102; Elizabeth, 96, 102;
John, 96, 102; Joseph, 78,
102; Mary, 78, 102
RICHARD, Elizabeth, 111
RICHARDS, Ann, 130, 156;
Catharine, 177; Elisabeth,
16; Hannah, 26, 29, 131,
153, 179; Isaac, 29, 102,
119, 130, 131, 156, 157,
162; Jacob, 131, 179;
Jane, 157; Joanna, 149;
Joshua, 130; Lawrence,
157; Lydia, 157, 162;
Mary, 130, 131, 156, 157,
179; Nathaniel, 157, 166;
Phebe, 102; Rachel, 179;
Rebecca, 157; Richard,
102; Samuel Emlen, 130;
Sarah, 29, 131, 153;
Thomas, 26, 29, 131, 153,
179; Tomzin, 119; William,
131, 149, 157, 177
RICHARDSON, Caleb, 131, 178;
Catharine, 80, 102; Dinah,
131, 142, 178; Elinor,
102; Elizabeth, 81;
Hannah, 131, 142; Isaac,
102, 131, 146, 178; Joel,
131, 174; John, 102, 175;
Joseph, 131, 142, 178;
Lawrence, 157; Lydia, 131,
178; Martha, 102; Mary,
131, 146, 157, 178;
Samuel, 131, 175
RICHTSTEIN, Catharina, 61;
Heinrich, 61; Margaret,
61; Margrith, 61; Sophia,
61
RIDDLE, Susanna, 77
RIED, Sarah, 75
RIFFELL, Catherine, 23; Isaac,
23; Jonathan, 23; Kezia,
23; Nathan, 23; Rachel, 23
RIGG, Sarah, 27
RING, Benjammin, 157;
Nathaniel, 157; Rachel,
157
ROBERTS, Abraham, 103; Ann,
16; Anna, 20; Aubrly, 102;
Elisabeth, 16; Elizabeth,
103; Ellen, 103; Evan,
102; Gaynor, 102; George,
103; Isaac, 29; Jacob,
103; Jane, 15, 16, 102,
103; Jasher, 95, 102;
Jehiu, 36; John, 15, 16,
102, 103; Jonathan, 32;
Margaret, 103; Mary, 28,
95, 102; Mordecai, 20,
102; Nichols, 102; Owen,
102; Pratt, 103; Robert,
103; Ruth, 19, 28, 102;
Sarah, 15, 103; Thomas,
103; Thomzin, 35; William,
21, 103
ROBINSON, Elizabeth, 157;
Eunice, 157; George, 157;
James, 157; John, 157;
Mary, 157
ROBISON, Hannah, 22; Prudence,
74
RODGERS, Hannah, 74
ROGERS, Abner, 103; Abraham,
31; Alice, 103; Ann, 14,
28, 103; Benjamin, 14,
103; Charles, 14; David,
14, 28; Esther, 103, 104;
Grace, 28; Hannah, 14, 28,
33, 99, 103; Isaac, 103;
Jacob, 28, 33, 103, 104;
James, 13, 28, 103; John,
13, 33; Jonathan, 13, 14,
103; Joseph, 13, 14, 28,
103; Mahlan, 28; Mary, 13;
Owen, 103; Phebe, 103;
Priscilla, 28, 103;
Rebecca, 13; Rebeckah, 14;
Rebekah, 13; Robert, 103;
Samuel, 14, 103; Sarah,
103; Thomas, 103; William,

13, 14, 28
ROHRBACH, Catharina, 71;
  Peter, 71
ROMAN, Asenath, 141; Hannah,
  143; Joshua, 141, 143;
  Rebecca, 141, 143
ROMANS, Rachel, 31
ROSETTER, Elisabeth, 66;
  Jacob, 66; Johannes, 66;
  Thomas, 66; Wilhelm, 66
ROSS, Albinah, 131; Alexander,
  131, 151; George, 131;
  John, 131; Joseph, 172;
  Katherine, 131; Lydia,
  131; Mary, 131, 151;
  Rebecca, 131
ROULES, Lacey, 157; Mary, 157
ROWEN, Amos, 167; Elizabeth,
  138, 142, 157, 167;
  Hannah, 157, 167; John,
  167; Mary, 167; Moses,
  157, 167; Phebe, 167;
  Sarah, 138, 167; William,
  138, 142, 157, 167
ROWLAND, Mary, 146, 155;
  Rachel, 163; Ruth, 153;
  Thomas, 153, 155, 163
RRR, Thomas, 77
RUSHTON, Ann, 108
RUSSELL, Alexander, 74;
  Hannah, 157; John, 157;
  Sarah, 157; Susanna, 103;
  Thomas, 157; William, 77,
  103
RUSTON, Elizabeth, 74
RYIN, --, 74

-S-
SAHUGER, Johannes, 68
SALERIN, Catharina, 39
SAMMS, Anna, 128; Nathaniel,
  128
SAMUEL, John, 103; Magdalen,
  103
SANDERS, Ann, 103; John, 103;
  Sarah, 103
SANDERSON, Henry, 74
SAUGER, John, 68
SCARLET, Hannah, 112, 136,
  157; John, 157, 160; Mary,
  157, 160; Nathaniel, 136,
  157; Phebe, 112, 131, 136;
  Shadrach, 112, 131;
  Shadrack, 136
SCARLETT, Mary, 141;
  Nathaniel, 141
SCHAERER, Conrad, 66;
  Dorothea, 66
SCHAUDERIN, Christiana, 37
SCHAUMER, Conrad, 37
SCHAUMERIN, Anna Maria, 37

SCHEERER, Catharina, 43;
  Conrad, 43; Rebecka, 43
SCHEIER, Conrad, 55
SCHEIMER, Adam, 66; Anna
  Catharina, 66; Edward, 66;
  Elisabeth, 66
SCHEIMMER, Catharina, 40
SCHELEYTER, Jacob, 47
SCHENDIERIN, Anna Maria, 38
SCHENIDER, Caspar, 70;
  Margareth, 70
SCHERARD, Jacob, 71; Maria, 71
SCHERARDIG, Abraham, 70;
  Henrich, 70; Jacob, 70
SCHERER, Catharina, 45, 46,
  48, 51, 53; Cathrina, 49;
  Conrad, 45, 46, 48, 49,
  51, 53, 56, 60, 63, 71;
  Dorathea, 60; Dorothea,
  56, 63; Elisabeth, 63;
  Jacob, 48; Johann Conrad,
  60; Johannes, 56;
  Magdalena, 45; Maria, 71;
  Sara, 49
SCHERERDIN, Christina, 47;
  Henrich, 47; Margareth, 47
SCHERIDAN, Abraham, 56; Anna
  Maria, 56
SCHEUMER, Magdalena, 58
SCHLEIER, Catharina, 56;
  Elisabeth, 60, 62;
  Heinrich, 60, 62; Jacob,
  60; Magdalena, 62
SCHLEYER, Henrich, 71;
  Magdalena, 71
SCHLEYN, Henrich, 49;
  Johannes, 49; Maria, 49
SCHMEHL, Elizabeth, 42;
  Johannes, 42; Peter, 42
SCHMICK, Cathrina, 49;
  Conrath, 51; Elisabeth,
  49; Henrich, 51; Jacob,
  49; Magdalena, 49; Maria,
  51; Peter, 49; Susanna, 49
SCHMID, Adam, 41, 71; Anna
  Mar., 48; Barbara, 49;
  Catharina, 41, 48, 51, 53,
  71; Cathrina, 49;
  Christina, 48;
  Danjel(Daniel), 60;
  Eleanor, 41; Elisabeth,
  41, 63, 64; Elizabeth, 41;
  Fridrich, 69; Friedrich,
  48, 70; Georg, 62;
  Gertraut, 41; Jacob, 41,
  45, 62, 69, 71;
  Jesajas(Isaiah), 57;
  Jesse, 65; Johan Jacob,
  48; Johanes, 57; Johannes,
  41, 48, 49, 53, 55, 59,
  60, 61, 62, 64, 65, 72,

73; John, 49, 62; Joseph, 55; Jost, 41, 45, 71, 72; Margrith, 56, 67; Maria, 53, 55, 57, 59, 60, 61, 62, 64, 65, 73; Maria Magdalena, 49, 64; Michael, 64, 67; Petronella, 70; Sara, 49, 62, 73; Simon, 49; Valantin, 41; Valentine, 41; Vallantin, 41; Vallentin, 49, 51, 71; Wilhelm, 63, 64
SCHMID(SMITH), Maria, 69
SCHMIDT, Angelina, 48; Catharina, 48; Elisabeth, 69; Vallantin, 48; Vallentin, 69
SCHMIDTH, Johannes, 69
SCHNEI, Johannes, 54; Susanna, 54
SCHNEIDER, Abraham, 49, 72; Andres, 68; Anna, 68; Anna Elisabeth, 40; Anna Margaretha, 68; Anna Maria, 38, 61, 69; Barbara, 42, 53; Carl, 55; Caspar, 37, 38, 42, 44, 58, 60, 66, 67, 68, 72; Casper, 65, 67, 73; Catharia, 51; Catharina, 37, 38, 51, 53, 54, 58, 61, 62, 63, 67, 69; Christina, 39, 70; Daniel, 38, 72; Danjel (Daniel), 57; Elisabeth, 48, 49, 51, 54, 57, 58, 59, 60, 66, 67, 68, 72; Eva, 51; Evann, 38; Georg, 39, 51, 53, 54, 58, 61, 63, 70; George, 62, 67; Hanna, 60; Hannes, 51; Heinrich, 65; Henna, 57, 58; Henrich, 67; Jacob, 37, 38; Joh., 40, 51; Joh. Georg, 40; Johan, 51; Johannes, 37, 38, 39, 40, 42, 48, 49, 51, 53, 54, 56, 57, 58, 59, 61, 67, 68, 69, 70, 72; John, 51; Magdalena, 38, 51, 54, 56, 68; Margareth, 38; Margrith, 58, 65; Maria, 59; Maria Barbara, 71; Maria Elisabetha, 40; Peter, 48, 61, 63; Rosina, 40; Sibilla, 38, 42, 55; Sibillla, 73; Susanna, 51, 53, 56, 58, 61, 65, 66, 67; Sybilla, 44; Thomas, 37, 38, 39, 42, 65, 69,

70, 71; Zusanna(Susanna), 57
SCHNEIDERIN, Anna Maria, 37; Catharina, 38
SCHNER, Anna Maria, 71; Wendel, 71
SCHOER, Conrad, 64; Dorathea, 64; Nicolas, 64
SCHOLL, Friderich, 62; Philippine, 62; Samuel, 62
SCHONFULTER, Barbara, 48; Elissabetta, 49; Peter, 48
SCHONHOLTZ, Gerthraud, 71; Martin, 71
SCHONHOLTZER, Barbara, 37; Catharina, 37; Elisabeth, 46, 47; Elisabetha, 45; Elizabeth, 37; Gertraut, 40; Jacob, 37; Johannes, 37; Martin, 37, 40, 71; Peter, 38, 45, 46, 47
SCHONHOLZ, Christina, 54; Johannes, 54
SCHONHOLZER, Elisabeth, 53; Maria, 53; Martin, 53
SCHORT, Elisabeth, 54; Hannes, 54
SCHOT, Elisabeth, 53
SCHOTT, Catharina, 45, 69; Hannes, 56; Heinrich, 46; Henrich, 45, 68, 69, 70; Johannes, 70; Magdalena, 56; Melchoir, 45
SCHOWALTER, Johannes, 67; John, 67; Susanna, 67
SCHREIDER, Adam, 63; Johannes, 63; Susanna, 63
SCHUEMAN, Elisabeth, 63; Hannes, 63
SCHUG, Danjel(Daniel), 57; Elisabeth, 57; Jacob, 57; Jospeh, 57; Maria, 57
SCHULER, Sara, 63, 68; Sophia, 63; Wilhelm, 63, 68
SCHUMANN, Anna Margaretha, 39
SCHUNCK, Catharina, 57; Catharina Elisabetha, 37; Cathrina, 48; Conrad, 37; Isaac, 38; Peter, 39, 48, 70; Simon, 39, 48, 57, 68, 70
SCHUNCKEN, Ana Margaretha, 37; Anna Margaretha, 37; Simon, 37, 38
SCHUND, Margareth, 69; Simon, 69
SCHUNHOLT, Elissabeta, 48; Peter, 48
SCHUNK, Anna Maria, 37; Benjamin, 44; Catharina, 60; Conrat, 44; Maria, 44;

Peter, 60; Simon, 37
SCHURZDERY, Margareda, 44
SCHWANER, Elisabeth, 67;
    Elizabeth, 67; Johannes,
    67; Susanna, 67
SCOFIELD, David, 21
SCOTT, Abram, 21, 22; Amos,
    23; Elizabeth, 21, 23;
    Esther, 23; Hannah, 95;
    James, 103; Jesse, 23;
    John, 103; Martha, 30;
    Rachel, 23; Rosseter, 23;
    Sarah, 106; Thomas, 23
SEAL, Abraham, 176; Benjamin,
    160; Caleb, 157;
    Elizabeth, 160; Joseph,
    157; Joshua, 157, 166,
    176; Lydia, 157, 166;
    Phebe, 160; Sarah, 157;
    William, 178
SEATON, Ruth, 152
SEELER, Catharina, 48;
    Elisabeth, 51; Elisabetha,
    47; Elizebeth, 49; Maria,
    51; Philip, 47; Phillip,
    48, 49, 51; Vallentin, 49
SEIBERT, Jacob, 69; Michel, 69
SEIFERT, Christina, 52;
    Elisabeth, 52; Heinrich,
    52
SEILER, Hieronimus, 41;
    Johannes, 41; Peter, 69;
    Phillip, 69
SEIVERT, Abraham, 38;
    Catharina, 38; Isaac, 39;
    Jacob, 38; Michael, 38, 39
SELLER, Elisabeth, 52; Georg,
    52; Philip, 52
SELTENREICH, Anna Maria, 52,
    54, 56, 58, 60, 62;
    Catharina, 52; Christina,
    60; David, 52, 54, 55, 58,
    59, 60, 62; Elisabeth, 55,
    56; Rebecca, 58
SERRILL, Alice, 84, 103;
    Isaac, 103; James, 84,
    103; Jane, 84, 103; Mary,
    103
SESTMAN(SASTMAN), Elisabeth,
    48; Henrich, 48; Johannes,
    48
SHARP, Abigail, 131; Ann, 131,
    154, 157; Benjamin, 131,
    140; Deborah, 131;
    Elizabeth, 131, 154;
    George, 131, 179; Hannah,
    140; John, 131, 154, 157;
    Joseph, 131; Mary, 131,
    178; Samuel, 131; Sarah,
    131; Thomas, 131
SHARPLESS, Abraham, 30, 31,
    157, 172; Ann, 18, 157;
    Benjamin, 131; Blakey, 18;
    Daniel, 103, 106; Dinah,
    157, 172; Edith, 131;
    Elizabeth, 78, 103;
    Esther, 178; Hannah, 103,
    106, 179; Isaac, 18;
    Jacob, 18; Jane, 12; John,
    78, 103; Joseph, 103, 153,
    178; Joshua, 18, 131;
    Lydia, 153, 178; Martha,
    126, 131, 153; Mary, 30,
    103, 153, 178; Mercy, 18;
    Nathan, 18, 36, 131;
    Phebe, 12, 27, 30, 178;
    Rachel, 18, 28, 131;
    Rebecca, 174; Rebekah,
    178; Samuel, 12
SHAW, Martha, 146; Mary, 138;
    Moses, 138, 146; Prudence,
    140; Rebecca, 21; Ruth,
    138; Thomas, 140
SHEPHERD, Pishmonday, 157;
    William, 157
SHEPPARD, Jane, 157; Solomon,
    157; William, 157
SHERIDAN, Abraham, 59; Maria
    Barbara, 59
SHERWARD, Pennell, 98; Ruth,
    98; Thomas, 98
SHEWAAARD, Caleb, 88; Hannah,
    88
SHEWARD, Caleb, 103; Hannah,
    103; James, 157; John,
    103; Moses, 103; Ruth,
    103, 144, 157; Samuel,
    144, 157; Thomas, 103
SHEWIN, Hannah, 143; William,
    143
SHNEIDER, Maria Barbara, 52
SHORTLEDGE, Enoch, 131;
    Hannah, 131; Isaac, 131;
    Jacob, 131; James, 131;
    John, 131; Joshua, 131;
    Phebe, 131; Samuel, 131;
    Swithin, 131
SHORTRIDGE, Isaac, 174
SHOTT, Catharina, 43;
    Melchior, 43
SHOTTIN, Catharina, 43
SHUNK(IN), Elisabeth, 40
SIDWELL, Ann, 158; Anne, 158;
    Elinor, 158; Elisha, 158;
    Hugh, 158; Mary, 158, 173;
    Nathan, 158; Richard, 158
SIEBERT, Catharina, 69;
    Michael, 69
SIMMONS, Henry, 131, 158;
    Mary, 131; Rachel, 131,
    158
SIMPSON, --, 76

INDEX 215

SINCLAIR, Abraham, 173; Ann, 131; Bery Berry, 131; Mary, 131, 158; Robert, 158; Samuel, 131; Sarah, 131; Thomas Lightfoot, 131; William, 131
SINKLER, Ann, 87, 104; Georg, 104; George, 87; Margaret, 138; William, 104
SLEIP, Anna Maria, 73; Elisabeth, 73; Peter, 73
SMEDLEY, Abigail, 104; Ambrose, 104; Amy, 104; Bennett, 104; Dinah, 104; Edith, 104; Elizabeth, 12, 104; Esther, 103; Francis, 104; George, 104; Hannah, 81, 104; Isaac, 12; Jane, 12; Jeffrey, 104; Joel, 12, 104; John, 104; Joseph, 29; Lydia, 12, 88, 104; Mary, 104, 105; Peter, 12; Phebe, 12, 108; Rachel G., 158; Rebecca, 29; Samuel, 12, 104; Sarah, 104; Thomas, 104, 158; William, 12
SMEDLY, Peter, 36
SMELDEY, Benjamin, 104; Esther, 104; Isaac, 104; Jacob, 104; Joll, 104; Lewis, 104; Rebecca, 104; Susanna, 104
SMITH, --, 77; Aaron, 177; Abram, 75; Alice, 155; Ann, 131, 162; Anne, 131; Daniel, 166; Dorithy, 158; Dorothy, 131, 144; Elizabeth, 28, 158, 179; Ephraim, 158; George, 104; Hannah, 28; James, 28, 155, 158; Jane, 104; John, 28, 77, 131, 149, 158, 162; Joseph, 76, 158; Joshua, 28; Lydia, 28, 131, 149, 177; Margaret, 158; Mary, 158, 174; Rachel, 155, 158; Ruth, 131, 158; Samuel, 28, 172; Sarah, 28, 131, 161; Thomas, 28, 131; William, 76, 104
SOHN, Anna Maria, 53; Joh. Georg, 53
SOLWIG, Eva Elisabeth, 68; Jacob, 68
SPACKMAN, Ann, 30; George, 25; Isaac, 20; James, 30; Mary, 30; Susanna, 30; Susannah, 30; Thomas, 30; Thomzin, 25

SPEAKMAN, Ann, 91, 140; Ebenezer, 158; Enoch, 145, 158; Hugh, 140, 158; Mary, 140, 145, 158; Rachel, 145; Sarah, 173; Thomas, 158
SPEARY, James, 11
SPECHT, Catharina, 39; Peter, 39
SPECHTIN, Elisabetha, 38
SPENCER, Aaron, 131; Asa, 131; Elizabeth, 131; Francis, 158; Hannah, 131; John, 104; Jonathan, 131; Joseph, 131, 158; Mary, 131; Phebe, 104; Rebecca, 158; Samuel, 131; Sarah, 104, 131, 158; Susanna, 32; Susannah, 104; Timothy, 104
SPIELMANN, Conrad, 69; Johannes, 69
STAHL, Christian, 40; John, 40
STALFORD, Elizabeth, 20
STALKER, Grace, 104, 105; Hugh, 104; Thomas, 104, 105
STALL, Amos, 27; Anna, 27; John, 27
STAMM, Conrad, 61; Maria, 61
STANFIELD, Jane, 20; John, 20; Mary, 20; Samuel, 20; Thomas, 172
STANLEY, Jane, 7
STANTON, Daniel, 19
STAR, James, 32; John, 32; Joseph, 32; Mary, 32; Rebekah, 32; Sarah, 32
STARR, Abraham, 132; Alice, 145; Ann, 10, 13, 33, 34, 153; Aquilla, 13, 34; Benjamin, 10, 35; Beulah, 13, 33; Deborah, 132; Elisabeth, 10; Elizabeth, 25, 105, 161; Hannah, 4, 20, 112, 141, 174; Isaac, 10, 104, 105, 132, 158; Isabel, 161; James, 4, 13, 20, 104, 132; Jane, 90, 104, 105; Jeremiah, 105, 132, 145, 153, 158, 159; John, 10, 13, 34, 105, 132; Joseph, 10, 13, 28, 104, 132; Margaret, 132, 148, 158; Mary, 13, 87, 132, 173; Merrick, 132; Moses, 132, 159; Phebe, 105; Rachal, 20; Rachel, 4, 104, 132, 144, 154, 158; Rebecca, 10, 13, 104, 153; Reuben, 174; Samuel,

132; Sarah, 4, 10, 13, 20, 28, 33, 141, 155, 159, 161; Susanna, 132; Thomas, 104, 132, 141, 155, 161; William, 10, 90, 104
STEEL, Andrew, 100, 105; Elizabeth, 77; Jane, 105; Sarah, 100, 105, 108
STEELE, James, 77
STEER, John, 159; Rachel, 159
STEGER, Adam, 71; Anna Catharina, 39; Catharina, 69; Elisabeth, 53, 63, 68; Eva Elisabeth, 38; Georg Adam, 39; Henrich, 72; Jacob, 52, 53, 63; Johannes, 63; Martin, 52, 53; Peter, 38, 39, 68, 69, 71, 72
STEIDLER, Catharina, 59, 64, 68; Eva, 59, 62; Isaac, 62; Johannes, 64; Peter, 59, 62, 64, 68
STEIN, Adam, 51, 54, 58, 62, 69, 70, 71; Catharina, 40, 51, 54, 58, 62, 71; Ida Elisabeth, 69; Johannes, 54; Margreth, 69; Margrith, 51; Sussannah, 40
STEIP, Elisabeth, 58, 62; Heinrich, 62; Jacob, 58; Peter, 58, 62
STEIPEN, Elisabeth, 56
STEMPLE, Jane, 105; John, 105; Leonard, 105; Rebecca, 105
STEPHAN, Barbara, 46; Catharina, 46; Conrad, 71; Magdalena, 71; Phillip, 46, 71
STEPHEN, Margaret, 173, 179
STEPHENS, Isaac, 159; Jonathan, 159; Margaret, 159; Rachel, 159
STERRIT, Rebecca, 76
STESSAN, Barbara, 42; Jacob, 42; Phillip, 42
STESTAN, Elizabeth, 69; Philip, 69
STEUDLER, Elisabeth, 57; Eva, 57; Peter, 57
STEYER, Elisabeth, 59; Elisabetha, 37; Gertraud, 59; Jacob, 37, 59; Peter, 37
STIKEL, Anna Maria, 43; Jacob, 43; Joh. Georg, 43
STODE, Ann, 146; John, 146
STORY, Betty, 174
STRAUSS, Susana, 66
STROUD, Caleb, 173; Edward, 166; John, 127, 132; Joshua, 173; Magdalen, 127; Magdalena, 132; Margaret, 132, 154; Martha, 173; Mary, 173; Samuel, 173
STUART, Hannah, 74; Mary, 74
STUBBS, Sarah, 171
STUDDY, William, 178
SUFFELL, Hannah, 24; Jesse, 24; John, 24; Mary, 24; Sarah, 24; Thomas, 24
SWAINE, Edward, 159; Francis, 159; Jane, 149; Sarah, 159
SWAYNE, Ann, 159, 161; ann, 132, 147; Benjamin, 132; Betty, 132, 159, 167; Caleb, 132, 133, 159; Catherine, 159; David, 132, 133, 172; Deborah, 133, 172; Edward, 142, 159, 164; Eli, 175; Elizabeth, 123, 132, 133, 147, 172; Francis, 123, 132, 133, 150, 159, 167; Hannah, 117, 132, 133, 159, 162, 164, 167; Isaac, 132, 159; Jacob, 133, 159, 172; James, 133, 159, 167; Joel, 132; John, 132; Jonathan, 132; Joseph, 132; Joshua, 132, 133; Lydia, 132, 133; Margaret, 132; Mary, 132, 147, 156, 159, 176; Nathan, 133; Orpha, 132; Phebe, 132, 133, 159; Rachel, 132, 133, 159; Rest, 132; Ruth, 132; Samuel, 117, 132, 133, 159, 162; Sarah, 117, 123, 133, 142, 150; Stephen, 133; Susanna, 132, 139, 159; Thomas, 132, 133, 172; William, 132, 133, 147, 156, 159, 161
SWAYRE, Elizabeth, 129; William, 129
SWITHIN, Hannah, 158; John, 158; Phebe, 158; Shortledge, 158
SWORD, Ebenezer, 75
SYBOLT, Gasper, 159; Rebeka, 159
SYMPSON, Isaac, 74

—T—

TAGGART, Ann, 149; Jacob, 149; Sarah, 149
TAGGERT, Rebecca, 76
TATNALL, Edward, 159;

INDEX 217

Elizabeth, 159
TAYLOR, Abijah, 105; Ann, 24, 100, 105, 133, 165, 167; David, 105; Deborah, 105; Elinor, 159; Elizabeth, 105, 160, 167; Grace, 27; Hannah, 130, 133, 137, 159, 170; Isaac, 105, 130, 133, 159, 165; Israel, 133, 169; Jacob, 165, 167, 177; James, 105, 133, 169, 179; Jane, 105, 133, 169; Jesse, 133, 169; Joel, 133; John, 105, 159, 169, 178; Jonathan, 105; Joseph, 105, 127, 133, 137, 153, 155, 159, 162, 169, 170, 179; Lydia, 133, 159; Margaret, 169; Mary, 76, 104, 105, 127, 153, 162, 171; Matthew, 19; Nicholas W., 160; Peter, 105; Phebe, 153; Rachel, 133; Rebecca, 130, 133; Rebeccah, 179; Richard, 159; Samuel, 105, 160; Sarah, 105, 155, 169; Simon, 133; Thomas, 133
TEMPLE, Clemens, 179; Daniel, 179; Elizabeth, 120, 133, 179; Hannah, 120, 133; Mary, 179; Mary W., 133; Samuel, 133, 179; Sarah, 179; William, 133, 179
THATCHER, Abigail, 138; Olive, 165; Richard, 138; Susanna, 138
THEIS, Christoph, 72; Justina, 72
THEISS, Christoph, 58; Justina, 58; Margrith, 58
THIEL, John, 67
THOMAS, Abel, 25; Abigail, 86; Abraham, 105, 106; Amos Yarnall, 106; Ann, 106; Anna, 15; Beulah, 106, 152; Charles W., 14; Christina, 44; Daniel, 30; Dina, 21, 105, 106; Dinah, 6, 96, 106; Eleanor, 21; Eli, 106; Elinor, 6; Elisabeth, 15; Eliza, 6, 106; Elizabeth, 4, 92, 105, 106, 145; Ellin, 25; Emmor, 106; Enos, 106; Esther, 81, 105; Evan, 105; Francis, 106; George, 14, 15, 16, 106; Gideon, 106; Grace, 8, 104, 105; Gwen, 105; Hannah, 15, 26, 98, 103, 105, 106, 160, 165; Henry, 107; Hezekiah, 81, 105; Hooper, 106; Isaac, 31, 106, 160, 165; Jacob, 16, 26, 28, 105, 106; James, 105, 106; Jane, 15, 106, 110; Jehu, 6; Jemima, 105, 106, 107; Jesse, 106; John, 6, 15, 19, 21; Jonah, 6, 21; Jonathan, 13, 81, 106; Joseph, 106; Judah, 6; Julian, 13; Lydia, 15, 16, 105, 106; Maria Catharina, 44; Martha, 94, 106; Mary, 13, 16, 82, 88, 105, 106, 160; Mary Ann, 106; Mathau, 105; Mordecai, 106; Mordecai H., 106; Nathan, 106; Peter, 4, 6, 105, 106; Phebe, 8, 15, 16, 78, 88, 105, 106, 107; Philip, 106; Priscilla, 82, 105, 106; Rachel, 105, 178; Rebecca, 12, 16, 21, 105, 106; Rebeckah, 13; Rebekah, 6, 28; Reuben, 10; Richard, 8, 15, 16, 26, 78, 105, 106; Robert M., 106; Samuel, 16, 105, 106; Sarah, 6, 15, 21, 45, 81, 105, 106, 107; Susanna, 106; Tamer, 107; Thamzin, 106; Thomzine, 26; Townsend, 106; Watkin, 105; Watson, 13; William, 16, 29, 44, 45, 105, 106
THOMPSON, Ann, 155; ann, 128; Barak, 133; Beulah C., 160; Daniel, 133, 144, 160, 162; David, 134; Eli, 133; Eliza, 156; Elizabeth, 128, 133, 144, 155, 160, 170; Emey, 139; Esther, 133; George, 134; Grace, 107, 155; Hannah, 20, 133, 160; Isaac, 20; James, 128, 139, 155, 160; Jane, 81, 148, 160; Jeremiah, 20; Joel, 133; John, 133, 145, 156, 160; Joseph, 20, 133, 134, 160; Katharine, 133; Lettice, 133; Levi, 133; Lydia, 133, 160; Mark, 160; Martha, 160; Mary, 145, 160; Moses, 107; Peter, 107; Rebecca, 119, 133; Richard, 133; Robert, 75, 134; Sarah, 20, 133, 160; Tacy, 148; William, 75, 133, 160

THOMSON, Elizabeth, 160;
  James, 160
TIBBERD, Phinehaus, 31
TILFORD, John, 76
TODD, Ann, 155; Deborah, 148;
  Jane, 146; John, 146, 154,
  155, 160, 163; Margaret,
  146, 160, 163; Martha,
  160; Mary, 154
TODHUNTER, Evan, 21; Hannah,
  21; Isaac, 21; Jacob, 21;
  John, 21; Joseph, 21;
  Margaret, 21; Mary, 21
TOMKIN, Ann, 25
TOMLINSON, Mary, 89
TOMSON, Ann, 154
TORRENCE, Robert M., 74
TOUCHSTONE, Rachel, 76
TOWNSEND, Amos, 107; David,
  15; Deborah, 107; Eliza,
  15; Esther, 91, 168, 174;
  Francis, 15; Hannah, 22;
  Jane, 15; John, 22, 107;
  Joseph, 36; Letitia, 160;
  Lydia, 15, 18; Mary, 5,
  107, 110; Priscilla, 15;
  Rachel, 15; Samuel, 15;
  Sarah, 15, 88, 107; Susan,
  15; Thomas J., 15;
  William, 160
TREEBEE, Joseph, 25
TREED, Christian, 58
TREGO, Benjamin, 107; Hannah,
  107; Margaret, 107; Mary,
  107; Sarah, 83; William,
  107
TREVILLA, Ann, 160
TRIMBLE, Ann, 8, 11, 25, 26,
  33; Daniel, 22, 25; Eliz.,
  77; Elizabeth, 168; Grace,
  8, 26; Hannah, 8, 11, 26;
  Isaac, 168; James, 74,
  168; Jane, 168; John, 8,
  129, 134, 168; Joseph, 28,
  168; Lyddia, 26; Lydia, 8,
  129, 134; Mary, 10, 25,
  168; Phebe, 8, 23, 107,
  166; Richard, 8, 26, 33;
  Samuel, 19; Sarah, 28;
  Susanna, 8, 26; Tamzin,
  35; William, 8, 11, 23,
  26, 36, 107
TROTH, John, 165
TROTTER, Hannah, 3; Margaret,
  3; William, 3
TRUMBLE, Grace, 15; Lydia, 15;
  William, 15
TURNER, George, 107; Sarah,
  107

-U-

UNDERWOOD, Alexander, 136,
  160, 161; Ann, 22, 24,
  136, 160; Elizabeth, 107;
  Joseph, 107; Ruth, 161;
  Samuel, 160; Sarah, 170;
  William, 161

-V-

VALENTINE, Ann, 24; George, 4,
  27, 36; Jacob, 4; Jane, 4,
  107; Jehu, 161; Jonathan,
  161; Lydia, 161, 179;
  Mary, 3, 4, 107; Phebe, 4,
  27, 107; Rachel, 4, 19,
  27, 31, 107; Robert, 3, 4,
  19, 23, 24, 107; Sarah, 4,
  107; Susanna, 4; Thomas,
  3, 4, 107
VANCE, Elizabeth, 107
VANCOURT, Daniel, 134; Mary,
  134
VANDER WEID, Joh., 58;
  Magdalena, 58
VARMAN, Mary, 138
VERNON, Aaron, 107; Gideon,
  84, 107; Hannah, 107;
  Isaac, 107; Jonathan, 22;
  Lydia, 107; Margaret, 107;
  Mary, 22; Moses, 107;
  Nehemiah, 107; Phebe, 84;
  Rachel, 107; Rebecca, 107;
  Susannah, 107
VORE, Christian, 107; Sarah,
  107

-W-

WAGENER, Bastian, 46, 47, 69;
  Caspar, 46; Elisabeth, 71;
  Magdalena, 47; Margaretha,
  46, 47; Margreth, 51;
  Peter, 71; Sebastian, 51
WAGNER, Anna Maria, 37;
  Bastian, 48; Catharina,
  38; Elisabeth, 37, 39, 56,
  65, 66; Georg, 54; Hannes,
  61; Jacob, 65, 66;
  Johannes, 38, 39, 48, 73;
  Margaretha, 48; Margrith,
  54, 56; Maria, 61; Peter,
  61; Sebastian, 37, 38, 54,
  56; Wilhelm, 65
WALER, Jane, 161; Joseph, 161
WALKER, Alexander, 75;
  Benjamin, 23, 99, 107;
  Isaac, 107; Isabel, 75;
  Isbella, 75; James, 74;
  Leah, 107; Rachel, 99,
  107; Ruth, 23, 99, 107;
  Sarah, 23, 107
WALL, John, 108; Mary, 81, 87,
  108; Ruth, 79; William,

INDEX 219

87, 108
WALLACE, David, 74; Sarah, 76
WALLICHIN, Maria, 63
WALN, Ann, 108; Hannah, 108;
 Jane, 108; Joseph, 108;
 Mary, 108; Richard, 108;
 Samuel, 108; Sarah, 108;
 Susanna, 108; William, 108
WALTER, Ann, 161, 175;
 Catharina, 52, 60;
 Catharine, 66; Hannes, 52;
 James, 133, 154, 161, 175;
 Jane, 133, 134; Johannes,
 60; John, 66, 161; Lydia,
 133; Martha, 161; Rebecca,
 161; Sarah, 154; Thomas,
 161
WALTON, --, 76; Abigail, 134;
 Elizabeth, 161; Hannah,
 134, 176; Isaac, 161;
 Jane, 75; Joseph, 176;
 Joshua, 21, 134, 161, 175;
 Rebekah, 176; Susanna,
 175; William, 176
WARD, Amy, 161; Philip, 161
WARFEL(HARPEL), James, 76
WARNER, Isaac, 134, 167; John,
 134, 161, 167; Joseph,
 134, 167; Levi, 134, 167;
 Lydia, 134, 161, 167;
 Mary, 134, 167; Nancy,
 134; Nanny, 167; Rachel,
 134, 167; Samuel, 21, 27;
 Sarah, 88; Simeon, 134;
 Simon, 167; Susanna, 99;
 William, 161, 167
WARREN, Daniel, 24
WATSON, Hannah, 13; William,
 13
WAY, Ann, 134; Deborah B.,
 134; Elizabeth, 9, 134;
 Francis, 9; Hanna, 43;
 Hannah, 134; Hugh, 43;
 Isaac, 134; Jacob, 134;
 James, 134; Jesse, 134,
 175; John, 43; Johsua,
 161; Joseph, 134; Joshua,
 9, 10, 24, 134; Lydia, 10;
 Lydia C., 134; Marshall,
 134; Martha, 10, 24; Mary
 Miller, 134; Moses, 134;
 Paschall, 134; Sidney,
 161; Thomas, 134; William,
 134
WAYNE, Jacob, 173; Mary, 173;
 Sarah, 173; Thomas, 173
WEATHERELD, Mary, 24
WEAY, Hanna, 43; Hugh, 13;
 Maria, 43
WEBB, Ann, 161; Benjamin, 161;
 Daniel, 161; Elizabeth,
141, 161, 165; George,
 161; Hester, 161; James,
 161; Jane, 161; Mary, 169;
 Sarah, 161; Stephen, 177;
 Thomas, 161; William, 161
WEBER, Eva, 54; Johannes, 54;
 Magdalena, 54
WEBSTER, Ann, 162; Elizabeth,
 162; Hannah, 144, 161;
 Isaac, 161; Jane, 144;
 John, 134, 144, 161, 162;
 Margaret, 161; Michael,
 162; Pamela, 150; Phebe,
 144; Rebecca, 134; Sarah,
 134, 161; Thomas, 134;
 William, 134, 161, 162
WEELY, Anna Catharina, 41;
 Joshannes, 41
WELLS, Catharine, 180;
 Elizabeth, 134, 180;
 Henry, 24; Isaiah, 180;
 John, 134, 180; Josiah,
 134; Katherine, 134; Mary,
 134, 180; Sarah, 134, 180;
 Susanna, 180; Susannah,
 134; Thomas, 134, 180
WELSH, Elizabeth, 169; George,
 75; Joseph, 74; Thomas,
 169
WELY, Jane, 19, 20
WENGARD, Jacob, 41; Phillip,
 41; Susanna, 41
WERLICH, Johannes, 71; Maria,
 71
WERLY, Maria, 57
WEST, Hannah, 162; Joshua,
 162; Lydia, 162; Mary,
 162; Phebe, 119; Samuel,
 162; William, 119
WEYAND, Jacob, 61, 73;
 Johannes, 61, 73;
 Magdalena, 55, 61, 73;
 Philip, 55, 65; Susanna,
 55
WEYANDT, Anna Catharina, 43;
 Philip, 43; Susanna, 43
WHALEN, Ann, 108; Catharine,
 108; Dennis, 108; Isaac,
 108; Israel, 108; John,
 108; Mary, 108; Phebe,
 108; Sarah, 108
WHELEN, Ann, 18; Dennis, 18,
 19; Isaac, 28; James, 18;
 John, 18; Joseph, 18;
 Jospeh, 29; Martha, 18;
 Phebe, 18; Sarah, 18;
 Townsend, 25
WHERRY, Joseph, 75
WHITAKER, Edith, 36; Phebe,
 74; Phineas, 36
WHITCRAFT, John, 77

WHITE, Elizabeth, 108, 133;
Hannah, 75, 162; Jane,
108; John, 134, 162; Mary,
133, 134, 162; Miriam,
141; Nathaniel, 108;
Nicholas, 108; Phebe, 108;
Samuel, 134, 162; Sarah,
96, 108; Thomas, 21, 96,
108; Uriah, 108; William,
132, 134, 162
WHITESIDE, Abram, 75; Hannah,
169
WHITSON, Elizabeth, 162;
Hannah, 179; Henry, 162,
179; Martha, 162; Thomas,
162
WICKERHAM, Rachel, 143;
William, 143
WICKERHSAM, Ruth, 151;
William, 151
WICKERSHAM, Abigail, 118, 134,
163, 169, 173; Abner, 162,
164; Ann, 162; Anna, 23;
Caleb, 162; Elizabeth,
162; Enoch, 162; Hannah,
112, 118, 134, 137, 171;
Isaac, 174, 178; James,
162, 178; Jane, 162;
Jesse, 23; John, 178;
Kezia, 162; Lydia, 112,
136, 137; Mar, 162;
Martha, 162; Mary, 162,
164, 178; Peter, 162;
Priscilla, 162; Rachel,
162, 163; Robert, 162,
168; Sampson, 162; Sarah,
162, 178; Thomas, 118,
134, 162, 178; William,
137, 162, 163
WILD, James, 76
WILEY, Abigail, 134; Allen,
163; Ann, 134; John, 134;
Joseph, 134; Mary, 29;
Rachel, 163; Sarah, 134;
Thomas, 163
WILKIE, --, 77
WILKINS, Hannah, 148
WILKINSON, Alice, 161, 163;
Eliza, 163; Elizabeth,
134, 140, 161, 163; Emey,
134; Francis, 134, 163;
Hannah, 134, 163; Joseph,
134, 140, 163; Mary, 163;
Moode, 134; Rebecca, 134,
146; Ruth, 134, 140;
Susanna, 134; Thomas, 161,
163; William, 134
WILKSON, Alice, 172;
Elizabeth, 172; Joseph,
172; Thomas, 172
WILLIAM, Jacob, 19

WILLIAMS, Abner, 109; Adino,
109; Ann, 108; Catharine,
29; Daniel, 12, 25, 163;
David, 22; Davie, 19;
Deborah, 13; Edward, 12,
109; Elisabeth, 13;
Elizabeth, 31, 170; Ellis,
16, 87, 108, 109; Enoch,
109; Esther, 108, 109;
Grace, 7; Hannah, 1, 30,
99, 108, 178; Hannah
Francina, 163; Isaac, 13,
30, 108; Israel, 1; Jacob,
1, 108; Jane, 1, 22, 94,
109; Jese, 87; Jesse, 108;
Joan, 108; Joann, 109;
John, 1, 12, 25, 29, 109,
163; Jonathan, 13;
Katharine, 12, 26; Lewis,
108; Lydia, 16, 87, 108,
109; Margaret, 108; Mary,
12, 13, 25, 30, 84, 108,
109, 163; Miriam, 108;
Mordecai, 13, 23; Nathan,
108; Orion, 163; Rehoboth,
109; Robert, 108, 109;
Ruth, 108; Sarah, 12, 23,
25, 34, 87, 94, 108;
Sibbila, 94; Sibbilla, 12,
25; Thomas, 84; Vincent,
108, 109; William, 12, 13,
27, 31, 108, 109
WILLIAMSON, Abraham, 109; Adam
Buckley, 109; Alice, 96,
109; Anne, 109; Azariah
Lewis, 109; Daniel, 109;
Elizabeth, 85, 109; Enos,
109; Esther, 98, 109;
Francis, 108; George, 109;
Gideon, 25; Hannah, 109;
Jane, 88, 102, 109; John,
109; Margaret, 96, 109;
Mary, 90, 108, 109;
Rebecca, 109; Robert, 96;
Sarah, 103, 109; Walter,
109
WILLIAMSTON, Sarah, 100
WILLIS, Betty, 147
WILLS, Betty, 163; Edward,
163; William, 163
WILLY, Allen, 163; Mary, 149;
Rachel, 163; thomas, 163
WILSON, Abner, 166; Agness,
174; Alisanna, 163; Amos,
135, 163; Amy, 153; Ann,
125, 135; Benjamin, 174;
Christopher, 163; David,
135, 152, 163; Dinah, 4,
163; Edward, 135;
Elizabeth, 26, 135, 163,
174; Ephraim, 135, 163;

INDEX

George, 174; Hanna, 66; Hannah, 135, 152, 163, 166, 177; Hugh, 135; Isaac, 135, 163, 171, 172, 180; Jacob, 31; James, 153, 163, 166; Jane, 74, 75, 135, 157; Jehu, 4; Jesse, 166; Joel, 135; John, 4, 21, 125, 135, 163, 166, 170; Joseph, 174; Joshua, 163; Joyce, 21; Lydia, 153; Margaret, 76, 135, 152, 159, 163, 166, 172; Martha, 135, 160, 174; Mary, 4, 26, 135, 166; N. N., 66; Oliver, 135; Phebe, 135, 166; Rachel, 135; Rebecca, 135; Rebeccah, 180; Samuel, 135; Sarah, 135, 163, 166, 177, 180; Seth, 4; Stephen, 135; Susanna, 172; susanna, 66
WINDLE, Abigail, 135, 163; Benjamin, 135; Cabel, 135; Caleb, 172; David, 135, 163; Dorithy, 158; Francis, 135, 163, 164; Joseph Kirk, 135; Lydia, 166; Mary, 163, 164; Thomas, 163; William, 164
WINTERS, Robert, 77
WITHERS, Jane, 74; Mary, 75
WITTMAN, Barbara, 37
WOLLASTON, Elinor, 135; Hannah, 164; James, 164; Jeremiah, 164; Martha, 135; Mary, 135, 164; Prissilla, 135; Sarah, 135; Thomas, 135, 164
WOLLISTON, Joseph, 76
WOOD, Cassandrew, 135; Elizabeth, 135, 168; Enos, 168; George, 135; Isabell, 168; Jacob, 168; James, 164; Joel, 135; John, 135, 168; Joseph, 135, 168; Joshua, 135, 168, 169; Josiah, 35; Lettice, 164; Lewis, 168; Lydia, 135, 179; Margaret, 119, 132, 135, 143, 159, 164; Mary, 132, 135, 159; Nathan, 135; Pishmonday, 157; Rebecca, 157; Ruth, 135, 167, 170, 172; Ruth Hayse, 172; Suanna, 179; Susanna, 135, 164; Thomas, 135, 157, 164, 179; William, 119, 132, 135, 143, 159, 164, 179

WOODCRAFT, Hannah, 27
WOODROW, Isaac, 161, 164; Lydia, 161, 164; Mary, 164; Ruth, 164; Sarah, 173; Simeon, 164; Sus., 74
WOODS, Elizabeth, 171; Esau, 171; Isabel, 171; Jacob, 171; John, 171; Joseph, 171; Joshua, 171; Lewis, 171
WOODWARD, Alice, 32, 109, 171; Ann, 13; Deborah, 135; Edward, 109; Elizabeth, 116, 135, 142, 158, 164; Hannah, 109; James, 13, 164, 172; Jane, 13; John, 164; Lettice, 164; Lettis, 172; Levi, 135, 164, 165; Lydia, 110, 137, 147; Mary, 135, 158, 164; Neal, 137, 147; Phebe, 147, 164; Rachel, 135; Rebeca, 135; Rebecca, 116, 135, 142; Samuel, 135, 164; Sarah, 135, 137, 164; Susanna, 135; Thomas, 116, 135, 142, 158, 164; Timothy, 135; William, 109, 110
WOOLERTON, Betty, 17; Dorcas, 34; James, 34
WOOLEY, John, 110; Phebe, 110; Thomas, 110
WOOLSTON, James, 115; Mary, 115
WORK, Aaron, 75
WORLHAUSER, Margrith, 58
WORRAL, Elisha, 110; Maris, 110; Rebecca, 110
WORRALL, Phebe, 87, 110; William, 87, 110
WORSLEY, Daniel, 136; Sarah, 136, 160
WRIGHT, Ann, 136; Elizabeth, 136, 160; Fishmore, 136; Hannah, 136, 137; Isaac, 136; Jacob, 164; James, 136, 137; John, 136; Margaret, 136; Martha, 136; Mary, 136, 137, 164; Patience, 151; Sibilla, 100; Thomas, 100, 136
WUNZIN, Eliesabetha, 46
WURSTLER, Catharina, 68
WYAND, Danjel, 58; Philip, 58; Susann, 67; Zusanna, 58

-Y-

YARNALL, Aaron, 110, 111; Abigail, 85, 111; Alice, 110; Allen, 110; Amos, 78, 88, 110, 111; Ann, 110;

Benjamin, 111; Catharine, 110; Daniel, 110, 111; David, 26, 110, 164; Dowse, 110; Elizabeth, 29, 96, 98, 104, 110; Ellin, 110; Enoch, 32, 110; Enos, 110; Francis, 110; George, 111; Hannah, 85, 102, 106, 110, 164; James, 110; Jane, 81, 87, 88, 102, 110, 111; John, 110; Jonathan, 110; Joseph, 87, 110; Lydia, 110, 111; Mary, 78, 85, 87, 106, 110, 111; Mordecai, 110; Moses, 32, 110, 111; Nathan, 164; Peter, 27, 110; Phebe, 84, 102, 110; Phillip, 164; Priscilla, 26; Rachel, 111; Rebecca, 110, 111; Reuben, 111; Samuel, 110; Sarah, 32, 83, 110, 111; Simeon, 98; Susanna, 106, 110, 111; Thomas, 32; Traver, 102; Truman, 111
YARNELL, David, 111; George, 79; Hannah, 111; Lydia, 79; Mordecai, 22; Sarah, 111

YEAGER, Elisabeth, 66; Johanes, 66; Peter, 66
YEARSLEY, Hannah, 2; Nathan, 34
YEGER, Anna Maria, 73; Georg, 68, 73; George, 73; Jacob, 68
YITTAL, --, 75
YOUNG, Ann, 75
YUMER, Robert, 75
YUNGBLUT, Elisabeth, 42; Johann, 42; Johannes, 42; Michel, 42
YUNGLUT, Margareth, 42

-Z-
ZEUG, Christina, 40
ZINCK, Barbara, 53; Catharina, 53; Catharine, 67; Elisabeth, 53; Heinrich, 67; Jacob, 53; Johannes, 53; Michael, 67
ZINK, Barbara, 56, 63; Danjel(Daniel), 58; David, 51; Johannes, 56; John, 63; Margrith, 56; Samuel, 63; Stephan, 58; Stephen, 51, 59; Susanna, 51, 58, 59

Other Heritage Books by Charlotte Meldrum:

Abstracts of Bucks County, Pennsylvania Land Records, 1684-1723

*Early Church Records of Burlington County, New Jersey
Volumes 1-3*

Early Church Records of Chester County, Pennsylvania, Volume 2
Charlotte Meldrum and Martha Reamy

Early Church Records of Gloucester County, New Jersey

Early Church Records of Salem County, New Jersey

Early Records of Cumberland County, New Jersey

Johnston County, North Carolina Marriages, 1764-1867

Marriages and Deaths of Montgomery County, Pennsylvania, 1685-1800

Other Heritage Books by Martha Reamy

*1860 Census Baltimore City: Volume 1, 1st and 2nd Wards
(Fells Point and Canton Waterfront Areas)*

*Abstracts of South Central Pennsylvania Newspapers
Volume 2, 1791-1795*

Early Families of Otsego County, New York, Volume 1

Early Church Records of Chester County, Pennsylvania, Volume 2
Martha Reamy and Charlotte Meldrum

Abstracts of Carroll County Newspapers, 1831-1846
Martha Reamy and Marlene Bates

Other Heritage Books by Martha and Bill Reamy:

*Erie County, New York Obituaries as Found in the Files of
The Buffalo and Erie County Historical Society*

*Genealogical Abstracts from Biographical and
Genealogical History of the State of Delaware*

History and Roster of Maryland Volunteers, War of 1861-1865, Index

Immigrant Ancestors of Marylanders, as Found in Local Histories

Pioneer Families of Orange County, New York

Records of St. Paul's Parish, [Baltimore, Maryland], Volume 1

Records of St. Paul's Parish, [Baltimore, Maryland], Volume 2

St. George's Parish Register [Harford County, Maryland], 1689-1793

St. James' Parish Registers, 1787-1815

St. Thomas' Parish Register, 1732-1850

The Index of Scharf's History of Baltimore City and County [Maryland]

www.ingramcontent.com/pod-product-compliance
Lightning Source LLC
Chambersburg PA
CBHW050141170426
43197CB00011B/1920